# ALTER EGOS

# ALTER EGOS

Hillary Clinton, Barack Obama, and the
Twilight Struggle Over American Power

## Mark Landler

RANDOM HOUSE

NEW YORK

Published in the United States by Random House, an imprint and division of Penguin Random House LLC, New York.

RANDOM HOUSE and the HOUSE colophon are registered trademarks of Penguin Random House LLC.

LIBRARY OF CONGRESS CATALOGING-IN-PUBLICATION DATA
Names: Landler, Mark, author.
Title: Alter egos : Hillary Clinton, Barack Obama, and the twilight struggle over American power / Mark Landler.
Description: New York : Random House, 2016. | Includes bibliographical references and index.
Identifiers: LCCN 2016002132 | ISBN 9780812998856 (hardback) | ISBN 9780812998863 (ebook)
Subjects: LCSH: Obama, Barack. | Clinton, Hillary Rodham. | United States— Foreign relations—2009– | BISAC: POLITICAL SCIENCE / Political Process / Elections. | HISTORY / United States / 21st Century. | BIOGRAPHY & AUTOBIOGRAPHY / Political.
Classification: LCC E907 .L364 2016 | DDC 327.73009/05—dc23
LC record available at http://lccn.loc.gov/2016002132

Printed in the United States of America on acid-free paper

randomhousebooks.com

987654321

FIRST EDITION

Book design by Simon M. Sullivan

*For Angela,*
*my alter ego*

Now the trumpet summons us again—not as a call to bear arms, though arms we need—not as a call to battle, though embattled we are—but a call to bear the burden of a long twilight struggle.

JOHN F. KENNEDY, INAUGURAL ADDRESS, JANUARY 20, 1961

# Contents

## Prologue

## The Warrior and the Priest

Barack Obama turned up unexpectedly in the press cabin of Air Force One as the plane was high above the South China Sea, about to begin its descent into Malaysia on a flight from South Korea. The president was not one for casual in-flight visits, saving these encounters for the trip home to Washington, when he would ruminate with reporters, off the record, about what he had accomplished overseas. So when he appeared on the afternoon of April 26, 2014, in the middle of a weeklong tour of Asia, something clearly was up. Wearing an open-necked blue shirt, gray slacks, and an unsmiling expression, Obama shook hands with the journalists on board that day: reporters from the four major news agencies; a network producer from CBS News; a correspondent for the *Los Angeles Times*. Before he reached the third row of seats, where I was standing with a hand outstretched, the president wheeled around, returned to the front of the cabin, and propped himself, arms crossed, against a gray bulkhead, next to a flickering television screen.

It was hard to know if Obama had ignored me intentionally: I was the last in a scrum of reporters, and the president likes to keep these pleasantries to a minimum anyway. But when he swatted away my opening question about China, a chill wind was clearly blowing.

"I'll answer that in a minute," the president said, "but first I want to say a few things."

Obama, it turned out, was angry about two articles that had run in *The New York Times* the previous day. One, by me and a colleague, Jodi Rudoren, declared that his trip had already been marred by a pair of setbacks: the failure to strike a trade deal with Japan and the collapse of his latest effort to negotiate a peace accord between Israel and the Palestinians. The other said his administration had underestimated the bellicose nature of North Korea's new ruler, Kim Jong-un. Obama wanted me to know he never expected to sign a trade agreement on that trip, nor, for that matter, did he bear any illusions about North Korea's boy dictator. The impromptu visit was meant to set the press straight about our coverage of his foreign policy. Obama viewed it as shallow, mistaking prudence for fecklessness, pragmatism for lack of ambition.

"Ben and I have been talking about giving a speech that lays out my foreign policy," he said, stealing a glance at his foreign policy amanuensis, Benjamin Rhodes, who had slipped quietly into a seat behind the reporters, next to the press secretary, Jay Carney, and seemed as unsure of what his boss was going to say as the reporters were.

"I can sum up my foreign policy in one phrase," Obama said, pausing a beat for his punch line. "Don't do stupid shit."

America's problems, he said, stemmed not from doing too little but too much, from overreach rather than inaction. The country's greatest disasters had come from blundering into reckless military adventures, whether in Vietnam or Iraq. The key to managing a sound foreign policy was to avoid entanglements in places where America's national interests were not directly at stake—Syria, for example, which was caught up in a sectarian war that would defy outside efforts to end it; or Ukraine, victimized by a predatory Russia but a country with which the United States conducted a negligible amount of trade. Warming to his theme, Obama offered a brisk tour of places his White House had *not* started new conflicts: the Middle East, Asia, eastern Europe. Historic achievements in foreign policy—Nixon's opening to China—were once-in-a-generation occurrences, he said. He might yet get one if the West negotiated an agreement with Iran to restrain its nuclear program. But in a world of unending strife and unreliable despotic leaders, hoping for more than that was simply not realistic. In such a world, Obama was content to hit singles and doubles, hewing to his foreign policy version of the Hippocratic oath.

As we touched down outside Malaysia's capital, Kuala Lumpur, Obama kept talking, bracing himself against the bulkhead as the tires squealed and ordering those who were standing in the aisle to sit down. ("I'm the only one who's allowed to stand," he said. "I don't want that liability.") Before returning to his cabin, where he would put on a jacket and tie and jog down the stairs to another red-carpet welcome in another distant land, Obama turned to the reporters and asked, "Now what's my foreign policy philosophy?"

"Don't do stupid shit," we replied sheepishly, like schoolchildren taught a naughty rhyme by a subversive teacher.

Obama smiled and then was gone as abruptly as he had come. His credo hung in the air, though. At one level, it seemed crude, almost juvenile, particularly coming from a man who cared deeply about words and believed in the power of language to convey ideas. And yet it had the ring of authenticity. More so than his shimmering oratory—his references to the "arc of history" or the "spark of the divine"—those four words seemed to capture what was for Obama the irreducible truth of being commander in chief of the world's remaining superpower.

As a White House correspondent for *The New York Times*, I had traveled to a dozen countries with the president over four years, from a state visit to Buckingham Palace, arriving in a thirty-car motorcade, to a secret mission in Afghanistan, flying at night over the Hindu Kush in Black Hawk helicopters. I questioned him at news conferences in the East Room and the Great Hall of the People, listened to him elaborate his worldview in speeches in London, Jerusalem, and Brisbane. And yet it was during a salty Saturday afternoon encounter in the back of Air Force One that Obama uttered what would become perhaps the signature slogan of his presidency—the foreign policy equivalent of "It's the economy, stupid."

Soon enough, "Don't do stupid shit" entered the vernacular. Obama repeated it in a meeting with columnists and editorial writers; his advisers cited it in interviews; it was even codified in a speech he gave the following month at the United States Military Academy at West Point—an address that will surely rank as one of the most ambivalent ever delivered by an American president. The elders of the foreign policy establishment debated the wisdom and meaning of the phrase, usually amending it, in a clumsy attempt to make it more family friendly, to "Don't do stupid stuff." To Obama's critics, it became shorthand for the president's weak and dilatory leadership—leadership, they said, that had relinquished America's historic and necessary role as the ultimate guarantor of world order. It seemed, in the wake of the Islamic State's brutal rampage across Syria and Iraq and Russia's de facto invasion of Ukraine, hopelessly inadequate to a storm-tossed world.

Among those critics was Hillary Clinton, his onetime rival who had become his loyal lieutenant and now aspired to be his successor. As secretary of state, she had been intimately involved in every major foreign policy debate of his presidency. She would run for the White House, in no small measure, as the custodian of his legacy. And yet, once Clinton had left his cabinet at the end of the first term, she was eager to start delineating her own views about the world. It was an inevitable distancing of herself from her former boss, and like all such partings, it wasn't pretty.

"Great nations need organizing principles," she said when she was asked in the summer of 2014 if Obama's phrase held any lessons for her. " 'Don't do stupid stuff' is not an organizing principle."

Dissent was not something I encountered in two years of covering Clinton at the State Department (I moved to the White House beat in 2011). She was robotically faithful and on message in those days, apt to start sentences with "As President Obama said . . ." or "President Obama has been very clear . . ." She told off aides who criticized him or his policies, a courtesy the White House didn't reciprocate. Loyal, disciplined, and determined to be a team player, Clinton rarely, if ever, showed public daylight between her and the president. For reporters who expected the kind of withering sniper fire between Foggy Bottom and the Oval Office that Clinton and Obama had exchanged in South Carolina during the 2008 primaries, their display of unity was stifling.

To travel with the secretary of state as I did, to forty-three countries on four continents, however, was to witness a woman completing a remarkable, decade-long metamorphosis—one that widened, rather than narrowed, her differences with the progressive president she had agreed to serve. Clinton was shedding the last vestiges of her image as a polarizing, left-wing social engineer in favor of a new role as commanding figure on the global stage, someone who could go toe-to-toe with the mullahs in Tehran or the cold warriors in Moscow. A loyal lieutenant, yes, but a general in waiting.

Under the surface, Clinton's Manichean worldview was always there. It turned up early, in her blunt closed-door prediction to an Arab foreign minister that the Iranians would spurn Obama's offer of an olive branch. Later, one could see it in her unstinting support of the military commanders in their request for a larger American troop deployment to Afghanistan than the president or even his Republican defense secretary wanted. Or in her support of the Pentagon's recommendation to leave a residual force of 10,000 to 20,000 troops behind in Iraq. It surfaced in her campaign for air strikes in Libya to prevent a slaughter by Colonel Muammar al-Qaddafi, and it fueled her case, the summer before she left the State Department, for funneling weapons to the rebels fighting Bashar al-Assad in Syria.

Avidly, if discreetly, Clinton played the house hawk in Obama's war cabinet.

That Clinton is much more hawkish than Obama is no revelation to anyone who watched them brawl in the winter of 2008. She accused her young opponent of naïveté after he said he would negotiate with America's adversaries "without preconditions." She warned Iran that if it ever launched a nuclear strike on Israel, the United States would "totally obliterate" it. Their differences, however, were largely submerged by Clinton's innate caution, relentless self-control, and the common cause the two rivals made when she agreed to join Obama's cabinet. He recruited her to repair an American image that had been shredded after eight years of George W. Bush's presidency. She, with her dreams of the White House deferred, recognized this as a way to burnish her national security credentials and keep her place on the world stage. The last thing Clinton wanted was a public rift with her new boss.

Once she was a private citizen, however, with the presidency again in her sights, the fissures between them became harder to conceal. Nor was she as inclined to do so. She came out against his ambitious Asia-Pacific trade pact, after having been one of its most enthusiastic advocates. She began to etch clear policy differences with him on Syria and Russia—a distancing his aides found opportunistic, if unsurprising. In August 2014, Clinton said Obama's refusal to arm the rebels in Syria left a security vacuum there and in Iraq, which had been filled by the brutal warriors of the Islamic State. Her criticism antagonized a president who already felt embattled. A few days later, the pair hugged in an awkward reconciliation at a birthday party in Martha's Vineyard for Vernon Jordan's wife, Ann. "I never saw them interact all evening," said a guest who watched their stilted body language from a nearby table.

Clinton still embraced central tenets of Obama's foreign policy; it was, after all, her foreign policy, too. In the fall of 2015, she articulated the case for his much-disputed nuclear agreement with Tehran to an audience at the Brookings Institution. But their public remarks only underscored how differently Clinton viewed the achievement than Obama. He called it "the strongest nonproliferation agreement ever negotiated." She called it a flawed deal worth supporting only if it was linked to relentless enforcement, a con-certed effort to thwart Iranian malfeasance in the Middle East, and an unwavering threat to use military force to prevent Iran from ever getting a bomb. "My starting point will be one of distrust," she said.

Clinton's break with Obama over Russia played out similarly. She had long been more suspicious of Vladimir Putin than the pres-ident, though she voiced those warnings, Obama's aides noted, only when Putin's sinister motives were already well established. At a Democratic fundraiser in California in March 2014, she likened his annexation of Crimea to Hitler's conquest of the Sudetenland in the 1930s. Eighteen months later, she said Obama's restrained response to Putin's bullying of Ukraine was inadequate. And when Putin intervened in Syria on behalf of Assad, Clinton sounded the trumpet of a new cold war. "All the Russian experts that thought that their work was done after the fall of the Berlin Wall, I hope that they will be dusting off their materials," she said. These re-tired cold warriors, she said, needed to draw up a battle plan for "how we try to confine, contain, deter Russian aggression in Eu-rope and beyond."

Their differences surfaced again during the bloody months at the end of 2015, when radical Islamists carried out killing sprees in Paris and California. The carnage propelled terrorism to the fore-front of yet another presidential campaign. Suddenly, the tangled conflict in the Levant was no longer just a riddle for foreign policy experts; it posed a direct threat to the homeland, throwing Obama on his back foot and playing out in the crude appeals to nativism and nationalism by the Republican candidates. Syria was where Clinton had first split with him over supplying arms to the rebels; now they split again over her call to impose a no-fly zone over northern Syria, as her husband had done in Iraq in the 1990s to protect the Kurds.

"Look," she told an audience at the Council on Foreign Rela-tions a few days after the attacks in Paris, "I have made clear that I have differences, as I think any two people do."

• • •

Barack Obama and Hillary Clinton are more than just two of the most riveting political figures of our time. They are protagonists in a great debate over American power—one that will decide not only who sits in the Oval Office but the direction she or he will take a nation that faces a new twilight struggle against the forces of disorder.

On one side of the debate stand those, like Obama, who believe the United States resorts too readily to military force to defend its interests, that American intervention in other countries usually ends in misery, and that the nation would be well-served by defining its interests more narrowly than it has for most of the post–World War II era. On the other side stand those, like Clinton, who believe that the calculated use of military power is vital to defending national interests, that American intervention does more good than harm, and that the writ of the United States properly reaches, as George W. Bush once declared, into "any dark corner of the world." Clinton and Obama have come to embody competing visions of America's role in the world: his vision restrained, inward looking, radical in its acknowledgment of limits; hers, hard-edged, pragmatic, unabashedly old-fashioned.

This book will explore that divide: how it played out in the major foreign policy debates of the Obama administration; how it will shape the president's legacy; how it could shape a Clinton presidency; and what it means for a nation exhausted after more than a decade of war yet facing a cascade of new threats, from the medieval jihad of the Islamic State to the nineteenth-century nationalism of Russia to the twenty-first-century muscle flexing of China. The book will go behind the speeches and press conferences to the Situation Room meetings and Oval Office huddles, the phone calls and emails, in which Clinton and Obama wrestled with their options, bringing their different worldviews to bear on an often uncooperative world.

It is a perennial debate in postwar America, sometimes framed as realism versus liberal internationalism, George Kennan versus Woodrow Wilson. The disciples of Wilson regard foreign policy as an idealistic enterprise, a means of transmitting liberal Democratic values throughout the world. The apostles of realpolitik view it pragmatically, as a means of safeguarding national interests. Obama and Clinton don't fit neatly into those boxes; it is too simple to say she is from Mars and he is from Venus. The reluctant warrior in the Oval Office was nevertheless an avid believer in drones, Navy SEALs, and other instruments of covert warfare. The hawk in the State Department was nevertheless committed to the diplomacy and multilateral institutions championed by Wilson. Realism and idealism coexist in both of them.

Clinton and Obama, it must be said, agreed more than they disagreed. Both preferred diplomacy to brute force. Both shunned the unilateralism of the Bush years. Both are lawyers committed to preserving the rules-based order that the United States put in place after 1945. Yet as that order has begun to fracture, they have shown very different instincts for how to save it. "The president has made some tough decisions," Leon Panetta, who served as Obama's defense secretary and CIA director, told me. "But it's been a mixed record, and the concern is, the president defining what America's role in the world is in the twenty-first century hasn't happened.

"Hopefully, he'll do it," Panetta said. "Certainly, she would."

Dennis Ross, a former aide to Clinton and Obama who played a behind-the-scenes role in the secret negotiations with Iran over its nuclear program, said, "It's not that she's quick to use force, but her basic instincts are governed more by the uses of hard power."

The differences between them are not ideological as much as generational, cultural, even temperamental. Clinton is a Midwesterner, a product of the Cold War who came of age during the Vietnam era and watched as her husband articulated a new rationale for humanitarian intervention in the Balkans in the 1990s. She is a woman aspiring to a job that has been held only by men. Obama is a child of the Pacific Rim who came of age after Vietnam and had no firsthand exposure to the Balkans campaigns (he was immersed in state politics in Illinois during those years). The formative foreign policy event of his lifetime was the American misadventure in Iraq.

Obama came into office as a counterrevolutionary, seeking to end Bush's wars and restore America's moral standing. But his ambitions were even larger than that: He set out to reconcile Americans to a world in which the United States was no longer the undisputed hegemon. He shunned the triumphalist language of American exceptionalism, declaring that the nation's unique character lay not in its perfection but in its unending struggle to live up to its ideals. He refused to be drawn into distant conflicts, with the much-regretted exception of Libya. He tied the nation's security to that of other nations, seeking cooperation on climate change and nonproliferation. And yet he also defended the just use of military force to defend the homeland or to avert genocide. "Our challenge is reconciling these two seemingly irreconcilable truths," Obama said in accepting his prematurely awarded Nobel Peace Prize in 2009. "That war is sometimes necessary, and war at some level is an expression of human folly."

Clinton is more conventional and more political. Her foreign policy is less a doctrine than a set of impulses, grounded in cold calculation and what one aide calls "a textbook view of American exceptionalism." She is at heart a "situationalist," somebody who reacts to problems piecemeal rather than fitting them into a larger doctrine. Her flexibility has led people to read different things into her foreign policy: Republicans accuse her of being an Obama retread; Obama loyalists grumble that she dramatized her divisions with the president on Syria and Russia for political reasons; Leslie Gelb of the Council on Foreign Relations warns that she could end up in thrall to the neoconservatives who led the United States into Iraq. "She takes the position that leaves her the least vulnerable," he told me.

Those characteristics make her a ready warrior but a cautious diplomat. Unlike most modern-day secretaries of state, Clinton kept her distance from peace negotiations between the Israelis and

Palestinians, judging them to be an uphill climb and not worth the risk of alienating Jewish voters at home. Obama made daring overtures to Iran and Cuba; it's not clear the United States would have achieved either, but especially the Iran nuclear deal, had Clinton been elected president in 2008 instead of him. Obama's statesmanship, Dennis Ross noted, flowed from a very different source than Clinton's: He tended to view adversaries in terms of their grievances toward the United States; Clinton views them more traditionally, in terms of their interests. "It leads you in a different direction," Ross said.

Predicting how a secretary of state would act as commander in chief is, at some level, a fool's errand. The last person to make the transition was James Buchanan in 1857; his presidency, which accelerated the slide toward the Civil War, was widely judged the greatest failure in the history of the Republic. Clinton might view the diplomatic stakes differently as president than she did as secretary of state. Militarily, she would face the same constraints Obama did, not just at home but abroad. The breakdown of the twentieth-century American order, Obama's defenders note, has made the world less amenable to any president's efforts to control it. "If you look at Obama and his rhetoric in 2008, you would have expected a transformational and maximalist president," said Joseph Nye, a Harvard political scientist who advises Clinton. "He was going to ban nuclear weapons. He was going to repair relations with the Muslim world. We were going to have a reset with Russia. These were ambitious goals, but he turned out to be a rather prudent retrencher. The pendulum is going to swing back somewhat now, and Hillary Clinton is probably going to be less of a retrencher. The question is how much leeway she'll have."

How well Clinton's hawkish instincts match the country is an open question. Americans are weary of war and remain suspicious of foreign entanglements. And yet, after the retrenchment of the Obama years, there is evidence that they are equally dissatisfied with a portrait of their country as a spent force, managing its decline amid a world of rising powers, resurgent empires, and lethal new forces such as the Islamic State. If Obama's minimalist approach was a necessary reaction to the maximalist style of his predecessor, then perhaps what Americans yearn for is something in between—the kind of steel-belted pragmatism that Clinton has spent a lifetime cultivating.

It is not easy to find a historic parallel for the relationship between Barack Obama and Hillary Clinton. In their ambitions and rivalry, they resemble Theodore Roosevelt and Woodrow Wilson—"the warrior and the priest," in the words of John Milton Cooper, Jr.—who staked out competing visions for America as a great power in the twentieth century: robust and adventurous; restrained and rule bound. But Clinton and Obama are from the same political party and worked in the same administration. The closer analogy, perhaps, is to Harry Truman and his secretary of state, Dean Acheson, who created the American-led order that Obama and Clinton are both fighting to preserve. Truman embodied the idealistic spirit of Wilson; Acheson reflected the balance-of-power realism of Roosevelt. "While the visions seemingly clashed," as G. John Ikenberry wrote, "they ended up working in tandem."

For Clinton and Obama, as for those men present at the creation, it was a story of dreams and disillusionment: Obama's attempt to reset relations with Russia, mocked by Putin on the battlefields of the Crimean War; Clinton's fervent plea to the president to rescue Libya from a madman, which ended up pitching the country further into madness, and hardened Obama against doing anything when the savagery moved to Syria. The young idealist who made an eloquent case for humanitarian military intervention in Oslo became the chastened realist who made a pinched argument for avoiding it at West Point four and a half years later.

It is a story with a rich supporting cast: Joe Biden, the windy vice president who honed his foreign policy over decades in the Senate and vied with Clinton for Obama's ear, arguing for an approach even more minimalist than the president's; Bob Gates, the Soviet-era spymaster and Bush holdover who became a Clinton ally; John Kerry, the patrician senator who succeeded Clinton at State and whose hell-for-leather style made her look staid by comparison; Richard Holbrooke, the Clinton friend and pathologically driven Democratic statesman, who never found his footing with Obama; and a cadre of advisers, from Ben Rhodes to Jake Sullivan—young men in a hurry, who exercised influence beyond their years as agents of their bosses. Looming just offstage was Bill Clinton, the forty-second president and citizen of the world, who once called the United States the "indispensable nation." He influenced his wife, both with his wide-angle worldview and through the challenges of his presidency, from the Balkans to Rwanda, which filtered into her views on Libya and Syria.

Ultimately, though, this book is about two supremely ambitious figures: the prickly, distant president who lectured reporters on his plane but could be refreshingly honest as he wrestled with problems; and the practiced, hyper-cautious secretary of state who knocked back drinks with her press corps but could never quite dispel the suspicion that her bonhomie was an act. These were archrivals who became partners for a time, trailblazers who shared a common sense of their historic destiny but different instincts about how to project power. As one prepared to relinquish the presidency, and the other made her long-awaited bid for it, how Hillary Clinton and Barack Obama view America's role in the world is a central question of our time.

Part I

**Worlds Apart**

# One

## From Cairo to Copenhagen

Hillary Clinton sat in the hideaway study off her ceremonial office in the State Department, sipping tea and taking stock of her first year on the job. The study is more like a den—cozy and wood paneled, lined with bookshelves that displayed mementos from Clinton's three decades in the public eye: a baseball signed by the Chicago Cubs star Ernie Banks, a carved wooden figure of a pregnant African woman, a statue of her heroine, Eleanor Roosevelt. The intimate setting lent itself to a less formal interview than the usual ones with Clinton in the nouveau opulence of her outer office, with its crystal chandelier, marble fireplace, and obligatory portrait of Thomas Jefferson, America's first secretary of state. On the morning of February 26, 2010, however, Clinton was talking about something more sensitive than mere foreign affairs: her relationship with Barack Obama. To say she chose her words carefully doesn't do justice to the delicacy of the exercise. She was like a bomb-squad technician, deciding which color wire to snip as the timer ticked down to zero.

"We've developed, I think, a very good rapport, really positive back and forth about everything you can imagine," Clinton said about the man she had described during the 2008 campaign as naïve, irresponsible, and hopelessly unprepared to be president. "And we've had some interesting and even unusual experiences along the way."

She leaned forward as she spoke, gesturing with her hands and laughing easily. There was more warmth than one had in exchanges with Obama, but less of an expectation that she might say something revealing. Clinton singled out, as she often did, the United Nations climate change summit in Copenhagen the previous December, where she and Obama had gate-crashed a meeting of leaders from China, India, and Brazil, and over the next seventy-five minutes persuaded the balky leaders to accept a nonbinding agreement that saved the summit from collapse. For Clinton and Obama, it was a bonding moment, proof that these former rivals could work together without a script.

It was also, in the tentative, early days of this rivalry turned partnership, extremely unusual.

A more telling anecdote, one Clinton never discussed publicly, had come six months earlier, in June 2009, when the new president traveled to Egypt to deliver a landmark speech to the Islamic world. Clinton was in the audience at Cairo University that day, drawing cheers and applause from the crowd that craned to see her as she entered the vaulted auditorium just before Obama, a handbag slung over her tan jacket. She had flown there overnight from a Latin American summit in Honduras, leaving in the middle of a rancorous negotiation over the diplomatic status of Cuba, so she wouldn't miss the most important address of Obama's young presidency. But the picture of solidarity belied a more complicated backstory: As the trip was getting under way, she had declined a request from the White House chief of staff, Rahm Emanuel, to peel off from the presidential entourage after the speech and fly to Jerusalem to meet with officials of Israel's new government.

For weeks, the content and choreography of Obama's big speech had been the subject of fierce debate inside the West Wing. Some of his advisers wanted him to seize the moment and lay down a new peace initiative for Israel and the Palestinians. Others disagreed, saying that in keeping with his pledge to wind down the Iraq War, his focus should be on a restart with the Islamic world. Some argued that Obama should visit Israel after Egypt to show America's solidarity with its other main ally in the region. Others, including Ben Rhodes, said no, that would turn this historic gesture into yet another exercise in American shuttle diplomacy, diluting his message that a new era was dawning for the United States in the Middle East.

Obama opted not to go. Emanuel, worried that skipping over Jerusalem would bruise the feelings of the Israelis, proposed that Clinton do damage control. He went way back with Hillary, having worked for Bill Clinton's campaign in 1992 and later in the White House as a senior adviser for policy and strategy. He and the First Lady had crossed swords during those years, but Emanuel had been there for the highs and lows of the Clinton presidency—from planning Bill's first inaugural to helping draft the statement in which the president admitted his affair with Monica Lewinsky. Emanuel was also a staunch defender of Israel; he had once served as a civilian volunteer for the Israeli Defense Forces. Despite those credentials and their long history, when Emanuel asked Clinton to go to Israel in Obama's stead and show the president's commitment to a close ally, she turned him down cold.

"She couldn't, wouldn't, and didn't," said a former senior administration official who was told of the exchange.

Those in Obama's inner circle thought her refusal smacked of self-interest, the reaction of a cabinet member who still thought and acted like an independent political figure. Clinton had her own long-standing ties to Israel and American Jews, and Obama's demand that Israel halt the building of settlements in the West Bank, which she had faithfully delivered that spring, had already landed her in hot water with both. In those early days, with the bitterness of the campaign still a raw memory, some people in the West Wing concluded that Clinton was more concerned about protecting her flanks than the president's. "There were times when it was like two principals," the official said, "and each was judging it through the lens of their own interests."

The lack of a high-level American visitor to Israel that summer would have lasting repercussions on the relationship between

Obama and the Israeli government. Many in Israel never overcame their suspicion of the new president; his personal rapport with Prime Minister Benjamin Netanyahu, cool to start with, would deteriorate into mutual loathing. Not only did Obama skip Jerusalem, Israeli officials say, he gave them no heads-up about what his message would be in Egypt. "The Cairo speech is a foundational document," said Michael Oren, who was Israel's ambassador to Washington during much of the Obama presidency. "That it was given without any consultation with us is just amazing." Among the president's top aides, the episode came to be seen as a major unforced error. Emanuel refused to discuss any exchanges he had with Clinton on the subject, but he did admit that the Cairo trip had been mishandled. "I will take my fair share of lumps on it," he told me. "You can't go to the region and not go to your closest ally. Someone should have gone: the president, the vice president, the chief of staff, the secretary of state."

Six months later, at the climate change summit in Copenhagen, it was Clinton who needed Obama to get on a plane.

She had gone to the meeting with mixed feelings. For days leading up to it, her advisers worried that she was walking into a minefield. There were deep divisions among the countries attending, and little hope of bridging them in time to produce an agreement. But Clinton had named a special envoy for climate change, Todd Stern, as a symbol of America's resolve to join the fight against climate change, and he sent a memo to Clinton's aides, urging that she come. Once there, Clinton found a situation so chaotic and dysfunctional that she likened it to an eighth-grade student council meeting. The summit had devolved into another grudge match between the developed and developing worlds. China, India, and Brazil were refusing to sign an agreement that would commit them to even incremental steps to curb emissions. Diplomats from 193 countries wandered the bright hallways of the Bella Center in a state of fretful entropy.

With failure looming, Clinton telephoned Obama and urged him to fly to Copenhagen to try to break the deadlock. His political advisers were opposed, not wanting to pull the boss away from a crowded domestic agenda for a diplomatic caper that looked as if it was going to end badly. Obama, though, had promised, like Clinton, to get serious about climate change. He trusted her diagnosis: that only the American president could broker a compromise. So on the evening of December 3, 2009, he ordered Air Force One fueled up for a flight to Denmark.

Twenty-four hours later, he was being briefed by an exasperated Clinton inside a small coffee bar in a shopping mall adjacent to the conference center that had been closed for the meeting. When it became clear that the Chinese delegation was trying to water down any agreement, holing up in a conference room with windows taped over to conceal their dealings from the Americans, Obama and Clinton decided to take matters into their own hands. They set off to confront the Chinese in person, fast-walking down a hallway and up a flight of stairs, panicked aides in chase, before they ran into a Chinese official in the doorway, waving his arms and shouting "Not ready yet."

Confusion swirled as Clinton and Obama tried to find out who was in the room with the Chinese. An advance person told them it was the Indians, the Brazilians, and the South Africans. Now Clinton was mad: The Indians had told American officials they had already left for the airport. A major developing country was lying to avoid dealing with the United States on climate change? She and Obama looked at each other in disbelief. "C'mon, let's just do this," he said to Clinton. She moved first, ducking under the outstretched arm of a Chinese security guard and barging into the room, which drew a collective gasp from the leaders huddled around a conference table. Obama was right behind her. "Hi, everybody!" he bellowed, like a dad coming home early to find his teenage kids throwing a keg party in the backyard. "Mr. Prime Minister, are you ready to see me now?" he said, turning to face the nonplussed Chinese premier, Wen Jiabao, who was anything but.

Taking seats at the cramped conference table, Obama and Clinton began sketching out the terms of a deal like the lawyers they were, their aides scribbling on pieces of paper that they pushed back and forth across the table. The nonbinding agreement to monitor pollution reduction standards and set a goal to limit the rise in global temperatures was a mushy compromise, one that would look even mushier six years later, when nearly two hundred countries agreed to a binding deal in Paris. In the annals of global climate change negotiations, Copenhagen does not occupy a place of honor.

For Clinton and Obama, however, that hardly mattered. Copenhagen was a crucible for them personally, proof that they had finally put the past behind them. To Rahm Emanuel, the episode showed that whatever their past tensions, they shared an elemental bond: Both were political animals, attuned to the practices and prevarications of other politicians. And foreign policy, he added, is just another form of politics. "Yes, there's *history*," Emanuel went on, dropping his voice half an octave to mock those who would argue that a spat between superpowers is really all that different from a food fight between Chicago aldermen. "Someone did this or that four thousand years ago. But every person you're dealing with is a person who's dealing with politics."

Copenhagen also drove home the sort of world Clinton and Obama would deal with over the coming years: messy, rife with shifting alliances, and hungry for American leadership, even if many resented that leadership. Though they often differed over how to assert America's role, Clinton and Obama were united in the belief that preserving a lawful world order should be a paramount goal of the United States in the twenty-first century. "I think they each had an *aha* moment in Copenhagen, both with each other and in terms of looking at everyone else," said Jake Sullivan, a thirty-nine-year-old lawyer who was Clinton's top policy adviser at the State Department.

Decoding the relationship between Barack Obama and Hillary Clinton has never been simple. They did not indulge in public rifts or emotional displays of unity; both are too disciplined for that. There was less heartfelt affection than flows between Obama and Joe Biden, but more quiet regard than flows between Obama and John Kerry. They respected each other without ever losing the undercurrent of competition that charged their clashes on the campaign trail. The Hillary-and-Barack story is less a soap opera than a dynastic saga, a tale of thwarted ambition and painstaking cultivation. In that sense, Cairo and Copenhagen are bookends for a relationship that is both genuine partnership and enduring rivalry.

At the beginning, they used humor to defuse the tension between them. When Clinton shook hands with the Brazilian president, Luiz Inácio Lula da Silva, in April 2009, he confessed that he had never expected Obama to be elected president. "Well, neither did I," she shot back. A few weeks later, Clinton returned from a visit to Mexico, then battling an outbreak of swine flu. "The second she got back from Mexico," Obama said during a stand-up routine at the annual dinner of the White House Correspondents' Association, "she pulled me into a hug and gave me a big kiss—told me to get down there myself."

While Clinton and Obama managed to poke fun at the bitterness of the campaign, the Cairo episode demonstrated that it was harder for Clinton to get over it than it was for Obama. "It's easier when you're the winner to put things aside," said David Axelrod, a veteran of the 2008 campaign who stayed on to advise the president and had his own complicated relationship with Clinton. "But Obama is not a vengeful person. He didn't view her negatively. He viewed her as a friend who he had to run against."

"There was a coolness right after the nominating process," he continued. "I mean, it's natural. Their first meetings probably were a little bit labored. But by the time she joined, it was a seamless transition." Clinton had a tougher time letting down her guard with Obama's aides, however. When Axelrod asked her office for her email address in June 2009, she clearly wanted to keep him at arm's length. "Does he know I can't look at it all day so he needs to contact me thru you or Huma or Lauren during work hours?" she replied to her chief of staff, Cheryl Mills, referring to her trio of close aides. Obama and Clinton still treated each other less as colleagues than as generals of rival armies that suddenly found themselves in an alliance of necessity. For the first few months, Joe Biden played the role of go-between, carrying messages from one camp to the other. "Hillary would say to me, 'How do you think I should present this to the president?'" the vice president told me. "And I'd say, 'Whoa, just present it to him.' And Barack would say, 'Does she know what a good job I think she's doing?' I'd say, 'Just tell her.'"

Biden, however, had his own complicated relationship with Clinton. The two knew each other well and met regularly for breakfast at the vice president's residence. But he could be condescending about her foreign policy experience, contradicting her in meetings and reinforcing the impression that she was the odd woman out.

Clinton, in fact, was far more isolated and unsure of herself in 2009 and 2010 than is commonly understood, several former aides said. She had trouble penetrating Obama's clannish inner circle and struggled to adjust to his centralization of national security policy making in the White House. Her anxiety was reflected in the bewildered emails she sent to her aides, inquiring about what was going on at the White House. Her staff worried that she was demoralized. "Secretary of Awesome," Cheryl Mills wrote on August 6, 2009, attaching a YouTube video of Clinton shimmying with the locals at a party in Nairobi, Kenya. "You shake your tail feathers girl!" she said. Plenty of Clinton's subordinates sucked up to her for the usual reasons of self-advancement, of course. But emails like this one from Mills were meant, as much as anything, to buck up her spirits.

Clinton coped with the stresses of her situation by stocking the State Department with people loyal to her and focusing her energy on areas such as development and public diplomacy that would burnish her image without getting in the way of Obama. But that left the State Department even more peripheral—"like a Palestinian enclave in the middle of Israel," in the words of one former official; "like the United States of Hillary," in the words of another. That was particularly dangerous in this administration, which proved to be the most White House–centric of the modern era, run by a rigorously self-contained president who relied on a small circle of trusted advisers.

At times, Clinton seemed like a kid in a new school, trying to elbow her way into the popular clique. On the morning of June 8, 2009, she emailed two aides to say, "I heard on the radio that there is a Cabinet mtg this am. Is there? Can I go? If not, who are we sending?" On February 10, 2010, she dialed the White House from her home, but couldn't get past the switchboard operator, who didn't believe she was really Hillary Clinton. Asked to provide her office number to prove her identity, she said she didn't know it. Finally, Clinton hung up in frustration and placed the call again through the State Department Operations Center—"like a proper and properly dependent Secretary of State," as she later wrote to one of her aides in a mock-chastened tone. "No independent dialing allowed."

In December 2009, rumors began circulating that the West Wing was maneuvering to oust Richard Holbrooke, her old friend and the special representative for Afghanistan and Pakistan. At the time, I called Jake Sullivan to check it out. He alerted Clinton, who asked him and Philippe Reines, her communications adviser, to see what they could find out. "People are deeply unhappy with our friend," Sullivan confirmed to her. Reines wondered if the White House had leaked the story, hastening to add, "There's no way they'd handle you that way." Nearly a year into the administration, it was clear that Clinton's people still did not entirely trust Obama's people.


As hard as it was for Clinton, it was even harder for their staffs to reconcile. Both sides suffered from a kind of post-traumatic stress disorder. Tommy Vietor, who drove a press van in rural Illinois during Obama's Senate campaign and later worked as his press secretary in Iowa, recalled that for months, the Obama and Clinton campaigns held daily conference calls with reporters in which they clubbed the other side in harsh personal terms. Every afternoon, he would pore over the Clinton transcripts, soaking up the attack lines like a toxin. "The people who went through that campaign manufactured a pretty visceral hatred for each other," said Vietor, who went on to be the spokesman for the National Security Council. "You magnify differences and internalize grievances in a way that is ridiculous."

When Clinton finally gave up and threw her support to Obama in June 2008, enemy combatants were forced to become comrades-in-arms. The Obama campaign hired prominent Clinton domestic policy advisers and folded together the foreign policy teams, making room for Clinton-era luminaries such as Holbrooke and Madeleine Albright. Friendships that had been put on ice for the previous eighteen months were reactivated. "It was weird because we wanted to rip each other's throats out a few minutes earlier," said Dan Pfeiffer, who was the Obama campaign's communications director and later held the same job at the White House.

That weirdness did not compare to what happened days after the election, when the president-elect told his aides he was going to ask Hillary Clinton to be his secretary of state. The idea had been percolating for a while, advanced by John Podesta among others, so it was not a total surprise. But the prospect was still jarring. When Pfeiffer, a fast-talking Beltway operative who runs everything through a political calculator, first heard the choice, he recalled thinking it was "brilliant and dangerous." On the one hand, Obama would bring his archrival into the tent, eliminating the prospect of her taking potshots at him from the Senate and short-circuiting speculation over whether she would challenge him again in 2012. On the other, he could not fire her without setting off a monumental political storm. That was no small risk for Obama to take, given their history and the bad blood between the two camps.

It also meant that Hillaryland—the Louis XIV–like court of advisers, staffers, supporters, fundraisers, and flatterers that she had cultivated—was going to take up permanent residence in Obama's administration. Clinton, it seemed, was determined to find a place for every one of them. As a condition of taking the job, she extracted an unheard-of promise from Obama: that she could fill the political posts in the State Department. These plums, typically a president's to hand out to his loyalists, instead went to Hillary to parcel out to hers. The only exceptions were ambassadorships and a handful of other posts, such as deputy secretary, which went to Jim Steinberg, an Obama adviser who nevertheless had once worked for Bill Clinton. Cabinet members are normally allowed to bring only a handful of close aides with them to their new job. A former aide to Bill Clinton recalled telling William Cohen, a Republican senator named defense secretary in 1996, that he could bring a single person with him to the Pentagon. Hillary ended up bringing close to one hundred to State.

Clinton's hiring binge—which Obama honored despite the cavils of his own staffers—had far-reaching consequences for the State Department she was to run. Never before had the nation's seat of diplomacy been so unabashedly political, with a constellation of Clinton-appointed special envoys and advisers, some of whom knew next to nothing about diplomacy. Ronan Farrow, the twenty-two-year-old son of Mia Farrow, advised Clinton on "global youth issues," irritating the Foggy Bottom–dwellers who resented that he got prime real estate on the seventh floor, where Clinton had her office. Kris Balderston, a genial backslapper from upstate New York who had worked for her in the Senate, was put in charge of a new effort to create public-private partnerships. The politicos raised money to build a U.S. pavilion at the world's fair in Shanghai; distributed clean-burning cookstoves to mothers in the developing world; created social networks for people from diaspora groups; and incubated a host of other projects. It was worlds away from writing cables or stamping visas, the traditional work of diplomacy done by the State Department.

Broadly speaking, these were the kinds of progressive social causes Clinton had championed since she left Yale Law School thirty-five years earlier—the building blocks of an activist worldview that would set her apart from Obama. "This is a woman who wants to elevate development to be equal with diplomacy," said Anne-Marie Slaughter, a former dean of Princeton's Woodrow Wilson School of Public and International Affairs whom Clinton recruited to run her Policy Planning shop. "It's as much about human security as state security." Slaughter codified the new approach in a classically Clintonesque document known as *The Quadrennial Diplomacy and Development Review*. She likened Clinton to the skipper of a World War II destroyer, trying to retrofit her aging vessel for the wars of today.

In the short run, though, Clinton's hiring set off fights over personnel. It pitted her chief of staff, Cheryl Mills, a diamond-hard lawyer who had defended Bill Clinton during his impeachment trial, against Denis McDonough, the equally combative head of Obama's foreign policy transition team, and occasionally against Rahm Emanuel. In 2009, Clinton offered the post of undersecretary of state for arms control to Ellen Tauscher, a Democratic representative from Northern California who had been a stalwart fundraiser for her and Bill. Tauscher, whose district contained two national weapons labs, knew her military hardware. But she had ousted a Republican incumbent in 1996, and Obama's aides feared they would lose her district, which included a necklace of affluent East Bay suburbs of San Francisco. It didn't help that Clinton had not told them of her plans in advance.

"You tell Hillary to go raise $500,000 to keep that seat Democratic," Emanuel snarled at Mills, according to a person who heard the exchange. (The mayor said he did not recall the incident, though, he said, "It does sound like me.")

Clinton was able to hire Tauscher, but she lost other battles. She wanted Joe Nye of Harvard—who coined the term "smart power," which was to become her mantra at the State Department—to be ambassador to Japan. The White House preferred John Roos, a low-profile Silicon Valley lawyer and top-tier Obama fundraiser. And she was blocked from bringing aboard Sidney Blumenthal, the former *New Yorker* writer, White House staff member, and long-time Clinton-family retainer, whom she envisioned as a senior adviser parked in the Policy Planning division.

It was hard to know who hated the idea of Blumenthal more: the White House or the State Department. Obama's aides regarded him as a conspiracy theorist who had practiced his dark arts against them during the campaign, planting negative stories about Obama's private life. Clinton's cadre of young staffers, some of whom knew Blumenthal only by reputation, viewed him as the Ghost of Clinton Past who would threaten their access to her. Even other Clinton political appointees questioned what he would bring to Policy Planning, which had been created in 1947 by George Kennan, architect of the Cold War containment policy, as an elite preserve for big thinkers. It fell to Emanuel, who had nicknamed Blumenthal "G.K." (for Grassy Knoll) when they were both working in the Clinton White House, to tell Hillary he was persona non grata—a message he delivered not long after she declined to travel to Jerusalem. Turnabout, it seems, was fair play.

It hardly mattered that Blumenthal didn't get a State Department building pass. He functioned as a shadow counselor throughout her tenure, sending her hundreds of emails—addressed to H—with advice on polishing her image, dealing with the Libyan war, fighting turf battles with the White House, even staying abreast of GOP politics. By turns high-minded tutor and down-and-dirty gossip, he was without peer as a correspondent. On Election Day in 2010, he told Clinton that House Speaker John Boehner was "despised by the younger, more conservative members of the House Republican Conference. They are repelled by his personal behavior. He is louche, alcoholic, lazy, and without any commitment to any principle." In March 2010, he advised her to put a stop to David Axelrod's freelancing in foreign policy, which he said had aggravated tensions with Israel. "Make Steinberg tell Donilon they need to rein in Axelrod," he wrote, referring to Tom Donilon, who was then the deputy national security adviser. "Axelrod has enough to do fixing the domestic messes he's made. Let it come from Steinberg. He's unhappy anyway." Blumenthal's animus against Axelrod was really about Obama. He sent Clinton a steady diet of articles analyzing the flaws in the president's foreign policy, his troubles passing his legislative agenda, and his eroding popularity.

As always, though, Blumenthal's favorite project was Clinton herself. In July 2009, he sent her a long memo critiquing the draft of a speech she was planning to deliver at the Council on Foreign Relations. The speech, an ambitious blueprint for Clinton's tenure, had been through countless rewrites at the State Department. Blumenthal took an acid pen to it. "There's no accounting of progress so far," he wrote. "The effect is downbeat in tone." The speech, he said, was guilty of "blithe liberal cultural imperialism" in asserting that people everywhere want the same things Americans do. Most brutally, he advised Clinton to cut way back on her mantra, smart power. "Slogans can become shopworn," he wrote, "especially those that lack analytical, historical or descriptive power."

Of all the political staffers that Clinton brought with her to Foggy Bottom, none was as personally important to her—nor as emblematic of the tribal loyalties of Hillaryland—as Huma Abedin. Born in Kalamazoo, Michigan, and raised in Jeddah, Saudi Arabia, by an Indian father and a Pakistani mother, the thirty-three-year-old Abedin began working for Hillary as a White House intern in 1996 when she was still a student at George Washington University. A sleek, striking woman with a charming, if somewhat remote, manner and a taste for Louis Vuitton handbags, Abedin traveled everywhere with Clinton, keeping her on schedule and in hand sanitizer. So close had she become to both Clintons that Bill once toasted her as his surrogate daughter; a jet-lagged Hillary once emailed her at 12:21 A.M. to take her up on her offer to come over to her house for a chat. If she was dozing when Abedin arrived, Clinton emailed, "Just knock on the door to the bedroom if it's closed."

At a meeting early in 2009 in the State Department, Abedin, who had the title of deputy chief of staff, was going through a list of requests from "the president." When the others in the room looked at her puzzled, she clarified, "Not President Obama. Our president. Bill Clinton." It was a jarring gaffe, evidence of just how deep and tangled those ties were. And yet it was understandable: By the last year of the first term, Abedin was, in fact, working for both presidents. Under an arrangement that later caused political headaches for Hillary, Abedin kept working part-time for her at the State Department while accepting a lucrative contract from a private consulting firm with ties to the Clinton Foundation. No other Clinton aide enjoyed that kind of latitude. But Abedin's offhand remark back in 2009 illustrated the challenges of working in the Obama administration for anyone raised in the Clinton ecosystem: They had to get used to staffing a staffer, not a president.

Jake Sullivan was rare in that he had straddled both worlds. This allowed him to play a vital role in the acculturation process. Brilliant, rail-thin, with a guileless mien that belied shrewd political instincts, Sullivan first showed his dexterous touch in 2008, advising Clinton on foreign policy during the primaries, then prepping Obama for his debates against John McCain. He shared the deputy chief of staff title with Abedin, but like her, he wielded outsized influence. If Huma was Clinton's right hand, he was her left. He was at her side in all 112 countries she visited as secretary of state—an ever-present, increasingly spectral figure, in a blue fleece, his eyes often deeply ringed after pulling another all-nighter on the road. Clinton described him as a "coolheaded, clear-eyed analyst of the problems we faced with our national security."

"He ended up being invaluable," she told me.

Even by the best-and-brightest standards of Washington, Sullivan's résumé is an overachiever's dream: high school debate champion in Minneapolis; editor of the *Yale Daily News* in college; Rhodes Scholar at Oxford; Yale Law School, an alma mater he shared with Clinton and to which he returned to teach after leaving the administration in 2014; clerk to Supreme Court justice Stephen Breyer. Sullivan, like Clinton and Obama, has a lawyer's cast of mind: He talks about having a "theory of a case" and dismisses flimsy arguments as "not dispositive." He knows he's often the smartest guy in the room. "It can feel like arrogance to say, 'I have an idea,' or 'I can do that'—especially if you're surrounded by smart and experienced people," he once told graduates of the Humphrey School of Public Affairs at the University of Minnesota. "But that's not arrogance. That's being constructive."

On Thanksgiving Day in 2010, Sullivan emailed Clinton to let her know he had circulated a call sheet to senior officials to develop recommendations for how she should handle Prime Minister Netanyahu on the phone the next day. "I'm taking a break from peeling potatoes," Sullivan explained. (His emails, often on sensitive subjects, would later land him in the middle of the storm over Clinton's use of a private email address and computer server while she was secretary of state.) Melanne Verveer, Hillary's chief of staff in the White House and her ambassador for global women's issues at the State Department, watched Sullivan in action on an overseas trip. Hours into the flight, when the cabin was dark and everyone else had dropped off to sleep, he was quietly speaking to the White House over a secure phone line. "Jake just never stopped," she said. "Everybody else could be out cold, and Jake was working those phones."

These qualities were not lost on Obama's whiz kids, Denis McDonough and Ben Rhodes. Sullivan was to become the primary transmission belt between Foggy Bottom and the West Wing, between Hillaryland and Obama-world. He was crucial to easing Clinton's isolation, especially with McDonough, a forty-six-year-old fellow Minnesotan, with whom he established a less contentious relationship than Cheryl Mills had.

A college football star from the town of Stillwater, where his nickname was "the Dude," McDonough shares Obama's lean frame, ascetic habits, and cautious worldview, forged in the post-9/11 era. He is an old-school Irish Catholic, prematurely gray, with a touch of the hair shirt about him—working brutal hours, giving up coffee and chocolate for Lent, biking the seven miles to work from his home in Takoma Park, Maryland, until his wife forced him to give it up after an accident. A family man who coached his kids' soccer games while taking nonstop calls from the White House, McDonough could be uncommonly decent: He was known for his graceful notes to visitors and staffers. But he could also be hard on those around him, especially in the first year of the administration, when he bullied journalists and others who dared criticize his boss. He clashed with Sullivan, too, once laying into him for remarks he made at Obama's daily briefing that McDonough thought undercut him. (Sullivan, friends said, was stung for days afterward.) For the most part, though, the two got along. Over hundreds of emails and phone calls, they worked to make sure Clinton's public statements did not conflict with the White House.

With Rhodes, Sullivan developed a friendship that would prove fortuitous. Separated in age by a few months, they each had their boss's ear and power beyond their years. The two are different: Rhodes is a city kid from Manhattan who smokes and likes a martini; Sullivan, a Midwesterner who drinks beer and roots for the Vikings and Twins. Rhodes is an idealist and a romantic (he has an unfinished novel in a drawer, "Oasis of Love," about a woman who joins a mega-church in Houston, breaking her boyfriend's heart); Sullivan is hardheaded and pragmatic. Rhodes thumbs his nose at the Clinton-era Democratic establishment; Sullivan is a card-carrying member of that establishment. And yet they hit it off, emailing or speaking several times a day. Often, it was over routine matters such as the wording of a Clinton statement; other times, it was to make history. The diplomatic openings to Burma and Cuba both had their roots in bull sessions between Rhodes and Sullivan, with Sullivan honing the concepts and Rhodes using his influence with the president to maneuver them through the risk-averse West Wing bureaucracy.

After Clinton left the State Department, she and the president would use their staffs—once the source of so much mutual enmity—to preserve a veneer of unity over how they had worked together and how they viewed the world. She gave parts of her memoir *Hard Choices* to Rhodes for review before publication to make sure her gentle airing of policy disagreements did not ruffle Obama. In early 2013, Sullivan became national security adviser to Joe Biden, a perch that allowed him to convey the White House's sensitivities to her. To help with the rollout of the book, Clinton hired Tommy Vietor, the Obama loyalist whose jaundiced views of her had been formed by the poisonous transcripts he read back in Iowa. She won him over when he was the NSC's spokesman, once sending him a sling with a State Department seal after he dislocated his shoulder while playing basketball. A quick study with an iPhone full of press contacts, Vietor was tasked with pushing back on reporters who would use the book to try to drive a wedge between her and Obama.

For much of Clinton's tenure, the State Department and White House were tormented by the anonymous owner of a Twitter account with the handle @NatSecWonk. This mystery tweeter, who posted from inside the administration and amassed a small but devoted audience, ridiculed everyone from Rhodes to Reines to various *New York Times* reporters. Sample: "I'm a fan of Obama, but his continuing reliance and dependence upon a vacuous cipher like Valerie Jarrett concerns me." Or, "Look, Issa is an ass, but he's on to something here with the @HillaryClinton whitewash of accountability for Benghazi," referring to Darrell Issa, the California Republican who plagued Clinton over the Benghazi attacks. @NatSecWonk was eventually unmasked as a forty-year-old NSC analyst named Jofi Joseph. He was sacked; he issued an apology and since has become a cautionary tale for using social media in the workplace, when your workplace happens to be the White House.

Before his fall, though, @NatSecWonk had Clinton squarely in his crosshairs, tweeting that she had "few policy goals and no wins" as secretary of state. It was a harsh verdict, but in the years after she stepped down—when John Kerry was a whirling dervish of activity, negotiating the Iran nuclear deal, seeking a political settlement in the Syrian civil war, trying to revive the Middle East peace talks—it was not an uncommon one. By comparison to Kerry, Clinton's record looked meager; her approach, cautious; her achievements, evanescent. @NatSecWonk was simply voicing what a number of people in the White House and State Department privately thought: Hillary Clinton had been a respectable but run-of-the-mill secretary of state.

Assessing Clinton's record requires a couple of stipulations. The first is that few secretaries of state in the modern era have compiled a spectacular list of wins. Henry Kissinger, the most famous of them, engineered the secret opening to China and negotiated the Paris Peace Accords, which ended direct American combat in Vietnam and set the stage for the war's messy final act. James Baker, arguably the most effective of them, helped steer the Cold War to a peaceful end, assembled a robust coalition for the Persian Gulf War, and orchestrated the Madrid peace talks between the Israelis and Palestinians, which became a model for future Middle East peace negotiations. Warren Christopher, Madeleine Albright, and Condoleezza Rice had no comparable achievements, while Colin Powell is remembered most for brandishing a vial of white powder in the UN Security Council and claiming, erroneously, that Saddam Hussein had weapons of mass destruction.

Even John Kerry's busy tenure has earned a mixed verdict, with his failed Middle East peace campaign balancing his breakthrough with Iran. Kerry, moreover, was blessed with timing: Clinton spent her first two years in a largely symbolic global rehabilitation tour for the United States, patching up relationships frayed by George W. Bush's invasion of Iraq. Then she was tasked with lining up the international sanctions that eventually forced the Iranians to the bargaining table. As Clinton somewhat plaintively put it, she "set the table" for Kerry's diplomatic banquet.

"For better or worse, we have sort of a heroic vision of diplomacy," Jim Steinberg told me. "Henry Kissinger is the epitome of this. But it's easy to overwrite the traditional role of leader-to-leader diplomacy. That's especially true in the twenty-first century, because the role of the state has changed." Clinton confronted a world that was more complicated than Kissinger's or Baker's—one in which a medieval Islamic caliphate conquered large parts of Iraq; in which the United States no longer faced a single Cold War rival but rather a babel of rising powers; in which economic and environmental factors, such as joblessness in the Middle East and rising seas in the Pacific, drove events as much as geopolitics.

A second stipulation is that a secretary of state's clout derives almost wholly from his or her relationship with the president. To the extent that the secretary is seen as a confidant or, better yet, a proxy of the commander in chief, he or she can get things done. Kissinger spoke to Richard Nixon several times a day, more than anyone else in Nixon's cabinet. "Shared personality traits made [them] effective collaborators," Robert Dallek wrote in his book *Nixon and Kissinger.* "Their combative natures made them distrustful of others, whom they suspected of envy and ambition to outdo them." Jim Baker was George H. W. Bush's consigliere before his cabinet officer, a status that gave him muscle in Washington and credibility abroad. "Baker used to say that he was President George H. W. Bush's man at the State Department, not the State Department's man at the White House," said Aaron David Miller, who served as an adviser to Baker and other secretaries of state.

Neither of those models was ever going to apply to Clinton and Obama. She would never have described herself as Obama's woman at the State Department. Clinton was a world figure coming into the job, with celebrity and a Rolodex of contacts that rivaled or exceeded Obama's. Nor did she have the deep familiarity with the president—the round-the-clock, backchannel access—that Kissinger had with Nixon. "I see the president when I need to see him; I talk to the president when I need to talk to him," Clinton told me, a bit defensively. She was clearly sensitive that outsiders would make unflattering comparisons. In December 2009, when she was considering a request from *Newsweek* for a joint interview with Kissinger, Clinton raised a potential red flag with her press aide, Philippe Reines. "The only issue I think that might be raised is that

I see POTUS at least once a week while K saw Nixon every day," she emailed. "Of course, if I were dealing with that POTUS I'd probably camp in his office to prevent him from doing something problematic. Do you see this as a problem?"

The formal, unequal nature of her relationship with Obama was perhaps best summed up by the importance she attached to their weekly meeting in the Oval Office. On a snowy Thursday morning in February 2010 when she was scheduled to meet the president, Clinton got an alarming phone call: Her husband Bill had been admitted to New York–Presbyterian Hospital with chest pains, and was in need of an urgent heart procedure. Instead of rushing home to him, Clinton kept her weekly appointment, taking her customary seat on the yellow sofa as she and Obama talked about an upcoming trip to the Persian Gulf, where she planned to turn up the heat on Iran over its nuclear program. "No one had any idea" she had a family emergency, said an official who was in the room that day. Afterward, she raced for a shuttle flight back to New York.

Further complicating life for Hillary, Obama brought an overweening self-confidence to the Oval Office. He was more than ready to answer the three A.M. phone call—the punch line from Clinton's famous attack ad—without putting her on the line. His tight grip was most evident on marquee foreign policy portfolios such as Iran and Russia. He had befriended Dmitri Medvedev in the hopes that a high-level bromance with the young Russian president might usher in a new era of goodwill. He wrote secret letters to Iran's supreme leader, Ayatollah Ali Khamenei, to entice the suspicious mullah into a dialogue. Obama handed the Iraq file to Joe Biden, a decision that Clinton did not contest because she viewed it as a loser. Even on issues that are supposed to be in a secretary of state's wheelhouse—peace talks between Israel and the Palestinians, for example—the White House set the strategy and Clinton was less an architect than an implementer.

Obama sanctioned the consolidation of foreign policy decision-making inside the West Wing. By 2010, the National Security Council staff had grown to 370 people, more than ten times its size under Kissinger. As it grew, it expanded beyond strategy into the day-to-day operations traditionally handled by the State Department and other agencies. Some of that reflected the addition of the Homeland Security Council, a post-9/11 creation that advises the president on terrorism or other threats. But a lot of it simply represented the secular shift of power away from the Harry S. Truman building, home of the State Department, to the Eisenhower building, home of the NSC.

So well-established was the Obama White House's penchant for control that when Antony Blinken—a suave, well-pedigreed adviser to Biden who later became the deputy national security adviser—moved to the State Department to be deputy secretary in January 2015, he knew just how to break the ice with his new colleagues at his first staff meeting. "I've been here one day and I've come to one conclusion," Blinken told them with a grin. "This micro-management of the inter-agency process by the White House has got to stop."

Clinton's aides pooh-poohed the notion that she was plotting a run for the White House from Foggy Bottom and shaping her tenure as secretary of state to further that ambition. But in some ways, she never stopped behaving like a candidate. Her emails show she kept a close eye on the political machinations of would-be rivals such as Joe Biden, Jim Webb of Virginia, and Andrew Cuomo of New York. She made time to speak to marquee Democratic donors such as Steven Spielberg and less well-known, but important, figures such as Lou D'Allesandro, a state senator from New Hampshire who had been a cochairman of Italian-Americans for Hillary in 2008. When one of her former policy advisers, Neera Tanden, asked her in early 2012 whether she should hold a reunion for alumni of the campaign, Clinton gave it her blessing. "I am very proud of all they—and we—did," she replied. "Onward!"

Tanden emailed Clinton with regular updates on one of her pet issues: the epic battle to overhaul the nation's healthcare system. At one point, she noted that Obama's legislation was moving closer to what Clinton had pushed in the campaign. ("If it does break that way," Tanden wrote, "I'll try to ensure I'm not the only one who notices.") When the bill was a few votes short of passage in the House in November 2009, a desperate White House enlisted Clinton to lobby two Blue Dog Democrats from Arkansas who were holding out (one switched his vote to a yes). On the morning of Christmas Eve in 2009, Clinton told a State Department colleague, she woke up early to watch the Senate hold a seven A.M. vote on the legislation. It passed 60 to 39.

Even Clinton's diplomatic efforts sometimes felt like a political campaign. When she first traveled to Beijing in February 2009, for example, Clinton got an earful from the Chinese about how the United States might not be represented at the Shanghai Expo the following year because it had not raised the money to build a national pavilion. "I was dumbfounded that so little attention had been paid to it," she told me. "Everyone knows China is going to be an enormously powerful player in the twenty-first century. They have an expo, which is a kind of rite of passage that countries like to do to show they have arrived. We're not there? What does that say?"

Her solution was to reactivate the Clinton fundraising network. Elizabeth F. Bagley, a prolific bundler—and the widow of the R. J. Reynolds heir Smith Bagley—had been installed at the State Department as one of her special advisers. She began calling around to the chief executives of PepsiCo, General Electric, and Chevron, asking for multimillion-dollar pledges and dangling sponsorship deals. "Great news from Chevron!" Bagley wrote in an email that was forwarded to Clinton, after the oil company committed $5 million to the $60 million project. Chevron's CEO, David O'Reilly, had promised Clinton in a letter that he would help. The State Department's lawyers were queasy—"Would Thomas Jefferson do this?" one asked—but they signed off, provided that Clinton did not personally squeeze anyone for cash.

Evidently, their queasiness did not extend to the American ambassador. Clinton's office asked Jon Huntsman, a former Republican governor of Utah whom Obama appointed as his envoy to China in 2009, to dial for dollars as well. The scion of one of Utah's richest families, Huntsman had won two terms as governor. (He later came back from Beijing in 2012 to run a long-shot bid for the GOP presidential nomination.) Though he endorsed Clinton's effort, he refused to take part in it. "I didn't want McNerney from Boeing coming into the office saying, 'OK, we gave you five million bucks for the Expo, we need some help on 757 orders,'" he said, referring to Boeing's chairman, James McNerney. "I just never wanted to be put in that position. Nor did I want to put them, the CEOs, in that position."

It didn't matter: Clinton's star power alone was enough to raise nearly $55 million in less than nine months. The following May, she traveled to Shanghai to see the House That Clinton Built, otherwise known as the USA Pavilion. It looked like a rental-car center at a big-city airport, with matte-gray walls and relentless corporate shilling inside (videos showcasing representatives from Chevron, General Electric, and Johnson & Johnson; environmentally friendly features sponsored by Alcoa; a gift shop with licensed merchandise from Disney). "It's fine," Clinton replied, lips pursed, when I asked her what she thought of it. "Can you imagine if we had *not* been here?"

During the last two years of her tenure, Clinton did less of this feel-good public diplomacy and more of the heavy lifting on sensitive issues such as Syria, Libya, Iran, China, and the periodic clashes between Israel and Hamas. Still, she was never going to be at the heart of the Obama foreign policy machine, and she knew it. That helps explain her aggressive focus on development while secretary of state. The grab bag of social projects that she embraced was one way to compensate for the limitations she faced in the traditional realm of national security. Clean-burning cookstoves, diaspora engagement networks, women's and girls' rights, the Shanghai Expo—it all added up to what Aaron Miller called "planetary humanism."

Planetary humanism, it must be said, did wonders for her public image. "Hillary Clinton's Last Tour as a Rock-Star Diplomat," was the headline of a *New York Times Magazine* profile in June 2012, which opened with her inspecting an exhibit of cookstoves in China. She was celebrated in gauzy profiles in *Vogue* and *Elle,* a run of good press unmatched in her political career. (Her first *Times Magazine* profile, in 1993, carried the headline "Saint Hillary," and it was not meant as a compliment.) The polarizing figure of the Clinton White House and the 2008 campaign had become the cool customer in oversized dark sunglasses, reading her BlackBerry on a C-17 military plane about to take off for Tripoli. That photo of her, taken in 2012, went viral on the Internet, giving rise to a popular meme, "Texts from Hillary." (Obama: "Hey Hil, Whatchu doing?" Clinton: "Running the World.")

Clinton's emails confirmed the suspicions of those of us who covered her: She and her aides had a campaign-like obsession with her image and press coverage. Poll numbers were analyzed as if the secretary of state were always about to face the voters in New Hampshire. In March 2011, Reines sent Clinton an email with the subject line, "65%!" He was referring to her favorability rating in the latest CNN poll, which was near her all-time peak. "This is why we cooperate with so many profiles," he explained, "and just wait until 19 million people read *People* next week."

The White House never stopped viewing Clinton through a political prism, either. On November 14, 2012, Israel began an intense air campaign against Hamas militants in Gaza in retaliation for rocket attacks on Israeli cities. A ground invasion loomed. Clinton was in Asia with Obama on what had become a farewell tour for the two of them. She told the president she thought she should fly to the region immediately to try to broker a cease-fire. Clinton had not come to the decision easily; the risks of failure were great and the consequences of thrusting herself into the middle of it unpredictable. As Obama and his aides debated whether to send her, however, the conversation turned to a familiar theme, according to a person who witnessed the exchange: Was Clinton just doing this to make herself look good?

Ironic, in that three and a half years earlier they had viewed Clinton's refusal to travel to Israel as proof of her political gamesmanship.

They sat side by side in the White House, he in a dark blue suit and tie, she in a raspberry jacket with turned-up collar, the camera lights reflecting off the prescription eyeglasses she had worn since suffering a concussion from a fall in her home. It was January 25, 2013, four days after Obama had been sworn in for a second term, and seven days before Clinton was to step down as secretary of state. The occasion was a joint interview on *60 Minutes,* the first time Obama had appeared on the program with anyone other than his wife. For all the attention it got at the time, the interview shed little light on the deeper mysteries of their partnership. Clinton laughed off a suggestion that anyone should read their appearance together as a preemptive endorsement for 2016. Obama paid tribute to her for reinvigorating the role of secretary of state and reminisced about their diplomatic derring-do in Copenhagen in 2009.

"I consider Hillary a strong friend," he replied, when asked how he would describe their relationship.

"I mean, very warm, close," Hillary said, leaning forward and gesturing with her hands, as she tried to offer more than a six-word answer to the question. "I think there's a sense of understanding that doesn't even take words because we have similar views, we have similar experiences that I think provide a bond that may seem unlikely to some, but has been really at the core of our relationship over the last four years."

The backstory, as usual, was more revealing.

Obama had asked his staff to look for ways he could thank Clinton publicly for her service in his cabinet. Ben Rhodes suggested to Philippe Reines that they do a joint interview in *Time* magazine; Reines countered with a joint appearance on *60 Minutes.* He had a bias for television over print and he already had been talking to one of the program's correspondents, Scott Pelley, about a one-on-one exit interview with Clinton. Pelley knew her well; he had traveled with her to Afghanistan in 2009 to report on the challenges she faced as secretary of state. The White House agreed but insisted that the interview be conducted by another *60 Minutes* correspondent, Steve Kroft, a favorite of Obama's. As a gesture, the president's offer was both magnanimous and controlling, a handy metaphor for two partners with their own agendas.

The choice of Kroft also carried a strange echo: Twenty years earlier, Kroft had asked Bill Clinton about his marital infidelities in a famous joint interview with Hillary on *60 Minutes*. It was, in many ways, her debut as a national public figure. As Obama and Clinton sat together, their conversation was a reminder that not only did she likely have a longer political future than he, but she also had a longer past—one that stretched back to 9/11 and the Iraq War, the storms of the Clinton years, and the 1992 campaign, when she had perched on a couch next to Bill, helping him save his campaign. At that time, Barack Obama was a thirty-year-old bachelor in Chicago, armed with a law school degree and a sense of destiny strong enough that he had already begun work on a memoir. His life story bore little resemblance to hers.

To understand the relationship they would forge, it helps to go back to their roots, to the different worlds in which they grew up and the different worldviews they acquired there.

# Two

## Origins

On October 2, 2002, a little-known Illinois state senator named Barack Obama spoke at a rally against the Iraq War in Chicago's Federal Plaza. "I am not opposed to all wars," he told the crowd. "I'm opposed to dumb wars." Eight days later, a globally recognized former First Lady rose in the well of the United States Senate to declare her position. The White House was making a frightening case that fall: Saddam Hussein, it claimed, was secretly developing chemical, biological, and nuclear weapons. The president wanted the backing of Congress to take military action against him. "This is probably the hardest decision I've ever had to make," Hillary Clinton said, a rueful smile on her face. "Any vote that might lead to war should be hard. But I cast it with conviction." With that, she put her imprimatur on George W. Bush's invasion.

No issue exposed a deeper fault line between Clinton and Obama than the Iraq War. For both, it was a defining moment, one that reverberated for years afterward, even into the 2016 election— propelling and thwarting their ambitions, guiding many of their decisions, and framing how they perceive America's role in distant conflicts. Obama's foreign policy was, sometimes to an extreme, a repudiation of the blunders of Bush's military campaign. In the summer of 2015, he lashed out at those who opposed his nuclear agreement with Iran, accusing them of the same blindness that led America into the sand trap of Iraq. His withdrawal of the last

American combat soldier from Baghdad in December 2011 fulfilled a cherished campaign promise. But it proved a hollow victory when the Islamic State swept across the Syrian border into the security vacuum left by the Americans. He was forced to send soldiers back to Iraq, leaving to his successor a dangerous piece of unfinished business.

Clinton, who joined fellow Democrats Joe Biden and John Kerry in voting to authorize the war, wrestled with that judgment for the rest of her Senate career. She insisted, unconvincingly, that the White House had misled her about its intention to pursue last-ditch diplomacy to get weapons inspectors back into Iraq before pulling the trigger. She castigated the Bush administration for its conduct of the war and, along with the then Senator Obama, opposed its plan for a troop surge in 2007—a position both later conceded taking for political reasons, given the war's unpopularity.

Clinton's vote to authorize the military action had been no less political, of course. She came to the Iraq debate as the junior senator from New York, home to West Point and the sprawling Fort Drum army base, as well as ground zero for the 9/11 attacks. Those attacks, she and Bill Clinton instantly grasped, demanded an unyielding response from New York's woman in Washington. In multiple phone conversations on September 11, she and Bill honed her message. The next day, on the floor of the Senate, Clinton issued her own declaration of war against those who had brought down the Twin Towers. Anybody who sheltered terrorists, she declared, or chose to "in any way aid or comfort them whatsoever, will now face the wrath of our country."

As a woman who aspired to be commander in chief in the post-9/11 era, Clinton was determined to show herself as sufficiently steely for the battles to come, whether it was striking the Taliban in Afghanistan or toppling Saddam in Iraq. During the Democratic primaries, six years after she cast her Iraq vote, Clinton stubbornly refused to apologize for it. She only disavowed it as "wrong, plain and simple" twelve years later in her memoir, *Hard Choices*. In the end, her vote helped cost her the nomination to Obama, who used his antiwar stance to set himself apart from his more celebrated opponent.

And yet, cold calculation alone did not bring Clinton and Obama to that fateful divergence in the fall of 2002. Their views on Iraq were the product of a lifetime of experiences, coming of age in different places and times, with different instincts about the use of military power and the role of the United States as an agent of change in the world. Clinton grew up in the buoyant aftermath of World War II, the daughter of a navy petty officer who trained young sailors before they shipped out to the Pacific. Her parents were patriotic and conservative, typical, she wrote, "of a generation who believed in the endless possibilities of America." Obama, born in 1961, experienced the Greatest Generation only in the person of his grandfather, Stanley Dunham, who had been deployed to France six weeks after D-Day. A salesman who peddled furniture and later insurance, Dunham traced a restless, itinerant path that left him disillusioned at the end of his life, his dreams shrunk to fit a little apartment he shared with his wife and grandson.

The fourteen years that separated them put Obama and Clinton on opposite ends of the Vietnam War, that great hinge event of the post–World War II era. It shattered America's self-confidence and seared a generation of Democratic foreign policy thinkers whose counsel had sent Lyndon Johnson to ruin in Southeast Asia. Clinton, who delivered an anguished antiwar speech at her college graduation in 1969, was a pure product of those turbulent times. Obama, on the other hand, was eager to turn the page from the sixties and its messy legacy, summing it up years later as the "psychodrama of the baby boomers—a tale rooted in old grudges and revenge plots hatched on college campuses long ago."

Even more than time, Obama and Clinton were divided by geography. She was raised in the middle of the country, in a reliably Republican, middle-class suburb of Chicago. He had a polyglot childhood in Hawaii and even more distant Indonesia—forever an outsider, suspended between worlds. When Hillary Rodham arrived at Wellesley College as a freshman in the fall of 1965, she had been outside the United States only once, to the Canadian side of Niagara Falls. When Barry Obama turned up at Occidental College in the fall of 1979, he had traversed the international dateline many times but scarcely set foot in the American mainland. Clinton viewed her country from the inside out; Obama from the outside in.

Obama's cosmopolitanism was embedded in his DNA. With ancestors on his mother's side from south-central Kansas and on his father's side from western Kenya, "he could not be of one place, rooted and provincial," wrote his biographer David Maraniss. "His divided heritage from Africa and the American heartland had defined him from the beginning." The peripatetic career of Obama's anthropologist mother—shuttling back and forth between Hawaii and Indonesia—guaranteed that her young son would grow up with an expatriate's view of the United States, subjecting his country to the dispassionate gaze of a third party.

In Jakarta, the teeming, tropical city where Obama lived from the age of six to ten with his mother, Stanley Ann Dunham, and stepfather, Lolo Soetoro, he quickly picked up the language, Bahasa Indonesia. Young Barry sang patriotic songs and ordered his fellow first-graders to fall into formation in their own tongue. He ran with local kids through the alleyways of his middle-class neighborhood, redolent with the smell of clove cigarettes and burning banana leaves, and echoing with the call to prayer. Though Ann sent her son back to Hawaii to live with his grandparents after three and a half years, Indonesia remained a touchstone for him. His mother lived and worked in Jakarta for twenty more years, and as he made summer visits there as a teenager, he developed an increasingly jaundiced view of the influence of Western countries, their oil companies, and even their development agencies, including Ann Dunham's employer, the Ford Foundation. This far-flung Southeast Asian archipelago became Exhibit A for Obama of all that is good and ill about American power.

In Obama's 2006 book, *The Audacity of Hope,* which planted
the seeds for his presidential campaign, he devoted a single chapter
to the "world beyond our borders"; it begins and ends with Indonesia. The country, he wrote, offers a "handy record of U.S. foreign
policy over the past fifty years." In 1967, the year he and his mother
arrived, Suharto, a military officer with a placid face and brutal
streak, seized power in a bloody coup. He was embraced and bank-
rolled by the United States. American aid poured in; American
economists helped him modernize his economy; the American military conducted joint exercises with his soldiers. "The scope of that
power," Obama wrote, "was hard to miss." The rising tide of prosperity brought Indonesians luxuries such as refrigerators and cars.
Jakarta, once a dilapidated colonial outpost, became a metropolis
with glittering skyscrapers, clogged highways, and five-star hotels.
In the name of Cold War geopolitical security, however, the United
States tolerated the unsavory side of Suharto's rule: a repressive
political culture, the arrest and torture of dissidents, sham elections, and the brutal quashing of ethnic uprisings in distant corners of the country, such as Aceh.

Though he doesn't mention it in his book, Obama became disenchanted with the work done by the Ford Foundation and other
development agencies. Years later, in college, he was influenced by
one of his closest friends, Hasan Chandoo, a Pakistani, who told
him that American largesse, in support of military dictatorships,
had done as much harm as good in the third world. In his earlier
memoir, *Dreams from My Father,* Obama recalled that the idealism of his mother was no match for the cynicism and corruption
that festered all around her. "She was a lonely witness for secular
humanism," he wrote with more than a tinge of condescension, "a
soldier for New Deal, Peace Corps, position-paper liberalism."

His Kenyan roots added another layer to this carapace of suspicion. Obama wrote about the unexpected rush of resentment he
felt, on his first trip to his father's homeland, in seeing the Western
tourists in Nairobi, "taking pictures, hailing taxis, fending off
street peddlers, many of them dressed in safari suits, like extras on

a Hollywood set." In Hawaii, these sunburned visitors were a source of amusement; in Kenya, he found their gawking innocence an affront. Nearly three decades later, in July 2015, Obama returned to Kenya as president. His perspective inevitably was different. Shielded by his armored limousine and Secret Service detail, he lamented not being able to go up-country to visit his father's village or wander the streets of Nairobi, drinking tea and eating *ugali* and *sukuma wiki* (maize flour and greens) with the locals. Obama reminded them that he, too, was the product of colonialism: the grandson of a cook in the British army, the son of an intellectual who had gone to America for an education.

Critics have caricatured Obama's views of America as latent anticolonial rage, stoked by his Kenyan father and left-wing mother. That always seemed a stretch, given that he barely knew his dad and left Jakarta as a fourth grader. But Obama has long criticized the mix of naïveté and cynicism with which the United States treated postcolonial countries. "It's all there," he wrote of Indonesia, "our tendency to view nations and conflicts through the prism of the Cold War; our tireless promotion of American-style capitalism and multinational corporations; the tolerance and occasional encouragement of tyranny, corruption, and environmental degradation when it served our interests; our optimism once the Cold War ended that Big Macs and Internet would lead to the end of historical conflicts."

Coming home to Hawaii in 1971, one might think, would have given Barry Obama a healthy dose of America. His father was a distant figure in those days; he visited only once, at Christmastime that year. In some ways, life in Honolulu—where the turquoise dazzle of Waikiki gives way quickly to strip malls and cookie-cutter housing tracts—was as ordinary for Obama as it was for Hillary Rodham in Park Ridge, Illinois. He ate Kentucky Fried Chicken with his grandparents, watched *How the Grinch Stole Christmas!,* and played basketball with friends. At Punahou, the elite private school to which he had won a scholarship, Obama fell in with a carefree crew known as the Choom gang for their enthusiastic pot smoking.

But if Obama's teenage years had the late-seventies, stoner am-
bience of *Dazed and Confused*, Hawaii remained a place apart. In
those days, recalled Mike Ramos, a high school friend of Obama's,
football games aired on television hours after they ended on the
mainland. Because of the six-hour time difference with the East
Coast, the big news of the day in the United States was over by the
time people in Hawaii were waking up. The 2,500 miles of water
between Hawaii and California is a psychological, not just a physical, gulf. "In Hawaii, you really are on the outside looking in,"
Ramos told me. "There was this subtle otherness that crept in."

During Obama's school years, that feeling of otherness was reinforced by a flowering of Hawaiian history and culture. Gabby Pa-
hinui and his band, Sons of Hawaii, revived the genre of traditional
Hawaiian-language music, which was played on the first radio station exclusively devoted to Hawaiian music. Punahou began offering a course in Hawaiian history, which explored the less attractive
aspects of America's annexation of the islands, starting with the
1893 coup d'état, in which "these guys sort of came in and overthrew the queen," Ramos said. Obama, in his memoir, described
"the ugly conquest of the native Hawaiians through aborted trea-
ties and crippling disease brought by the missionaries" and "the
carving up of the volcanic soil by American companies for sugarcane and pineapple plantations."

There is little evidence that Obama dwelt too much on this
shabby history—by his own account, he wrestled more in those
years with his evolving sense of racial identity—but it fed into the
ambivalent view of the United States that he brought to the mainland. At Occidental College in Los Angeles, surrounded by a new
group of friends, including Hasan Chandoo and two other Pakistani students, Obama engaged in lengthy bull sessions about politics and foreign policy, conversations that sharpened his views
about the limits of American power. A telling moment came in a
freshman political science class, a few months after the signing of
the Camp David Accords. Obama represented a group that had
been assigned to critique a paper by fellow students in which they

argued that the peace treaty between Israel and Egypt would protect American interests and have a broader beneficial effect on the Middle East. He disagreed.

"We feel that the group's paper proceeds from the faulty premise that Egypt and Israel can solve the delicate problem of the Palestinians, with the U.S. overseeing and insuring the whole process," Obama wrote. "This takes a naïve faith in American ability to control the world according to its whims. In actuality, this has not been the case for some time—the U.S. today has limited influence in the Middle East, and must be viewed as a participant, rather than a controller of the world system."

Thirty years later, a newly elected Barack Obama attempted to play the peacemaking role in the Middle East that the eighteen-year-old Barry Obama had written off as a fool's errand. His chief emissary in that effort was his secretary of state, Hillary Clinton. Despite their combined celebrity and skills of persuasion, the two failed to bring together the suspicious Israelis and Palestinians—a result that seemed to vindicate the young Obama's conclusion that Americans habitually overestimated their ability to shape events in distant lands.

If Hillary Clinton harbored her own doubts about Obama's foray into Middle East peacemaking, they hinged on tactics, not on any reservations about the capacity of the United States to be a force for good in the world. For a person of her generation and upbringing, that was an unspoken assumption. In 1960, her ninth-grade history teacher, Paul Carlson, painted the world as a life-or-death struggle between godless communism and the American way—with only one acceptable outcome. "Remember, above all else," he exhorted the class, "better dead than red!"

Clinton, who at that time channeled the anticommunist, Republican views of her father, Hugh Rodham, wholeheartedly agreed. Political conversion was to come later, when Vietnam and the sixties swept over the Wellesley campus. But even after she had become First Lady, Clinton acknowledged in an interview with NPR, "my political beliefs are rooted in the conservatism that I was raised with." That was especially true of her foreign policy instincts. She talks often about her girlhood dream of becoming an astronaut, citing the rejection letter she got from NASA as the first time she encountered gender discrimination. Her real motive for volunteering, she wrote, may have been because her father fretted that "America was lagging behind Russia."

Hugh Rodham, a tightfisted drapery salesman, ran his house like the navy instructor he had once been. One of Clinton's biographers, Carl Bernstein, vividly described him in his living room lounge chair in front of a TV set, "barking orders, denigrating, minimizing achievements, ignoring accomplishments, raising the bar constantly for his frustrated children—'character building,' he called it." It left a deep impression. Years later, in a desert encampment outside Riyadh, Clinton found herself seated next to King Abdullah of Saudi Arabia, facing a giant flat-screen television showing images of off-road motorcycle racing (the king liked to conduct meetings with the TV on so others couldn't hear his conversation). The sight of it struck those of us traveling with her as bizarre, but she told us later it was strangely reminiscent of her father.

"She was Methodist, born in the Midwest, in the middle of the century," Lissa Muscatine, a friend and former speechwriter for Clinton, told me. "She was on the edge of these various social movements, but not quite there yet. She just has a very deep faith in the power of this country to do good in the world and to protect its people."

As a young woman, Clinton was as parochial as Obama was international. Part of it was a lack of linguistic talent: She was so hopeless at French in college that her professor told her, "Mademoiselle, your talents lie elsewhere." Even now, Clinton politely refuses to make the token gesture of uttering a few words in the native tongue when she lands in a country because she would mangle them so badly. (Obama, by contrast, never tires of showing off his limited Bahasa or Swahili.) Hillary did not make her first trip to Europe until after she left Yale Law School in 1973, when Bill Clinton took her to England to see Westminster Abbey, the Houses of Parliament, Stonehenge, and the Lake District. There, he made the first of many marriage proposals to his besotted but indecisive girlfriend.

Even Vietnam touched Clinton differently than it did many other members of her generation. During the tumultuous year of 1968, she was still making her transition from Republican to Democrat, going to the conventions of both parties. That summer, as a Republican college intern in Washington, she spoke up in a large meeting with a Wisconsin congressman, Melvin Laird, questioning him about the wisdom of LBJ's escalating involvement in Southeast Asia. Laird, who was later Richard Nixon's defense secretary, defended the policy, though he had his own misgivings. The future lawyer seemed less concerned about the quagmire of Vietnam than its constitutional implications, particularly after Nixon's decision to expand the war into Cambodia in 1970. Nor was Clinton a visible participant in the teach-ins and other antiwar rallies that roiled the Yale campus during her years as a law student in New Haven.

"During our law school years of 1969 to 1972, many of us were heavily involved in efforts to end the war in Vietnam," said Greg Craig, a classmate who went on to work as a White House lawyer for both Bill Clinton and Barack Obama. "I don't remember Hillary having much to do with that." (In 2008, he broke with Hillary to support Obama.)

Clinton, fired by her Methodist faith and a deepening social conscience, channeled her passions in another direction: alleviating poverty and defending the legal rights of children. Drawn to the work of Marian Wright Edelman, the founder of the Children's Defense Fund, Clinton began a two-decade odyssey that would make her a leading figure in the field of children's advocacy. "I realized," she wrote, "that what I wanted to do with the law was to give voice to children who were not being heard." She would carry those passions all the way to the White House.

• • •

Hillary Clinton's first two years as First Lady were, more than anything else, the story of her crusade to overhaul the American
healthcare system. Much has been written about this quixotic
effort—the intense secretiveness, the thousand-plus pages of regulations, the hubris, the "Harry and Louise" TV ad, which turned
the public against the project. What is pertinent to this book is how
completely the healthcare debate consumed her, and how the failure of it left her casting about for a new purpose. It's not that Clinton never looked abroad: She liked to remind people that as First
Lady of Arkansas, she brought Muhammad Yunus, the Bangla-
deshi social entrepreneur, to visit to see if his micro-credit programs could lift poor towns in the Ozarks. But just as her husband
never forgot James Carville's famous line about the 1992 campaign,
Clinton styled herself as a First Lady who cared about kitchen-
table issues.

Healthcare reform collapsed in August 1994. That November,
Republicans swept to power in both houses of Congress, having
turned the midterm elections into a referendum on Clinton-style
big government. It was a humiliating defeat for Bill Clinton, but
even more devastating to Hillary because she was identified with
the Great Society–style project that had done the most damage.
She became radioactive in the West Wing, blamed by the president's
advisers for wrecking his presidency. Demoralized and adrift, she
considered withdrawing entirely from a political role. "I didn't
want to be a hindrance to my husband's administration," she told
her staff.

It was not evident in those dark days, but the death of healthcare
was the beginning of Clinton's foreign policy career. In March
1995, she and her daughter, Chelsea, set off on a twelve-day, five-
nation tour of South Asia, where Hillary road tested the themes
that would echo through dozens of trips in the decades to come.
Flying from Pakistan to India, Sri Lanka to Nepal, Clinton visited
girls' schools, health clinics, and orphanages. She held earnest ex-

changes with women entrepreneurs who had been helped by micro-loans. She leavened one of her speeches with words from a poem written by an Indian schoolgirl: "Too many women, in too many countries, speak the same language. Of silence." In Nepal, she and Chelsea rode an elephant.

The response was immediate and enthusiastic. The polarizing Hillary of Washington was a hit overseas. She was exasperated when reporters traveling with her asked why she had not spoken out earlier on behalf of women's rights. "I had been working for 25 years on improving the status and dignity of women and children in America," she wrote. But Clinton's message played better over-seas, where she was greeted as a First Lady in the tradition of Jac-queline Kennedy, not as an ambitious left-wing social engineer trying to ram health insurance down the throats of Americans. Sty-mied in her ambitions to perfect her own society, Clinton realized that she could propagate her American values to a wider audience as a global ambassador.

As Carville later told her, "You spent two years trying to get people better healthcare and they tried to kill you. You and Chelsea rode an elephant, and they loved you!"

South Asia was merely a warm-up for China. In September 1995, six months after the trip with Chelsea, Clinton agreed to go to Bei-jing to attend the United Nations Fourth World Conference on Women. The trip prompted hand-wringing all over Washington: China hawks in Congress complained it would send the wrong message. (Beijing had just jailed Harry Wu, a Chinese dissident who had returned to his country from the United States.) Political aides in the West Wing feared she would somehow embarrass her husband. China hands at the State Department argued that Sino-American diplomacy should be left to the diplomats. "They were concerned it might offend the Chinese," the late Sandy Berger, na-tional security adviser at the time, told me. "They were rather bu-reaucratic about it. My view was, this was a great opportunity for the United States, for her to speak and represent us."

Clinton anguished over her speech, working on it during a family vacation in Jackson Hole, Wyoming, a stopover in Hawaii, and the eleven-hour flight to Beijing. She and her aides had tried to keep a tight grip on the draft to prevent it from being watered down with insertions from every government agency. Lissa Muscatine, her speechwriter, recalled padding up the darkened aisle of the plane to Clinton's cabin, passengers dozing on both sides, to hand her the final version. As she took the sheaf of papers, Clinton looked at her for a moment without saying anything. "I just want to push the envelope," she said quietly. Muscatine, a onetime newspaper reporter not given to mawkish emotion, was "just blown away," she recalled. "I thought, 'This is why I do this.' This was why I was willing to be up in the middle of the night on a plane, looking at a blank screen."

Clinton's speech proved the most successful of her career, and the most enduring as well. With blunt, unsparing language and a methodical piling-up of the horrors visited on girls and women in some societies ("doused with gasoline, set on fire and burned to death because their marriage dowries are deemed too small"; "denied food, or drowned, or suffocated, or their spines broken, simply because they are born girls"), Clinton built to a rhetorical climax. "If there is one message that echoes forth from this conference," she declared, "let it be that human rights are women's rights and women's rights are human rights, once and for all."

It was a memorable line from someone who, unlike Obama, does not often come up with memorable lines. The role of women in the developing world gave Clinton a frame through which to champion human rights, which she carried throughout her career. So it was a supreme irony that when Clinton traveled to Beijing fourteen years later on her maiden voyage as secretary of state, she told reporters that lecturing the Chinese leaders on human rights did not make sense because the two countries needed to work together on other pressing problems, from climate change to the North Korean nuclear threat. The idealism of Eleanor Roosevelt had given way to the realism of Henry Kissinger.

That duality, however, has long coexisted in Clinton. At eighteen, she posed a revealing question in a letter to a Methodist youth minister, Donald Jones, who was hugely influential in her spiritual quest. "Can one be a mind conservative and a heart liberal?" she asked. The dichotomy between mind and heart—which her biographers have cited to explain why her outrage over Vietnam did not move her to take to the streets—flows through Clinton's foreign policy, as it does through her politics. It would surface again as she began to play a subtle but influential role in Bill Clinton's kitchen cabinet on matters of war and peace.

In April 1993, fewer than one hundred days into the Clinton presidency, the Muslim town of Srebrenica was under siege by Bosnian Serbs. The author and Holocaust survivor Elie Wiesel visited the White House at that time and gave a talk about the "perils of indifference." Afterward, the president invited him up to the family quarters, where they were joined by Hillary; her chief of staff, Melanne Verveer; and Richard Holbrooke, who would later become special envoy to the Balkans. Bill Clinton, Verveer recalled, gave Wiesel a status report on the fighting in Srebrenica and asked him, "What would you do?"

"Elie was quite clear," she said. "We have to act."

His words had a big impact on Hillary. By then, she wrote later, she already believed "the only way to stop the genocide in Bosnia was through selective air strikes against Serbian targets." Her husband agreed, but he couldn't sell it to the European allies. So he defaulted to a fruitless strategy of offering the Serbs concessions to try to lure them into peace talks. It took another two years—and the slaughter of more than eight thousand in Srebrenica—before NATO, led by the United States, carried out air strikes, forcing the Serbs to the table and leading to the Dayton Accords. Six years later, in March 1999, she advised her husband to order air strikes in Kosovo, where the Serbs were trying to wipe out ethnic Albanians.

"I urged him to bomb," she said to *Talk* magazine, recounting a phone call she made to Bill while on a trip to North Africa. "You cannot let this go on at the end of a century that has seen the major holocaust of our time. What do we have NATO for if not to defend our way of life?"

Among those who shared Hillary's hawkish views on the Balkans was Madeleine Albright, a fellow Wellesley graduate ten years her senior, then serving as ambassador to the United Nations. "What's the point of having this superb military that you're always talking about if we can't use it?" she famously said to Colin Powell, the chairman of the Joint Chiefs of Staff, when he recited a list of objections to intervening in Bosnia. In the summer of 1995, Albright wrote President Clinton a blunt memo, arguing that the United States needed to make a renewed push for air strikes, even if it meant withdrawing the UN peacekeeping force that was there. Hillary took notice, and when Bill was mulling who should replace Warren Christopher as secretary of state in his second term, she made a full-court press for Albright.

"Hillary said to him, 'Why wouldn't you name Madeleine? She's closer to your views than anybody else, she expresses them better than anybody else, and besides, it would make your mother happy,' " Albright told me. "I would never have been secretary of state if it hadn't been for Hillary."

The two traveled together and became fast friends. On a trip in September 1996 to Prague, the city of Albright's birth, they walked the cobblestone streets of Old Town Square, window-shopped, and sat in a café, talking about World War II over dumplings and cabbage. "I got the sense, and it clearly came through later, that she understood what American power was about," Albright recalled. *The New York Times* portrayed the outing as an audition for Albright with the First Lady, but their kinship was genuine, deepened in part by their shared experience of marital strife. "One of the stranger dinners of all time was Hillary, Queen Noor, and me," Albright recalled about an evening she organized with the queen of Jordan after the Monica Lewinsky scandal, "each of us connected to a husband who was either dead, divorced, or in a state of dishonor." (Albright's husband, Joseph, left her for another woman when she was forty-five.)

Apart from her lobbying for Albright, detecting Hillary's fingerprints on the foreign policy of Bill Clinton is not easy. Unlike with healthcare reform, where she ran the president's task force, she did not take part in NSC debates or buttonhole either Sandy Berger or his predecessor as national security adviser, Anthony Lake. But nobody doubted that she made her views known to her husband—"I suspect in the evening," Berger said. "The president had such great respect for her views and her judgment. I often thought in the morning I heard some echoes of Hillary in something he said. So I suspect they talked about these things privately."

Sometimes, her keen interest in issues caught people off guard. In October 1996, George Mitchell, whom Clinton had named as his special envoy to Northern Ireland after his retirement from the Senate, traveled to Chautauqua, New York, to help the president prep for the first debate of his reelection campaign against Bob Dole, the Republican nominee (the Yankee Mitchell played the cranky Dole in the mock debates). On their first evening together, Clinton invited Mitchell to dinner, and the former senator found Hillary sitting at the table. For the first hour, he recalled, they talked only about his diplomatic efforts in Northern Ireland, an initiative she continued as secretary of state. "She was very emotionally involved in it," Mitchell told me.

On rare occasions, the president's men got a glimpse of what Hillary was telling him behind closed doors. On December 15, 1998, the first couple was flying home from the Middle East after a visit laden with symbolism. Benjamin Netanyahu had taken them to Masada, the mountaintop fortress where the Jews made their last stand against the Roman army nearly two thousand years ago. They had sung Christmas carols at the Church of the Nativity with Yasser Arafat. In the conference room on Air Force One, Clinton was being briefed by Berger and another NSC official, Bruce Rie-

del, about a chronic headache: Saddam Hussein's refusal to allow
United Nations weapons inspectors back into Iraq.

Weeks earlier, the Pentagon had drawn up plans to carry out air
strikes against Iraqi sites where Saddam was suspected of hiding
weapons of mass destruction. But each time Clinton was about to
pull the trigger, Saddam would make just enough of a concession
to unravel the solidarity of America's allies and forestall a military
attack. There were political complications as well: Clinton faced
an impeachment vote in the House because of the Lewinsky affair;
calling in an air strike at that moment would inevitably carry an
echo of *Wag the Dog*. But with the Muslim holiday of Ramadan
fast approaching, his advisers on the plane warned him that time
was running out.

"He was a reluctant warrior who, I think, in his heart of hearts
wished Iraq would just go away," Riedel recalled.

The briefing over, a weary Clinton walked out of the room to get
some sleep in his cabin at the front of the plane. The First Lady
stayed behind, along with Riedel and Berger, who continued hash-
ing out the issues. The two men were plainly worried that if Clinton vacillated again, it would damage his credibility. Hillary, who
had been leafing through magazines, said nothing during the briefing but listened to their back-and-forth. Suddenly, she spoke up.
"Don't let him off this time," she said. "You got to make sure you
get him. Don't let him sneak out of this one."

The "him" she was referring to was her husband, not Saddam
Hussein.

The next day, Clinton signed off on Operation Desert Fox, sending waves of F-16 fighters, B-52 bombers, and Tomahawk cruise
missiles to strike nearly one hundred Iraqi targets, including Saddam's palaces and the barracks of his Republican Guard. The list
of targets suggested to some that the purpose of the attack was as
much to destabilize the Iraqi regime as to destroy Saddam's weapons. Two months earlier, Clinton had signed legislation that made
"regime change" in Iraq official United States policy. Desert Fox, it
turned out, was the precursor to George W. Bush's war.

• • •

Standing in the Senate that October day in 2002, Hillary Clinton drew heavily on what she had seen as First Lady to justify her vote on Iraq. Her husband, she noted, had resorted to military force against the country. Saddam, she said, citing multiple intelligence reports, had begun replenishing his chemical and biological stockpiles, and restarted his nuclear program, as soon as the missiles of Desert Fox stopped flying. She credited Bill with shifting U.S. policy from containment to regime change, even if the method he had in mind for forcing out Saddam was the ballot box, not the Eighty-second Airborne. Clinton reminded her audience that, similar to Bush with Iraq, her husband had been unable to obtain the UN Security Council's authorization for air strikes in Kosovo because of the opposition of a veto-wielding Russia. The United States and its NATO allies went ahead with a seventy-eight-day bombing campaign anyway, and it halted a campaign of ethnic cleansing against thousands of ethnic Albanians. Leadership, she said, sometimes requires going around the United Nations.

"Perhaps my decision is influenced by my eight years of experience on the other end of Pennsylvania Avenue in the White House, watching my husband deal with serious challenges to our nation," she said. "I want this president, or any future president, to be in the strongest possible position to lead our country, in the United Nations or in war."

Clinton disavowed her Iraq vote later on the grounds that the intelligence was faulty and that Bush misused the authority he was being granted. In fact, she failed to read a ninety-two-page classified National Intelligence Estimate provided to the senators, which offered a far more hedged assessment of whether Saddam possessed these weapons than the five-page unclassified version, including objections raised by the State Department and the Energy Department. The case Clinton laid out in 2002, however, faithfully reflects her worldview: the need for military force, the argument for regime change, the virtues of strong presidential leadership, and the necessity to act unilaterally when American interests are at stake and the world is not going along. As Obama said, speaking of Indonesia, "It's all there."

At the time Obama made his Iraq speech in Chicago, nobody much cared what he thought. He was still two years away from the Democratic convention address that would catapult him to the national stage. Only a few seconds of grainy footage from that day in Federal Plaza survive. But as with Clinton, the case Obama made against going to war against Saddam Hussein still reflects his worldview: his dismissal of the neoconservative agenda of armchair warriors such as Dick Cheney and Paul Wolfowitz; his repeated references to Iraq as a "dumb war," and his observation that Saddam "poses no imminent and direct threat to the United States"—the same rationale he would cite as president for not intervening against Bashar al-Assad in Syria.

"Even a successful war against Iraq will require a U.S. occupation of undetermined length, at undetermined cost, with undetermined consequences," Obama said. Invading Iraq unilaterally and on such dubious grounds, he added, "will only fan the flames of the Middle East, and encourage the worst, rather than best, impulses of the Arab world."

Even the throwaway lines in Obama's speech seem eerily predictive today. He referred to Egypt and Saudi Arabia as "so-called allies," and asked why the United States hadn't done more to stop them from repressing their populations and corrupting their economies so thoroughly that they had spawned a generation of angry, hopeless young people. Both countries saw their relations with the United States fray during the Obama presidency, under the twin strains of the Arab Awakening and Obama's eagerness to seek a nuclear accommodation with their archenemy, Iran. Rather than start a war in the Middle East, Obama challenged Bush to press nuclear-armed states such as Russia, India, and Pakistan to lock down their weapons stockpiles. That reflected an interest in nonproliferation that dated back to Obama's college days. At Columbia, where he had transferred from Occidental in 1981, he got an A on a paper he wrote on arms negotiations between the Soviet Union and the United States. He also wrote an article for the college's weekly magazine, *Sundial*, about two campus groups that were advocating a nuclear freeze.

When Obama graduated in 1983, he felt as if he were being drawn to a career much like his cosmopolitan upbringing—a prospect that left him uninspired. "Was I going to give in to what I felt was the gravitational pull of graduate school," he wrote, "getting a degree in international relations and working in the State Department, in the Foreign Service, or working for an international foundation?" Instead, he followed a path not unlike the young Hillary Clinton: He packed up his Honda Civic, drove to Chicago, and began work as a community organizer. For the next six years, his life was rooted in a place where the big questions were about asbestos in housing projects, not the throw-weights of nuclear missiles.

In fact, Barack Obama would not turn his attention back to world affairs in any sustained way until he was elected to the Senate in 2004. During the years that Hillary Clinton watched her husband struggle with Bosnia and Kosovo—scoring military successes that weaned the Democratic Party off an antiwar bias that had prevailed since Vietnam—Obama was getting married, teaching law at the University of Chicago, and launching his political career in Illinois. The lessons of the Balkans seemed to pass him by. In *The Audacity of Hope*, he devoted one paragraph to Bill Clinton's foreign policy. "In the eyes of the public, at least," he wrote, "foreign policy in the nineties lacked any overarching theme or grand imperatives."

Once in Washington, however, Obama tried to make up for lost time. He won a seat on the Senate Foreign Relations Committee and rekindled his interest in nuclear nonproliferation. In 2005, he traveled to Russia and Ukraine with Senator Dick Lugar, the Indiana Republican who had channeled money to the Russians to help secure their warheads. After touring a fortified Soviet-era nuclear storage facility, Obama recalled, they were fed "borscht, vodka, potato stew, and a deeply troubling fish Jell-O mold."

Casting about for fresh foreign policy ideas in the turbulent years after the Iraq invasion, Obama consulted Susan Rice, a Democratic foreign policy expert, and Samantha Power, a journalist and academic. Both spoke passionately about the need for America to intervene militarily on humanitarian grounds when the situation demanded it. Power had written the Pulitzer Prize–winning book *A Problem from Hell,* which was a blistering indictment of the Clinton administration's failure to do more to halt the genocide in Rwanda; Rice, a junior aide on Bill Clinton's National Security Council, was haunted by guilt over America's inaction there.

For all his attraction to idealists such as Power and Rice, Obama was drawn instinctively to the realist camp—a line of thinkers, from Kennan to Kissinger, who thought that foreign policy should reflect a cold-blooded weighing of national interests, not ideals. Obama spoke approvingly of the realism of George H. W. Bush, who did not pursue Saddam's army to Baghdad after the Gulf War. He struck up a dialogue with Zbigniew Brzezinski, who served as national security adviser to Jimmy Carter and became a leading light among Democratic realists. "I said to myself after talking to Obama, 'This is a very bright, very intelligent guy who seems to have a broadly gauged view of how the world is changing,'" Brzezinski told me. "And I still stick to that. I think what really has not been entirely up to par—and I have to qualify that because he has inherited a messy situation from his predecessor—has been the response to the dilemmas, particularly in the Middle East."

Years later, when Obama came under fire for his refusal to carry out threatened air strikes in Syria or his reluctance to intervene in Libya, the White House would reflexively bring up the Iraq precedent—so much so that critics began to complain that the president needed a strategy that was something more than "not-Iraq." In his heart, however, Obama remained as much a skeptic about America's capacity to control events outside its borders as he had been as a college freshman.

In January 2006, as a senator with presidential ambitions, Obama joined two other lawmakers on a tour of the Middle East.

He went to Iraq, where he saw firsthand the results of what he had dubbed, four years earlier, a "dumb war." And he spent a week in Israel and the West Bank, where, flying by helicopter over the stony hills, he recalled being unable to tell the Jewish towns from the Arab ones. Gazing over the holy sites in Jerusalem, Obama wrote these words:

> From the promenade above Jerusalem, I looked down at the Old City, the Dome of the Rock, the Western Wall, and the Holy Sepulcher, considered the two thousand years of war and rumors of war that this small plot of land had come to represent, and pondered the possible futility of believing that this conflict might someday end in our lifetime, or that America, for all its power, might have any lasting say over the course of the world.
>
> I don't linger on such thoughts, though—they are the thoughts of an old man.

A young man, too.

# Three

## Hillary and the Brass

It was the end of a whirlwind five-day trip to the Persian Gulf, and Hillary Clinton was anxious to get back to Washington. She wanted to keep three appointments with President Obama the next day. Instead, she was cooling her heels in the VIP lounge at the King Abdulaziz International Airport outside Jeddah, her aging Air Force Boeing 757 grounded by a faulty fuel valve. While she paced the room in a flowing red pashmina—checking her BlackBerry and making stilted small talk with reporters—her aides worked the phones, trying desperately to find her another ride home.

Salvation came in the form of General David Petraeus, the commander of the Pentagon's Central Command, who also happened to be in Saudi Arabia that day, lunching with King Abdullah at his desert encampment outside Riyadh. Petraeus got a call through military channels that Clinton was stranded and agreed to divert his smaller Boeing 737 to Jeddah to pick her up, along with a few close aides, and take her back to Washington. "I said, 'Look, she's the secretary of state,'" he told me. "'We're going to have to disembark a fair number of people, but let's do this.'" The general even gave up his private compartment at the back of the plane to Clinton, an act that was equal parts chivalry and protocol: Because she was the ranking government official on board, it was now technically her aircraft, with the secretary of state's seal transferred from her stalled plane. Throwing down a couple of blankets, Petraeus stretched out and tried to get some sleep.

"The only place where I could get flat was the space between seats that face each other," the general recalled, having made a characteristically thorough study of the cabin layout.

Clinton and Petraeus both enjoy telling the story, and why not? It is a grace note in a methodically managed, mutually advantageous relationship—one that began warily in the toxic atmosphere of the Iraq War but was cemented in the war councils of the Obama White House. As a member of the Senate Armed Services Committee, Clinton impressed Petraeus on multiple visits to Iraq, connecting with his troops and peppering him with incisive questions about his counterinsurgency strategy. But in September 2007, she alienated him by publicly questioning his assessment of the progress made by George W. Bush's troop surge. Accepting his assertions, she scoffed, would require a "willing suspension of disbelief." Petraeus viewed it as a crass, if predictable, political move by a candidate facing a primary challenge from the antiwar Obama. It didn't help that Hillary had chatted amiably with the general in a Senate cloakroom before putting a shiv in him during the televised hearing. A chilly period followed until Clinton, soon after taking office as secretary of state, invited Petraeus for a conciliatory glass of wine in her Georgian house in Washington. From then on, there would be no daylight between her and this son of a Dutch-born sea captain.

Clinton's cultivation of men with medals didn't end with Petraeus. She became even closer to General Jack Keane, a retired army vice chief of staff who was the intellectual architect of the Iraq surge and a mentor to Petraeus. A burly, independent-minded New Yorker who grew up in Manhattan housing projects and goes to the opera at the Met, Keane spent dozens of hours with Clinton over the last decade—over lunch, drinks, and dinner—tutoring her on Iraq, Afghanistan, and the threat posed by the Islamic State. In all those conversations, Keane said, the only major issue where they split was the surge, which she opposed. In 2008, after Iraq had been stabilized, she told him, "Well, Jack, you were right all along." (The country's stability didn't last.) Clinton also forged links with Stanley McChrystal, the ascetic warrior who led the counterinsurgency campaign in Afghanistan until he was fired by Obama after his aides made derogatory remarks about almost every member of his war cabinet to *Rolling Stone* magazine. She was the exception. "Hillary had Stan's back," one of the aides told the reporter, Michael Hastings.

Most important, she built an enduring alliance with Robert Gates, the defense secretary and Bush holdover, with whom she shared a Midwestern upbringing, a taste for a stiff drink after a long day of work, and a deep-seated skepticism about the intentions of America's foes. In the administration's first high-level meeting on Russia in February 2009, when Gates was still sniffing out his new colleagues, aides to Obama proposed that the United States make some symbolic concessions to Russia as a gesture of its goodwill in resetting the relationship. Clinton, the last to speak, brusquely rejected the idea, saying, "I'm not giving up anything for nothing." Her hardheadedness made an impression on Gates, a former CIA officer who had been faulted for his agency's failure to anticipate the collapse of the Soviet Union and was deeply wary of a changed Russia. He decided, there and then, she was someone he could do business with.

"I thought, 'This is a tough lady,'" he told me.

Clinton's cultivation of the military reflected her instinctive comfort with the brass as well as a shrewd political calculation: lining up with the Pentagon would prevent the State Department from being marginalized at a time when the internal foreign policy debates that really mattered were about how to end two wars. Her most recent predecessors, Condoleezza Rice and Colin Powell, had lost out in knife fights with the defense secretary or the vice president. Drawing close to Gates would make the State Department and Pentagon allies, not adversaries, in dealing with a clannish White House staff. Gates, too, complained about the controlling nature of the West Wing, but as a Republican and a Bush veteran who had been asked to stay on, he was given more deference by the White House. "A lot of the things that Secretary Clinton had foisted upon her and agreed to, he couldn't imagine having to deal with and never would have tolerated," said Geoff Morrell, the Pentagon press secretary at the time.

For Clinton, it was a variation on a familiar theme: Just as the ambitious senator from post-9/11 New York tried to make herself bulletproof on national security, the new secretary of state was trying to establish her bona fides in a wartime administration. But her affinity for the armed services is also rooted in a traditional worldview in which the military plays the central role in projecting American power. It stands in sharp contrast to Obama, who kept his generals at arm's length, complained he was bullied by his commanders over how many additional troops to send to Afghanistan, and favored covert special operations over conventional military campaigns.

"Hillary is very much a member of the traditional American foreign policy establishment," said Vali Nasr, a foreign policy strategist who advised her on Pakistan and Afghanistan at the State Department. "She believes, like presidents going back to the Reagan or Kennedy years, in the importance of the military—in solving terrorism, in asserting American influence. The shift with Obama is that he went from reliance on the military to the intelligence agencies. Their position was, 'All you need to deal with terrorism is NSA and CIA, drones and special ops.' So the CIA gave Obama an angle, if you will, to be simultaneously hawkish and shun using the military."

Clinton's old-school hawkishness collided with Obama's new approach in unpredictable ways. She backed General McChrystal's recommendation to send 40,000 more troops to Afghanistan, before endorsing Gates's fallback proposal of 30,000. (Obama went along with that, though he stipulated that the soldiers would begin to pull out again in July 2011, which she viewed as a mistake.) She supported the Pentagon's plan to leave behind a residual force of 10,000 to 20,000 American troops in Iraq. (Obama rejected this, largely because of his inability to win legal protections from the Iraqis, a failure that was to haunt him when the Islamic State overran much of the country.) And she argued for the United States to intervene in Libya to avert a slaughter of civilians in Benghazi by Colonel Muammar al-Qaddafi. It was the only place where she and Gates parted company; he warned that nothing good would come of the United States starting another war against a Muslim country.

Clinton swung Obama in favor of military action, perhaps the clearest case in which she carried the day. But Gates's warnings were well-founded. The United States and its allies developed no plan for dealing with the violence that erupted after Qaddafi's ouster, and Obama watched in horror as Libya descended into anarchy. In the case of Afghanistan, Clinton's vote created a winning bloc in Obama's cabinet for a major troop surge. But she contributed to what critics, even inside the Pentagon, viewed as the "over-militarization" of the conflict. The keys to solving Afghanistan were diplomatic as well as military: rooting out the rampant corruption of the Afghan regime and reducing the constant meddling of its neighbor, Pakistan. By falling in behind the Pentagon, Clinton's State Department did not play as central a role as it should have in helping extricate America from its wars.

"I think one of the surprises for Gates and the military was, here they come in expecting a very left-of-center administration and they discover that they have a secretary of state who's a little bit right of them on these issues—a little *more* eager than they are, to a certain extent," said Bruce Riedel, the former intelligence analyst who conducted President Obama's initial review on the Afghanistan War. "Particularly on Afghanistan, where I think Gates knew more had to be done, knew more troops needed to be sent in, but had a lot of doubts about whether it would work."

For those who closely followed Clinton's career, her embrace of the military was no surprise.

• • •

In 1975, the year Hillary Rodham married Bill Clinton, she said she stopped in at a marine recruiting office in Arkansas to inquire about joining the active forces or reserves. She was a lawyer, she explained; maybe there was some way she could serve. The recruiter, she recalled two decades later, was a young man of about twenty-one, in prime physical condition. Clinton was then twenty-eight, freshly transplanted from Washington, teaching law at the University of Arkansas in Fayetteville, and wearing Coke-bottle eyeglasses. "You're too old, you can't see, and you're a woman," he told her. "Maybe the dogs will take you," he added, "dogs" being a pejorative reference to the army.

"It was not a very encouraging conversation," Hillary said at a lunch for military women on Capitol Hill in 1994. "I decided maybe I'll look for another way to serve my country."

Though Clinton repeated the story in the fall of 2015 over breakfast with voters in New Hampshire, there have long been suspicions it is apocryphal. She did not mention it in her memoirs, Bill gave a different account of it in 2008, substituting the army for the marines, and there is no documentary evidence it ever happened. Why would a professionally minded Yale Law graduate, on the cusp of marriage, suddenly want to put on a uniform? Ann Henry, an old friend who taught at the university after Clinton moved to Little Rock, recalled that during those days, female faculty members, as an exercise, would test the boundaries of careers that appeared closed to women. "I don't think it's made up," she told me. "It was consistent with something she would have done." Others speculated it was some kind of subversive antiwar stunt. Hillary had, after all, spoken out against Vietnam at Wellesley.

Many painted her with the same brush as Bill, whose dodging of the draft and attendance at antiwar protests saddled him with an antimilitary reputation that took him years to overcome. His push to end antigay discrimination in the military, which resulted in the

"Don't Ask, Don't Tell" law, only deepened the suspicion. Even his salute was found wanting. But Hillary's history was always more complicated. People who know her well said the impulse to enlist was in keeping with her conservative Midwestern upbringing—the navy petty officer's daughter with a traditional streak. How else to explain a young woman who, at the height of the antiwar protests in 1968, when she was already well into her metamorphosis from Goldwater Girl to liberal activist, still managed to attend the Republican convention?

Clinton's next exposure to the military did not come until she was First Lady eighteen years later. Living in the White House is, in many ways, like living in a military compound. A marine stands guard in front of the West Wing when the president is in the Oval Office. The Military Office operates the medical center and the telecommunications system. The navy runs the mess, the marines transport the president by helicopter, the air force by plane. Camp David is a naval facility; when the first family goes there for the weekend, they are guarded by the marines. The daily contact with men and women in uniform, Clinton's friends said, deepened her feelings for them.

In March 1996, Clinton visited American troops stationed in Bosnia. The trip became notorious years later when she claimed, during the 2008 campaign, to have dodged sniper fire after her C-17 military plane landed at an American base in Tuzla. (Chris Hill, a diplomat who was on board that day and later served as ambassador to Iraq under Clinton, recalled children handing her bouquets of spring flowers; not snipers.) But she didn't fake the good vibes during her tour of the mess and rec halls. With her teenage daughter at her side, she bantered and joked with the young servicemen and -women—an experience, she wrote, that "left lasting impressions on Chelsea and me."

When Clinton was elected to the Senate, she had strong political reasons to care about the military. The Pentagon was in the midst of a decades-long, politically charged process of closing military bases; New York State had already been a victim. Plattsburgh Air

Force Base was closed in 1995, a loss of 350 civilian jobs for that hard-luck North Country town. New Yorkers were determined to protect their remaining bases, especially Fort Drum, home of the army's Tenth Mountain Division, which sprawls over one hundred thousand acres in rural Jefferson County. In October 2001, a month after 9/11, Clinton traveled to Fort Drum at the invitation of General Franklin "Buster" Hagenbeck, who had just been named the division's commander and would be deployed to Afghanistan a month later. Like many, he had preconceptions of Clinton from her years as First Lady; the woman who showed up at his office around happy hour that afternoon did not fulfill them.

"She sat down," he recalled, "took her shoes off, put her feet up on the coffee table and said, 'General, do you know where a gal can get a cold beer around here?'"

It was the start of a dialogue that stretched over two wars. In the spring of 2002, Hagenbeck led Operation Anaconda, a two-week assault on Taliban and al-Qaeda fighters in the Shah-i-Kot Valley that was the largest combat engagement of the war to date. (It later came under fire for shoddy communications between air and ground forces.) When the general came back to Washington to brief the Joint Chiefs of Staff, Clinton took him out to dinner on Capitol Hill for her own briefing. They also spoke about the Bush administration's preparations for war in Iraq, something Hagenbeck was following with anxiety. The general, it turned out, was more of a dove than the senator. He warned her about the risks of an invasion, which was then being war-gamed inside the Pentagon. It would be like "kicking over a bee's nest," he said.

Hagenbeck forgave Clinton for her vote to authorize military action. "She made a considered call," he said. And "she was chagrined, much after the fact." He viewed her subsequent vote against the Iraq surge as at least defensible, given that "people are going to argue for years over the role of the surge." For him, what mattered more than Clinton's voting record was her unstinting public support of the military, whether in protecting Fort Drum or backing him during a difficult first year in Afghanistan.

Clinton's education in military affairs began in earnest in 2002, after the Democratic Party's crushing defeat in midterm elections moved her up several rungs in Senate seniority. The party's congressional leaders offered her a seat on either the Senate Foreign Relations Committee or the Senate Armed Services Committee. She chose Armed Services, spurning a tradition of New York senators, from Jacob Javits to Daniel Patrick Moynihan, who coveted the prestige of Foreign Relations. Armed Services dealt with more earth-bound issues such as benefits for veterans and the Selective Service System, and it was the preserve of Republican hawks such as John McCain. But after 9/11, Clinton viewed Armed Services as better preparation for her future. For a politician looking to hone hard-power credentials, it was the perfect training ground. She dug into it like a grunt at boot camp.

Andrew Shapiro, her foreign policy adviser, lined up ten experts—including Bill Perry, who had been defense secretary for her husband, and Ashton Carter, who would become Obama's fourth defense secretary—to tutor her on everything from grand strategy to defense procurement. She met quietly with Andrew Marshall, the octogenarian strategist at the Pentagon who labored for decades in the blandly named Office of Net Assessment, earning the nickname Yoda for his Delphic insights. She went to every committee meeting, no matter how mundane. Aides recall her on C-SPAN3, sitting alone in the chamber, patiently questioning a lieutenant colonel.

Thirty years after she said she was rejected by a marine recruiter in Arkansas, Hillary Clinton had become a military wonk.

Jack Keane is a bear of a man with a jowly, careworn face, Brylcreem-slick hair, and the supreme self-confidence of a retired four-star general. He speaks well, with a trace of a New York accent that gives his arguments a rat-a-tat-tat urgency. He is a well-compensated member of the military-industrial complex, sitting on the board of General Dynamics and serving as a strategic adviser to Academi, the controversial private-security contractor once known as Blackwater. He is the chairman of an aptly named think tank, the Institute for the Study of War. Though he is one of a parade of cable-TV generals, Keane is the resident hawk on Fox News, where he appears regularly to call for the United States to use greater military force in Iraq, Syria, and Afghanistan. He doesn't shrink from putting boots on the ground, and has little use for civilian leaders, such as Barack Obama, who do.

He is also perhaps the greatest single influence on the way Hillary Clinton thinks about military issues.

Keane first got to know her in the fall of 2001, when she was a freshman senator and he was the army's second-in-command, with a distinguished combat record in Vietnam, Somalia, Haiti, Bosnia, and Kosovo. His bond with David Petraeus had been forged in 1991, when he saved the younger man's life after he was accidentally shot in the chest during a military exercise. Fifteen years later, Keane would enter the annals of military history as the leader of a vocal insurgency inside the Bush administration that argued that the remedy for a floundering campaign in Iraq was to double down on it, a strategy that would become known as the surge. But with Clinton, his agenda was more modest: He wanted to make her a home-state booster for Fort Drum and another New York institution, West Point. Keane had expected her to be intelligent, hardworking, and politically astute, but he was not prepared for the respect she showed for the army as an institution, or her sympathy for the sacrifices made by soldiers and their families. Keane was confident he could smell a phony politician a mile away; she did not strike him as that.

"I read people; that's one of my strengths," he told me. "It's not that I can't be fooled, but I'm not fooled often."

Clinton took an instant liking to Keane. "She loves that Irish gruff thing," said one of her Senate aides, Kris Balderston, who was in the room that day. When Keane got up after forty-five minutes to leave for a meeting back at the Pentagon with a Polish general, she protested that she wasn't finished yet and asked for another appointment. "I said, 'OK, but it took me three months to get this one,'" Keane told her drily.

Clinton exploded into a raucous laugh. "I'll take care of that problem," she promised.

She was true to her word: The two were to meet dozens of times over the next decade, discussing the wars in Afghanistan and Iraq, the Iranian nuclear threat, and other flashpoints in the Middle East. Sometimes he dropped by her Senate office; other times they met for drinks at Bistro Bis, a popular restaurant on Capitol Hill. He escorted her on her first visit to Fort Drum and set up her first trip to Iraq. Once, Clinton's aides scheduled lunch in the Senate dining room. She ordered them to move it to a nearby restaurant and showed up full of apologies, saying she did not want to put the general in an awkward position, being seen with such a political figure in such a public venue. By mutual agreement, they steered clear of politics. The one time Clinton strayed into that terrain, Keane asked, "Are you sure you want to go there? I think you instinctively know you're not going to like my response."

Everything else, though, was on the table. At a meeting in Clinton's Senate office in January 2007, Keane tried to sell her on the logic of the surge. The previous month, he had met with President Bush in the Oval Office to recommend that the United States deploy five to eight army and marine brigades to wage an urban counterinsurgency campaign; only that, he argued, would stabilize a country being ripped apart by sectarian strife. His presentation, delivered at the request of Bush's national security adviser Stephen Hadley, angered some of Keane's fellow generals, who didn't want to change course. But it had a big impact on the commander in chief, who soon ordered more than twenty thousand additional troops to Iraq.

Clinton was another story. "I'm convinced it's not going to work, Jack," she told him. She predicted that the American soldiers patrolling in Iraqi cities and towns would be "blown up" by Sunni militias or al-Qaeda fighters. She did not buy his argument that they would be protected by the local population, once the locals realized that the Americans were there to halt the cycle of sectarian bloodshed. "She thought we would fail," Keane recalled, "and it was going to cause increased casualties."

Politics, of course, was also on her mind. Barack Obama was laying the groundwork for his candidacy in mid-January with a campaign that would emphasize his opposition to the Iraq War and her vote for it. He was setting off on a fundraising drive that would net $25 million in three months, sending tremors through Hillaryland and establishing him as a formidable rival. Clinton needed to put together her own campaign quickly to prevent him from making even greater inroads. Although she disagreed with Keane about Iraq, Clinton asked him to become a formal adviser to her on national security. "As much as I respect you," he replied, "I can't do that." Keane's wife had health problems, which had moved up his retirement from the army, and he did not, as a policy, endorse candidates. (That didn't stop Donald Trump from invoking him as an expert source during a Republican debate.) Sometime during 2008—he doesn't remember exactly when—Clinton made a major concession on the surge. "She said, 'You were right, this really did work,'" Keane said. "On issues of national security," he said, "I thought she was always intellectually honest with me."

He and Clinton continued to talk, even after she became secretary of state. Several times in 2009, Clinton's aides rearranged her schedule to make time for calls or meetings with Keane. In June 2010, Clinton emailed her secretary, "I want to see Jack Keane for a drink." More often than not, they found themselves in sync. Keane, like Clinton, favored more robust intervention in Syria than Obama was willing to undertake. In April 2015, the week before she launched her candidacy, Clinton asked him for a briefing on military options for dealing with the fighters of the Islamic State. Bringing along three young female analysts from the Institute for the Study of War, Keane gave her a two-hour-and-twenty-minute presentation. Among other steps, he advocated imposing a no-fly zone over parts of Syria that would neutralize Syrian president

Bashar al-Assad's air power, with a goal of forcing him into a political settlement with opposition groups. Six months later, Clinton publicly adopted this position, further distancing herself from Obama.

"I'm convinced this president, no matter what the circumstances, will never put any boots on the ground to do anything, even when it's compelling," Keane told me. He was sitting in the library at his home in McLean, Virginia, lined with books on military history and strategy. His critique of Obama was hardly new or original, but it faithfully reflected the thinking of Clinton and many of her policy advisers. "One of the problems the president has, which weakens his diplomatic efforts, is that leaders don't believe he would use military power. That's an issue that would separate the president from Hillary Clinton rather dramatically. She would look at military force as another realistic option, but only where there is no other option."

Befriending Keane gave Clinton instant entrée to his informal network of active-duty and retired generals. The most interesting by far was David Petraeus, a cerebral commander who shared Clinton's jet-fueled ambition and a life story that mixed heady success with humbling setbacks. Both would be accused of mishandling classified information—Clinton because of her use of a private server and email address to conduct sensitive government business, a decision that erupted into a political scandal and cast a shadow over her presidential campaign; Petraeus because he had given a diary containing classified information to his biographer and mistress.

On Clinton's first trip to Iraq in November 2003, Petraeus, then a two-star general commanding the 101st Airborne Division, flew from his field headquarters in Mosul to the relative safety of Kirkuk to brief her congressional delegation. "She was full of questions," he recalled. "It was the kind of gesture that means a lot to a battlefield commander." On subsequent trips, as he rose in rank, Petraeus walked her through his plans to train and equip Iraqi Army troops, a forerunner of the counterinsurgency strategy in Afghanistan. It worked to their mutual benefit: Petraeus was building ties to a prominent Democratic voice in the Senate; Clinton was burnishing her image as a friend of the troops. "She did it the old-fashioned way," he said. "She did it by pursuing relationships."

"Her star power with the troops was evident," Petraeus continued. Sometimes that caused tensions with her fellow lawmakers, who were largely ignored while she was being mobbed by the soldiers. "They would line up. Everybody wanted to be in a photo with Senator Clinton. The other members of the delegation would be back in the vehicle, and occasionally you'd hear, 'C'mon, Hillary.'"

When Petraeus was sent back to Iraq as the top commander in early 2007, he gave every member of the Senate Armed Services Committee a copy of *The U.S. Army/Marine Corps Counterinsurgency Field Manual,* which he had edited during a tour at Fort Leavenworth. Clinton read hers from cover to cover. During a hearing, she seized on a ratio in the manual to challenge him on whether the United States would ever be able to field enough forces in Iraq, as a percentage of the population, to conduct a viable counterinsurgency. "We were sailing through," the general recalled, "and all of a sudden, lo and behold, there was Clinton." Petraeus conceded her point: Even with the surge, there would not be enough troops on the ground to meet his recommended ratio of soldiers to locals. But he argued the gap would be narrowed by the use of contractors and, later, the introduction of trained Iraqi troops.

"It was a very penetrating line of inquiry," he said of Clinton's interrogation. "Welcome to the National Football League."

The next time Petraeus went to Capitol Hill, nine months later, domestic politics had turned savagely against the war. He was there with the American ambassador to Iraq, Ryan Crocker, to report on the status of the surge. Both men believed the influx of troops had contributed to a measurable reduction in civilian deaths from roadside bombs and other insurgent attacks in the country. But they faced five senators running to be president of a nation fed up with the war. (In addition to Clinton and Obama, there were Joe Biden,

Chris Dodd, and John McCain.) With the exception of McCain, all were itching for a fight; the general's friend Clinton drew the most blood. "You have been made the de facto spokesmen for what many of us believe to be a failed policy," she said, glaring at him and Crocker.

Although Clinton's reservations about the surge were valid, her opposition to it, like her vote for the war, came back to haunt her. This time, it was her ally Bob Gates who resurrected the ghost. In his memoir, Gates wrote that she confessed to him and the president that her position had been politically motivated because she was then facing Obama in the Iowa caucuses. (Obama, he wrote, "vaguely" conceded that he, too, had opposed it for political reasons.) Clinton pushed back, telling Diane Sawyer of ABC News that Gates "perhaps either missed the context or the meaning, because I did oppose the surge." Her opposition, she told Sawyer, was driven by the fact that at that time, people were not going to accept any escalation of the war. "This is not politics in electoral, political terms," Clinton said. "This is politics in the sense of the American public has to support commitments like this."

The next time she found herself in a debate over sending troops into harm's way, she voiced no such reservations.

"We need maps," Hillary Clinton told her aides.

It was early October 2009 and she had just returned from a meeting in the Situation Room, where Obama's war cabinet was debating how many additional troops to send to Afghanistan. The Pentagon, she reported, had used impressive color-coded maps to show its plans to deploy troops around the country. The attention to detail made Gates and his commanders look crisp and well-prepared; the State Department looked wan by comparison. At the next meeting, on October 14, the team from State unfurled its own maps to show the deployment of the "civilian surge," the army of aid workers, diplomats, legal experts, and crop specialists who were supposed to follow the soldiers into Afghanistan.

Clinton's fixation with maps was typical of her mind-set in the first great war-and-peace debate of the Obama presidency. She wanted to be taken seriously, even if her department was less central than the Pentagon. One way to accomplish this was by promoting the civilian surge, the pet project of her friend and special envoy to the region, Richard Holbrooke. "She was determined that her briefing books would be just as thick and just as meticulous as those of the Pentagon," a senior adviser recalled. She also didn't hesitate to get into the Pentagon's business, asking detailed questions about the training of Afghan troops and wading into the weeds of military planning. If she was overseas during one of the meetings, Clinton made sure to take part remotely. After an exhausting day in which she had spoken at Moscow State University and then visited the Russian republic of Tatarstan, Clinton put on headphones in her cabin and listened to the discussion in the Situation Room as she flew through the night, high above the Volga River, on her way home.

Much has been written about the troop debate, a three-month drama of dueling egos, leaked documents, and endless deliberations that crystallized the portrait of Obama as an overly methodical professor-in-chief. The story is typically framed as a test of wills between the Pentagon's wily military commanders and an inexperienced young president, with Joe Biden playing the role of devil's advocate for Obama. While that portrait is accurate, it neglects the role of Clinton. By siding with Gates and the generals, she gave political ballast to their proposals and provided a hawkish counterpoint to Biden's skepticism. Her role should not be overstated: She did not turn the debate, nor did she bring to it any distinctive point of view. But her unstinting support of McChrystal's maximalist recommendation made it harder for Obama to choose a lesser option.

"Hillary was adamant in her support for what Stan asked for," Gates told me. "She made clear that she was ready to support his request for the full forty thousand troops. She then made clear that she was only willing to go with the thirty thousand number because I proposed it. She was, in a way, tougher on the numbers in the surge than I was." Gates believed that if he could align Clinton; the chairman of the Joint Chiefs of Staff, Mike Mullen; the commander of Central Command, David Petraeus; and himself behind a common position, it would be hard for Obama to say no. "How could you ignore these Four Horsemen of national security?" Geoff Morrell said.

Just as Clinton benefited from her alliance with the military commanders, she gave them political cover. "Here's the dirty little secret," said Tom Nides, her former deputy secretary of state for management and resources. "They all knew they wanted her on their side. They knew that if they walked into the Situation Room and they had her, it made a huge difference in the dynamics. When she opened her mouth, she could change the momentum in the room."

David Axelrod recalled one meeting where Clinton "kicked the thing off and pretty much articulated their opinion; I'm sure that's one that they remember. There's no doubt that she wanted to give them every troop that McChrystal was asking for." Still, Clinton didn't prevail on every argument. Obama added a crucial condition of his own: that the soldiers be deployed as quickly as possible and pulled out again, starting in the summer of 2011—a deadline that proved more fateful in the long run than a difference of ten thousand troops. Clinton opposed setting a deadline for withdrawal, arguing that it would tip America's hand to the Taliban and encourage them to wait out the United States—which, in fact, was exactly what happened.

"The president was walking a very fine line," Axelrod said. "At the end of the day, he yielded to the wisdom of the group to the degree that he sent more troops. But in return, he got a commitment to limit the length of the mission. What he wasn't going to do was sign a blank check. What came out of it was a much more truncated approach to how these troops were going to be deployed and then scaled down."

Clinton's role in the debate was not without costs to her relationship with the White House. Her insistence on playing ditto-head to Gates rankled Obama's political aides, who felt she helped box in the president on a troop deployment he did not want, and that could pose real political dangers to him. As Bob Woodward of *The Washington Post* reported, Clinton at one meeting declared, "Mr. President, the dilemma *you* face . . ." Her use of "you," not "we," suggested that somehow, Afghanistan was Obama's problem, not hers, rekindling suspicions that she was not really on his team. Axelrod and Emanuel were drawn to Biden's more minimalist option. Rather than send a massive force to Afghanistan to re-build the country—a hugely expensive project—Biden proposed a smaller counterterrorism force that would target the Taliban and al-Qaeda and improve the training of Afghan troops.

In the final days of the debate, Clinton also found herself at odds with her own ambassador in Kabul. He, too, held different views than she did on the wisdom of a surge, which he had put into writing. On November 6, 2009, in a long cable addressed to Clinton, Ambassador Karl Eikenberry made a trenchant, convincing case for why the McChrystal proposal, which she had endorsed two weeks earlier in a meeting with Obama, would saddle the United States with "vastly increased costs and an indefinite, large-scale military role in Afghanistan." The Afghan president, Hamid Karzai, was "not an adequate strategic partner," Eikenberry wrote. Pouring in more American soldiers and money, he said, would only increase the country's dependence and "deepen the military involvement in a mission that most agree cannot be won solely by military means." It would make more sense to intensify diplomacy with Afghanistan's neighbor Pakistan, which offered a better chance to be a "game changer" in the struggle to vanquish the Taliban and al-Qaeda.

A few days later, the cable was leaked to my *Times* colleague Eric Schmitt, and the latest rift in the administration spilled into the open. Such leaks are not unusual in Washington: McChrystal's original assessment of the state of the war, and his call for more troops, had been leaked to Woodward two months earlier. This amounted to a counterpunch by the doves. Much of Eikenberry's analysis proved prescient, particularly his warnings about the threadbare partnership with Karzai. It carried an extra sting because he was a retired army three-star general who had been the commander in Afghanistan from 2005 to 2007. Clinton had not asked for the cable; Eikenberry had been encouraged to lay out his views by Doug Lute, who coordinated Afghanistan policy in the White House and shared the suspicion that Obama was being bulldozed into a larger-than-necessary surge. Clinton was furious, fearing it could upset a debate in which she and the Pentagon were about to prevail.

The episode laid bare a vexed relationship between Clinton and Eikenberry, one of the few generals with whom she didn't hit it off. A soldier-scholar with graduate degrees from Harvard and Stanford, Eikenberry was brilliant but had a reputation among his colleagues for being imperious. He clashed with two of her most trusted aides, Holbrooke and Jack Lew, the deputy secretary of state directly responsible for the civilian surge. Clinton had a similarly chilly relationship with Lute, another retired army lieutenant general with a graduate degree from Harvard, who also fought with Holbrooke. "She likes the nail eaters—McChrystal, Petraeus, Keane," a former aide said. "Real military guys, not these retired three-stars who go into civilian jobs."

Eikenberry wanted to function as a sort of proconsul in Afghanistan—the civilian equivalent of McChrystal—coordinating the work of the United Nations, the World Bank, and other nonmilitary agencies. But he represented only the United States while McChrystal commanded a multinational force. And the cable poisoned his relations with Karzai. Clinton viewed him as insubordinate on other grounds: In October 2010, he turned up at a NATO meeting in Brussels after having been told not to come. She and Gates both wanted the White House to remove him—a bitter, ultimately futile effort that goes unmentioned in Clinton's book but is covered by Gates in juicy detail. The ambassador, Gates concluded, was "under an umbrella of protection at the White House."

Neither Gates nor Clinton ever informed Eikenberry that they had tried to get rid of him, Eikenberry told me. While he declined to discuss the cable, his doubts about the investment of American blood and treasure were unchanged years later. "It is possible that the Afghan state will not collapse and the country again serve as a major base for international terrorism," he said. "But even if we achieve this much, it will have come at great human and fiscal cost, and over a thirteen-year period when we should have been more focused on the geopolitical challenges posed by China and Russia."

What the cable made clear was the degree to which the Afghanistan debate was dominated by military considerations. While Clinton did raise the need to deal with Pakistan, her reflexive support of Gates, Petraeus, and McChrystal on troops meant she was not as powerful a voice for diplomatic alternatives as she could have been. (Ironically, Eikenberry, the retired general, gave more weight to political considerations.) "She contributed to the over-militarizing of the analysis of the problem," said Sarah Chayes, who was an adviser to McChrystal in Afghanistan and later to the chairman of the Joint Chiefs of Staff Mike Mullen. Clinton also naïvely accepted Hamid Karzai's pledge in 2009 that the Afghans would stand up a security force capable of securing major cities within three years, and the entire country within five years—a timetable that proved illusory. In October 2015, six years after that promise, the persistent violence in Afghanistan and the legacy of Karzai's misrule forced Obama to reverse his plan to withdraw the last American soldiers by the end of his presidency. A few thousand troops will stay there indefinitely.

Clinton talked a lot about the civilian surge but never quite translated it into reality. The whole project always had a whiff of the utopian nation-building that Obama had disparaged in his mother's fieldwork in Indonesia: lawyers helping Afghans set up clean courts, agricultural experts helping them plant sustainable crops, civil servants helping them build efficient public agencies. In the end, the State Department proved inadequate to the task of deploying civilians in anywhere near the numbers needed to make a difference on the ground. The problem was institutional and cultural: The State Department Clinton inherited had been depleted during the Bush years, while the wartime Pentagon had been put on steroids. State still relied on the army to train its recruits, which it did in typically grand style, converting a complex of dilapidated buildings in rural Indiana that had once been a farm colony for "feeble-minded" boys into the simulacrum of a war-torn Afghan city. Though the State Department eventually sent about 1,250 people to Afghanistan, 700 of them never ventured beyond the fortified walls of the embassy in Kabul. Unlike the military, it could not order its diplomats into life-threatening assignments. At the Pentagon, which was managing a vast, deadly campaign with 100,000 troops, there was little sympathy for these limitations.

"The culture inside the State Department is, 'They're big-footing us,' but then they don't *want* to do it," Chayes said. "The military is dying for the State Department to play a bigger role, but it doesn't, either because it doesn't have the resources or it doesn't have the derring-do."

Midwestern roots and flat vowels aside, Hillary Clinton and Bob Gates were not natural buddies. They didn't agree on politics and had very different career paths: Clinton, an actor on the political stage; Gates, an operator in the shadowy world of intelligence. In July 2007, they crossed swords over Iraq: Clinton, then a senator, lashed out in a conference call with reporters after one of his deputies brushed aside her request for a briefing from the Pentagon on when it planned to begin pulling troops out of Iraq. Gates rushed to smooth her feathers, sending her a contrite letter by messenger. In his memoir, he painted a strangely shaded portrait of her. He lavished praise on Clinton as "smart, idealistic but pragmatic, tough-minded, indefatigable, a very valuable colleague, and a superb representative of the United States all over the world." But he also noted that the White House kept her on a short leash. From forcing an unwanted deputy on her to shielding an ambassador she regarded as insubordinate, the White House, in Gates's telling, all but put her in a gilded cage.

Still, Gates and Clinton both knew how to ride the political winds. And they had reasons to make common cause that went beyond Afghanistan. In the spring of 2009, she backed him when he asked Obama to block the release of Abu Ghraib–like photographs that documented the abuse of prisoners in Iraq and Afghanistan by American military personnel. Clinton had just returned from Baghdad, where the commander, army general Ray Odierno, warned her that the images would expose the troops to reprisal. (Obama agreed; the photos remain concealed.) Gates returned the favor by lobbying Congress to raise the State Department's budget. Diplomats, he said, needed to pick up some of the work of nation-building that had been done by soldiers.

Gates was acutely aware of the deficiencies of the civilian surge, but he never called out the State Department or allowed his subordinates to do so. Clinton had backed him on troops, and he was going to protect his relationship with her. A veteran of six administrations, Gates had witnessed corrosive battles between the Pentagon and the State Department—Caspar Weinberger vs. George Shultz under Ronald Reagan; Donald Rumsfeld vs. Colin Powell under George W. Bush—and he was determined not to repeat the cycle with Clinton. They shared a bigger common adversary: the West Wing. It would not be "career enhancing," Gates warned his staff, to get caught sniping at the secretary of state. There was symbolic power in a public alliance between diplomat and warrior, and they choreographed their relationship like tango dancers. After appearing together on a panel at George Washington University in October 2009, in which they finished each other's sentences, the two decamped to Blue Duck Tavern, a rustic-chic West End restaurant, for a cozy dinner. Their aides leaked it to the press before the check arrived.

The symbolism, however, was always in service of a policy goal, large or small. In July 2010, Clinton and Gates met in South Korea on the sixtieth anniversary of the start of the Korean War. They traveled up to the demilitarized zone, where they studiously avoided eye contact with a North Korean soldier who glared at them through the window of the guard post that straddles the border. Back in Seoul that evening, they got together for a drink in the bar of the Grand Hyatt hotel, discussing East Asian security over the racket of a Korean cover band. Seoul was on a razor's edge during that period. Four months earlier, North Korea had torpedoed a South Korean Navy corvette, the *Cheonan,* killing forty-six sailors. For weeks, the State Department and Pentagon had been debating how to respond to North Korea's belligerence and reassure their loyal Korean ally. The tentative plan—developed by Clinton's deputy at State Jim Steinberg—was to dispatch the aircraft carrier *George Washington* into coastal waters to the east of North Korea as a show of force.

But Admiral Robert Willard, then the Pacific commander, wanted to send the carrier on a more aggressive course—into the Yellow Sea, between North Korea and China. The Chinese foreign ministry had warned the United States not to do that, which for Willard was all the more reason to do it. He pushed Mullen, who in turn pushed Gates, to reroute the *George Washington.* Gates agreed, but he needed the commander in chief to sign off on a decision that could have political as well as military consequences.

In a weekend conference call with the president and a handful of his top aides, Gates laid out the case for diverting the *George Washington* to the Yellow Sea—that the United States should not look like it was yielding to China. Clinton strongly seconded it. "We've got to run it up the gut!" she had said to her aides a few days earlier, invoking an old football play in which the player carrying the ball barrels through the middle of the defensive line. The Vince Lombardi imitation drew giggles from her staff who, even eighteen months into her tenure, still marveled at her old-school hawkishness. Obama, though, was not persuaded. The *George Washington* was already under way; changing her course was not a decision to make on the fly.

"I don't call audibles with aircraft carriers," he said, one-upping Clinton on her football metaphor.

# Four

## Holbrooke Agonistes

In the winter of 2009, President Obama was in the Situation Room, polling his national security team about what to do in Afghanistan, where a United States preoccupied by Iraq had allowed the Taliban to regroup, threatening the gains American troops had made in six years of fighting. After going around the conference table soliciting opinions, he turned to a video screen on the far wall that flickered with the image of Richard Holbrooke. Holbrooke, whom Obama had named his special representative for Afghanistan and Pakistan a few weeks earlier, was joining the meeting from Kabul.

A broad-shouldered, barrel-chested man with tousled graying hair and a voice that bristled with portent, Holbrooke was the most storied diplomat of his generation. In a restless career that had spanned nearly fifty years, from Kennedy to Obama, he had accompanied Averell Harriman to Paris for the Vietnam peace talks in 1968; been named the youngest assistant secretary of state for East Asian and Pacific affairs in the history of the State Department, at age thirty-six; served as Bill Clinton's ambassador to Germany and representative to the United Nations; and brokered the Dayton Accords, ending the cruel civil war in Bosnia. He thought he knew how to talk to presidents.

"Not since Clark Clifford counseled Lyndon Johnson on the Vietnam War has a commander in chief faced such a momentous decision," Holbrooke intoned, glancing down to read from notes.

"Richard," Obama interrupted. "Do people really *talk* like that?"

A chagrined Holbrooke clammed up while the younger aides in the room traded eye-rolling glances. Moments like that made it clear why Richard Holbrooke was going to be a bad fit in the Obama administration. A man of high drama and an acute sense of his place in history, he ruffled feathers in a White House that prided itself on a lack of drama and operated on the principle that the president—and the president alone—makes history. Holbrooke was, in short, not Obama's kind of guy.

But he was Hillary's kind of guy. She relished his larger-than-life persona, tolerated his excesses, and defended him against the dart throwers in the White House. She would save his job several times, most dramatically in March 2010, and grieved after his sudden death from a torn aorta nine months later. At his memorial service at the Kennedy Center, Clinton delivered a heartfelt eulogy, reminiscing about the Teletubby-like yellow "sleeping suit" he used to change into on overnight plane trips, and recounting how he once trailed her into a ladies' room in Pakistan to badger her about something or other. "There was no escaping him," Clinton said.

It was clear she didn't want to.

Holbrooke is a rare case in which personal chemistry helps illuminate the deeper differences between Clinton and Obama. The same characteristics that endeared him to Clinton rubbed the president the wrong way. The Henry Luce–American Century worldview he brought to the table was inspiring to Clinton but hopelessly outdated to Obama. He was the embodiment of the generational clash between a young president who came of age after Vietnam and an older secretary of state steeped in the triumphs and tragedies of Democratic foreign policy—many of which bore Holbrooke's imprint.

It was this Democratic establishment that the upstart senator from Illinois had taken on and beaten in the election. Although Holbrooke was folded into the Obama foreign policy campaign team after Clinton's defeat—playing a cameo role in an epic cast of three hundred advisers—he was forever marked as a Clinton man. At times, it felt almost like Obama's aides used him as a proxy for their lingering resentments against Hillary. Certainly, Holbrooke exemplified Clinton's view of the American role in the world: brash, intrepid, confident that the United States was indispensable to cracking the world's toughest problems. She admired his wearing-down of the Serbian dictator Slobodan Milosevic at Dayton in 1995, which had produced a major foreign policy achievement for her husband. She liked the way he threw himself at impossible missions, speaking with such passion about helping Afghans to grow crops other than opium poppies, that she dubbed the native New Yorker "Farmer Holbrooke."

It didn't hurt that Holbrooke had cultivated her for years. He supported her candidacy in 2008 and was assumed to be a lock for secretary of state in a Hillary Clinton administration. When she ended up at the State Department, she wanted him to be her deputy, a request Obama's aides denied. They were still bruised by his sharp elbows during the campaign, when he had warned Democratic foreign policy experts who were supporting Obama that they were putting their careers at risk. But Clinton insisted on giving him a major role, and the White House couldn't argue, given his résumé. With his long interest in Afghanistan, desire to be in the thick of things, and appetite for intractable problems, it was no wonder Holbrooke angled for the Afghanistan and Pakistan portfolio.

"He wanted to be a 'Great Man,' so he could change history," Clinton said in her eulogy, as Obama shifted uncomfortably in his chair behind her onstage. "He was, and he did."

Holbrooke, however, fatally misread his new president and the political currents in which Obama was operating. He was unable to navigate the shoals in a White House–centric administration. He talked out of both sides of his mouth, appearing to back a troop surge in the Situation Room but privately telling journalists and his friends in New York it would never work. He ran a talented but chronically disorganized shop in the State Department, and he talked constantly with reporters at a time when the White House was determined to control the public narrative. In the end, he fell short of the Olympian goal he set for himself—negotiating a political settlement with the Taliban—though his defenders argue that some in the White House stymied his efforts in a petty attempt to deny him another Dayton.

In the years since his death, the stories of Holbrooke's humiliations have become the stuff of Foggy Bottom lore. There was the time Jim Jones, the national security adviser, promised he would soon get rid of Holbrooke in a letter to Ambassador Karl Eikenberry in Kabul, and then accidentally copied it to a long list of administration officials. Or the time Holbrooke was kept waiting on a tarmac overseas, with no flight, while junior White House aides emailed each other about whether the Pentagon should approve a military jet to pick him up. Or how he could never get a one-on-one with the president, whom he had asked, rather poignantly, at their first meeting to call him Richard rather than Dick because that's what his wife wanted.

Five months before his death, Holbrooke, with history on his mind, began recording a diary that offered a window into his anguished frame of mind. The recordings, often made late at night, burn with his ambition to broker a deal with the Taliban, but also with his frustration with a White House that did not value his experience or heed his advice. Obama, he noted, had promised to pursue direct talks with Iran during the campaign, even at the risk of being labeled naïve by Clinton. But when Holbrooke proposed opening a channel to the Iranians to win their support for a political settlement in Afghanistan, Obama's aides rejected him. "It's hard to explain that one," he lamented, calling it a "singular failure of this administration." Left unsaid was the fact that Holbrooke might have been the wrong salesman for the idea, given the White House's abiding suspicion of his ambition.

For veterans of the Obama administration, Holbrooke serves as a kind of Rorschach test: he was either the victim of a callow, insular White House, so determined to keep him on the sidelines that they were willing to put their entire Afghan policy at risk; or he was a Clinton-era relic who made enemies, refused to be a team player, and failed to adapt to the age of Obama.

To some, he was both.

"The game he wanted to play was this high-stakes, high-drama game," said Vikram Singh, a former deputy to Holbrooke who is now vice president at the Center for American Progress, a left-leaning think tank. "It's not like Richard tried to change himself to fit the no-drama tone and tenor of this administration, which surprised me and did not serve him well." Derek Chollet, a onetime Holbrooke speechwriter who worked in the Obama White House, said his old boss's Vietnam references had sent eyes rolling in the Clinton years, too. The difference was that Clinton's aides viewed him as a talent worth the cost; Obama's did not. "Rather than seeing Holbrooke as an asset to be used," he said, "they saw him more as someone who had to be tolerated—and barely tolerated, at that."

Holbrooke recognized he had a potential ally in Hillary early in her husband's administration. In March 1995, writing in *Foreign Affairs* magazine, he had described the American and European response to the Yugoslav civil war as "the greatest collective security failure of the West since the 1930s." His hyperbolic criticism didn't sit well with his friends on the NSC staff, whom, after all, he was casting in the role of Hitler's appeasers. Hillary, though, agreed with him. That summer, when Holbrooke was put in charge of negotiations to end the war in Bosnia and was frustrated by Bill Clinton's reluctance to take military action, he privately reached out to her for help. Bosnia, he warned, was a "cancer on the presidency"—a message that she wasted no time passing on to Bill. Three years later, when his critics tried to derail his nomination as ambassador to the United Nations, the First Lady stood by him. Holbrooke, she wrote, "had acquired fervent enemies, generally for reasons to his credit. He was ferociously intelligent, strong, often blunt and fearless."

After the Clintons left the White House and Hillary began her own political ascent, Holbrooke became a constant presence in her life, buttering her up in ways large and small. Each year, he and his wife, Kati Marton, invited her to a holiday dinner at their elegant apartment on Central Park West. One year, Hillary expressed admiration for the work of the Salvation Army; at the dinner the next year, Holbrooke hired a Salvation Army marching band to parade through his dining room, playing Christmas carols. By 2007, Holbrooke was a leading voice on her foreign policy advisory team. That was when he warned fellow Democrats such as Susan Rice and Philip Gordon about the career consequences of signing up with Obama instead of Clinton.

When Obama was elected, he invited Holbrooke to his transition office in Chicago to interview for secretary of state. It was all rather perfunctory: The president-elect had already zeroed in on Clinton for the job. But she had to undergo a vetting process. If that turned up something troublesome enough to disqualify her, Holbrooke would be a credible fallback. The session went badly; Obama seemed immune to his blustering charm. "He took to his first meeting with the president-elect a freight train of negatives—the collected grievances of those who disliked him or with whom he had disagreed in the past," said Frank Wisner, a diplomat whose friendship with Holbrooke dated back to Vietnam. "He was bigger than life when he came through the door, and he had all these enemies, lots of them. He angered a lot of people because he had this incredible drive and determination."

Finding a suitable job for Holbrooke was never easy. He had ended up on thin ice in virtually every government post he had held, going back to the Carter administration. Jimmy Carter ordered Zbigniew Brzezinski to cut him out of a meeting with Deng Xiaoping because he was worried that Holbrooke, with his overbearing personality, would upset the delicate negotiations. At the outset of the Clinton administration, he wanted to be ambassador to Japan but was rebuffed by the national security adviser, Anthony Lake, an old colleague with whom he'd long had a complicated relationship. Feeling shut out, a frustrated Holbrooke took off for Southeast Asia and Europe and found himself, improbably, on New Year's Eve in a freezing hotel room in war-torn Sarajevo.

"If I don't make my views known to the new team, I will not have done enough to help the desperate people we have just seen," Holbrooke wrote in his journal. "But if I push my views, I will appear too aggressive. I feel trapped." He could have written the same words sixteen years later, after Obama's election left Holbrooke jockeying again for a job in a Democratic administration. But there was one difference: Obama was ready to act in Afghanistan in a way that Bill Clinton had not been in Bosnia.

Though Holbrooke initially regarded the Afghanistan assignment as yet another consolation prize—for not being named deputy secretary of state—he set about turning his new gig into something worthy of his stature. He insisted on being called the special representative for Afghanistan and Pakistan (SRAP), a designation meant to underscore he was the president's emissary, not some run-of-the-mill special envoy. He coined the phrase "Af-Pak" and was delighted to see it enter the diplomatic lexicon (never mind that some Pakistanis regarded the term "Pak" as an ethnic slur).

Assigned a nondescript warren of offices outside the State Department's cafeteria that used to house the cashier, Holbrooke quickly assembled a mini-empire of experts from the Pentagon, the CIA, and other agencies. He attracted big names such as Barnett Rubin, a leading scholar on Afghanistan from New York University; Vali Nasr, an Iranian-born academic who had written widely on the Islamic world; and newcomers such as Rina Amiri, an Afghan-born woman who bravely advocated for women's rights in her native country. He also drew from his New York social world, naming Ronan Farrow as an adviser. Holbrooke had known Farrow since he was fifteen, taking him on as a speechwriter in 2004 as a favor to his celebrity mother, Mia Farrow.

Holbrooke's empire building antagonized his State Department colleagues, particularly in the Bureau of South and Central Asian Affairs, which he Balkanized to create the SRAP office. In bureaucratic matters, he had all the finesse of a steamroller. When Clinton named Tom Nides, an affable investment banker, as a deputy secretary of state with a portfolio that included the civilian surge into Afghanistan, Holbrooke invited him to lunch at Kinkead's, a seafood place on Pennsylvania Avenue.

"I just want to make sure you know this," Holbrooke said, as they unfolded their napkins. "I don't work for you."

"Richard, I'm sure you don't work for me," Nides replied, even though he clearly outranked him.

In Holbrooke, however, the White House had someone with peerless credentials for the job. As a young diplomat in Vietnam, he had developed firm views about counterinsurgencies, the centerpiece of Obama's strategy in Afghanistan (he believed they bred a crippling dependency). In the Balkans, he had learned the value of backing up American diplomacy with the threat of NATO bombing raids. As a private citizen, he had traveled to Afghanistan in 2006, where he had met with a jailed Taliban militant as well as with President Hamid Karzai. Holbrooke relished the thin air of the Hindu Kush; he viewed Afghanistan as an even greater challenge than Vietnam. Given his age, then sixty-seven, it would probably be the last big one of his life.

Barney Rubin, who knew more about the Taliban than anyone in the government, argued there was an opening for reconciliation talks, even in early 2009. But nobody was listening to him. Most believed the Taliban were in no mood to negotiate; they were waiting to see what the new president would do. Days after Obama took office, he had asked Bruce Riedel, a savvy former CIA analyst and foreign policy adviser to his campaign, to conduct a quick policy review on Afghanistan. Though Holbrooke was nominally a cochairman of the exercise, he felt shunted aside, especially when he learned that Riedel had presented his recommendations to the president during a flight to Los Angeles on Air Force One (the first of several times that Holbrooke would be left off the presidential plane). Riedel's forty-four-page report, drawn up in barely two months, called for a "fully resourced counterinsurgency campaign" that would require thousands of American soldiers and civilians to secure the country, train Afghan troops, and help Afghans build the institutions for a stable society. The report flatly rejected the idea of reconciliation, saying the Taliban were "not reconcilable." It became the template for how the administration dealt with Afghanistan in the years to come.

Holbrooke's response was to busy himself in other areas that could help the country, like the upcoming Afghan elections, for which he desperately wanted to find a candidate to challenge Karzai. He threw himself into such projects as sending crop specialists from the Agriculture Department to Afghanistan to wean its farmers off poppies. At a meeting in February 2009, while the Riedel report was still being written, Holbrooke began laying out his agrarian vision for the country. Suddenly, Bob Gates cut him off.

"Aw, Richard, nobody in the Department of Agriculture has a clue about how to farm anything," he said. "That's not what the Department of Agriculture does. The Department of Agriculture pays people *not* to farm. If you want farmers, you should go to Texas A&M or someplace like that, where they actually know what they're talking about."

If Gates thought Holbrooke was looking for help in the wrong places, his insights about agriculture in Afghanistan were on target. Years earlier, he had written that the Bush administration's policy of eradicating poppy crops—by burning, spraying, or tilling them under—was counterproductive because it left Afghan farmers penniless, hopeless, and ripe for recruitment by the Taliban. "It wasn't just a waste of money," Holbrooke told *The Washington Post* in early 2009. "This was actually a benefit to the enemy."

His solution was to set up a system of credit to entice farmers to diversify into legitimate crops such as saffron or pomegranates. Ignoring Gates's jibe, he pushed the USDA to send fifty-two experts to Afghanistan on one-year assignments, where they offered the farmers advice on irrigation and helped install windmills and open nurseries. He got a kick out of Clinton's "Farmer Holbrooke" nickname because it was so incongruous for a Manhattan-born urbanite whose prior exposure to agriculture consisted of the organic farm stands he passed on the way to the Hamptons.

Clinton's patience with Holbrooke was not limitless, however. In one meeting with Pakistani officials, when he wasn't letting other people speak, she told him to pipe down. Other times, she advised him not to pick fights. At a long session at her house in 2009, she and Jake Sullivan counseled Holbrooke about how to deal with the White House. "She would rein him in, and she would just say, '*Stop, Richard,*'" Rosemarie Pauli, Holbrooke's longtime chief of staff, recalled. "And he would listen to her, because he respected her." When Holbrooke clashed with Clinton, they tended to make up quickly. On August 9, 2010, he recorded in his diary, they had argued over a strategy memo he was writing for the president on the reconciliation process. Two hours later, Clinton called Holbrooke back to say that the blowup had been a misunderstanding, and that they should start over. "Hillary," he said, "does not like to apologize or ever say she was wrong, so I understood that to be a gesture."

In July 2010, Holbrooke brokered an agreement between Pakistan and Afghanistan that would allow Afghan farmers to transport their goods across Pakistan to sell in India. It wasn't as glamorous as Dayton, but it reinforced Holbrooke's argument that to stabilize Afghanistan, Pakistan needed to be more cooperative. Shortly after Clinton presided over the handshakes in Islamabad, Holbrooke turned up in the filing center, next to a swimming pool at the American embassy, where the diplomatic press corps were racing to make their deadlines. He had brought along Pakistan's ambassador to Washington, Husain Haqqani, and a case of warm champagne. As the reporters hunched over their keyboards, he filled plastic cups and delivered a detailed briefing, unfazed that they were too busy to listen.

Clinton and Holbrooke shared a propensity to wear out people with their enthusiasm for wonky issues. But unlike Clinton, who views the world as a series of problems to be solved, one after the other, Holbrooke considered himself a grand strategist. Even as his office was churning out arcane reports on agricultural diversification, he was looking for ways to play a decisive role in Afghanistan's future. His first foray into the country's internal affairs would backfire badly.


Holbrooke's low opinion of Hamid Karzai was no secret when he joined the administration. In a March 2008 op-ed column for *The Washington Post,* he criticized Karzai for not arresting the fearsome Uzbck warlord Abdul Rashid Dostum after he had attacked and brutalized a rival commander, allegedly with a beer bottle. "Excuses were made," he wrote, "but none justified his open disregard for justice." When Karzai was running for another five-year term as president in August 2009, Holbrooke openly rooted for someone to knock him off. He expressed admiration for one of the challengers, Ashraf Ghani, a well-spoken former World Bank official who had been finance minister, even encouraging James Carville to offer him advice. Holbrooke was ridiculed for his infatuation with Ghani, who, though a member of the dominant Pashtun tribe, lacked a political base. (Holbrooke was a better political handicapper than he got credit for: Ghani finally won the presidency in 2014 after surviving a grueling election against his rival, Abdullah Abdullah.)

On August 21, the morning after Afghans had gone to the polls, Holbrooke was in Kabul, warning colleagues that there might have to be a runoff. With so many allegations of vote rigging, Holbrooke expected Karzai would not get the necessary 50 percent of the vote. At a tense lunch later that day, Karzai accused Holbrooke of meddling. "There can't be a runoff," Karzai said. "There won't be a runoff." In an interview later, Holbrooke acknowledged it was a "frank exchange"—diplomatic code for a shouting match. The damage had been done: His relationship with Karzai was in tatters, and his detractors in the White House now had an opening to undermine him.

Holbrooke was right about the need for a runoff. But when it came time for the United States to have a "come to Jesus" moment with Karzai, the White House chose John Kerry, then the chairman of the Senate Foreign Relations Committee, to be the messenger. Kerry spent hours with Karzai, strolling through the gardens of the presidential palace. He told him about his own frustrations with allegations of voter fraud in Ohio, where he had lost in 2004 to George W. Bush, and Al Gore's misery four years earlier in Florida. Clinton, barely a year past her own bitter defeat, called Karzai to back up Kerry's words. Karzai acquiesced to a runoff that November, but after Abdullah pulled out, he was declared the victor.

"John performed brilliantly in every respect," Clinton told me. "It really came from deep down inside him. He understood the difficult intellectual and psychological struggle that Karzai was going through." Kerry's yeoman's service made him a prime candidate to succeed Clinton as secretary of state in a second term. Holbrooke, who was angling to succeed Clinton himself, had to watch as his job was done by someone else.

When Obama made his first trip as president to Afghanistan in March 2010, three months after ordering the deployment of thirty thousand additional American troops there, his special representative was left off Air Force One. The snub hurt Holbrooke with the status-conscious Afghans and Pakistanis, and it revealed that his problems in the White House went beyond Obama's campaign veterans. His bigger foes, it turned out, were Jim Jones, the laid-back marine general serving as national security adviser, and Doug Lute, the hardworking Bush administration official whom Obama kept on to run Afghanistan policy in the NSC. "Lute and Jones just blocked him," a Holbrooke loyalist said. "He never had a chance with them."

It was characteristic of Holbrooke not to gripe about these indignities, at least in public, or to allow them to slow him down. During this period, he was quietly working on Clinton to back his plan for reconciliation talks with the Taliban. She was frankly skeptical, but Holbrooke arranged a tutorial on the complexities of Afghan society, bringing in his experts to talk to her about the tribal links between the Taliban and Pashtun society. "He would say, 'Don't listen to me. Listen to Barney, listen to Vali, listen to Rina,'" Vali Nasr recalled. "And she would listen. I'm not saying she was sold, but she would say, 'Why do you think that? How would that work?'"

Holbrooke's problem was not Clinton. She accepted the argument that there had to be a political solution to the war, though in the early days, she saw more promise in trying to peel off lower-level Taliban fighters than in engaging the high command. His problem was the American generals fighting the war. In early 2009, Clinton brought Holbrooke together with David Petraeus for a get-to-know-you glass of wine at her home, after her own entente with Petraeus. He and Holbrooke began to meet regularly for dinner, and they propagated the narrative of a soldier-diplomat buddy act. It was good copy, and it made sense since a winning war effort would demand a high degree of civilian-military coordination. But behind the scenes, they tangled—a tug-of-war between two supremely ambitious figures that David Axelrod likened to the battle of wits between Sherlock Holmes and Professor Moriarty. Petraeus called Holbrooke his wingman, ostensibly evidence of their tight bond. Holbrooke held his tongue in public, but he bridled at the phrase, complaining to his wife, Kati, "Since when did the diplomat become the general's wingman?"

The fastidious Petraeus was put off by Holbrooke's slapdash style. The general once turned up for a meeting in the middle of an interview I was conducting with Holbrooke in early 2010. Rather than kick me out, Holbrooke invited me to stay on for a while, which left Petraeus visibly uncomfortable. As he held forth on the problems in Afghanistan, Holbrooke rested his stocking feet on a low coffee table. Petraeus stared at his wiggling Gold Toes before interrupting him to ask, "Richard, why aren't you wearing shoes?" Holbrooke, who had bad feet and liked to pad around the office shoeless, waved his hand dismissively, declaring that he was more comfortable without them. Petraeus, glancing down at his own spit-shined shoes, was nonplussed.

Above all, Petraeus did not want Holbrooke's diplomacy to interfere with his war planning. When I asked the general about the prospects for reconciliation in June 2010, shortly after he had replaced Stan McChrystal as the commander of the International Security Assistance Force, Petraeus made clear it was premature to enter into negotiations with the Taliban while his troops were still fighting to root them out of Afghan villages and towns. "This will not end like the Balkans," he told me.

"Petraeus is strongly opposing all this," Holbrooke recorded on August 6. "He says it's too early and he wants to do it only when he says the time is right, which he says will be next year. Frankly, I just don't believe him. I think the situation will still be an ambiguous muddle, with elements of progress and elements of retrogression."

Holbrooke persisted, however. Despite resistance from the Pentagon, the CIA, and some in the White House, he eventually won Obama's backing to open a secret channel to a Taliban emissary who claimed to represent the one-eyed Taliban leader, Mullah Muhammad Omar. He was an Afghan named Syed Tayyab Agha. Because the contact was so tenuous, Holbrooke opted not to go himself. He sent his deputy Frank Ruggiero and an official from the NSC, Jeff Hayes. To cover his bases with Petraeus, Holbrooke sent the pair to brief the general in Afghanistan after the meeting. "Petraeus was not at all interested," said an administration official who took part in the session. "His response was, 'Did you talk about ceasefires? They said, 'No, that would come at the end of any process.' And he said, 'Good. As long as you didn't talk about ceasefires, then I've got no issue with it.' He was so nervous that the White House was going to blow the whistle and say, 'Stop your military campaign.'"

Petraeus had reason to worry: At the White House, Holbrooke's ideas on reconciliation were slowly gaining traction. Obama was not especially eager to talk to the Taliban but he was eager to wind down the war, and he recognized one might open the door to the other. Clinton and Bob Gates, though staunch supporters of the military's counterinsurgency strategy, were attuned to the political pressures facing the president. But Holbrooke's tensions with Obama's aides continued to plague him. In this case, the infighting may have gotten in the way of pursuing a path to peace.

At issue was who would lead the talks with the Taliban. Holbrooke and Clinton assumed that, naturally, it would be the hero of Dayton. But Jones and Lute could not bear the thought of Holbrooke reenacting his Balkans triumph in Afghanistan. Lute was resentful of his high-handedness. He thought the United States, as a combatant, should not be at the table cutting a deal between the Taliban and the Afghan government. And anyway, Karzai, who had distrusted Holbrooke since the election, would never abide him as a mediator. So Lute came up with the idea of giving the assignment to Lakhdar Brahimi, a wizened Algerian diplomat then serving as the United Nations representative in Kabul. "Brahimi is a distinguished UN diplomat who knew Afghanistan and had a trusting relationship with Karzai," Lute told me. "The UN had convening power among key players that the U.S. did not."

Clinton had gotten wind of this scheme in advance and told Obama she opposed bringing in the UN envoy. When Lute and a colleague presented it to the president, they got a withering response. "This is screwed up," the president said, according to someone who was in the room. "You guys come in here knowing that Secretary Clinton opposes this, and ask me to do an end-run around her?" (Lute said he did not recall the meeting with Obama and would not have tried to circumvent Clinton.)

It was not the first time Clinton had saved Holbrooke's skin. A few months earlier, while Clinton was on a trip to Russia, General Jones had summoned Holbrooke to his corner office in the West Wing and told him he should plan his departure from the administration. A stunned Holbrooke, thinking he had just been fired, retreated to his rented house in Georgetown to consider his options. Tom Donilon, an old friend then serving as Jones's deputy, advised him to do nothing. But Rosemarie Pauli—whom he had asked to come to the house, along with his press assistant, Ashley Bommer—urged him to appeal to the secretary of state. Holbrooke's first call was to Jake Sullivan, whom he woke in a Moscow hotel room in the middle of the night.

A few hours later, Sullivan briefed Clinton, and another campaign to save Holbrooke began. She had asked Strobe Talbott, a mutual friend of hers and Holbrooke's, to be part of an informal support group for him. The day after she returned from Russia, Talbott emailed her about a lunch he'd had with Donilon that was dominated by White House complaints about Holbrooke. "It sounded quite ominous re his immediate boss, and not great re the ultimate one," he wrote, referring to Jones and Obama. Sullivan put together the equivalent of a legal brief for Clinton, itemizing the achievements of the SRAP staff and explaining the distinctive nature of Holbrooke's leadership. Armed with that, she requested a meeting with the president.

"Jim Jones can't fire Richard Holbrooke," Clinton told Obama, according to two people who were briefed on their exchange. "I can. You can. If you want to fire him, it's certainly your prerogative, but you'll be doing it over the objections of your secretary of state." Obama countermanded Jones, and Holbrooke lived to fight another day.

Nothing better exemplified Holbrooke's troubles with the White House than the September 2009 issue of *The New Yorker*. It contained a long, admiring profile of him under the headline "The Last Mission." While it did not trigger his dismissal, as would the explosive profile of Stan McChrystal in *Rolling Stone* a year later, it shared some of the same features: an exotic backdrop and a colorful narrative, based on unusual access to a swashbuckling hero who was not named Barack Obama. As soon as the magazine hit newsstands, Denis McDonough called Holbrooke on the carpet. He was particularly incensed that Holbrooke had allowed the writer, George Packer, to sit in on a meeting between him and Karzai. The State Department spokesman, P. J. Crowley, gave Clinton a heads-up on the article via Cheryl Mills. "Richard strayed shall we say from discussion of our strategy," he emailed. Holbrooke's cultivation of reporters had long been a sore spot with Obama's aides, who tried to keep tight control over such contacts; this piece made them neuralgic.

It is true that Holbrooke was catnip to journalists, in part because they recognized him as a kindred spirit. A onetime news clerk at *The New York Times*, editor of *Foreign Policy* magazine, and columnist at *The Washington Post*, Holbrooke had moonlighted as a writer even as he established himself as a top-shelf diplomat. He offered reporters unsolicited critiques of their works, and his obsession with their coverage was comical. Dozing on a flight out of Afghanistan one night in 2010, I suddenly felt a silent presence over my left shoulder; it was Holbrooke peering at the half-written article on my open laptop. When I snapped the computer shut, he shrugged his shoulders and started a conversation about something else.

For all his palaver with journalists, Holbrooke was a better dispenser of analysis than scoops. When I asked him in the fall of 2010 whether the United States was ready to talk to the Taliban, he replied that it was an "over-the-horizon" issue. Not that far over the horizon, in reality: He was about to send his deputy to the first secret meeting, in a village outside Munich, Germany, with the Taliban emissary, whom he had dubbed A-Rod after the not-yet-disgraced New York Yankees slugger. Holbrooke said little about his alienation from the White House and never publicly criticized the president.

In December 2009, Obama traveled to West Point to announce the troop surge. Holbrooke, who told Clinton privately that he had deep doubts about the plan, was, as usual, not invited to go with him. So, instead, he flew to Brussels, where he convened a meeting of Af-Pak representatives from other countries and delivered a briefing on Obama's decision. It all looked very coordinated but it was largely a way for Holbrooke to save face, to paper over being sidelined back home. However brave a front he put up, he privately despaired over his lack of entrée to the Oval Office.

Holbrooke's audio diary became an outlet for his frustration with the White House. He was wounded when Clinton and Donilon told him that the president wanted him to drop his constant references to Vietnam. "I was very struck by this," Holbrooke said, "since I thought there were obviously relevant issues." He mixed jabs at Donilon ("Tom's strengths are political and public affairs; he doesn't have a strategic sense") and Rahm Emanuel ("He's smart, he's quick, but he's just not very nice, at least not to me") with tidbits about his own Gatsby-like social life (an eightieth-birthday party for George Soros, held under a tent for five hundred at a Hamptons horse farm). But the recordings also captured the unabashed patriot and incurable romantic in Holbrooke. He talked about seeing a revival of *South Pacific* at Lincoln Center in August 2010 and being struck by the America of Rodgers and Hammerstein, a country at the zenith of its power after World War II. "The contrast with today," he said, choking up. "It was very powerful, and I just kept thinking of where we were today, our nation, our lack of confidence in our own ability to lead, compared to where we are in 1949, when it came out, evoking an era only five to seven years earlier, when we had gone to the most distant corners of the globe and saved civilization."

By that fall, Holbrooke's friends were advising him to leave on his own terms. He told them to mind their own business, but they were beginning to worry about his health. Though he was a sturdy man, his punishing work and travel were catching up with him. At lunch with Frank Wisner at the Metropolitan Club in New York, the two were tucking into their customary menu of congressional navy bean soup and two-dozen Cherrystone clams. Holbrooke, who ate with the same brio he did everything else, nicked the tip of his nose with the edge of a clamshell, and blood spurted out. "We had to get napkins to staunch the flow, and I said, 'What the hell's wrong with you?'" Wisner recalled. It was then that he learned his friend was taking heavy doses of Coumadin, a blood-thinning drug prescribed to people with heart disease.

A few days after the secret Taliban meeting in Germany—the

first step in his gambit to negotiate a settlement with the Taliban—Holbrooke suffered the tear in his aorta that would kill him. The previous evening, he had dined at a Georgetown restaurant, 1789, with Michael Abramowitz, a former *Washington Post* reporter and the son of another renowned American diplomat, Morton Abramowitz. He recalled Holbrooke being subdued and tired but engaged. They chatted about trends in journalism (mostly negative, in Holbrooke's view) and geopolitics (he saw the Caucasus as the next major flashpoint).

The next morning, Holbrooke dropped in on David Axelrod at the White House to plead yet again for a one-on-one with the president. Axelrod told him he would see what he could do. His assistant, worried about Holbrooke's flushed appearance, offered him a glass of water. Then he went to Clinton's office, where, during a session with her and Jake Sullivan, his face abruptly turned dark red and he was suffused by pain. Holbrooke was rushed to George Washington University Hospital, where he underwent twenty-one hours of emergency surgery and became the focus of a worldwide vigil. Hamid Karzai and President Asif Ali Zardari of Pakistan both called Kati Marton on her cellphone to offer their best wishes. In a twist Holbrooke would have appreciated, his heart surgeon, Farzad Najam, was from Pakistan.

Even in physical agony, Holbrooke's combination of charm and intensity didn't leave him. Told by the attending physician, Jehan El-Bayoumi, that he needed to relax, he said, "You have to promise me that you're going to end the war in Afghanistan." OK, she said, and then she asked him to close his eyes and imagine being on a beach. "I don't like beaches," he said. When she asked him what he wanted to imagine, Holbrooke replied, "a beautiful woman." Suddenly, his eyes opened.

"You!" he exclaimed.

It is hard to know if things would have gone differently in Afghanistan had Richard Holbrooke not died on December 13, 2010. Some in the administration argue that Lute's attempts to block Holbrooke from talking to the Taliban, by promoting a UN envoy in his place, paralyzed the process at a critical juncture. If the White House had simply made Holbrooke the negotiator, a former NSC official said, "the talks with the Taliban would have started earlier and progressed further." But Obama was determined from day one to withdraw American soldiers from Afghanistan. By telegraphing his intentions so early and often, he may have foreclosed the possibility of any meaningful negotiation with the Taliban. They knew they could wait out the Americans.

The bittersweet postscript to Holbrooke's last mission is that two months after he died, Clinton finally opened the door to reconciliation. In a speech at the Asia Society dedicated to her old friend, Clinton challenged the Taliban: "Break ties with al-Qaeda, give up your arms, and abide by the Afghan constitution, and you can rejoin Afghan society." It was a familiar demand, but there was a twist: She now was saying that the Taliban could meet these criteria as a result of negotiations, not as a precondition for them. That made diplomacy possible in a way it had not been before.

With the door to talks open, the White House explored various channels, some rather far-fetched. One involved negotiating with the Taliban through an intermediary, Hamid Gul, a retired Pakistani general who had been the head of Pakistan's powerful spy agency, the Inter-Services Intelligence Agency, or ISI, which had long had ties with the Taliban. On the American side, the emissary was to be Bruce Riedel, author of the first Afghan review. Like many of these schemes, the idea went nowhere.

Holbrooke's successor, Marc Grossman, plunged into a delicate negotiation with the Taliban and Karzai, who was deeply suspicious of American efforts to broker a settlement without him. Grossman was a career diplomat as low-key as Holbrooke was larger-than-life, but he had one advantage: no baggage with the White House. In one of his first meetings, he revived Holbrooke's idea of reaching out to Iran for help on Afghanistan. "Everyone said, 'Sure, go ahead,'" a senior official recalled. Amazed at meeting so little resistance, Grossman asked his State Department colleagues to explain. "The White House didn't allow Dick to do that," one told him, "because they thought the only reason Dick wanted to talk to the Iranians was to be the one to talk to the Iranians."

Grossman's overture to Iran was unrequited; his diplomacy with the Taliban was doomed by Karzai's suspicions and a chain of clumsy miscommunications over a political office the Taliban opened in Qatar. The militants hung a sign and raised a flag over the building, drawing fierce protests from Karzai, who said they were presenting themselves as a government-in-exile. When the United States finally achieved a diplomatic breakthrough with Iran five years later, the credit went to John Kerry, and, ultimately, to Obama. In the end, the only deal ever struck with the Taliban was a prisoner swap in which five of their fighters held in Guantánamo Bay, Cuba, were exchanged for Sergeant Bowe Bergdahl, an American soldier who walked off his base in Afghanistan and was captured and held by the Taliban for nearly five years. Given the army's later charges that Bergdahl was a deserter, it was not much of a deal—a threadbare alternative to the grand bargain Holbrooke had in mind, not to mention a lingering political headache for the president.

"Richard was a big-picture guy in a small-picture administration," said Husain Haqqani, who met him for breakfast at the Four Seasons Hotel in Georgetown the day before he became ill and recalled Holbrooke venting frustration at his inability to build trust with Pakistan's military commanders. "How could you have a special representative who was not special, and not representative of the president?"

A few weeks after Holbrooke's death, his widow, Kati Marton, was invited to lunch at the White House mess by Samantha Power, who had been one of his acolytes. She ran into Denis McDonough, who expressed his sympathies and said, "Kati, if there's anything we can do, let us know."

"Only because Samantha was next to me, did I not say, 'I wish you had made that offer to Richard when he was alive,'" she told me. "That the president couldn't take ten minutes because Richard wasn't cool enough, wasn't a temperamental soul mate? That speaks to a very specific lacuna in the president's character—that he's not ultimately comfortable beyond his very narrow zone."

Marton, a writer and former ABC News correspondent, waged a campaign to bury her husband at Arlington National Cemetery, even though he did not meet the requirement of having been an active or retired member of the military. She asked Clinton and the former chairman of the Joint Chiefs of Staff Mike Mullen to send letters on his behalf. Holbrooke's "public service was inextricably intertwined with our military," Clinton wrote on September 8, 2011, "and, more than once, Richard found himself on the front lines, the living embodiment of 'one mission, one team.'" Six weeks later, the army secretary, John McHugh, wrote back to Marton to say, "Ambassador Holbrooke, unfortunately, is not eligible to be laid to rest at Arlington." Marton thinks the White House could have intervened to waive the rule.

Holbrooke's eldest son, David, made a nuanced HBO documentary about his father, *The Diplomat*. His research for the film left him with a more philosophical view of Holbrooke's ordeal. Looking back, he says, his father's generational disconnect with Obama could have been foretold in an encounter his son had with the president on the day Holbrooke was appointed. Shaking Obama's hand, David, who was forty-three at the time and plays respectable, middle-aged basketball, told him, "Any time you want to ball up, let me know." Obama laughed and asked him what kind of game he had; David, who is six foot six, replied that he resembled Horace Grant, the solid, if unspectacular, power forward who played for the 1990s Chicago Bulls. "My dad would probably have said Bob

Cousy," David said, referring to the Boston Celtics superstar whose heyday was in the fifties and sixties.

Clinton has said little in public about Holbrooke's travails. Privately, friends say, she is still offended by the way the White House treated her friend. In her memoir, she did not bother to quote from Obama's eulogy, in which he placed his envoy in a line of diplomatic giants from Dean Acheson to Clark Clifford. Much has been made of the cringeworthy dynamics at his memorial service: the pinched president, praising the man he never had time for; the emotional secretary of state, mourning the man who didn't leave her alone. Perhaps the strangest moment, missed by all but the lip-readers in the front row, came when one of Holbrooke's oldest friends, Leslie Gelb, described him as being "like Odysseus"—"a leader of men, and women, and interns." The audience cracked up at the word "interns," but Bill Clinton, who was sitting onstage where the acoustics were poor, didn't catch it.

He leaned over to Hillary for clarification.

"Interns," she mouthed, her eyes narrowing. "He said 'interns.'"

Obama's remarks were faultlessly dignified but utterly impersonal. Only once, for a moment, did his mask drop. "So full of life," he said of Holbrooke's over-the-top energy, "he was a man both confident in himself and curious about others." At the word "confident," a smile flashed across Obama's face and he cast a knowing glance at the audience. Though he placed Holbrooke in the pantheon of Democratic statesmen, it was precisely this status that made Obama and his aides suspicious of him. They were determined to break free of that cohort and its well-worn nostrums—nostrums to which Clinton wholeheartedly subscribed. In the process, however, they failed to benefit from the decades of experience he brought with him. "I can understand the desire to think more creatively and to change things and to think there's an old guard," said Dan Feldman, a Holbrooke deputy who later served as the special envoy, "but not at the expense of losing institutional memory and history."

In retrospect, the president's aides admitted, they could have handled some things differently. "If Obama having a one-hour lunch with Holbrooke would have made him feel that much better, we could have done that," Ben Rhodes told me. The White House also could have made it clearer that when it forbade him from giving television interviews, it was because, in the throes of the Great Recession, the administration wanted only economic officials on television. Afghanistan was a distraction for a domestically focused president. That speaks to a larger truth about Holbrooke: His job title never matched his self-image.

"I don't think the president was aware that there was so much drama surrounding Richard Holbrooke," Rhodes said, in a comment that would have cut his special representative to the quick.

After Holbrooke's death, the drama was hard for Obama to avoid. In the flood of elegies to him, a narrative took hold: His relentless turf battles with the White House had worsened his health problems; the rigors of his last mission somehow had precipitated his death. The president began to take it personally. At a White House meeting on Afghanistan a few weeks later, said a person who was there, Obama complained, "I'm sick of people writing about how I killed Richard Holbrooke."

## Part II

# War and Peace

# Five

## Below the Waterline

"Is anyone reading the newspaper?" Hillary Clinton asked incredulously. "Is anyone watching television?"

Her colleagues assembled around the conference table in the Situation Room squirmed in their chairs. They had just been praising a classified report about the CIA's drone program in Pakistan, which the agency had presented to the NSC's Principals Committee in the spring of 2012. The report was part of a high-level review Barack Obama had ordered of the covert policy of targeted killings, the cornerstone of his counterterrorism campaign against al-Qaeda. "Mr. President," it began, "under your leadership, we have conducted . . ." The headline numbers looked promising: the number of accidental civilian casualties from drone strikes in the rugged frontier between Pakistan and Afghanistan had dropped markedly as a percentage of the total casualties; the Hellfire missiles fired from Predator drones were hitting the bad guys with greater precision, the report claimed.

"Oh, that's great," said one senior official.

"Good data," said another.

"It shows that this is not the picture everyone paints," chipped in a third.

Clinton, as was her habit, had asked the national security adviser, Tom Donilon, who was chairing the meeting, to let her speak last. She proceeded to shred the whole exercise. "It doesn't matter what our analysts are saying," Clinton told her startled colleagues. The numbers didn't begin to capture the damage the drone program was doing to America's image abroad. "First of all, the narrative is out there," she said. "The bigger question, folks, is, 'What the heck are we doing with drones? What is our policy? Do we have an answer for the American public? Do we have an answer for the left? Do we have an answer for our international allies, who want to know under what criteria, under what conditions, under what international law, are we using them?'"

There were no good answers to Clinton's questions that day, just as there had been no answers at any of the other White House meetings held to discuss this new type of war, which had, like it or not, become America's calling card in some of the world's most dangerous places.

Hillary Clinton did not, and does not, oppose Obama's use of covert operations in fighting terrorism. She endorsed the CIA plan to dispatch a team of Navy SEALs to raid Osama bin Laden's hideout in Abbottabad, Pakistan—albeit in a heavily hedged calculation, with a list of pros and cons long enough to fill a yellow legal pad. She backed the firing of Tomahawk cruise missiles from American ships to hit terrorist targets in Yemen, a quasi-secret program to help the Yemenis combat the al-Qaeda franchise that had taken root there. She favored sending drones from a secret CIA base in Afghanistan to strike terrorists in Pakistan, even if the Pakistanis seethed at the intrusion into their territory. "She was supportive of what we had to do to deal with al-Qaeda," Leon Panetta, the CIA director at the time, said. "Both of us knew very well that the key was to ensure that Pakistan, regardless of their concerns, would stand back and allow us to continue those operations."

But Clinton was deeply frustrated by the lack of coordination between the CIA and the State Department about the timing of drone strikes; they sabotaged the work of her diplomats on a regular basis. She fought for her ambassador in Islamabad to have the right to veto what he judged to be ill-chosen strikes, and for the White House to be more open about the program, which it never publicly acknowledged, so that she and other officials could defend it, particularly when they traveled to the countries where drones were being used.

Clinton got a taste of the damage these strikes inflicted on America's reputation and image abroad in a way that Obama did not. The president carried out his drone war within a tight circle of counterterrorism advisers who compiled a list of targets to be killed or captured and had the boss sign off on them. They were driven by a single overriding goal—to prevent another act of terrorism on American soil without committing more American ground troops—and not overly concerned about how their tactics might bruise feelings abroad. Obama never visited Pakistan as president; Clinton went three times as secretary of state. Each time she did, she got bombarded with questions about the strikes—What about civilian casualties? Why not let the Pakistanis do it themselves? Why was this any different from what the terrorists are doing?—none of which she was allowed to answer because of the program's covert nature.

Her firsthand exposure gave Clinton a more jaundiced perspective than Obama on targeted killings as an instrument of foreign policy: how they could turn public opinion against the United States; how they could be exploited by foreign governments to create a negative, sometimes false, narrative; how they could undercut the diplomatic outreach of the State Department or the development work of USAID; how they could radicalize societies, even as they "removed fighters from the battlefield," to use the White House's preferred euphemism. By 2009, the CIA's insistence on not confirming the existence of the program was a charade because the strikes were routinely reported in the Pakistani press. It was a charade that came at a high cost, Clinton believed: Because no government official could publicly talk about the program, the United States could not articulate a persuasive moral or legal case for why it needed to be in the killing business.

"She was fine with the lawful use of drones as a tool, but very uncomfortable with using drones as a *strategy*," said Harold Koh, who served as the State Department's legal adviser from 2009 to 2013. "She doesn't believe they are a strategy."

An eminent legal scholar and ardent political supporter of Clinton, Koh knows better than anyone the ethical and legal conundrum posed by these weapons. As a Yale Law professor with a deep interest in human rights, Koh had been a fierce critic of George W. Bush's post-9/11 counterterrorism policies, from the waterboarding of suspected terrorists to their indefinite detention at Guantánamo Bay. In his role at the State Department, he worked hard to reconcile Obama's targeted killings with international law, opening himself up to charges of hypocrisy in the process. After leaving the government in 2013, Koh went to Oxford University in England, where he had studied as a Marshall Scholar, to square that circle. Obama's failure, he told the Oxford Union in a speech titled "How to End the Forever War?," was not the drone strikes themselves, but the president's opacity about them: refusing to talk about drones made it impossible to explain their utility or to defend their legality.

"Because the administration has been so opaque, a left-right coalition running from Code Pink to Rand Paul has now spoken out against the drone program," he said. This fueled "a growing perception that the program is not lawful and necessary, but illegal, unnecessary, and out of control. The administration must take responsibility for this failure, because its persistent and counterproductive lack of transparency has led to the release of necessary pieces of its public legal defense too little and too late."

In a vaulted hall at Oxford, Koh was echoing what Clinton had said a year earlier in the windowless confines of the Sit Room.

It took Obama three years to offer his first candid defense of drones, and when he did, it wasn't in a speech at West Point or a press conference at the White House. Instead, he chose a Google Hangout, a live video chat carried on YouTube. Obama's press staff liked these social media channels as a way to reach young people, and when he sat down for the group video chat on January 30,

2012, his audience asked a typical mix of trivial and tough questions. By then, outside investigators estimated, the United States had carried out 257 strikes in Pakistan, killing up to 2,500 people (of which 15 percent to 22 percent were believed to be civilians). Amid the requests for Obama to show off his dance moves or tell how he and Michelle planned to celebrate their twentieth wedding anniversary came this from Evan in Brooklyn, New York: "Mr. President," the young man asked, "you've ordered more drone attacks in your first year than your predecessor did in his entire term. These drone attacks cause a lot of civilian casualties. I'm curious to know how you feel they help the nation, and whether you think they are worth it."

Drones don't kill a lot of civilians, Obama replied. They are precision tools, aimed at enemies whose names are on a list, not, he said, "a bunch of strikes, willy-nilly." Paras Patel, a medical student from Detroit, wasn't satisfied. But don't these incursions, he asked, send a message that the United States is too ready to interfere in other countries? Obama conceded the risk, but said that drones allowed the U.S. government to go after terrorists in places that were beyond the reach of local troops and would otherwise require a much more intrusive and dangerous military intervention. Most of the strikes he had ordered, he said, were in a part of northwest Pakistan along the Afghan border. It was the first time Obama confirmed what everyone knew. This remote, mountainous, and violent place—a safe haven for al-Qaeda since 9/11—was in America's crosshairs.

"It is important for everybody to understand that this thing is kept on a very tight leash," he said. "It's not a bunch of folks in a room somewhere, just making decisions."

Except, to a great extent, that's what it was.

From the moment Obama took office, he made it clear he would continue the targeted killing program he inherited from George W. Bush. His resolve was hardened at the end of his first year when a Nigerian man nearly blew apart a Northwest Airlines plane bound for Detroit by igniting explosives hidden in his underwear. The

Christmas Day plot failed and the 290 passengers on board arrived safely. But Obama viewed it as a political near-death experience for his administration—one that erased his early ambivalence about many of the counterterrorism methods used by his predecessor. Not only was he sure that targeted killings were the smart way to fight terrorism, he was determined to run the program from the West Wing.

Obama entrusted the grim business of selecting targets to John Brennan, his chief counterterrorism adviser. The sixty-year-old spymaster had lost his initial shot at being CIA director in the first term because of comments he made that were viewed as soft on the Bush administration's use of rendition and torture, and ran counter to Obama's pledge to end both practices. Assigned a claustrophobic, bunker-like office in the White House basement, Brennan oversaw a group of more than one hundred people across the government whose job was to compile what the press dubbed the "kill list." He arguably wielded more power than he would have in the wood-paneled suite at CIA headquarters in Langley, Virginia. (He ended up as the agency's director in the second term.)

The son of Irish immigrants from County Roscommon, Brennan has the hulking physique, rough-hewn features, and bristle-cut hair of a New York City police captain, circa 1940. Jesuit educated and a workaholic, he studied Arabic during a junior year abroad in Cairo and served as the CIA's station chief in Saudi Arabia in the mid-1990s, when nineteen American servicemen were killed in a truck bombing at the Khobar Towers. He was one of a trio of national security aides, along with Denis McDonough and Tom Donilon, whom Obama called "the grim Irishmen." When the Irishmen were waiting for him in the Oval Office, the president could be sure they weren't there to chat about last night's game or which pop star was going to perform that evening in the East Room. Brennan was on hand for the hardest conversations of all: whether Obama should approve a drone strike that would kill a person, sometimes many people, in a distant land. Inevitably, given his Irish Catholic roots and image of rectitude, some began to think of him as the president's confessor.

Obama leaned heavily on Brennan's knowledge of Islamic extremism, of Saudi Arabia, and of Yemen, where he had forged close ties to President Ali Abdullah Saleh. "The purpose of these actions is to mitigate threats," Brennan told my colleagues Scott Shane and Jo Becker in 2012. "It is the option of last recourse. So the president, and I think all of us here, don't like the fact that people have to die. And so he wants to make sure that we go through a rigorous checklist: the infeasibility of capture, the certainty of the intelligence base, the imminence of the threat, all of these things."

Brennan wasn't the only official who amassed uncommon authority to wage this hidden war. Leon Panetta, Obama's first CIA director, asked the president in the fall of 2009 to expand the agency's fleet of armed drones and to petition the Pakistanis to widen the territory over which they were allowed to fly. Neither decision was straightforward. "The politics in Pakistan," he told me, "were very complicated." But Panetta got both. It was a tribute to his bureaucratic agility—Clinton described him as a "shrewd, blunt, and colorful Washington operator"—and to Obama's broader reflex in the first term, which was to give the agency whatever it wanted.

At the same time the CIA was building its secret air force, the White House cast around for nonmilitary ways to combat terrorism. Denis McDonough was put in charge of an early effort to diagnose why the United States had such a poor image in Pakistan, and vice versa, and to devise ways to improve each. After the enormity of the task became clear, the project faded. The State Department later developed plans for a center to counter extremist propaganda, which would pool experts from several agencies to try to discredit or preempt the anti-American messages of jihadi groups. But it ran into resistance from Obama's advisers, who viewed it as encroaching on the NSC's turf. When Clinton presented the idea at a meeting with the president and his homeland security staff in July 2010, he exploded in frustration. "I don't know what I have to do to get people around here to listen to me," he said. "I've been asking for this kind of plan for more than a year!" McDonough and Brennan were stung by his reprimand. But rather than leaping into action, they took it out on the State Department, waiting another year to authorize the center.

"Some of us were in the awkward position of working for a guy who said during the campaign that he wanted to do this in a smarter way," said Daniel Benjamin, who coordinated counterterrorism policy for Clinton at the State Department. "Then the kinetic piece became so dominant that it was hard to get a hearing for all the other stuff."

The White House, some concluded, was paying lip service to the other stuff. "It was a constant theme from very early on. It was the mantra no one ever did anything about: We can't solve this by drone strikes alone, we can't shoot our way out of this," said Dennis Blair, who had a brief, stormy tenure as Obama's director of national intelligence in 2009 and 2010.

A blunt, brainy navy admiral who once commanded the Pacific Fleet, Blair came in knowing the Clintons better than he knew Obama. He had been a Rhodes Scholar at Oxford with Bill. The two were not close, but in the turbulent year of 1968, Blair asked Clinton to deliver a graduation speech in his place at an American military high school in London. (Blair was busy studying for his exams; Clinton had decided to skip his.) It was a risky move—swapping a straight-arrow Naval Academy grad for a bearded anti-Vietnam protester—but Clinton threaded the needle. He paid tribute to those who served while making it clear that he disagreed with the policy. Decades later, when Clinton was president, the Pentagon sent Blair, then a fast-rising navy officer, to the CIA to serve as its liaison to the agency. There, Blair honed his views about the proper role of intelligence agencies in American foreign policy—views that he brought to an Obama war cabinet that included his former classmate's wife.

Blair and Hillary should have been natural allies. He thought the

United States relied too much on covert operations instead of old-fashioned diplomacy. In some countries in the Middle East and South Asia, the CIA station chief had more clout with the local government than the ambassador, a situation that understandably grated on the career diplomats. Nowhere was the tension between diplomats and spies greater than in Pakistan, where the Pakistani spy agency, the ISI, mirrored the CIA's influence. The conflict led to a shouting match between Clinton and Panetta over who got to sign off on drone strikes there. Blair, in his role atop the intelligence establishment, hoped to right that balance. Early in 2010, he approached officials at the State Department about ways he could help bolster the influence of ambassadors in the region. Had he succeeded, Clinton would have been a big winner. He did not. The admiral's outsider status and impolitic manner crippled him with Obama and his aides. After a string of clashes with Panetta—the most bitter after he tried to take away the CIA's traditional right to name the senior American spy in foreign countries—Blair was fired by the president that May.

The first thing to know about America's relationship with Pakistan, Richard Holbrooke liked to say, is it exists both above the waterline and below the waterline. The visible part consists of the traditional diplomacy and development that the United States conducts with hundreds of countries. The submerged part consists of covert counterterrorism operations—sometimes in conjunction with the Pakistani authorities, sometimes not. The trick was not to let the below-the-line activities swamp the above-the-line ones. With the White House stepping up drone strikes in 2009 and 2010, Holbrooke saw the waters rising fast. "All we're delivering to these Pakistanis are drones," he lamented, more than once, to his State Department colleagues.

It wasn't quite true. On October 28, 2009, the White House delivered Hillary Clinton. Her first visit to Pakistan as a secretary of state was designed to promote diplomacy and development. She may have arrived with the stealth of a Predator; the traveling press was given few advance details of her itinerary for security reasons. But her three days of town-hall meetings and media interviews proved to be the opposite of a drone strike: a conspicuously public display of American outreach. Holbrooke, who had urged Clinton to make the trip and accompanied her at every step, desperately wanted to move the dialogue between the United States and Pakistan beyond security. Clinton had a parallel hope: to lift the debate to new psychological ground—not the sunny uplands of mutual trust and understanding, exactly, but to a place where the two sides could speak more openly about the grievances they nourished in the dark.

The catch was, Clinton couldn't talk about—let alone defend—the drone program, perhaps the most immediate source of Pakistani suspicion. It was like sending a defense attorney into the courtroom and telling her she couldn't put one of her key witnesses on the stand.

The extent to which tensions over Islamic extremism overshadowed the relationship became clear right away. A few hours after Clinton's plane landed, a powerful car bomb ripped through a teeming market in Peshawar, the gateway into Afghanistan, ninety miles northwest of the capital. More than one hundred people were killed. It was Pakistan's most serious terrorist attack in two years, and the worst ever in Peshawar, an ancient city now on the front lines of a deadly Taliban insurgency. It was also a grim reminder of the rift with Washington: The Americans complained Pakistan wasn't doing enough to hunt down militants; the Pakistanis griped that the withdrawal of American troops from Afghanistan had allowed those extremists to export their terror across the border. Pakistani TV played Clinton's remarks condemning the attack on a split screen: the other half had images of parents carrying the bloodied bodies of their children through a hellish landscape of smoke and fire.

Clinton had brought with her $125 million in aid to help Pakistan repair and upgrade its aging power plants to cut down on power failures. It was part of an effort by Holbrooke to cull the hundreds of U.S. projects in Pakistan and funnel money into a few high-profile programs that would tangibly improve the lives of Pakistanis. "For months," she said, "families have endured sweltering heat and evenings spent in the dark, without appliances or televisions or computers"—not to mention the petty crime that spikes when the lights go out. It was all true, but it was lost on a day when Pakistanis were convulsed by a crime wave of a totally different magnitude.

Pakistan's news media—a noisy babel of newspapers, cable news channels, and websites—relentlessly fed the narrative of America's cynical motives. Exuberant, gossipy, and conspiratorial, they pandered to the conviction of many Pakistanis that the United States was a faithless partner that sent drones to violate their airspace, CIA assassins to roam their streets, and was only biding its time until it abandoned them again, just as it had after Pakistan helped it fight the Russians in Afghanistan. All this made the news media a prime target for Clinton's charm offensive; Philippe Reines, her communications guru, told the public affairs staff in the embassy to "bring 'em on."

Clinton prepped exhaustively for the questions and was plainly worried about land mines. Drones were the obvious one. But two days before the trip, she emailed Jake Sullivan to ask about a related issue: reports in the Pakistani press that Blackwater, the private security contractor with a notorious history in Iraq, had agents in Karachi, masquerading as aid workers, who were planning assassinations of Taliban and al-Qaeda leaders for the CIA and the military's Joint Special Operations Command. "Do we have good answers for the Blackwater allegations? What exactly are they? And what's been said before?" Sullivan emailed back to assure Clinton that Vali Nasr, Holbrooke's adviser on Pakistan, was drafting talking points.

Clinton's swordplay with Pakistani journalists over the next three days was as combative as she expected. It made her fencing with the political press in Iowa and New Hampshire look dainty by comparison. On her first afternoon, seven TV anchors arrived to interrogate her at the American embassy, a sprawling compound that was fortified in 1979—after being burned to the ground by a mob—and reinforced again after 9/11. Interrupting Clinton and speaking over one another, they peppered her on the strings Congress had attached to a $7.5 billion aid program for Pakistan ("We believe the bill had a sort of hidden agenda") and allegations that American contractors were illegally carrying weapons on the streets of Pakistani cities ("Will you allow Pakistani soldiers to patrol like this, carrying illegal weapons in their hands in the streets of Washington?"). Drones figured high on the list.

"If the United States government is so sincere in helping Pakistan through its problems," one asked, "why is it that you are constantly using drone attacks inside Pakistan? Why not transfer that technology to the Pakistani military that you have praised yourself?"

"I don't really talk about that," she replied. "I think that's something the military-to-military relationship has to deal with."

Why, she was asked, had the United States disregarded a resolution against drone strikes by the Pakistani parliament? (The strikes were governed by an unwritten agreement between the ISI and the CIA.)

"Well, I think on all of these issues, there has to be a recognition that we're in the middle of a war," she said.

The next day, Clinton faced the Pakistani public in Lahore. Security was extraordinary: The Pakistani police and military had turned the densely populated Punjabi city of ten million, one of the most dynamic, culturally sophisticated in South Asia, into a ghost town. Clinton's motorcade hurried along deserted boulevards, past Mughal and Victorian buildings that looked shuttered. Even the side streets had been cleared, vast black curtains hung between the buildings to deprive the curious of a glimpse of her convoy of armored vehicles. Clinton's security detail was on edge; this was one of the most dangerous places she had visited. At the Government

College University, a public institution established during the British Raj, Clinton faced a carefully screened audience of students. But as soon as she took her seat on the stage, the pounding resumed.

"The drone attacks are being carried out in our country on our people," said a young woman from King Edward Medical University. "They are causing so much collateral damage at the same time." Why, she asked, wouldn't the United States share intelligence on targets with the Pakistani military and let Pakistan carry out the strikes itself?

"Well, I will not talk about that specifically," Clinton replied. "But generally, let me say that there's a war going on."

At another town-hall interview back in Islamabad, this one with Pakistani women, the moderator, Saima Mohsin, noted that a United Nations committee had raised questions about whether drones violated international law because they were a form of extrajudicial killing. "Yet they continue," she said to applause, "and the Pakistani people have begun to resent them and associate them with U.S. policy toward Pakistan as a whole."

"What's important here is that there's a war going on," Clinton responded, "and I won't comment on that specific matter."

"Do you think, and does the Obama administration feel, that the loss of life and how people feel about them in Pakistan is worth the minimal successes you get?" another questioner asked.

"Well, again," Clinton said, "I'm not going to comment on any particular tactic or technology."

"What is actually terrorism in U.S. eyes?" a female student from Peshawar University asked moments later. "Is it the killing of innocent people in, let's say, drone attacks? Or is it, again, the killing of—a vengeful killing of innocent in different parts of Pakistan, like the bomb blast two days ago in Peshawar? Which one is terrorism, do you think?"

In case Clinton missed the point, the moderator added, "Do you perceive both victims as victims of terrorism?"

"No, I do not," she said. "I do not."

Clinton's silence on drones was all the more awkward because she was so outspoken about other touchy issues. On the Pakistani complaints about the strings attached to U.S. aid: "Pakistan doesn't have to take this money," she said. "Let me be very clear: You do not have to take this money." On a claim that the aid was puny compared to the $700 million that the United States supposedly paid Kyrgyzstan for access to a single military base: "That's wrong. We negotiated the contract," she said. On reports the United States was secretly building a barracks for one thousand marines on the embassy grounds in Islamabad: "Untrue. Totally untrue," she said. "That is the kind of thing that sort of poisons the well." Above all, Clinton was unsparing about the double game Pakistan had long played with Muslim extremists: publicly condemning and fighting them, while quietly giving certain groups sanctuary and succor, either through the military or the ISI. "Al-Qaeda has had a safe haven in Pakistan since 2002," she told a roundtable of Pakistani newspaper editors in Lahore. "I find it hard to believe that nobody in your government knows where they are and couldn't get them if they really wanted to. And maybe that's the case. Maybe they're not getable. I don't know."

Clinton's remarks were widely broadcast in Pakistan and drew starchy, if unconvincing, denials from the government. "If we knew where al-Qaeda's leaders were, or if we had meaningful intelligence on their whereabouts shared with us, we would act against them," a senior Pakistani official told me that day (then he asked me not to use his name). Other Pakistanis praised her candor. "Right on the target," Anwar Iqbal, a correspondent for the Pakistani paper *Dawn*, emailed Huma Abedin. "It was much needed. I think it will have a positive impact. Let her be more open, more forthcoming."

At home, her bluntness was cheered by the White House, which was fed up with the prevarications of the Pakistani government. Her performance earned her some of the best press clips of her tenure at the State Department. "Hillary Rodham Clinton's first trip to Pakistan was never going to be easy," *The New York Times* said in an editorial. "Mrs. Clinton challenged Pakistan's government to do more to shut down Al Qaeda, but she was, rightly, determined to use this visit to also broaden the relationship."

For Clinton, the truth telling on al-Qaeda was cathartic ("I was just tired of the BS," she later told a senior Pakistani official), but she hated not being able to answer any of the questions about drones. Had she done so, she probably would have articulated a case not unlike the one Obama made to the bloggers on Google. "Reports of civilian casualties from drone strikes—often, but not always, untrue—fueled anger and anti-American sentiments," she wrote four years later in her memoir. "Because the program remained classified, I could not confirm or deny the accuracy of these reports. Nor was I free to express America's sympathies for the loss of any innocent life, or explain that our course of action was the one least likely to harm civilians, especially when compared to more conventional military action, such as missiles or bombers—or the costs of leaving terrorists in place."

Clinton returned from that trip determined to advance her argument that the White House needed to be more transparent about drones. She had some allies, even in the intelligence community. Michael Leiter, the director of the National Counterterrorism Center, also favored more openness. "Because we were keeping things covert," he told me, "it was making it tougher to do counter-messaging, and it was giving the Pakistanis a free pass." But Clinton was elbowed aside by the CIA, which warned Obama that if the government ever publicly acknowledged the program, it would lose its legal authority and have to be shut down. The reality was that the State Department had little say. America's relationship with Pakistan was driven by security, and thus firmly anchored in the realm of soldiers and spies.

Coordination between the CIA and the State Department was so poor that the agency sometimes carried out drone strikes just hours after the departure of a senior American official from Pakistan.

One strike occurred while John Kerry, then a senator, was on a plane returning from sensitive meetings with Pakistani leaders, in which he had been negotiating the return of the tail section of a Black Hawk helicopter that had been left behind after the aircraft crash-landed during the raid on Osama bin Laden's compound. "I hit the effing roof," Kerry recalled in an interview. "I was incensed. We were making an agreement to try to get something done. And *kaboom*! We do this thing that just drove people nuts." From Dubai, where he was changing planes, Kerry called Tom Donilon to lodge a furious complaint. Some at the State Department began to suspect deliberate sabotage. "It became a joke," said one former senior official. "How many hours after a principal went there would there be a drone strike?"

The silence from the United States allowed the Pakistani government to weave a narrative on drones that suited its own interests. Its story changed over time. The truth is, Pakistan's military and intelligence always had a more complex view of drones than they liked to admit publicly. The strikes began under Bush with the assent of Pervez Musharraf, the general-turned-president, and included agreements on what targets were out of bounds. At times, Musharraf even took credit for the strikes. But when Obama stepped up the program, it became a political headache for the Pakistani government. And when the CIA stopped consulting the ISI about targets, it began hitting people whom the Pakistanis wanted to protect. Suddenly, the Pakistani intelligence establishment viewed the strikes as a threat rather than a benefit. The ISI began mobilizing street protests against the United States.

"The issue was always: Who are the drone strikes killing?" said Husain Haqqani, the former Pakistani ambassador to the United States. "When the drone strikes killed people that Pakistan didn't want killed, there were protests. When the drone strikes killed people that Pakistan didn't mind being killed, there were no protests."

Few people understand the murky links between the Pakistani authorities and Islamic extremism better than Haqqani, a journalist who was once kidnapped and roughed up by Pakistani intelligence agents. As ambassador, he had regular access to Holbrooke and Clinton. To Clinton's credit, Haqqani said, she saw that the United States was losing the PR war. "This was Hillary being a politician. Hillary's greatest achievement was that she was a politician as secretary of state." But it wasn't enough just to recognize the problem. "I used to say, 'You guys need to have a narrative on drones,'" he recalled. "The problem was, the CIA didn't want to talk about it."

Cameron Munter is a diplomat of the old school, an affable sixty-two-year-old Cornell grad who studied in Freiburg and Marburg and got a PhD in modern European history at Johns Hopkins. He likes a beer at lunch and sprinkles his conversation with German phrases. Like many Foreign Service officers of his generation, he is an admirer of Richard Holbrooke, who pushed him for ambassador to Pakistan at the recommendation of Chris Hill, after Holbrooke could not find other candidates for the job. Munter had been a deputy to Hill, another Holbrooke acolyte, in Baghdad, where he earned a reputation for getting along with men in uniform. That would be important in a country where the generals called the shots. When Obama had a ceremonial hail and farewell with Munter just before he left for Islamabad in October 2010, he took him by the arm as he was walking out of the Oval Office and told his envoy what he wanted out of America's relationship with Pakistan.

"No terrorist attacks," the president said.

Munter arrived in Pakistan just as that relationship was about to go into a death spiral—"an elevator that had no bottom floor," as Dan Benjamin put it. In January 2011, a CIA contractor named Raymond Davis was arrested in Lahore after fatally shooting two Pakistani men on a motorbike who had pulled up next to him in a traffic circle. Davis radioed for help and a Toyota Land Cruiser sent by his colleagues hit and killed a motorcyclist while trying to reach the scene. To enraged Pakistanis, the killings confirmed what they had complained about to Clinton when she visited fifteen months earlier: American intelligence contractors, shielded by diplomatic immunity, were roaming the streets with illegal weapons. Pakistani authorities knew Davis worked for the CIA and were in no mood to give him special treatment. He was charged with murder and tossed in jail. The White House sent John Kerry to help Munter negotiate his release. Two months later, Munter and the head of the ISI, Lieutenant General Ahmad Shuja Pasha, struck a novel agreement. The families of Davis's victims would be paid $2.3 million in "blood money," a recognized form of compensation under sharia law, and Davis was released.

Since the United States was sticking to Davis's cover as a diplomat, even in private conversations with Pakistani officials, it fell to Clinton as secretary of state to thank the Pakistani authorities for releasing the CIA contractor and to Ambassador Munter to meet him on the tarmac at the Lahore airport for his flight to Afghanistan and freedom.

On March 17, two days after Davis was released, the CIA carried out one of its deadliest drone attacks yet. It fired missiles into a meeting of tribal elders in a village in a frontier region known as North Waziristan. As many as forty-four people were killed, and though one was a well-known Taliban militant, the reaction in Pakistan was immediate and sulfurous. The military condemned the strike, viewing it, with some justification, as CIA retribution for the jailing of Davis. Anti-American protesters poured into the streets of Lahore, Karachi, and Peshawar. The attack had been a so-called signature strike, in which the CIA targeted people involved in suspicious patterns of behavior rather than suspects it had identified. To Munter, this definition of a combatant was dangerously elastic. "My feeling is, one man's combatant is another man's—well, a chump who went to a meeting," he said to a reporter in 2012.

The biggest shock was yet to come with the May 2, 2011, commando raid on Osama bin Laden's compound in Abbottabad, a spectacular violation of Pakistan's sovereignty that left the country's leaders angry and humiliated. But even without bin Laden, the situation had become untenable for Munter. Drones were a major bugbear in the relationship. "It's all everyone wants to talk about," he told a colleague. The ambassador clashed with the CIA station chief in Islamabad, demanding the right to call off strikes—particularly signature strikes—if he judged they would be too damaging. Back at Langley, CIA officials viewed Munter as weak-kneed and emotional, a stark contrast to his predecessor, Anne Patterson. Steely and discreet, Patterson kept whatever disputes she had with the CIA within the embassy. She never uttered the d-word. Munter, on the other hand, spoke openly about drones with his staff and took his case to higher authorities. In June 2011, a month after the bin Laden raid, he was speaking via a secure video link to an NSC meeting that included Clinton and Leon Panetta. Again, he asserted his right as the ambassador to have final say over drone strikes. As my colleague Mark Mazzetti reported, Panetta cut him off in midsentence; "I don't work for you," he said.

Even some of Clinton's aides were impatient with Munter. They thought he was being absolutist in a situation that required flexibility. His complaints were getting in the way of Clinton's effort to maintain relations with the CIA. But when he clashed publicly with Panetta, she had little choice but to stand up for her ambassador. Turning to Panetta, she said he was wrong to assert that the agency could carry out drone strikes in Pakistan over the objections of the ambassador. Under Title 22 of the United States Code, Munter was the president's representative in the country and therefore outranked any other American official on the ground.

"No, Hillary, it's you who are flat wrong," Panetta replied.

The other people in the Situation Room were aghast. The spectacle of two cabinet members shouting at each other at an NSC meeting was unheard of in the Obama administration, where such public feuding was discouraged. Like a parent rushing to change the TV channel when something lurid comes on, Tom Donilon hushed Clinton and Panetta. He worked out what was billed as a compromise between the CIA and the State Department, but in fact was a major defeat for State. If Munter vetoed a strike, the agency could appeal to either the deputy secretary of state or to Clinton herself. If both upheld him, the CIA could have State overruled by the White House. Looking back four years later, Munter said he had no quarrel with Clinton. "I think she backed me," he said, "but State just lost the fight.

"I'm not a pacifist," Munter insisted. "There's a case to be made for drones. But you need to make every effort to use them judiciously. Even the perception of indiscriminate use can take its toll."

Exhausted and disillusioned, Munter resigned in May 2012 after only eighteen months on the job.

Clinton and Panetta, by contrast, quickly made up. Their relationship, after all, dated back to her husband's White House, when Panetta was the budget director, looking for spending cuts, and Hillary was the First Lady, looking to expand healthcare. Compared to that war, a turf battle over who got to sign off on drone strikes was small beer. "My good friend Leon Panetta," she gushed in her memoir, heaping praise on him. In Panetta's book, which was hard on Obama, he described Clinton as "a luminous representative for the United States in every foreign capital." In the cold calculus of Washington, the mutual admiration society made sense: Clinton was the cabinet's superstar; Panetta, the author of what would be its most sensational triumph.


Clinton had neatly listed her points in two columns on a yellow legal pad. She was being asked to give her judgment on Panetta's proposal to send Navy SEALs on a nighttime mission to kill or capture Osama bin Laden deep in the heart of Pakistan. It was the ultimate black op, a covert mission that posed far graver risks to Obama's presidency than any of the drone strikes he had authorized. Though it was a gut decision, that didn't mean Clinton shouldn't approach it like a lawyer—anticipating all the liabilities, taking into account all the pros and cons. She had qualms about the intelligence suggesting that bin Laden was hiding in the walled compound in Abbottabad. Moreover, she feared a military incursion like this would wipe out whatever progress she and other American officials had made with the Pakistanis over the previous two and a half years.

"Much of her analysis was about Pakistan and the relationship," Bill Daley, the White House chief of staff, recalled of the two months of taut deliberations. "That would end it."

For Clinton, there was a broader, if unspoken, irony to finding herself in this debate at all. Back in the 2008 campaign, she and Obama had clashed over a scenario not all that different from the one under consideration. He declared that if the United States had "actionable intelligence about high-value terrorist targets" in Pakistan, and the Pakistanis refused to act on it, then the United States should go in by itself. Clinton had ridiculed his threat as the posturing of a foreign policy naïf. "He basically threatened to bomb Pakistan," she scoffed during a Democratic debate in February 2008, "which I don't think was a particularly wise position to take."

In the spring of 2011, the high-value target was bin Laden, and the intel, if not airtight, was certainly actionable. For a few tense weeks, Clinton was one of a small circle of officials who filed down to the Situation Room twice a week to study satellite photos of the compound in Abbottabad, where a mysterious solitary figure paced the courtyard. Should they send in helicopters with a team of Special Forces soldiers? Should they use a drone strike? Or should they bomb the site into oblivion with a B-2 bomber?

In thirty-six years of deliberating military operations, Bob Gates told the group, he had learned the essential truth of Murphy's Law: If something can go wrong, it will. Bombing the house rather than sending in a SEAL team, he said, would at least mitigate those risks. Joe Biden was more adamant. He amplified Gates's doubts and echoed Clinton's prediction that it would wreck the relationship with Pakistan. Michael Morell, the CIA's deputy director, was cautious—he spoke for those in the agency who had been burned by the erroneous reports of weapons of mass destruction in Iraq—

but he thought the weight of the evidence suggested bin Laden was in the house.

Michael Leiter had been brought into the debate at the beginning of April. As he absorbed the magnitude of the risks, he became convinced that the White House needed one more critical scrub of the CIA's evidence—a so-called red team composed of people who were not part of the original planning. He sold Donilon and Brennan on the idea and put together a three-person team: two from the National Counterterrorism Center, including his lead analyst on al-Qaeda, and one from the CIA. After poring over the data, each came back with their own estimate of the odds bin Laden was in the compound: 40 percent, 60 percent, and 75 percent.

"What do you think the odds are?" the president asked Leiter, after he presented the red team's findings.

"I think it's probably fifty-fifty," Leiter replied. "But even if I accepted the lowest number, forty percent, that's thirty-eight percent higher than we've had for the last decade."

On April 28, Obama asked for a final show of hands. Panetta recommended going ahead, as did Mike Mullen, the chairman of the Joint Chiefs of Staff, who expressed confidence in the training of the SEALs. Donilon, Brennan, and McDonough, the "grim Irishmen" who were the top three officials in the NSC, all came out in favor. So did Daley, in part because he thought that if it ever emerged that the White House had information on the whereabouts of bin Laden and failed to act on it, Obama would be crucified. Gates remained reluctant. When it was Clinton's turn to speak, she recited the pluses and minuses on her legal pad before throwing in with the yes camp.

"I concluded the chance to get bin Laden was worth it," she wrote. "As I had experienced firsthand, our relationship with Pakistan was strictly transactional, based on mutual interest, not trust. It would survive. I thought we should go for it."

Three days later, the same group gathered again on a Sunday to watch the raid unfold. After the surviving helicopter landed at its base in Afghanistan, the tense vigil in the Situation Room gave way to frantic activity. Clinton and her colleagues had each been assigned a list of counterparts to call to inform them of the raid before it was made public. Leiter, standing at a glassed-in phone booth next to the operations center, heard one of the watch officers trying to find a phone number for Bill Clinton, so Obama could call him. "You don't have his number?" the officer said to one of Clinton's former staffers. "I'm sorry, I thought you still worked for President Clinton."

That problem, at least, was easy to solve, Leiter thought. He went to find Hillary to ask her if she could provide her husband's number. It's in my BlackBerry, she said with a chuckle. Together, they walked to a lead-lined cabinet next to the entrance to the Situation Room, where the officials had to stash their cellphones before entering the inner sanctum of national security.

In the years since the bin Laden raid, the Situation Room debate has been mythologized almost as much as the heroics of the SEALs— the actions of every player subject to interpretation and reinterpretation. In the White House's telling, Clinton played a cautious role. "She wasn't in any way, shape, or form a cowboy about it," Daley said. "Bin Laden was a forty-nine to fifty-one percent call," another official said. "She happened to be fifty-one percent." At a retreat with Democratic lawmakers six months later, the vice president lumped Clinton in with those who had given Obama an equivocal go-ahead.

"Every single person in that room hedged their bet, except Leon Panetta," he recalled. "Leon said go. Everyone else said, forty-nine, fifty-one."

"He got to me," Biden said. "He said, 'Joe, what do you think?'"

"I said, 'You know, I didn't know we had so many economists around the table,'" the vice president continued. "I said, 'We owe the man a direct answer. Mr. President, my suggestion is, don't go. We have to do two more things to see if he's there.'"

The dig at Clinton was unmistakable.

Biden later changed his story. After he and Obama left the Situation Room, the vice president said in October 2015, he privately told the president "he should go, but to follow his own instincts." Biden's protean memory does not change the fact that Clinton spoke out in favor of the raid while he did not. Just as Gates valued her support during the debate over sending troops to Afghanistan, Panetta valued her vote that day. "She ultimately had the same confidence that I did," he told me. "It was the confidence of the SEALs to conduct that operation."

By the spring of 2012, when Clinton asked her colleagues in the Situation Room if they read the papers or watched TV, Obama was doing his own hard thinking about how America was conducting the drone wars. He had ordered the review to develop new policies governing the use of drones and expanding the ability of officials to talk about them. Part of this was driven by Obama's conviction that he needed to take the United States off the perpetual war footing that had followed the 9/11 attacks. Part of it was his weariness with the relentless criticism from the left.

"It's enough," he told John Brennan in the middle of 2012. "I don't want to be just remembered as the drone president."

As was often the case with Obama, the review culminated in a speech. In this case, he aimed to do nothing less than chart a vision for how the United States should combat terrorism in the post-9/11 era. The address, which Obama delivered at the National Defense University on May 23, 2013, was larded with the lawyerly arguments and rhetorical flourishes typical of him. It was obvious the president had grappled with the legal and moral issues raised by drones, but it was equally obvious that he remained wedded to their efficacy and was determined to keep using them. "To say a military tactic is legal, or even effective, is not to say it is wise or moral in every instance," Obama observed. But drones were still a lower-cost alternative to the military adventurism of George W. Bush. "Invasions of these territories," he said, "lead us to be viewed as occupying armies, unleash a torrent of unintended consequences, are difficult to contain, result in large numbers of civilian casualties and ultimately empower those who thrive on violent conflict."

Most telling was what was missing from the speech: any mention of drones in Pakistan. Even when Obama was urging Americans to exorcise their post-9/11 demons, he refused to lift the veil on this part of the shadow war, thus protecting its legal standing. The president also needed Pakistan if there was to be any solution to Afghanistan. "You would think that over the course of seven years, given how much controversy it has engendered, he might abandon that faith," said Ben Rhodes, who drafted the speech. "He never has. He's seen it produce significant results. He really does see it as preventing the use of larger-scale force. In his mind, the justification is both the success as a counterterrorism tool and also, frankly, the preference as an alternative to different types of military force."

There is an undeniable logic to that argument. And yet, to those who tried to preserve the remnants of a relationship between the United States and Pakistan during the Obama years, his single-minded reliance on drones came to symbolize a broader refusal to project American power in more direct ways. Vali Nasr, the Holbrooke aide who wrote Clinton's talking points for her interviews with the Pakistani journalists, left the State Department in 2011, discouraged because he felt she and Richard Holbrooke had been drowned out by the CIA in the debate about how to balance diplomacy with counterterrorism. Targeted killings became the go-to mode of American engagement. The primacy of the drone, Nasr said, was the key to understanding Obama's foreign policy, as well as where it diverged from Clinton's.

"It's not like they had a disagreement about al-Qaeda's threat," he said. "But Hillary was of the belief that regional stability, engagement, and the U.S. military is more important to this." For Obama, drones not only opened the door to withdrawing troops from Afghanistan and Iraq; they were a way to avoid getting drawn into future entanglements, military or diplomatic, which would sap the nation and distract from his domestic agenda. "It allows you to be disengaged," Nasr said. "We don't need to be in Iraq, we don't need to invest in the Arab Spring. We don't need to worry about any of this; all we need to do is to kill the terrorists. It's a different philosophy of foreign policy. It's surgical, it's clinical, it's clean."

"Basically," Nasr said, "he's the drone president."

# Six

## Peacemakers

Barack Obama's first visit to the UN General Assembly in late September 2009 was meant to set a bold new course for his country. He would tell the world the United States had sworn off the excesses and unilateralism of the George W. Bush era. He would demonstrate a new American commitment to combating climate change. He would lay out his vision of a world free of nuclear weapons. He would signal his willingness to engage Iran. And he would redress Bush's tardiness in tackling the great unfinished diplomatic business of our time: a peace accord between the Israelis and the Palestinians. It was a goal he had set on his first full day in the Oval Office, when he placed his two first overseas phone calls to the president of the Palestinian Authority and the prime minister of Israel.

The day before Obama spoke to the United Nations, however, he found himself a few blocks away, in a room at the Waldorf Astoria hotel, face-to-face with the reality that bridging ancient rifts in the Holy Land wasn't going to be any easier for him than it had been for his predecessors. He was meeting that afternoon with Israeli prime minister Benjamin Netanyahu and Palestinian Authority president Mahmoud Abbas; the mood was tense. The two were no closer to sitting down for direct talks than when Obama had taken office eight months earlier. Neither trusted the other, neither was ready to take a risk, and neither was feeling pressured by the administration's peacemaking efforts to date, which had been handled by George Mitchell, the laconic former senator from Maine then serving as the president's Middle East envoy.

Obama was frustrated with both men, but he was also frustrated with Hillary Clinton. His secretary of state had made only one visit to Jerusalem and the West Bank all year, in March, before Netanyahu had even formed a government. Obama's aides had not forgotten her refusal to go to Jerusalem after his speech in Cairo. She had put neither her sweat nor her prestige into his signature diplomatic project. "The sense was, she wanted to keep a distance from this whole thing," said Michael Oren, Israel's ambassador to Washington from 2009 to 2013. "She didn't think it was winnable."

At a separate meeting with Clinton in New York that week, Obama chided her, telling her that she needed to travel to the region more often, according to two people who witnessed the exchange. She needed to become more personally involved in steering the process rather than delegating it to Mitchell. She needed, in short, to get in the game.

"We cannot continue the same pattern of taking tentative steps forward and then stepping back," an impatient Obama said to the press after meeting individually with Netanyahu and Abbas at the Waldorf. "Success depends on all sides acting with a sense of urgency. That is why I have asked Secretary Clinton and Senator Mitchell to carry forward the work that we do here today." His comments seemed aimed as much at Clinton and Mitchell as at the two Middle East leaders.

For Obama, the peace process was about more than pacifying a swath of eternally contested land between the Mediterranean Sea and the Jordan River. He subscribed to the argument, then in vogue, that ending the Israeli military's occupation of the West Bank would be a kind of silver bullet. It would reduce the seething antagonism of Muslims toward Israel and its great defender, America. And in so doing, it would help him achieve an even more cherished goal: extracting the United States from the bloody morass of the Middle East. To shake loose a perennially calcified process, Obama decided to give the Israelis a blunt message: They needed to halt the construction of Jewish settlements in the Palestinian territories. Persuading the Israelis to stop, he believed, would give the Palestinians hope and the United States fresh credibility as an honest broker.

His messenger was to be Hillary Clinton, who had her own longstanding ties to Israel and the American Jewish community. She also had a lifetime of experience in how to navigate the Middle East from her husband, Bill, the last president to make Middle East peacemaking a priority from his first days in the White House.

For Hillary, though, plunging into the peace process was not that simple. She had recommended that the president appoint George Mitchell as the special envoy, and Mitchell made clear he did not want her getting too involved, especially in the early days. Moreover, she had qualms about Obama's demand that Israel freeze its settlements. While she shared his belief that settlements were pernicious—their steady march across the sunbaked hilltops of the West Bank eclipsing the dream of a viable Palestinian state—she feared, correctly, that pounding the Israelis on the issue would provoke a nasty confrontation. Clinton, who was eager to demonstrate her loyalty to her new boss, dutifully advocated the settlements policy. But she kept getting the tone wrong, first overstating the president's demands and then giving the Israeli government too much credit for its belated, incremental response.

Within a year, Obama's tough-love approach had poisoned his relationship with Netanyahu, soured the Israeli public, and alienated pro-Israel voters in the United States. Tensions between the United States and Israel had spiked to their highest levels since 1991, when George H. W. Bush, furious at Prime Minister Yitzhak Shamir's refusal to halt settlements, held up $10 billion in loan guarantees for Israel. The feud put Clinton, with her political ambitions, in an awkward spot. "There was a tension between wanting to be supportive of the president, but not wanting to be identified as hostile to Israel, for which Obama was unfairly labeled, starting with the Cairo speech," said Martin Indyk, who was ambassador to Israel under Bill Clinton and has advised Hillary.

Clinton's successor, John Kerry, didn't let the fear of being branded anti-Israel stop him from making a determined, if fruitless, effort to broker a peace deal during Obama's second term. To those who risked their reputations in the Middle East, there was something uncourageous about Clinton's hands-off approach. "She took very little action to bring about peace," Jimmy Carter, who brokered the Camp David Accords in 1978, told *Time* magazine. "It was only John Kerry's coming into office that reinitiated all these very important and crucial issues." Kerry and Clinton, of course, were in very different places as secretary of state: He was a statesman in the sunset of his career with little to lose, making one last swing for the history books; she was a closely watched politician on a stepping-stone to the White House, eager to avoid alienating a powerful voting bloc. "Hillary," Indyk said, "would have been labeled as a failure by her political rivals in a way that Kerry wasn't."

Taking risks for Middle East peace is different for a president than for someone who aspires to be president. Clinton need look no further than her husband as a model. Bill Clinton spent countless hours mediating between Yasser Arafat and Ehud Barak, the Israeli leader at the time. In the mists of Camp David, he came tantalizingly close to conjuring an agreement between them. Hillary, free to set her own policy rather than carry out someone else's, might well view such a challenge as irresistible. In November 2015, she wrote an op-ed piece in the *Forward,* a Jewish newspaper, explaining how she planned to mend ties with Israel as president. At the top of her list: revive the peace process. "I will never stop working to advance the goal of two states for two peoples living in peace, security and dignity," Clinton declared.

But she would go about it differently than Obama has. Clinton would draw closer to Israel rather than distance herself from it, for political reasons and out of the conviction—shared by her husband—that only a tight hug with the United States can embolden Israelis to take the risks of a territorial accommodation with the Palestinians. As with other elements of her foreign policy, Clinton's approach would likely be more conventional than Obama's, less a break with the past than an echo of it.

Her differences with the president over the peace process were largely submerged during Obama's first term. Clinton, ever the loyal soldier, carried out a policy with which she had reservations. But they played out in pitched battles between aides in the White House and State Department; in the adroit way that Israeli officials were able to manipulate the administration; and in periodic tensions between the president and the secretary of state over her role. Clinton made a series of public statements about Israel at the end of her tenure, and particularly after she left the State Department, that revealed the gaps between her and Obama. Their tangled joint ownership of the peace process says a lot about how these two view America's role in the Middle East, and especially the nature of its relationship with Israel.

Barack Obama came into the White House determined to be a different kind of peacemaker. He was convinced that George W. Bush and Bill Clinton had erred in prizing harmony with Israel above all else. Its ceaseless expansion of settlements was turning the two-state solution into a mirage, an outcome that would further inflame Arabs and leave Israel more isolated and vulnerable. The United States, by tolerating rather than resisting the settler movement, had lost credibility with the Palestinians and the Arab world. It was enabling Israel's myopic leaders. He also thought that reaching an agreement with Iran on its nuclear program was worth risking the wrath of the Israelis, who viewed the Iranians as an enemy bent on the destruction of the Jewish state. To achieve that goal and put the relationship back into balance, Obama needed to tell the Israelis some inconvenient truths. In that regard, he was not unlike his predecessors, dating back to Eisenhower, who entered office intent on keeping a distance from Israel, only to pull it close later.

At a meeting in the Roosevelt Room on July 13, 2009, which was to become fabled among those who obsess about America's relationship with Israel, Obama was challenged by a dozen American Jewish leaders about why he was picking a fight with the Israeli government. "The lesson of history is that there should be no public daylight between the United States and Israel," Malcolm Hoenlein, the executive vice chairman of the Conference of Presidents of Major American Jewish Organizations, told him. "The enemies of both countries will exploit any public differences."

Obama was having none of it. "Look at the past eight years," he replied, according to people who were in the room that day. "Eight years, no daylight. Eight years, no progress."

It wasn't just about creating daylight with Israel. Because of his background and worldview, Obama was instinctively more sympathetic to the Palestinians than his predecessors had been. Even before he was sworn in, he talked to his aides about reaching out to Mahmoud Abbas, the shuffling eighty-year-old career politician who had succeeded Arafat as president of the Palestinian Authority. Ziad Asali, a physician who founded the American Task Force on Palestine, thinks Obama's exposure to Muslims as a child gave him a more nuanced perspective, even if the Islam of Indonesia is different from that in the Arab world. "He felt he understood Arab and Muslim issues better than most people because he had lived in Indonesia," Asali said.

There has been fervid speculation about Obama's ties to Rashid Khalidi, a Palestinian American scholar who was an occasional dinner partner when they both lived in Chicago. A dedicated Palestinian nationalist, Khalidi is an outspoken critic of Israel's policies. Conversations with him and his wife, Mona, Obama once said, had opened his eyes to his biases and blind spots. "It's for that reason that I'm hoping that, for many years to come, we continue that conversation," Obama, then a state senator, said at a going-away party for his friend, who was moving to New York. The two fell out of touch as Obama's political fortunes rose, however, and if Khalidi was the future president's Arab Svengali, he suggests it had little effect. "Careful examination of the record," he wrote with some bitterness in 2013, "shows that the Obama administration in fact followed very much the same trajectory in dealing with Palestine and Israel as most previous administrations over the past 35 years."

Obama may have learned about Palestinian grievances at Rashid Khalidi's dinner table, but he was introduced to Chicago's establishment by a very different crowd. As he ran for the Senate from Illinois, Obama's friends say his views on the Middle East were shaped by a circle of prominent liberal Jewish friends in Chicago: David Axelrod; the industrialist Lester Crown; and especially Abner Mikva and Newton Minow. Close friends, Mikva and Minow each had distinguished public careers: Mikva, a Democratic member of Congress and federal judge, and Minow, the only chairman of the Federal Communications Commission ever to become a household name after he called American TV a "vast wasteland." The pair introduced Obama to their wealthy friends in law and business, and they talked to him about the Israeli-Palestinian conflict. Zionists imbued with the social justice ideals of the civil rights movement, they combined loyal support for Israel with a gimlet eye toward its policies.

"Mikva and Newt Minow are truly mentors of Obama's," Axelrod said. "They come out of a Chicago Jewish community that's progressive and more apt to be J Street than AIPAC," he added, referring to the dove and hawk of the two main pro-Israel lobbying groups.

Later, as Obama prepared to run for president, he was influenced by another Jewish son of Chicago: Rahm Emanuel, the city's future mayor, who was then a congressman rising into the ranks of the House Democratic leadership. When Obama was elected, he asked Emanuel to become his chief of staff. With his volunteer service in the Israeli military and experience in the Clinton administration, Emanuel had his own ideas about how to handle Netanyahu. He wasn't shy about expressing them to his new boss, becoming

Obama's de facto chief adviser on Israel. In 1998, as a young aide, he had watched Netanyahu, during a previous stint as prime minister, hold up a peace deal with Bill Clinton at the Wye River Summit in Maryland to try to extract a last-minute concession to release Jonathan Pollard, the American intelligence analyst who had been convicted of spying for Israel and sentenced to life in prison in 1987. (Clinton refused; Pollard was eventually paroled in 2015.) "In Rahm's view, the only way to deal with Bibi is to pressure him," said Dennis Ross, a longtime Middle East diplomat who watched the drama unfold with Emanuel and later worked for both Hillary Clinton and Obama.

Obama also was receptive to George Mitchell, the Senate lion recruited to be special envoy by Hillary. She had gotten to know Mitchell in the 1990s when he chaperoned her health-reform package in Congress, and later, through his work on Northern Ireland. By peace process standards, Mitchell was a fresh face: a Catholic from Maine with a Lebanese-born mother. His only prior involvement in the conflict had come in 2001, when he led an investigation for Bill Clinton into the causes of the second intifada, the Palestinian uprising; it found fault on both sides and recommended both a settlement freeze and the resumption of peace talks. Obama and Clinton hoped he would bring a new approach to an issue that had been dominated for years by a fraternity of career peacemakers: Ross, Indyk, Daniel Kurtzer, Robert Malley, Aaron David Miller, and a handful of others. On his first tour of the region in February 2009, Mitchell met more than a dozen Gulf monarchs and Arab strongmen. He returned with a clear message: "There has to be a settlement freeze."

"What the president decided was that the atmosphere was so difficult, the hostility was so high, that we had to try to create a change in the atmosphere that would permit a reduction in hostilities, so the partners could actually sit and talk to each other with some hope of success," Mitchell told me during an interview in his New York law office, high above Rockefeller Center. "One of the real problems is that not only do the two societies have a high degree of mistrust, but the two leaders do. We tried to accelerate a reduction in hostilities by asking people to do positive things."

Some former officials believe Obama over-interpreted the message from Mitchell's trip. Arab leaders, they said, were less concerned about settlements and their corrosive effect on the peace process than they were about the threat of a nuclear-armed Iran. But the emphasis on settlements played into the president's biases. He thought the United States needed to prove to the Arabs that it could change Israel's behavior. And that meant getting tough with the Israelis.

In making Clinton his designated hammer, Obama could hardly have chosen anyone with more history.

Being married to Bill Clinton had given Hillary a front-row seat for the most sustained effort at peacemaking of any president since Jimmy Carter. From presiding in his first year over the South Lawn handshake between Yasser Arafat and Yitzhak Rabin that sealed the Oslo Accord to laying down the Clinton Parameters a few months before he left office, Clinton never stopped trying to untie the knot between Israelis and Palestinians. When Hillary talks about the rigors of the peace process, she reflexively falls back on anecdotes involving Bill, Yasser, and Ehud at Camp David. His near miss there was an object lesson to her about the perils of peacemaking.

But Hillary had made her own journey through the minefield of Middle East politics as First Lady, which left another kind of imprint on her. In 1998, she spoke via satellite to a gathering of Israeli and Arab teenagers in Villars, Switzerland. Responding to a question from a young Israeli, she used the word "Palestine" and said creating an independent Palestinian state was "very important for the broader goal of peace in the Middle East." Her comments created a flap: She was asked why she was referring to a country that did not exist, and the White House disavowed her comments, which had not yet become official American policy. A year later, after

Clinton had declared she was running for Daniel Patrick Moynihan's New York Senate seat, she wandered into far deeper trouble during a visit to the West Bank city of Ramallah.

At a ceremony with Palestinian health officials, Clinton did not react when Suha Arafat, the wife of Yasser Arafat, accused Israeli military forces of using "toxic gases" against Palestinians, causing cancer in women and children. Instead, she gave Arafat a polite kiss. Clinton's gesture, which she later likened to a handshake, outraged Jewish groups and whipped up a storm of hostile newspaper editorials in New York for days following the visit. Arafat's speech was translated from Arabic to English, but Rob Malley, an NSC official who was traveling with the First Lady, and other members of her delegation were distracted and were not listening as closely as they should have been. The full import of Arafat's remarks set in only hours later, when Sandy Berger, the national security adviser, called Malley in alarm to ask what had happened.

Back in New York, Clinton's high command panicked. Her advisers were terrified she had just lost the Jewish vote and perhaps the election. ("Shame on Hillary," said a front-page headline in the *New York Post*.) As soon as she got back to the United States, they sent her on a fence-mending tour with local Jewish leaders. Thanks in part to the goodwill attached to the Clinton name, the crisis passed. But Hillary spent years after that conscientiously building up her record in the Senate as a friend of Israel—and trying to avoid another misstep. "I think that has haunted her," said an adviser to Clinton who helped shape her Senate campaign. "The thing about the Arafat kiss is that she learned very quickly that there are deep waters in New York that you have to be very, very careful about how you handle."

Clinton brought that sense of caution to the State Department. She was willing to manage the situation in the Middle East but she had no desire to plunge into shuttle diplomacy, like Condi Rice had or John Kerry had. That was time-consuming, with low odds of success and high odds of offending someone. The advantage of a name-brand envoy like Mitchell was that she could leave the daily grind of peacemaking to him: the tedious strategy sessions with the

Israelis in the King David Hotel; the dusty motorcade rides to the Muqata, the Palestinian leadership compound in Ramallah; the eleven-hour flights from Joint Base Andrews to Ben Gurion Airport, which had eaten up so much of Rice's time in her final year. Clinton would weigh in when necessary, when there was a deal to be cut or an impasse to be broken.

The trouble is, secretaries of state can't outsource the Middle East. As Denis McDonough said to me, "There's core-course curriculum, and then there's extra credit. This is always seen as a core requirement for a secretary of state." He didn't criticize Clinton but his meaning was clear: She couldn't avoid the Middle East. Since the days of Kissinger and Baker, leaders in the region have looked to the secretary of state to set the tone and tempo of the peace process. Mitchell's diligent spadework was no substitute for the voice of the nation's chief diplomat, especially one named Clinton.

It was her misfortune to find herself caught between a new president determined to challenge Israel and an incoming Israeli leader determined to rebuff American challenges. Clinton did her best to head off the collision. On her first trip to Israel in March 2009, when Israelis were still jockeying over their new coalition, she held a private meeting with Tzipi Livni, the outgoing foreign minister and head of the opposition Kadima party. Clinton pleaded with Livni to accept a deal that would create a national unity government, rather than a right-wing coalition led by Netanyahu's Likud party. Livni declined because she could not get the terms she wanted from Likud. Clinton said nothing about her lobbying afterward. "We look forward to working with the new government when it is formed," she said blandly at a news conference. But she dropped a bread crumb: "Now, that doesn't mean that as good friends, which we are, we might not have opinions that we will express from time to time."

It wasn't the first time a Clinton had meddled in Israeli politics to try to spoil Netanyahu's chances. In 1996, Bill Clinton, convinced that a Netanyahu election victory would dash his peace plans, wrapped his opponent, Shimon Peres, in a warm embrace. The White House coordinated messages with Peres, opening a back channel to his campaign through two Democratic consultants, Zev Furst and Doug Schoen. Clinton gave Peres a high-profile ride on Air Force One and warned the Israelis a week before the vote to choose peace, that is, Peres. Netanyahu won 50.4 percent to 49.5 percent. At their first Oval Office meeting a few weeks later, Netanyahu lectured Clinton about Arab-Israeli relations, leaving the president to splutter, "Who's the fucking superpower here?"

Netanyahu got his first taste of the new regime when he visited the White House in May 2009. Obama pressed him in the Oval Office to curb the growth of settlements and told him that George Mitchell was trying to line up reciprocal gestures from Israel's Arab neighbors. These included reopening trade offices that had existed in the 1990s and obtaining rights for El Al planes to fly over Saudi Arabia. At a dinner at the State Department that night, Hillary Clinton pulled Netanyahu aside and told him a freeze was very important to the president. "I can't do that," he told her, according to a person who was there.

A week later, after a meeting with the Egyptian foreign minister, Clinton stepped before the cameras in the Benjamin Franklin Room of the State Department. A reporter asked her whether she would be satisfied if the Israeli government halted the construction of new settlements, but not construction in existing settlement blocs—so-called natural growth—an idea then being floated. "He wants to see a stop to settlements," Clinton replied, referring to Obama. "Not some settlements, not outposts, not natural growth exceptions. We think it is in the best interests of the effort that we are engaged in that settlement expansion cease. That is our position."

In fact, that wasn't the White House position. Under the freeze Mitchell was then discussing with the Israelis, they could continue to build within existing settlement blocs—when a growing family wanted to add a few rooms to their house, to use the anodyne example often invoked by the Israelis; just not outside the existing perimeter of the settlements. Clinton had "plussed up" Obama's position, in the words of one former official. "She added a few flourishes to it," said another, more sympathetic to her. Either way, her three "nots" reverberated widely. The Israelis were furious, while Obama's aides were annoyed that Clinton had locked them into a harder-line position vis-à-vis Netanyahu than was the case.

Clinton did not mention the episode in her book, writing only "I delivered the president's message as forcefully as I could." Yet it was one of the most telling moments of her first year in the Obama administration. She had been the public advocate for a policy with which she had reservations, a policy she knew would provoke the Israelis and dismay her pro-Israel supporters. Advocating positions one doesn't agree with is part of the job for any senior government official, of course. But she went overboard in her stridency, a rare miscalculation that has various possible explanations. One is that Clinton fell into a gap between the administration's rhetoric and the actual deal that Mitchell was negotiating with the Israeli government. Another is that because she did not believe the policy in her bones, she instead viewed it as a kind of loyalty oath to her new boss, and thus over-cranked her tone.

"Hillary was playing the good soldier," Dennis Ross said. "As someone who understood White Houses, she knew she had to prove herself, not just to Obama but to the Praetorian Guard."


While Clinton was tripping over settlements, Obama suffered a setback of his own. At the urging of his national security adviser, Jim Jones, he agreed to stop in Saudi Arabia, before giving his speech in Cairo, to pay a visit on the aging monarch King Abdullah. The purpose was to extract the reciprocal gestures that would help grease new peace talks with Israel. Obama struck a respectful tone, saying he wanted to "come to the place where Islam began and to seek His Majesty's counsel and to discuss with him many of the issues that we confront here in the Middle East." The king took Obama to his lavish desert retreat outside Riyadh, the same Arabian Nights–style tent city where he later hosted Clinton. In the air-conditioned splendor under his big top, Abdullah, head of the House of Saud and custodian of the two holy mosques, proceeded to school his young visitor in the stubborn enmities of the Middle East.

"We will be the last to make peace with the Israelis," the king said when the president broached his proposals, according to two White House officials who were on the trip.

Obama's political aides, led by Rahm Emanuel, were beside themselves. They assumed General Jones had the meeting wired. Now their boss had been humiliated by a key American ally on his first trip to the region. The episode had two consequences: Jones became an increasingly marginal player in the West Wing (he would leave the following year); and the White House poached Dennis Ross from the State Department, where he had been advising Clinton on Iran, to oversee Middle East policy at the NSC. The move was engineered by Emanuel and Tom Donilon, whose influence was growing as Jones's waned. Donilon wanted to give the NSC more "strategic heft." Bureaucratic shuffles like this are the ambient hum of Washington, but Ross's move turned out to have an outsized impact on Obama's approach to Israel. It pulled him back to a more conventional, less confrontational approach.

A soft-spoken academic from the Bay Area, Ross had served under almost every president, Democratic and Republican, going back to Carter. In the 1990s, he was at Bill Clinton's right hand in Camp David, devising proposals to bridge gaps between the two sides. Hillary, who sat in on the briefings Ross gave her husband, got to know him well. In November 2000, days after she had been elected to the Senate, she asked him to accompany her to the funeral of Leah Rabin, the widow of Israel's slain leader Yitzhak Rabin. With a network of contacts across the Middle East and the ability to write and speak lucidly about its infuriating complexities—"providing context," he likes to call it—Ross's value to Clinton was obvious. When she became secretary, she recruited him to be a special adviser on the Persian Gulf and Southwest Asia, aka Iran. He took an office at the State Department next door to another inveterate Washington operator, Richard Holbrooke.

The rap on Ross is twofold: that he tilts toward Israel and that he favors endless, incremental diplomacy over the bold, game-changing approach that Obama seemed to want when he came into the White House. In May 2011, King Abdullah II of Jordan held a closed-door meeting with Middle East experts, administration officials, and journalists, in which he offered his view of Obama's efforts to restart the peace process. He said he was encouraged by what he had heard from the State Department and the Pentagon about their willingness to pressure Israel for concessions. "But not from the White House," Abdullah said, according to people in the room, "and we know the reason why is because of Dennis Ross."

The Hashemite king was on to something, but it wasn't just Ross. By then, Obama had concluded that making Emanuel his Israel whisperer had been a bad bet. Axelrod and Emanuel both worried that the rancor between Obama and Netanyahu was taking a political toll on their boss and threatening other Democrats. In 2008, he had won the White House with the support of nearly eight in ten Jewish voters. But Republicans, who had swept to control of the House in 2010, were painting him as hostile to Israel. Pro-Israel Democrats were raising alarms, warning that he could lose 10 to 20 percentage points of the Jewish vote in 2012. The political team was counting on Ross to help put the relationship with Israel on a more even keel.

Understandably, Clinton was miffed. Ross had originally chosen to work for her over Obama; now he was jumping ship, further evidence of where the real power resided. Years later, Ross said he never would have gone to the State Department if he had read the Clinton-Obama dynamic better. "I knew her and felt certain she would dominate the policy process much like Jim Baker during Bush 41," he wrote. "That turned out to be wrong." Obama, he said, was the "decision maker, and everything—not just the financial crisis—was going to run through him." Moreover, the president's men saw to it that Ross was given broad latitude, which allowed him to wander into all sorts of issues, chief among them the peace process. That was a manageable headache for Clinton but a dire threat to Mitchell. One of the enduring mysteries for those who worked for Mitchell is how a political pro who had been a master of the Senate could not transfer those skills to the administration. Part of the problem was simple geography: Mitchell had remarried in 1994 and started a new family in New York. He was determined to spend much of his time in the city. But his absences from Washington handicapped him in the intramural skirmishes, which began even before Ross got to the White House.

In May 2009, when Ross was still overseeing Iran at the State Department, he and Mitchell were in a meeting with the president. Obama asked Ross for his views on the settlements push, and he responded that no one had ever asked an Israeli leader to do what this administration was asking. Mitchell, on the spot, heatedly defended the policy. Netanyahu, he said, might be ready to take a risk on the peace process if he felt confident about America's nuclear diplomacy with Iran—a right-back-at-you gesture to Ross, who was responsible for that. The exchange didn't change Obama's mind on settlements, but he said to Mitchell, "You've got your work cut out for you."

Two months later, Ross and Mitchell clashed again in front of the president, this time over Mitchell's plan to jump-start peace negotiations between Israel and the Palestinians by pressing them to resolve all the major issues that divided them: borders, security, the political status of Jerusalem, and the right of return for Palestinian refugees. That would never work, Ross declared: The gaps between the two sides were too wide. Better to start with small steps and build up gradually to a broad agreement. Mitchell, who was slow to anger, fumed that Ross was trying to discredit his approach. "Boy, you got him pretty worked up," Donilon said to Ross afterward.

The Israelis, ever the savvy interpreters of Washington power politics, lost no time in exploiting this new dynamic. Ross had a legitimate reason to be in touch with Israeli officials because of his work on Iran's nuclear program, a source of deep concern to the Israelis. Netanyahu, with Ross's quiet encouragement, began expanding that channel to include issues related to the Palestinians. "The Israelis are unique among our allies in that they get to choose the interlocutor on our side," said Steven Simon, a senior NSC official who worked on Middle East policy with Ross. On their side, the Israelis fielded a low-profile lawyer and trusted aide to Netanyahu, Yitzhak Molcho. Israel's positions on the Palestinian issue were now communicated to the Oval Office via a chain that ran from Netanyahu to Molcho to Ross to Donilon to Obama. Mitchell was effectively cut out. He still met with Netanyahu and remained the primary interlocutor with Mahmoud Abbas, but his position was compromised. Ross had seized control of the peace process, such as it was.

Clinton, meanwhile, kept stumbling on settlements. After pressing the Israelis without success for months in 2009 to halt all construction, the White House finally extracted a concession from Netanyahu: He would stop new construction for ten months in the West Bank, though not in East Jerusalem. At an eleven P.M. news conference with the prime minister in Jerusalem on Halloween night, Clinton pronounced the moratorium "unprecedented." Strictly speaking, she was right: No Israeli leader had ever frozen building on that scale. But to a White House that had demanded a much broader halt, it looked like a modest step. The Palestinians quickly dismissed it as inadequate; their Arab allies exploded in indignation; and the same White House aides who had complained about Clinton's earlier overreach on settlements now said she had been played by the Israeli leader.

Four months later, the Israelis vindicated this cynical view. The Jerusalem municipal authorities approved 1,600 new housing units in Ramat Shlomo, a Jewish housing development in East Jerusalem, the sliver of territory that had been excluded from Netanyahu's agreement the previous October. Worse, they did it during a visit by Vice President Biden. "They'd promised us repeatedly there would be no surprises," Mitchell recalled. "This was a big surprise." For Mitchell, the experience summed up his frustrations. Earlier that day, he had won an agreement from Netanyahu to begin indirect talks with the Palestinians. At four P.M., after a quick trip to Ramallah to check in with Abbas, Mitchell returned to Jerusalem to announce the talks. At six P.M., he briefed Biden, then boarded his own plane to fly home. While he was in the air, news of the building in East Jerusalem broke.

Obama and Emanuel were livid, more so than Biden himself. Once again, it fell to Clinton to play the heavy. She administered a forty-three-minute tongue-lashing to Netanyahu by phone, telling him Israel had insulted the vice president and the country. He insisted he'd known nothing about the plans. Clinton's reprimand stung; years later, Netanyahu still brought it up with colleagues. Yet he was publicly unrepentant. Flying to Washington ten days later for the annual meeting of AIPAC, Netanyahu told reporters that Israel had no plans to cave to American pressure on settlements. In an email, Jake Sullivan told Clinton that he heard the Israelis "sounded a bit cocky."

"They always sound cocky," she replied. "In the air or on the ground."

By the summer of 2010, Clinton and Obama had undergone a role reversal on the peace process. Netanyahu's ten-month settlement freeze was fast ticking away. Clinton and Mitchell had become convinced that unless the president himself launched direct talks between Netanyahu and Abbas, the two sides would walk away, maybe for good. Obama, however, was disenchanted: His bitter tug-of-war with Netanyahu over settlements, combined with his growing sense that no Israeli gesture was ever going to satisfy Abbas, had led him to conclude that neither man was up to the challenge. Privately, an aide said, Obama suspected that Netanyahu only wanted the imagery of peace talks to get Israel through the next UN General Assembly, a gathering that increasingly show-cased Israel's international isolation.

"How do we know this isn't going to break down in three weeks?" Obama asked his aides of the talks.

No one could give him a convincing answer.

Still, on September 1, a reluctant Obama stood in the East Room to launch his own version of Camp David. He was flanked by Net-anyahu, Abbas, and the leaders of Egypt and Jordan, the only two Arab states that had ever made peace with Israel. "Too much blood has already been shed, too many hearts have already been broken," the president declared. "This moment of opportunity may not re-turn soon again." If Obama showed little of the passion of Jimmy Carter or the roll-up-your-sleeves energy of Bill Clinton, it was un-derstandable. After just two more meetings between the leaders, the Israeli freeze, such as it was, expired. Abbas, who had dithered for eight of the ten months before agreeing to talk, declined to come back to the table.

At last, it was Clinton's turn to roll up her sleeves. She launched a desperate campaign to persuade Netanyahu to extend the freeze—and her experience in those difficult months may explain why she didn't want to get involved in the first place. The low point, argu-ably, came on November 12 in a conference room at the Loews Re-gency Hotel in Manhattan, where the Israeli leader was staying. Clinton found herself in an eight-hour bargaining session over a onetime ninety-day extension of the freeze. Her hope was that this step, however attenuated, would be enough to lure Abbas back.

She tried everything, even floating the early release of Jonathan Pollard. (A good rule of thumb: The appearance of Pollard in any negotiation with the Israelis was a sign of desperation.) A skilled, bare-knuckles bargainer with a cast-iron backside, Netanyahu turned every session into an endurance test. Once, during a mara-thon call, a frustrated Clinton began silently banging the phone on her forehead. Their arguments were loud and frequently profane. Like almost everyone, Clinton calls Netanyahu by his childhood nickname, Bibi; often it was attached to the f-word. On November 12, she watched as his negotiators haggled over every point, no matter how picayune. At one point, Molcho and Mitchell fell into a mind-numbing technical discussion over which half-finished houses could be completed under a grandfather clause. Suddenly, a hand slammed down on the table. It belonged to Dan Shapiro, an NSC senior director who would go on to be the ambassador to Israel.

"This is insane!" he shouted. "You know what you want. You know what we want. Let's just get it over with."

Shapiro's explosion electrified both sides. Jake Sullivan was thrilled that his colleague had cut through all the nonsense; Michael Oren slipped him a note that said, "This is your finest moment." It broke the logjam: Netanyahu finally agreed to extend the freeze. But the price was steep: The United States offered to give Israel twenty F-35 stealth fighter jets, worth $3 billion. Clinton later told Tony Blair she found the whole exercise a "nasty business." Nor was there any guarantee it would satisfy the Palestinians, who always seemed to be looking for reasons not to enter any negotiation.

A few weeks later, the deal collapsed, the victim of resistance in Netanyahu's right-wing cabinet and bickering over whether Israel would pay for the planes. With it went any chance for a breakthrough during Clinton's years as secretary of state.

For all the harsh words and histrionics, Clinton and Netanyahu managed to get along. Clinton worked hard at it. "She had a jaundiced view of Bibi from her experience in the White House," said Martin Indyk, who tangled with Netanyahu as the special envoy for Israeli-Palestinian negotiations under Kerry. "But her approach combined the need to show she could get along with the elected prime minister of Israel with an understanding of how to deal with him." Both admired the politician in each other; there were even flashes of affection. When Michael Oren told Netanyahu that Clinton had been hospitalized after falling in her home, the prime minister called him back on his cellphone three times in an hour for updates on her condition. (A less sentimental explanation, a longtime Netanyahu watcher said, was that he was intrigued by the possibility that a tough adversary was about to leave the scene.)

The same was not true of Netanyahu and Obama. After a promising first meeting, their relationship deteriorated rapidly into mutual suspicion, even contempt. The accumulated slights and snubs were symptoms of a deeper chasm between them: one, a progressive Democrat who saw the world in hues of gray; the other, a Manichean Likudnik, who saw it in black and white. Obama, like Clinton, called the prime minister Bibi. But it was, bar none, the worst relationship he had with any foreign leader.

An important milestone in this painfully public unraveling came on May 19, 2011, when Obama gave his most important address on the Middle East since the Cairo speech two years earlier. The Arab world was coming apart, with angry crowds flooding the streets and dictators toppling from Tunisia to Yemen. To the president, the upheaval argued for taking another shot at ending the Israeli-Palestinian conflict, which for so long had been a rallying cry for aggrieved Arabs. He planned to propose that the two sides resume talks to create a Palestinian state on the basis of Israel's borders before the 1967 Arab-Israeli war. Israel would swap the Palestinians some land on its side of the border to offset the settlements on the West Bank. The formula was hardly revolutionary, but Obama's public endorsement would give it new life. Ross knew this would antagonize Netanyahu; he tipped off Yitzhak Molcho the night before.

That phone call set off a diplomatic storm that captured the state of Israel's relations with the United States. Molcho, who had been boarding a flight to Washington to prepare an upcoming visit by Netanyahu, was called back to Jerusalem by the prime minister. The next morning, Molcho got on the phone with Ross and Tom Donilon, while an agitated Netanyahu called Clinton. Molcho pressed for Obama to water down the speech. There was no way, he said, Israel could defend itself with pre-1967 borders. The White House refused, though Donilon and Ross, anxious to mollify Netanyahu, tweaked other lines to soften its tone. The line-by-line negotiation went on all morning, delaying Obama's arrival at Foggy Bottom by thirty-five minutes.

Speaking under the twinkling chandeliers of the Benjamin Franklin Room, the president did his best to draw a connection between the Israeli-Palestinian conflict and the broader turmoil in the region. "At a time when the people of the Middle East and North Africa are casting off the burdens of the past," he said, "the drive for a lasting peace that ends the conflict and resolves all claims is more urgent than ever." In fact, the opposite was true: The Arab uprisings had made the Israeli-Palestinian conflict a sideshow. Far from pressing both sides to seek a deal, the chaos throughout the region made Netanyahu and Abbas even more risk averse.

As Ross expected, Obama's reference to the 1967 borders lit a fuse. A day after the president spoke, Netanyahu himself arrived in Washington, loaded for bear. Sitting next to Obama before the fireplace in the Oval Office, he delivered an extraordinary public rebuke. Israel, he said, "cannot go back to the 1967 lines, because these lines are indefensible." Pre-1967 Israel, he reminded Obama, was half the width of the Washington Beltway, his reference to a local landmark somehow making the lecture even more patronizing. He said he had no plans to negotiate with a "government that is backed by the Palestinian version of al-Qaeda," referring to Hamas. And he dismissed out of hand another longtime Palestinian demand: that Israelis accept the descendants of Palestinians who had been displaced by the state of Israel. "It's not going to happen," he declared. "Everybody knows it's not going to happen."

Obama looked at Netanyahu stone-faced. Out of camera range, his aides were fuming. The chief of staff, Bill Daley, asked Ron Dermer, a Netanyahu adviser who would later become Israel's ambassador to Washington, whether his boss made a habit of going to people's houses and lecturing them. It could have been worse: Before Netanyahu left for the White House, anxious members of the Israeli delegation pulled him into the courtyard of Blair House, across the street. They pleaded with him to soften his statement so it was aimed less at Obama and more at the Palestinians.

Obama could be just as peremptory toward Netanyahu. In March 2010, during a White House meeting about—what else?—extending the settlement freeze, he left the prime minister and his aides in the Roosevelt Room for more than an hour while he went to have dinner with his wife and daughters in the family quarters. Just before he left, the president turned to Netanyahu and said, "I have some homework for you," according to an Israeli in the room. "You don't give a head of state homework," this person added. The White House laid out cheese and crackers for the Israeli delegation, which ended up staying until two thirty A.M. in what proved a futile effort to find a formula to extend the freeze. What infuriated Netanyahu most about the episode, an American official recalled, was less that Obama left for dinner in the middle of it than that he brought his guest into the West Wing through a rear entrance where there were no cameras to record his arrival.

Despite these snubs, Israeli officials insisted that Netanyahu's problems with Obama were not, at heart, personal. The two did fine at their first meeting in 2007, arranged in a hurry by their aides, who found an empty janitor's office at Ronald Reagan Airport in Washington for them to chat. Obama was just gaining traction in his primary challenge against Clinton, and Netanyahu, who fancied himself an astute observer of American politics, was impressed with the young senator. "He's got it," he told his aides afterward. "He can beat Hillary." Instead, it was Obama's decisions—from pounding Israel on settlements to cutting a nuclear agreement with Israel's archenemy, Iran—that poisoned the relationship. "There is tremendous personal animus from Obama toward Bibi," a senior Israeli official said. "There is no animus from Bibi toward Obama." But, he added, "Bibi has deep contempt for his worldview. He hates the liberal, leftist worldview. He has very little patience for it."

Obama viewed Netanyahu as a big talker who never backed up

his words with actions. In a private conversation in July 2010, the Israeli leader told the president he was ready to move on a peace accord with the Palestinians if Israel's security could be assured. Obama quickly dispatched Ross and General James "Hoss" Cartwright, the vice chairman of the Joint Chiefs of Staff, to Jerusalem with ideas about how to do that. But when Netanyahu came to the White House two months later for face-to-face talks with Abbas, he put nothing on the table. Obama felt betrayed: He had regarded Netanyahu, with his rock-solid Likud credentials and commanding political stature, as the one Israeli leader who could pull his people into a difficult peace with the Palestinians. His refusal to try struck Obama as an unpardonable lack of courage.

That perception of cowardice bled into the dispute over Iran. Netanyahu regularly threatened that Israel would strike Iran militarily if it felt its existence was being threatened. Given Israel's track record—it had bombed a Syrian nuclear reactor in 2007—the United States took the threat seriously. But Netanyahu, for all his bluster, had less appetite for military action than most Israeli leaders. By the fall of 2014, Obama's aides concluded that he had missed his chance to launch a preemptive strike on Iran's nuclear facilities, a decision they chalked up to his gutlessness. "The thing about Bibi is, he's a chickenshit," an unnamed senior administration official told Jeffrey Goldberg of *The Atlantic* for an article on the crisis in the relationship.

Netanyahu was understandably outraged by the slur. It says something about how deep the mutual loathing had become that in the guessing game of which mysterious American official had uttered that slur, senior Israelis threw out a startling name: Barack Obama.

On November 30, 2012, Israeli authorities announced plans to move ahead with settlements in a strategically sensitive part of East Jerusalem known as E1. Even by Israel's standards, this was highly provocative: Putting up houses in that area would limit access to the cities of Ramallah and Bethlehem, all but foreclosing the dream of a viable, contiguous Palestinian state. "This is not just another few houses in Jerusalem or another hilltop in the West Bank," Daniel Kurtzer, a former American ambassador to Israel and Egypt, told me at the time. "This is one of the most sensitive areas of territory, and I would hope the United States will lay down the law."

That evening, Hillary Clinton was the keynote speaker at the Saban Forum, an annual gathering organized by the Brookings Institution and paid for by the Israeli-American media baron Haim Saban. It was two months before she would leave the Obama administration to return to private life, but already she exuded a sense of liberation, a cabinet member about to reclaim her identity as an independent political figure. Before Clinton took the podium at the Willard Hotel, there was a fulsome video tribute to her diplomatic career that featured testimonials from Benjamin Netanyahu, Ehud Barak, and Tzipi Livni. With its stirring images and references to her even brighter future, it could have been the first commercial for her 2016 campaign. "I just have an instinct that the best is yet to come," said Tony Blair, capturing the giddy mood in the room. When it was her turn to speak, Clinton said, "I prepared some remarks for tonight, but then I thought maybe we could just watch that video a few more times."

She might as well have done that. The speech that followed was the kind of pro-Israel boilerplate that would have gotten a presidential candidate from either party a standing ovation at AIPAC's annual meeting. "America has Israel's back," she said, in a typical platitude. "America and Israel are in it together," she said in another. She deplored the Palestinian Authority's efforts to seek recognition at the United Nations and promised never to allow Iran to acquire a nuclear bomb. And what of the new settlements in E1? The secretary of state who had once declared "not some settlements, not outposts, not natural growth exceptions," said only, "These activities set back the cause of a negotiated peace." It was the blandest possible response, which took no account of the stakes involved. Clinton, though she had not yet left office, already viewed Israel through the lens of domestic politics.

In March 2015, a few weeks before Clinton announced she was running for president, she got a phone call. It was Malcolm Hoenlein, the American Jewish leader who had asked President Obama six years earlier why he was willing to allow daylight to show between the United States and Israel. Clinton, he said, assured him that she wanted "to return the special U.S.-Israel relationship to constructive footing."

Translation: No more daylight.

# Seven

## Sinking Sands

It was a crisp, clear Saturday morning in late January 2011, patches of snow on the ground, when the cellphone in Frank Wisner's pocket began buzzing. Wisner, a lawyer and diplomat who had served as American ambassador to Egypt, had a shotgun in his hands and his eye trained on the sky above him. He was shooting ducks at the Clove Valley Rod & Gun Club, an exclusive four-thousand-acre range in the woodlands east of Poughkeepsie, New York, that has attracted hunters from Dwight D. Eisenhower to Dick Cheney. The caller was Bill Burns, an old colleague of Wisner's then serving as the ranking career diplomat in the State Department. Cellphone reception at the range was wretched, but Wisner heard enough, amid the static, to hop in his car and drive the seventy miles back to his apartment in New York City. "Would you give us a hand and try to get a message to Mubarak, on behalf of the president?" Burns asked him that morning. "The secretary would like you to consider this."

For Wisner, a bluff, bullet-headed seventy-seven-year-old who came of age at a time when American diplomats jumped at the chance to parachute into the world's trouble spots, there was only one answer: Yes. He spoke again with Burns, Dennis Ross, and Tom Donilon that day and the next, going over the script of what he was to say to Egypt's longtime president Hosni Mubarak, whose people had suddenly risen up in revolt against him. He asked for, and got, a ten-minute phone call with Obama. Wisner told Burns he was comfortable with the plan to ease Mubarak gently into yielding power, but he warned against any threats to cancel U.S. military aid. "It will do no good," Burns emailed Clinton that morning, relaying his argument, "and only spark angst in the wider region and within the Egyptian Armed Forces—the one national institution likely to survive all the current uncertainty."

On Sunday, Wisner was driven to a distant section of the tarmac at John F. Kennedy International Airport, where he boarded a blue and white Air Force 757 bound for Cairo. He landed the next day at ten A.M., and was driven straight to Mubarak's palace through streets empty but for a single tank guarding a traffic circle. Omar Suleiman, the vice president, was waiting for him at the door. A suave general who spoke perfect English, Suleiman was a familiar figure to Wisner from his days as ambassador, when Suleiman had run Egypt's feared military intelligence service. Now he was Mubarak's right-hand man. Clearly agitated, Suleiman badgered Wisner to preview the message he was bearing. Wisner declined until he was taken inside, where he found the president holed up, grimly resisting the call of protesters in Tahrir Square that he step down.

"I was never a chum or a pal," Wisner told me of the man who had ruled Egypt with an iron hand for three decades. "I had a lot of time for Mubarak; I still do. He was a great friend of this country for many, many years. He stayed too long in office, which is a different matter."

Wisner delivered a two-part message from Obama, according to officials who briefed him: that Mubarak not permit his security forces to crack down on the demonstrators, and that he set a timetable for the transfer of power. Wisner repeated the message to make sure it got through. When he left the palace two hours later, he felt sure that Mubarak wanted him to believe there would be no blood on the streets. He also sensed, even if the president didn't say it, that Mubarak knew his time was up. The Egyptian leader was a proud man, though, and he made clear he would not be stampeded into a departure date.

Back at the American embassy, Wisner dictated a summary of his meeting and took part in a secure video conference call with officials from the White House and the State Department. They were impatient to see results from Wisner's mission, but he told them that Mubarak needed time to come to terms with the finality of his situation. Wisner was still counseling patience the following Saturday, after he had returned to New York. By then, Tahrir Square had turned bloody, with pro-Mubarak thugs, some on horseback, storming the protests, and the security forces opening fire. Wisner spoke, via satellite, to the Munich Security Conference, a high-level meeting where world leaders gather to discuss geopolitics. (Clinton was there.) The United States should not hustle Mubarak out the door, Wisner warned the group. He had an important role to play through the end of his term in September, seven months away. "It's his opportunity to write his own legacy," he said.

At the time Wisner was speaking, Clinton and her aides were in meetings elsewhere in the Bayerischer Hof, the elegant nineteenth-century hotel where the conference was held. They did not see his video presentation as it happened. Shortly afterward, Jake Sullivan walked to the nearby Charles Hotel to brief Clinton's press corps. He blanched when a reporter read him Wisner's remarks from a BlackBerry.

When the president was told about Wisner's speech that afternoon, he hit the roof. Four days earlier, Obama, prodded by a circle of younger aides who worried that he was not reacting enough to the tumultuous events in Tahrir Square, had shifted from patiently nudging Mubarak to demanding that he begin the transition "now." As his press secretary Robert Gibbs memorably embellished it, "Now started yesterday." But in Munich, his own emissary was arguing that yesterday didn't start for seven months. And Clinton was reinforcing Wisner's languid timetable: An orderly transition, she said at the conference, would require constitutional amendments, the assembly of voter rolls, the creation of political parties, and the emergence of credible opposition leaders after thirty years of repression. All that would take time. The previous day, Clinton told Sullivan she felt she had gone too far in publicly pressuring Mubarak to accept a swift handover. "I'm afraid what I said yesterday is being used to support the idea that we are pushing his leaving," she emailed Sullivan. He replied that the State Department had softened its message from "the transition must begin now" to "negotiations must begin now."

When Obama gets really mad, his aides said, he doesn't raise his voice or unleash a stream of profanity. Rather, his speech becomes clipped; his words pointed. "What was Wisner doing speaking at the Munich Security Conference?" a clipped and pointed president asked Clinton by phone before she flew home. "And why was he saying different things than I have?" Obama told her to put a stop to the mixed messages.

"He took me to the woodshed," Clinton later wrote.

It was the angriest phone call Obama ever made to Clinton, one that laid bare stark differences in how they thought the United States should respond to the first of the great Arab uprisings.

The State Department, on White House orders, immediately disavowed Wisner. He was speaking as a private citizen, a spokesman said, not a presidential emissary. Bill Burns, who had suggested Wisner for the job, was chagrined to see a respected elder stumble after he had dutifully carried out his instructions. White House aides, never shy about playing Monday-morning quarterback, clucked that Wisner had been too close to Mubarak. One NSC adviser said he had floated the idea of sending Richard Armitage, a Republican diplomat even more bullet-headed than Wisner, who would have been tougher. Clinton's aides evinced little sympathy, saying Wisner should have kept his mouth shut. But she was gentler: Wisner said she spared him the gory details of her conversation with Obama, and told him she regretted how it had worked out. Though Wisner was not a Clinton person, he had served as her husband's ambassador to India and had been a lifelong friend of her friend Richard Holbrooke. They shared a dais, along with Obama, at his memorial service.

Reflecting on his misadventure four years later, Wisner abjured bitterness or regret. Sensitive to the obligations of an envoy, he insisted that he had followed his talking points to the letter. He got out of sync with Obama, but that was because they were in different time zones and Wisner did not realize how much the president's position had shifted. He still thought his remarks in Munich were valid, if impolitic. But he acknowledged the White House may have been right in concluding that events in Tahrir Square had gone too far for an orderly transfer of power.

"Would it have been possible," he mused, "for Mubarak to organize a transition, assuming he wanted to? Or was there too much emotion on the street? I suspect it was too late. But the right American strategy was to seek a responsible transition."

Frank Wisner's story is worth recounting not because he was right about Egypt—though he may well have been—but because in its tensions and contradictions, it set the stage for how Obama and Clinton would respond to the cascading upheavals in the Arab world. From Egypt and Bahrain to Yemen and Libya, the president and his secretary of state struggled to reconcile values with interests, democratic hopes with geopolitical realities—often wrapping themselves around the axle in the process. Their struggle culminated in the horrors of Syria, where the United States ended up a bystander to the deadliest war of the twenty-first century.

How Obama and Clinton reacted to these upheavals says a lot about their instincts and views of America's role in the world. Clinton generally prized stability and loyalty to allies; Obama worried more about not being on what he considered the "right side" of history. Clinton put faith in America's ability to influence events in storm-tossed countries; a more skeptical Obama was determined to limit American involvement. But they didn't always revert to type. As the uprisings mutated—becoming less democratic and more sectarian—Clinton and Obama evolved in their positions. Sometimes they all but reversed roles. The same idealistic president who stood up for the fervent young crowds in Tahrir Square refused to call it a coup when Egypt's generals put Mubarak's democratically elected successor, Mohamed Morsi, in chains two years later. The same realist secretary of state who wanted to stick with Mubarak and warned of the need for an orderly transition in Egypt, talked Obama into joining a risky NATO bombing campaign in Libya to stop Colonel Muammar al-Qaddafi from slaughtering his own people in Benghazi.

The zigzagging made for an unnerving spectacle, laying bare not just the differences between Obama and Clinton but also the contradictions in their own positions. Clinton worried that Egypt would be portrayed as the first major break between her and the president. When *The New York Times* was preparing a story on the behind-the-scenes wrangling over Mubarak while she was in Munich, Clinton emailed Sullivan to ask "Is this a State-WH rift story? A POTUS-S rift? There's more (and less) than meets the eye." She had a point: The Arab Awakening was perhaps the biggest foreign policy challenge to arise during the Obama presidency, and the first such crisis the president and his secretary of state had faced in real time. It was bound to test them. In the six tumultuous weeks between Cairo and Benghazi, three decades of American thinking about the Middle East had been upended. "We've had a way of engaging with Egypt for the last twenty to twenty-five years," said Brian Katulis, an expert in the Middle East and a senior fellow at the Center for American Progress. "The uprising threw a huge dust cloud in the face of policy makers."

And yet it's incorrect to say the administration had no warning it was coming. The previous August, Obama had ordered his staff to produce a report assessing the risks for violent upheavals in Arab countries. The eighteen-page classified document, known as *Presidential Study Directive 11* (PSD-11), identified four countries—Egypt, Jordan, Yemen, and Bahrain—as ripe for popular revolt, and offered a country-by-country analysis. "There's no question Egypt was very much on the mind of the president," said Samantha Power, then an NSC staffer, who wrote the report with Dennis Ross and a development expert, Gayle Smith. "You had all the unknowns created by Egypt's succession picture," she said, "and Egypt is the anchor of the region."

Revolution was also on Clinton's mind when she spoke to Arab leaders in the Gulf emirate of Qatar on January 13, 2011. The region faced an explosion of unrest and extremism, she warned, if the leaders did not liberalize their political systems and curb the corruption that permeated their societies. "In too many places, in too many ways," she declared, "the region's foundations are sinking into the sand." These proved to be the most prescient words she would utter as secretary of state.

Tahrir Square crystallized an internal debate, stretching back to Obama's first days in office, about how he should respond to unrest abroad. The president came in reflexively opposed to anything that smacked of the freedom agenda of George W. Bush, which he felt had come to be seen by Muslims as coercive and hypocritical. In his first speech to the United Nations in September 2009, Obama erected four main pillars of American engagement with the world; spreading democracy was not one of them. In June 2009, he said little on behalf of the young people at the vanguard of Iran's doomed Green Movement. Dissidents inside Iran had urged the United States not to champion the protesters because it would tarnish them domestically. But the decision left Obama's advisers queasy, especially after the Iranian regime sent paramilitary thugs into the crowds with hoses and truncheons.

Obama's aides regularly tried to inject references to democratic values into the president's speeches. At midnight the day before that first UN address, Ben Rhodes and Denis McDonough summoned Michael McFaul, a Stanford University political scientist and Russia scholar who had just joined the NSC, to the Waldorf Astoria to help craft some last-minute language on democracy. McFaul had just finished cowriting a book called *Advancing Democracy Abroad,* a manifesto for promoting democracy without the my-way-or-the-highway unilateralism of Bush. When Obama walked into the room, McFaul, who hadn't been told the president would be joining them, realized his job was to persuade him to add a fifth pillar to his speech. Obama pushed back: The world is a complex place, he said; the collapse of regimes creates conflict. But he agreed to add a short coda on the American belief in universal values.

Until Cairo, McFaul, Rhodes, and other aides had measured their victories in terms of getting a few worthy lines stuck into an Obama speech. Now, with tens of thousands of people in Tahrir Square calling for Mubarak's fall, the idealists suddenly had a chance to influence an honest-to-God revolution. But they faced a wall of opposition: Clinton, Gates, and Biden were urging Obama not to throw an old friend at the heart of America's Middle East policy overboard; Tom Donilon agreed, as did a stream of worried callers from Israel and the Persian Gulf. Mubarak, for all his autocratic tendencies, had been a steadfast, dependable ally who had honored Egypt's peace treaty with Israel. In private conversations, Clinton reminisced fondly about the friendship that she cultivated with his wife, Suzanne Mubarak, during reciprocal visits to Cairo and Washington when Bill was president.

Obama's war council played to his pragmatism; his staffers played to his sense of history.

Clinton and Gates raised the specter of Iran's 1979 Islamic Revolution, which had the same populist roots as Egypt's uprising, but was hijacked by mullahs who turned Iran into a repressive Shiite theocracy and an implacable enemy of the United States. The ayatollahs, in this narrative, were the Muslim Brotherhood; Obama was Jimmy Carter. McFaul argued that the better analogies were the Philippines, Chile, or South Korea—countries the United States had nurtured from autocracy or Communism to democracy. That would make Obama Ronald Reagan, not Carter. Rhodes talked about Wael Ghonim, the fearless young Google executive who had started a Facebook page to spread the word about the demonstrations. He was detained and interrogated by Mubarak's police for eleven days, and after his release, gave an emotional interview on Egyptian television that made him the face of Tahrir Square. What was the value of Obama's presidency, if not to fight for people like him?

At times, the tug-of-war seemed less between Obama's top advisers than within Obama himself. When a circle of aides asked him, amid the hue and cry of the protests, to predict the outcome, he replied, "What I *want* is for the kids on the street to win and for the Google guy to become president. What I *think* is that this is going to be long and hard."

Obama, who had built his foreign policy on the goal of extracting the United States from the Middle East, struggled to understand this convulsing region. His government was of little help. It could churn out country-specific assessments such as PSD-11, but no one could create a larger mosaic of what was happening. The idealists on the NSC who pushed democracy knew little about the Arab world. The Arabists in the State Department's Bureau of Near Eastern Affairs were hidebound and lacking in imagination; they prized stability—read, Mubarak—above all. The CIA's Middle East analysts failed to foresee the chain reaction: how the uprisings leapt from country to country in an arc of instability that stretched from Tunisia to Syria. At night, in the residence, Obama resorted to surfing the blogs of experts on Arab affairs or news sites to get a local take on events. He sounded out journalists such as Fareed Zakaria about their visits to the region. The president, Zakaria said at the time, was "searching for a way to pull back and weave a larger picture."

To the extent that Obama ever formed that larger picture, he remained as cynical about Arab leaders as he had been in 2002, when he first came out against the Iraq War. Back then, he pointed to "our so-called allies in the Middle East"—Egypt and Saudi Arabia—as a better target for George W. Bush's pressure than Saddam Hussein's Iraq. "He thinks they are pre-civilized," said a person who has discussed the region with him.

For Bill Daley, the White House chief of staff, who stood firmly in the stability camp, it was clear how the Egypt debate was going to play out. "This was the eighty-seven-year-old doddering, hack politician versus the young revolutionaries with their iPhones," said Daley, whose father, Mayor Richard J. Daley, ruled Chicago like a pharaoh for twenty-one years and died in office. "This is like my dad in some ways: He's the old politician trying to hold on, while the young guys try to throw him out."

In the end, it was the old man, not the kids, who tipped the scales. Speaking to the Egyptian people on February 1, 2011, the day after he saw Wisner, Mubarak was imperial, defiant, and condescending. "This is my country," he said, announcing he would not stand for reelection but would stay until the end of his term. "This is where I lived, fought, and defended its land, sovereignty and interests, and I will die on its soil." Obama watched the speech with his aides in the Situation Room. Unlike Clinton, he had no nostalgic memories of a younger Mubarak, who succeeded the assassinated Anwar Sadat, or his gracious wife; he found Arab strongmen to be dissembling and unreliable. Fed up, he asked to be patched through to Mubarak.

"I know the last thing you want to see is Egypt collapse into chaos," Obama told him. "How can you help manage the change?"

"You don't understand my people," Mubarak replied. "I do understand my people."

"Let's talk tomorrow," Obama pressed.

"We don't need to talk tomorrow," Mubarak said. "You'll see. It'll all be done in a few days."

The two men never spoke again. After the phone call, Obama reconvened his National Security Council. He was clutching the text of a statement on Egypt that he planned to deliver to the American people in forty-five minutes. It included a line calling on Mubarak to step down. He polled the group: Clinton, Gates, and Biden urged him to hold off making the statement, or if he did, to take out the line about Mubarak leaving; the backbenchers, led by Rhodes, pleaded with him to go ahead. To the surprise of some in the room, John Brennan lined up with those who wanted to jettison Mubarak.

"He's toast," Brennan said.

Normally, a president does not announce a decision this momentous on the spot. But with his TV appearance less than an hour away, there was no time to put it off. Obama told the group he planned to call on Mubarak, a stalwart American ally for three decades, to step aside. Things had gone too far, the president said; the only way he could cling to power would be through an unconscionable use of force. Speaking from the grand foyer of the White House a few minutes later, Obama declared, "What is clear, and what I indicated tonight to President Mubarak, is my belief that an orderly transition must be meaningful, it must be peaceful, and it must begin now."

Nine days later, with the bloody clashes in Cairo and other cities across the country causing Mubarak's support in the Egyptian army to crumble, Obama told a college audience in Marquette, Michigan, "We are witnessing history unfold." The United States, he said, would "do everything that we can to support an orderly and genuine transition to democracy in Egypt." At the White House, Rhodes, McFaul, and Samantha Power savored another small victory: the words "democracy in Egypt."

"We finally got him to say that phrase," one of them exulted. A bigger victory came the next day when Omar Suleiman wanly announced that Mubarak had quit. A euphoric group gathered in McFaul's office in the Executive Office Building, cracking open bottles of booze and watching images on Al Jazeera of the delirious crowds in Cairo.

At that moment, the movement justified the optimistic label "Arab Spring." It seemed the fulfillment of one of Obama's favorite aphorisms: "The arc of the moral universe is long, but it bends toward justice." Within a few months, though, the promise of Tahrir Square had wilted.

Clinton, it turned out, had been right to worry about what came after Mubarak. After decades of authoritarian rule, Egypt had no real political parties. Its most cohesive opposition movement, the Muslim Brotherhood, had been ruthlessly repressed for decades. The White House signaled that it would be open to working with the Brotherhood so long as it was part of an orderly transition. McFaul was assigned to compile lessons from other such transitions: how to draft a constitution, how to sequence elections, and so on. (Ross dubbed him the head of the "nerd directorate.") But Egypt's generals weren't interested in any advice from the nerds. They scheduled parliamentary elections without laying the groundwork for the emergence of parties. Predictably, the Brotherhood won a thumping victory.

Obama, having championed democracy, had little choice but to support the winning party and its president, Mohamed Morsi. But the Brotherhood, to the surprise of few outside the West Wing, soon showed it had no plans to follow through with democratic reforms. Far from getting on the right side of history, Obama and Clinton were blamed by bitter Egyptians for taking sides with the Islamists. When Clinton visited Cairo in July 2012, her motorcade was pelted with tomatoes and shoes, while demonstrators chanted "Monica, Monica"—showing, if nothing else, that Egyptian crowds knew their Beltway scandals.

"How do I correct this image that we support the Muslim Brotherhood?" a frustrated Clinton asked Ross.

In hindsight, people close to Clinton said, the White House erred by wading into the debate. The Egyptian army would probably have removed Mubarak with or without Obama's disavowal of him. The president, by putting his finger on the scale, gained little favor with the protesters and lost credibility with other important constituencies in Egypt and throughout the region, especially in the Persian Gulf. "The lesson," said a senior official who worked with Clinton at the State Department, "is keep your powder dry because what you think you are accomplishing by being on the right side of history, you are not accomplishing."

In July 2013, thousands of antigovernment protesters were again thronging Tahrir Square—this time calling for Morsi's head. The Egyptian army obliged, ousting his hapless government, throwing him in jail, and ordering a bloody crackdown on the Muslim Brotherhood. Fireworks erupted in the square, but at the headquarters of the Republican Guard, where Morsi was believed to be held, soldiers fired on pro-Morsi crowds, killing at least fifty. The next day, Obama, clad in khakis and a dark blue golf shirt, gathered his advisers in the Situation Room to begin what turned into a Star Chamber–like debate over whether the United States should call the army's ouster a coup. At issue was $1.3 billion a year in military aid, which by law could not be given to a regime that had seized power in a coup d'état.

The State Department's top lawyer, Mary McLeod, said it was an open-and-shut case. To the admiration of some in the room, she refused to back down, even under intense pressure from officials who warned that cutting off the aid would further shake the region. Finally, the White House finessed the issue by deciding it did not have to make a call. "We will not say it was a coup; we will not say it was not a coup; we will just not say," an NSC spokeswoman said, channeling Dr. Seuss. Obama subsequently did hold back a little aid, though by March 2015, he had reinstated all of it, sending Egypt twelve F-16 fighter jets and twenty Harpoon missiles. The generals were back in charge, and the White House was resigned to dealing with them, even at the price of the democratic values Obama had championed two years earlier.

"Nobody had the energy to do the right thing," a senior White House official said.


Hillary Clinton's sermon to a roomful of stone-faced sheikhs in Qatar about the looming Arab revolt came four weeks before Mubarak fell. But it seemed to anticipate everything that happened during the first year of the Arab upheavals. In early January 2011, before the first protesters had taken to Tahrir Square, Clinton met with her staff to plan a coming trip to the Persian Gulf. She told them she was frustrated by the sclerotic pace of change in the region and wanted to say something that might get through to its leaders. At two A.M. on January 13, in a staff room at her hotel in the Qatari capital, Doha, Jake Sullivan and Dan Schwerin, one of her speechwriters, pored over a draft. They were noodling with a sand metaphor, which they worried might be a cliché or convey the wrong image. ("There's no way to climb out of quicksand," Schwerin noted.) They settled on "sinking into the sand."

Unlike Obama, Clinton is not a sparkling orator. With a couple of notable exceptions—her UN women's conference address in Beijing in 1995; the eighteen-million-cracks-in-the-glass-ceiling concession speech in 2008—she doesn't hit the high notes of Obama. Her speeches are laden with laundry lists and rest on familiar formulations (on the State Department beat, I lost count of the times she said something was "not only . . . but also"). Obama has his well-worn riffs, too: He often describes a thorny dilemma as a "false choice"—as in, the "false choice" between our freedom and our security. ("It's not a false choice," a Clinton aide once pointed out to me. "It's an actual choice.") But in Oslo, where he accepted the Nobel Peace Prize, or in Selma, where he marked the fiftieth anniversary of a bloody civil rights march, Obama was eloquent in a way that very few politicians could match.

There was little reason to think Clinton would surprise her audience when she walked into the gloomy ballroom of the Ritz-Carlton hotel that morning. She was speaking to a group called the Forum for the Future, which brings together leaders from rich countries and the Arab world to talk about political reforms. The rule of thumb at such gatherings is to utter well-meaning platitudes. On this day, though, Clinton spoke like a Puritan preacher, Jonathan Edwards in a charcoal jacket and headband. Her message seemed even more powerful because she was at the end of a four-day tour of the Persian Gulf that had showcased the failed promise of the Arab world: from the medieval autocracy of Yemen—where men with traditional curved daggers in their belts stared coldly as her motorcade snaked through the sandstone alleys of Sanaa's old city—to the engorged, self-satisfied fief of Qatar, still exulting from winning the 2022 soccer World Cup, for which it would soon employ a virtual slave-labor force of migrant workers to build stadiums in the desert.

"Those who cling to the status quo may be able to hold back the full impact of their countries' problems for a little while," Clinton said, "but not forever. If leaders don't offer a positive vision and give young people meaningful ways to contribute, others will fill the vacuum. Extremist elements, terrorist groups, and others who would prey on desperation and poverty are already out there, appealing for allegiance and competing for influence."

"So this is a critical moment," she declared, "and this is a test of leadership for all of us."

Clinton scolded her hosts for their corruption. Try to open a business in an Arab country as a foreigner, she said, and "you have to pass money through so many different hands. Trying to open up, you have to pay people off. Trying to stay open, you have to pay people off. Trying to export your goods, you have to pay people off. So by the time you pay everybody off, it's not a very profitable venture."

If Clinton was right about the sinking sand, though, she found it harder to strike the right tone when it entrapped a strategic American ally. A month before her broadside in Qatar, she was in Bahrain, home to the U.S. Navy's Fifth Fleet. The postage-stamp kingdom, ruled by Sunnis but with a majority Shiite population, did not have as repressive a record as the worst of the Arab states. But it had begun arresting lawyers and human rights activists, a precursor to the larger crackdown to come. At a meeting in the capital, Manama, on December 3, 2010, a member of Bahrain's parliament asked Clinton if she was alarmed by the signs of repression. "I see the glass as half full," she replied. "I think the changes that are happening in Bahrain are much greater than what I see in many other countries." Three months later, Bahraini security forces opened fire from a helicopter on protesters in Pearl Square, a traffic circle not far from where Clinton had spoken.

That wasn't the only faulty prediction she made that morning in Manama. Asked by a student whether she had another White House run in her future, Clinton smiled and said, "I think I'll serve as secretary of state as my last public position and then probably go back to advocacy work, particularly on behalf of women and children."


Scarcely had Clinton and Obama tried to deal with the turmoil in Egypt when they were confronted with a crisis in the country next door. Three weeks after protests flared in Libya's restive east, Muammar al-Qaddafi had ordered his tanks to put down a rebellion in the ancient seaside city of Benghazi. Mobilizing artillery, planes, and ships, Qaddafi pounded one city after the other on the road to the rebel stronghold. Once in Benghazi, he vowed to hunt down the rebels house-to-house like rats.

Libya posed a different kind of dilemma. It was not an ally of the United States, nor did it have clear strategic implications for American national security. Its uprising began with Arab Spring–like protests but rapidly spread into a civil war that split the country along geographic and tribal lines. It featured a cartoonish villain in Colonel Qaddafi, who had bedeviled presidents going back to Ronald Reagan, but had been more of a curiosity than a curse since 2003, when he signed a deal with George W. Bush to give up his weapons of mass destruction (indeed, he had been modestly useful in the battle against al-Qaeda). Rich in oil and gas, Libya was of far greater consequence to the Europeans—in particular to French president Nicolas Sarkozy. He had been embarrassed by the ouster two months earlier of the strongman Zine al-Abidine Ben Ali in Tunisia, a former French colony, and he was itching to reassert himself.

None of this argued for American military intervention, and at first, Clinton and Obama were united in their skepticism. Clinton, as usual, was acutely sensitive to the Pentagon's perspective; Bob Gates was implacably opposed to military action. Libya was not a vital U.S. interest, he argued, and Americans should not get into another war against a Muslim country. Nearing the end of his tenure, Gates had become grouchy—impatient with a White House that he thought was blind to the lessons of history and with a president who he felt was overly swayed by a coterie of young political aides. "They made exactly the same mistake in Libya that they accused Bush of in Iraq," he told me. "Failure to plan for what comes after the bad guy is gone."

Gates was backed up by his commanders. Mike Mullen, the chairman of the Joint Chiefs of Staff, said, "We're stretched in too many places, as it is," a former NSC official recalled. Mullen gave a tutorial on no-fly zones—the most obvious short-term response to Qaddafi—describing how the Pentagon would have to launch waves of bombs and missiles to take out his radar sites and command-and-control centers. That would be costly, Mullen said, and would not by itself shift the struggle in favor of the rebels. James Clapper, a retired air force general who was the director of national intelligence, cast doubt on whether there was even a viable rebel force on the ground to support. Hoss Cartwright, the vice-chairman of the Joint Chiefs of Staff, was open to intervening, but only if there was evidence that Qaddafi was moving his stockpiles of chemical weapons. (He still had some because the uprising had halted the internationally supervised operation to destroy them.)

On March 10, 2011, Clinton told Congress that if the United States waded into Libya without the imprimatur of the international community, it would find itself in a conflict that could escalate unpredictably. "And I know that's how our military feels," she said. That wasn't how her husband felt, however. The same day she was tapping the brakes on Capitol Hill, Bill Clinton told a women's conference in New York that he favored imposing a no-fly zone. "Nobody wants to see an arms race in Libya," he said, "but it's not a fair fight." Obama's aides were furious. They told Daley, whom they viewed as a Bill handler because of his days in the Clinton cabinet, to put a muzzle on his former boss.

By then, however, Hillary had been hearing the case for military action from many others. On February 21, her friend Sidney Blumenthal had sent her an email pointing out that Britain's former foreign secretary David Owen was calling for a no-fly zone over Libya. "What do you think of this idea?" she asked Jake Sullivan.

On March 3, John Kerry, usually the White House's most faithful defender in the Senate, had used a budget hearing to press Clinton to support a no-fly zone. "The global community cannot be on the sidelines while airplanes are allowed to bomb and strafe," he said. Kerry won an attaboy from Senator John McCain, the Arizona Republican, who had been flaying Obama for his inaction. But he got unhappy phone calls from senior State Department officials.

With Qaddafi's tanks bearing down on Benghazi, even other Arab nations began to pound the war drums, adding to the pressure that was building on Capitol Hill. On March 12, the Arab League voted to ask the United Nations to authorize a no-fly zone over Libya—a major symbolic step that would give the United States political cover for getting involved. A more concrete step came two days later when Clinton met in Paris with Abdullah bin Zayed, the boyish, aristocratic foreign minister of the United Arab Emirates, whom she refers to by his initials AbZ. (American officials are fond of abbreviating the names of Gulf sheikhs this way: Mohammed bin Zayed, the crown prince of Abu Dhabi, is known as MbZ.) The Emiratis, AbZ told her, were willing to send fighter planes. Still, there was no decision by the Americans.

Clinton spent February and March of 2011 shuttling among Geneva, Paris, Rome, and London for emergency meetings on Libya. She was prodded relentlessly by Nicolas Sarkozy, David Cameron of Britain, and Silvio Berlusconi of Italy to join a NATO operation. At a dinner meeting on March 14 in Paris with the foreign ministers of the G-8 countries, Washington's indecision became excruciating. One by one, the Europeans called for action, staring pointedly at Clinton. "This is pathetic," the Italian foreign minister, Franco Frattini, spluttered. "We need leadership, we can't just do nothing." Clinton's aides sweated and scanned their BlackBerrys in vain for new instructions from the White House. When it was her turn to speak, Clinton had to punt. "I agree with Franco," she said. "It's a very dangerous situation."

Things were about to change, however. At ten P.M., after her dinner with the foreign ministers, Clinton met at her hotel with Mahmoud Jibril, a former economic official in the Qaddafi regime who had emerged as the head of Libya's embattled opposition. The meeting was orchestrated by Bernard-Henri Lévy, the flamboyant French writer and philosopher. Lévy had turned Libya into a cause célèbre, hitching a ride into the country from Egypt in a vegetable seller's truck at the height of the uprising. He later introduced Sarkozy to the rebel leaders. With his flair for self-promotion and legion of detractors, Lévy is to French intellectuals what Richard Holbrooke was to Washington policy wonks. Clinton was beguiled, describing him as a "dramatic and stylish figure, with long wavy hair and his shirt open practically down to his navel." Her fascination lingered: Eighteen months later, she asked her aides to track down a copy of Lévy's documentary film about the Libyan civil war, *The Oath of Tobruk,* in which Sarkozy heaps praise on Clinton's role. ("I think Harvey [Weinstein] made it and showed it at Cannes last spring," she wrote.)

While Lévy waited in the next room, Clinton was joined by Chris Stevens, a fifty-year-old lawyer and diplomat whom she had recently named as her special envoy to the Libyan rebels. A fluent Arabic speaker with deep roots in the Arab world—he had served in Tripoli, Damascus, Cairo, and Riyadh—Stevens symbolized the promise of American engagement in Libya. Clinton wanted him to help her take stock of one of the men who proposed to shape the country's future. Mahmoud Jibril laid out a compelling case for military action. He reminded Clinton of Rwanda and the Balkans, two cases where the world—translation: her husband—had failed to stop mass killings. "My belief is that the fifty-minute encounter with Jibril was decisive," said Lévy, who was briefed afterward by Stevens. "Before, she had no clear position at all; she did not know. He moved, convinced, and persuaded her. She was impressed. She was moved in a human way, not only political."

Gates viewed Clinton's change of heart less dramatically. "My sense is, she was trying to be more responsive to our allies," he told me. Either way, right after the meeting, she dialed into the Situation Room. The Europeans were ready to take the lead in a NATO mission, she reported to Obama, the Arabs told her they would take part in it, and from what she had seen of the opposition leaders, they were worthy of American support.

"I met them, I looked them in the eye," Clinton said in an interview with my colleague Michael Gordon and me the day before she stepped down. "I was able to go back and say to the president, 'These are people you can count on, you can bet on, and we need to help them.'"


History hung over the Libya debate.

For Clinton, it was reminiscent of the Balkans, where her husband had sat back and allowed Europe to take the lead for the first two years of his presidency. The conflict metastasized until July 1995, when the horrors of Srebrenica finally jolted Bill to seize control of events. He mounted a NATO air campaign, committed twenty thousand ground troops, and sent Richard Holbrooke to broker the Dayton peace agreement. The Europeans, by and large, thanked him for it. "They grumble that we dominated Dayton," Secretary of State Warren Christopher wrote in a private memo to Clinton in December 1995, "but they really know that it wouldn't have gotten done otherwise."

For Susan Rice, the UN ambassador, it was the ghosts of Rwanda. She had been a twenty-eight-year-old aide on Bill Clinton's NSC in 1994, when the United States stood by while Hutus armed with machetes murdered eight hundred thousand Tutsis. Clinton later said the failure to prevent that was his greatest regret as president. Even more shameful, the question of whether to intervene to halt the slaughter never rose to the top levels of the NSC. Rice, whose portfolio included peacekeeping operations, questioned using the term "genocide" about Rwanda because it could put the president in an awkward position in midterm elections. Years later, she told Samantha Power, then writing for *The Atlantic,* "I swore to myself that if I ever faced such a crisis again, I would come down on the side of dramatic action, going down in flames if that was required."

Power, as it happened, was now on the NSC herself. Seared by her own experience as a journalist in the Balkans, she had written about America's chronic inaction in the face of mass killings, from the Armenian genocide and the Holocaust to Cambodia and Srebrenica. Speaking up from the backbench in the Situation Room, Power articulated the most fervent, unwavering voice in favor of intervention. The United States, she argued, had a moral obligation to protect the 630,000 people of Benghazi, who faced imminent extermination by Qaddafi's forces. Power was essentially invoking the "Responsibility to Protect," a foreign policy principle that calls on countries to intervene to prevent genocide and other mass atrocities. Known by its sterile acronym R2P, the concept has its roots in the weak responses to Rwanda and the Balkans. It was adopted at a United Nations summit in 2005 and has been widely endorsed, including by the United States, but remains the subject of scorn from some on the right, who view it as a threat to American sovereignty.

At first, Obama bristled at the lecture. "This isn't an opportunity for you to write a new chapter of your book," he snapped at Power, according to people who were in the room. But her arguments stuck with him. In laying out his case for joining the NATO campaign, the president came as close as he ever had to embracing R2P. "To brush aside America's responsibility as a leader, and more profoundly, our responsibilities to our fellow human beings under such circumstances would have been a betrayal of who we are," Obama said in a speech to the nation on March 28, 2011, from the National Defense University in Washington. "Some nations may be able to turn a blind eye to atrocities in other countries. The United States of America is different."

It was the first, and last, time that R2P would find a receptive audience with Barack Obama.

Some news accounts painted the Libya debate as an archetypal gender battle, pitting Power, Rice, and Clinton—the three Valkyries, in the phrase popularized by Maureen Dowd—against a roomful of reluctant men: Obama, Biden, Gates, Mullen, Daley, Brennan, and Donilon. (Gayle Smith, an NSC development official who also favored military action, joked to colleagues that their group should be named vagina.com.) Clinton doesn't play up the gender divide in her book beyond a line noting that Power and Rice both favored intervention. One explanation is it wasn't quite that clean a divide: Ben Rhodes argued for military action, as did Tony Blinken, then serving as national security adviser to Biden.

A more likely explanation is that the Three Amigas made for a strained sisterhood. Power and Rice both had chilly relations with Clinton dating from 2008, when they spurned her for Team Obama. Power, in the heat of the campaign, fatefully referred to Hillary as a monster. "I have regretted it pretty much every day since," she told NBC News in 2013, having put herself through an act of contrition that included a Holbrooke-brokered meeting with Clinton in which Power begged forgiveness. (She and Clinton became civil, if not chummy.) With Rice, who has scratchy relationships with friends as well as foes, there was no single rupture. She and Clinton met regularly at the State Department, where Rice kept an office and worked most Fridays so she could see more of her family in Washington. But Clinton's view, a former White House official said, was that Rice "works for them, not for me."

Clinton arrived at her recommendation for military action later than either Power or Rice, and then only after she had determined that the building blocks for an effective intervention were in place. To Jim Steinberg, Clinton's deputy, that made her an influential voice in turning the debate, not merely a third of a female triumvirate calling on Obama to act. "She opposed ineffective demonstrative action, like stand-alone no-fly zones, because they wouldn't achieve the objective," Steinberg said. "But she was prepared to act if there was a comprehensive strategy that could achieve the result."

The girls versus guys narrative paints Obama as a curiously passive figure, buffeted by the clamor of voices around him. There's no question he was reluctant to act until the end of the debate, and without Clinton's strong push, probably wouldn't have. That said, he leaned forward on Libya in a way he had not done on Egypt and would not do on Syria. At an NSC meeting the afternoon of March 15, 2011, the president declared that he was ready to act, but was dissatisfied with his options. He bought Gates's argument that a no-fly zone would not make a difference. But rather than use that as a pretext to avoid military action, he told his war cabinet to reconvene—minus the backbenchers—at nine P.M. that evening, and bring some better ideas.

"Let's make a difference," he told the group.

At the later session, Obama and his aides discussed the growing certainty that Britain and France would seek a UN Security Council resolution authorizing a no-fly zone. They debated abstaining or even vetoing it. But then Obama fastened on the idea of a larger operation, in which NATO warplanes would bomb Qaddafi's tanks and trucks to halt his advance on Benghazi, once American missiles had taken out Libya's air-defense system. The no-fly zone would, in effect, become a no-drive zone. He ordered Susan Rice to obtain authorization for "all necessary measures" to protect civilians.

While Obama was stiffening his spine, Rice was sparring at the United Nations with the Europeans, who were telling her they would go ahead with or without the United States. Earlier that evening, Rice had called France's ambassador, Gérard Araud, reaching him in his car. "You're not going to drag us into your shitty war," she told him. The equally sharp-tongued Araud replied that France wasn't a "subsidiary of the United States of America, Inc." At eleven P.M., after Obama had decided to back the NATO campaign, she called the Frenchman again to say, "OK, we're a go." Rice was not trying to avoid military action, her former aides insisted, merely a European-style no-fly zone, which the White House feared would be inadequate. Araud's interpretation was that the United States was bowing to the inevitability of European action. Whatever the reality, Rice maneuvered expertly through the Security Council to win a 10–0 vote. Russia abstained, and Vladimir Putin later condemned the air strikes as a medieval crusade by the West.

For the president, it was a risky and uncharacteristic decision, one that would have profound ramifications for his presidency, for the future of America in the Middle East, and for America's relations with Russia. The broader Security Council authority turned the NATO operation from a quick-strike humanitarian mission into a prolonged military campaign, exactly the kind of entanglement Obama had run against in 2008 and tried to avoid in the White House. The alliance's bombing raids continued for seven months, ending only with the killing of Colonel Qaddafi on October 20, 2011, after rebel soldiers flushed him out of a drainage pipe near his family home of Sirte.

Obama's hard line on Libya is often overlooked because he coupled it with clear restrictions. First, the United States would not deploy any ground troops—"boots on the ground," in the military parlance that has become a Sunday talk show cliché. Second, the United States would leave the bulk of the combat to the Europeans. It would provide what Obama called "unique capabilities on the front end"—destroying the regime's air defenses, jamming its communications, gathering intelligence—but French and British planes would rain the fire on Qaddafi's convoys. The goal, in Denis McDonough's phrase, was to "cabin" America's involvement.

This outsourcing of the mission was turned into a devastating bumper sticker when an unnamed senior administration official told Ryan Lizza of *The New Yorker* in May 2011 that Obama was "leading from behind." The White House chafed at the suggestion of weakness, and with some reason, given that it had committed eleven vessels, including guided-missile destroyers and nuclear attack submarines, and dozens of aircraft, from B-2 bombers to F-16 fighters. What was less understood at the time was that the president was drawing bright lines, not just to manage the expectations of America's gung ho allies but to rein in his own wartime bureaucracy.

In the linoleum-lined hallways of the Pentagon, the State Department, and USAID, midlevel officials rubbed their hands together gleefully at news of the NATO operation. After watching Iraq and Afghanistan slip away, Libya presented one more chance to get nation-building right. Without the limits Obama imposed, the government's muscle memory would have kicked in, and its interventionist machinery would have begun grinding. " 'No boots on the ground' was there to prevent the U.S. government from doing what it would normally do," said Jeremy Shapiro, a former State Department official who worked on Libya and Syria, referring to the inevitable influx of experts from USAID, the Treasury Department, and other agencies who would follow the troops into the country. "And it was still a constant struggle."

Even with these limits, the rapid growth of the mission was striking. By the end of March, less than two weeks after the operation began, the United States had launched nearly 200 Tomahawk cruise missiles, flown 370 attack missions, and dropped 455 precision-guided munitions. It was intercepting Libyan radio transmissions and conducting a full-blown psyops campaign, broadcasting messages in Arabic and English that encouraged Libyan soldiers to turn against Qaddafi and abandon their posts.

In his speech at the National Defense University, Obama said he had decided to act only because he thought the United States had a "unique ability" to avert a slaughter. The goals of the mission were to protect the Libyan people from "immediate danger" and to establish a no-fly zone. "Broadening our military mission to include regime change would be a mistake," Obama said. "If we tried to overthrow Qaddafi by force, our coalition would splinter. We would likely have to put U.S. troops on the ground to accomplish that mission, or risk killing many civilians from the air. The dangers faced by our men and women in uniform would be far greater. So would the costs and our share of the responsibility for what comes next."

Those last words would prove prophetic, nowhere more than in the ashes of Benghazi.

# Eight

## Post-Q

"Did we survive the day?" Hillary Clinton emailed Jake Sullivan shortly after 8 P.M., as if writing from an underground bunker.

"Survive, yes," he replied, five minutes later.

It was October 10, 2012, one day shy of a month since Chris Stevens and three other Americans had been killed in a fiery assault on the American diplomatic outpost in Benghazi. A House committee had just finished grilling two senior State Department officials and two former security officers in Libya about the state of security at the compound on the day of the attack. The lawmakers wanted to put Clinton herself in the dock. She was the first secretary of state since Cyrus Vance in 1979 to have an ambassador murdered in the line of duty. The murky circumstances of the attack, and the administration's shifting accounts of it afterward, fueled a cycle of hostile questions that led right to the doorstep of her seventh-floor office.

So intense was the flak that it all but obscured the events of September 11, 2012. The first phase of the attack—the one that killed Stevens and Sean Smith, a thirty-four-year-old State Department information management officer—lasted barely forty minutes. At 9:42 P.M., a gunman tapped his AK-47 on the window of a guard post and ordered the Libyan contractor inside to open the gate. Within seconds, dozens of men in fatigues and balaclavas swarmed into the compound. They were followed by Mitsubishi SUVs and

Toyota pickup trucks mounted with machine guns and flying the black flags of jihad. Volleys of gunfire and the explosion of hand grenades alerted the small contingent of diplomatic security agents that they were under attack. The Libyan militia members hired to defend them scattered into the darkness.

Stevens had retired to his room for the night; Smith was playing Eve, a popular online role-playing game. As the attackers sprinted toward the main residence, the agent guarding the two men rushed them into a safe haven at the rear of the building. A mesh steel door separated them from the attackers, who rampaged through the villa, overturning furniture and smashing computers and TV sets. The intruders tried unsuccessfully to break into the safe haven, poking their guns through holes in the mesh. The Americans were cut off from reinforcements; the other agents couldn't reach the residence because of the gunfire. Soon, the attackers were hauling jerry cans filled with diesel fuel from a nearby barracks, which they used to set the building alight. As black smoke and acrid fumes filled the rooms, Stevens, Smith, and the agent crouched on the floor, gasping for breath. The agent managed to clamber through a window, but Stevens and Smith were not behind him. Again and again, he went back into the heat and the darkness to look for them; they were dead of smoke inhalation inside.

The five remaining guards, badly outgunned, couldn't hold the compound. They piled into an armored vehicle and careened through the gate, under heavy fire, to a small CIA annex a mile away. It was no sanctuary: the militants soon began pounding the building with gunfire and RPG rounds; the Americans desperately returned fire. At about 5 A.M., a seven-person emergency response team from the embassy in Tripoli arrived to join the fight. But minutes later, a mortar landed on the roof, killing Glen Doherty and Tyrone Woods, both former Navy SEALs, and badly wounding another security agent. By 6:30, the situation was verging on hopeless, so the Americans decided to evacuate. They fled to the airport, under the escort of friendlier Libyan militias, where they boarded a chartered plane for Tripoli.

"Two of our officers were killed in Benghazi by an Al Queda–like [*sic*] group," Clinton emailed her daughter at 11:12 that night, using Chelsea's email pseudonym, Diane Reynolds. "The Ambassador, whom I handpicked and a young communications officer on temporary duty w a wife and two young children. Very hard day and I fear more of the same tomorrow."

Clinton was right to fear more hard days, though perhaps not for reasons she could have imagined in those first harrowing hours.

The questions about security—who knew how dangerous the situation was in Benghazi and when did they know it—began immediately. By the time of the House hearing on October 10, Republicans were at an angry boil. They seized on the fact that the State Department had rejected a request from the embassy in Tripoli to extend the deployment of sixteen American soldiers guarding the post. "What would it have took to give the guys on the ground who've been there for months, where you haven't been—what would it have took to get the additional security personnel?" asked Representative Jim Jordan of Ohio. It was part of a pattern of inexcusable security lapses by Clinton's department, Jordan and other lawmakers said, covered up by a secretary of state desperate to save her political skin and a White House, in the final weeks before an election, that had misled the American people about the nature of the attack.

To say that Benghazi was politicized doesn't begin to capture the torch-and-pitchfork atmosphere in the room that day. The Republicans were led by Darrell Issa, a showy California businessman who made a fortune selling car alarms and had risen to be chairman of the powerful House Committee on Oversight and Government Reform. With Obama facing voters in twenty-seven days, Benghazi was Issa's best chance to put a Democratic administration under a harsh magnifying glass. He and his GOP colleagues badgered and interrupted the State Department witnesses, so much so that after the hearing, the ranking diplomat—Patrick Kennedy, the undersecretary for management—called in reporters to make sure they heard his much-disputed assertion: The State Department had not neglected the security in Benghazi.

"Pat helped level set things tonight," Sullivan emailed Clinton that evening. "We'll see where we are in the morning."

Things did not get better the next morning.

Benghazi shadowed Hillary Clinton's 2016 campaign just as it had shadowed Barack Obama's 2012 reelection campaign, but the threat it posed to her was more ominous and lasting. For Obama, the attack called into question his counterterrorism credentials, specifically his claim that the United States had largely dismantled Osama bin Laden's terror network. The White House's slowness to acknowledge that Benghazi was a terrorist attack, critics said, revealed a president who did not want to admit, on the eve of an election, that al-Qaeda was alive and well. Once Obama was re-elected, however, the critics mostly turned their sights elsewhere.

For Clinton, the attack was the basis for a broader indictment of her character. It began with the accusations that she rejected requests for more guards in the weeks leading up to the attack. It escalated with questions about her statements in the aftermath of the incident. She, too, did not initially characterize it as terrorism and cited anti-American demonstrations elsewhere in the Middle East—propagating the narrative, her critics said, that Benghazi was merely a protest gone awry. The questions flared up again in March 2015 with the disclosure—as a result of a congressional investigation into the attack—that she had used a private account for her email while secretary of state. And it culminated in another contentious House hearing three years after the first one, with the same Republican lawmaker, Jim Jordan, brandishing Clinton's email to her daughter as proof that she was telling her family a different story than she was telling the public.

By then, the dispute had little to do with who was responsible for the tragic events of that night in Libya. With the facts of the case picked over in seven congressional investigations, thirty-two hearings, and eleven government reports, Benghazi was instead used as shorthand for a pattern of unscrupulous behavior by Clinton. It had become a right-wing talisman, much as Whitewater and Vince Foster had been in the 1990s.

Clinton's reflexive defensiveness didn't help. It stoked the suspicions of her critics, tested the loyalty of her defenders, and gave oxygen to the story. Nor did it help that one of her regular sources of intelligence on Libya turned out to be her confidant Sidney Blumenthal, who had no expertise in the country and whom the White House had denied a job at the State Department. He sent "H" dozens of emails with analysis and gossip about Libya, some of it cogent, some of it cockeyed (a plot by Britain and France, for instance, to split off the eastern part of Libya from the rest of the country). The intel in Blumenthal's emails came from Tyler Drumheller, an ex-CIA officer seeking to do business with the transitional government there. A controversial figure at the agency, Drumheller had served as chief of clandestine operations in Europe from 2001 to 2005, and got to know Blumenthal during the Bush administration, when he publicly criticized George W. Bush for mishandling intelligence to justify the invasion of Iraq.

A colorful former spook with a history of attacking a Republican president; a conspiracy-minded journalist-turned-Clinton-defender; a stream of emails to Hillary that read like outtakes from a bad spy novel. For the driven band of partisans employed by the Benghazi-Industrial Complex, as *Politico* once dubbed the scandal, it was like uncovering a rich new vein of ore in a depleted mine.

These details emerged, as they typically do in investigations involving the Clintons, slowly and only under unrelenting pressure. My colleague Michael Schmidt, who broke the story of the private email account in *The New York Times,* followed the forensic trail. In the summer of 2014, the State Department was gathering documents related to Benghazi to provide to a House select committee— yet another one—looking into the tragedy. Lawyers noticed that Clinton's emails came from a personal, not a government, account.

That raised questions about whether the State Department had access to all the documents it needed to complete its investigation. So the department began negotiating with Clinton's lawyers to hand over her emails. In December, Clinton's staff delivered dozens of boxes containing some 50,000 pages of emails to Foggy Bottom. Two months later, the State Department handed over about 900 pages related to Benghazi to the select committee.

Benghazi turned up another startling revelation about Clinton's email practices. Not only did she use a private address—clintonemail.com—she routed all her traffic through a server kept at the family home in Chappaqua, New York. After delivering roughly half of the emails to the State Department, her campaign said she had the server wiped clean. Clinton claimed she handed over all the emails (30,490) that were relevant to her work as secretary of state; she said the other 31,830 were personal—those related to her yoga routines or the flower arrangements at Chelsea's wedding. The decision about what to turn over, however, was made by Clinton's lawyers, not by State Department officials or government watchdogs. That raised questions about whether she had tried to get rid of damaging or even merely unflattering emails. Under intense pressure, Clinton later turned the server over to the FBI, which opened its own investigation into the security of her email arrangement and discovered the server hadn't been wiped clean after all.

Clinton's first attempt to calm the storm came in a hastily called news conference after a gender-equality conference at the United Nations on March 10, 2015. It was one of the most misbegotten exercises in damage control in the annals of American politics. Behind Clinton's right shoulder hung a tapestry reproduction of the *Guernica,* Picasso's antiwar masterpiece, with its images of a horse gored by a spear and a soldier lying dismembered on the ground. In front of her, across a rope line, stood a slavering press corps that had been kept waiting for hours. It wasn't clear which was more terrifying. "When I got to work as secretary of state," Clinton told the reporters, "I opted for convenience to use my personal email account, which was allowed by the State Department, because I thought it would be easier to carry just one device for my work and for my personal emails instead of two.

"Looking back," she admitted, "it would've been better if I'd simply used a second email account and carried a second phone, but at the time, this didn't seem like an issue."

Her explanation satisfied no one. Why couldn't she put personal and official email accounts on a single device, the reporters asked? If it was too cumbersome to do that with a 2009-vintage Black-Berry, why couldn't she have entrusted multiple smartphones to her personal aide, Huma Abedin, who carried lots of other things for the secretary? Why did she wait nearly two years after leaving to turn over her emails? Did she send or receive any classified communications? Was her email secure from hackers?

Other things didn't add up: A month earlier, Clinton had told a technology conference in Silicon Valley that she used a BlackBerry, an iPhone, and two generations of iPads. "I don't throw anything away," she joked. "I'm like two steps short of a hoarder." It's plausible to argue she would not have been so technologically ambidextrous in 2011, except that in August of that year, she sent an email to Blumenthal from her iPad, explaining that Hurricane Irene had left her without BlackBerry coverage. At the United Nations, she said her deleted emails included "personal communications from my husband and me." But Bill Clinton, his spokesman said, had "sent two emails in his life."

The press conference was a tense, chilly encounter that dredged up all the psychological baggage of Clinton's twenty-five-year relationship with the news media: their palpable suspicion of her; her ill-concealed dislike of them. ("Look, she hates you. Period. That's never going to change," an unnamed Clinton campaign veteran once told *Politico*.) For reporters who had covered Clinton at the State Department, it was as if the last six years had never happened. That had been a halcyon period when she struck an entente cordiale with the press. No longer was Clinton the above-the-fray secretary of state who could conduct a ninety-minute farewell interview with the diplomatic press corps and not get a single question about her political future. ("That's because you're such good journalists," she purred, when one of the reporters pointed it out. "You wouldn't get an answer anyway.") Now she was facing a political press pack that cared little about her diplomatic accomplishments and promised to be unrelenting in its pursuit of issues such as the email flap, which reinforced the narrative that the Clintons mock transparency and play by their own rules.

Nobody asked her about Benghazi that day. Why would they? As with Whitewater, where a penny-ante real estate deal led to Monica and the blue dress, it was beside the point. By that time, Benghazi had already been through a few cycles in the scandal machine: The security questions had given way to a tempest over the talking points that the CIA compiled to explain the attack, which suggested it grew out of a spontaneous protest against a YouTube video demeaning the Prophet Muhammad. The White House had been forced to retract that account when a later investigation determined there was no protest outside the compound that night. Susan Rice's use of the erroneous talking points on five Sunday morning talk shows the weekend after the attack dashed her dreams of replacing Clinton as secretary of state. (Never mind that David Kirkpatrick of *The New York Times* concluded, after an exhaustive on-the-ground investigation, that the attack had, in fact, been "fueled in large part by anger at an American-made video denigrating Islam.")

To Hillary's defenders, Benghazi was the latest example of a generation-long conspiracy to discredit the Clintons. To her critics, it was the latest in a litany of scandals that raised profound questions about her trustworthiness and fitness for high office. To others, who recalled the nonpartisan investigations of 9/11 or the 1983 embassy bombing in Beirut, it was a sad symptom of the corrosion of American political discourse: the murder of an idealistic diplomat and his brave compatriots exploited for partisan gain.

To some, it was all three.

It all reached a kind of absurd climax when the House Select

Committee on Benghazi interrogated Clinton in October 2015. The eleven-hour ordeal shed no new light on the attacks, serving mainly as a reminder that Clinton had the fortitude of a battleship. But the hearing irreparably discredited her Republican tormentors, led by their chairman, Trey Gowdy. The ranking Democrat, Representative Elijah Cummings of Maryland, captured the Grand Guignol nature of the spectacle. "I don't know what we want from you," he said to a bruised but unbloodied Clinton. "Do we want to badger you over and over again until you get tired and so we do get the gotcha moment?"

Yet Cummings, in his zeal to defend Clinton, didn't confront the real scandal of Benghazi, either. It wasn't about talking points or emails or Sid Blumenthal; it was about why the intervention had left Libya in such shambles. The unending partisanship short-circuited a much-needed debate over the lessons of Libya. At issue was not just the conduct of Clinton and her State Department; the president and his entire war cabinet were involved. At issue was not just whether the United States properly protected its diplomats in a dangerous country, but also whether it had adequately planned for a peaceful postconflict society. Libya raised the most basic questions about the limits of liberal interventionism in the age of Obama.

The paramount issue, in other words, was not what Clinton did or didn't do in the days after Benghazi; it was what she and Obama did or didn't do in the weeks and months after the president, at the urging of his secretary of state, fired Tomahawks into Tripoli.

On a leaden, chilly morning in May 2014, Barack Obama helicoptered to a windswept bluff above the Hudson River for the commencement exercises at West Point. The commander in chief told the 1,064 cadet graduates of the U.S. Military Academy that the nation they were being called to serve would avoid military misadventures abroad, even as it confronted terrorist threats from the Middle East to Africa. "We have to develop a strategy that matches this diffuse threat," he declared. "We need partners to fight terrorists alongside us." Rather than sending American soldiers to the world's hot spots, he said, the United States would train local troops to fight al-Qaeda in Yemen, support a multinational peacekeeping force in Somalia, and work with Europe to stand up a security force and border patrol in Libya.

It was Obama's only reference to Libya in the speech, even though that had been the major military intervention of his presidency. But then again, nobody wanted to talk about Libya in those days. Overshadowed by the charnel house that Syria had become, it languished in the shadows. The transatlantic project to build a Libyan security force never got off the ground. The same was true of the soldiers who were supposed to be trained to patrol its borders. Libya became a magnet for jihadi fighters who traveled there freely from around the region; soon, it had its own Islamic State franchise.

It's no exaggeration to say Libya has descended into a state of *Mad Max*–like anarchy. Rival militias—some affiliated with ISIS or al-Qaeda; others merely bloodthirsty—fight over its major cities. Awash in weapons, divided between east and west, and bereft of functioning state institutions, Libya is a seedbed for militancy that has spread west and south across Africa. It has become the most important Islamic State stronghold outside Syria and Iraq, drawing fighters from as far away as Senegal and forcing the United States to send warplanes back to the country in the winter of 2016 to strike their training camps. It supplies jihadi fighters to ISIS and Jabhat al-Nusra in Syria. It sends waves of desperate migrants across the Mediterranean, where they drown in capsized vessels within sight of Europe. It stands as a tragic rebuke to the well-intentioned activists in Paris and Washington.

It would be preposterous to blame this state of affairs entirely on Clinton or Obama. Nicolas Sarkozy, David Cameron, and other leaders of the gung ho European contingent deserve a share of the blame, as do the Libyans themselves. Mahmoud Jibril and his countrymen pleaded for the world's help and money but stubbornly rejected outside peacekeepers, which could have given their country the space to develop new institutions and blunted the rise of the militias. The same Arab countries that backed the NATO intervention are now funneling weapons and money to rival militia groups, turning Libya into a lethal proxy war like the one raging in Syria.

Still, there was a basic contradiction at the heart of Obama's decision to intervene that contributed to this unraveling. His focus on a front-end solution—consciously trying to avoid the nation-building missteps of George W. Bush—foreclosed any meaningful American role in the postwar stabilization or reconstruction of Libya. There would be no peacekeepers, trainers, or advisers. That distinguished Libya from Iraq and Afghanistan, but also from Bosnia, Kosovo, and virtually every other American intervention since World War II. The absence of boots on the ground deprived the United States of leverage in dealing with Libya's new leaders. While these leaders squabbled among themselves in Tripoli, the radical jihadi groups helped themselves to assault rifles and machine guns from Colonel Qaddafi's ransacked armories. As in Iraq half a decade earlier, the lack of security proved to be Libya's undoing: The militias poured in to fill the vacuum left by Qaddafi. What had been hailed by many as a "model intervention" turned out to be a blueprint for chaos.

"Those of us who felt we had to intervene had to be more decisive in terms of what we would do the day after," Dennis Ross said. "Obama was reluctant to get sucked in, but we should have explained more strongly to him why we needed to go in with a peace-keeping force. What we did in Libya is the equivalent of what Bush and Rumsfeld did in Iraq. We replaced the government. If you create a vacuum, you have to fill it, or bad forces will fill it."

Obama had every reason to worry about mission creep in Libya. What began as a humanitarian intervention with a specific, limited objective—averting a slaughter of civilians in Benghazi—soon became a grinding, months-long campaign to uproot Qaddafi's troops from all the cities they occupied. On April 14, 2011, less than a month after the air strikes started, Clinton and other foreign ministers hammered out a communiqué in Berlin, in which NATO declared that Qaddafi's departure was a political objective. A month earlier, Obama had ruled out regime change as a goal of the mission; now it was the alliance's formal writ. "We got caught in a strategic tautology," said Derek Chollet, who as the director of strategic planning at the NSC chaired a task force on "post-Q" planning. "Civilian protection never stopped being the mission. But Qaddafi wasn't relenting, and the civilians couldn't be protected as long as Qaddafi was in power."

Having catalyzed the debate over military action in the Situation Room, Clinton now took charge of the efforts to keep the balky NATO coalition together and lay the groundwork for the "post-Q" era. It was not easy work: The French and the Turks bitterly disagreed on the scope of the combat mission; the rebels, beset by tribal feuds and rivalries, offered a rotating cast of leaders. With their military campaign against Qaddafi bogging down, they implored the United States to supply them with heavier weapons. That prospect rattled nerves in the White House: Joe Biden and other senior officials worried that American guns could end up in the hands of radical Islamist groups or be used to inflict atrocities on civilians (prefiguring arguments that they would make against arming the rebels in Syria more than a year later).

Clinton, however, was open to it, provided the United States could keep the gun-running operation at arm's length. On April 8, 2011, she forwarded an email from Sidney Blumenthal to Jake Sullivan that raised the potential for a stalemate between Qaddafi's force and the rebels. "The idea of using private security experts to arm the opposition should be considered," Clinton noted. She may have been influenced by her husband. A few days earlier, Bill Clinton told ABC News he would be open to funneling weapons to the rebels. "I sure wouldn't shut the door to it," he said.

As spring gave way to summer and the fighting dragged on, Hillary began making an aggressive case internally. Part of her argument, former officials said, was that Qatar and the United Arab Emirates were actively arming extremist rebel groups in Libya. Unless the United States reinforced the more moderate and secular elements, it would cede influence in shaping the country's future, after Qaddafi was finally gone. "Her view was 'We've got to think about not just how we change the balance of power on the ground now, but the balance of power in the future,'" Ross recalled.

Clinton won the debate. Sometime that summer, the president signed a secret order authorizing the transfer of weapons, including Humvees, counter-battery radar, and antitank missiles, to select rebel militias. The program was modest, but it established Clinton's instinct for putting American skin in the game—a position she would take again in the summer of 2012 during the far more protracted debate over arming the Syrian opposition. Within weeks, the Libyan rebels began to turn against Qaddafi's army.

It's hard to remember, given how bad things later became, that the "post-Q" era began with promise. Despite the initial complications in the military operation, Libya was a success story for much of 2011 and even into 2012—one that bore Clinton's stamp every step of the way.

To rally political and financial support for Libya, she helped create a Contact Group, which grew to thirty-eight countries and met monthly in London, Rome, Abu Dhabi, and other diplomatic watering holes. Rarely did a country in the throes of violent change have so many people rooting for it. Partly it was a reaction to Qaddafi's brutish forty-two-year rule. But Libya also had a lot to recommend it: a manageable population of 6.6 million, concentrated near the Mediterranean coast; rich natural resources; and no religious or ethnic splits of the kind that sundered Iraq and Syria. In July 2011, Clinton freed up additional money for Libya by helping settle a debate in the administration about when the United States should recognize the rebels, who had created a National Transitional Council, as Libya's legitimate government.

That same month, Clinton sent a delegation to meet secretly in Tunisia with representatives of Qaddafi to try to work out his departure. Derek Chollet was one of the three emissaries at that meeting, held on July 16 in the splendor of the American ambassador's seaside residence in Tunis. (The other two were Gene Cretz, Chris Stevens's predecessor as ambassador to Libya, and Jeff Feltman, an unflappable diplomat then serving as assistant secretary of state for Near Eastern affairs.) The Americans delivered a blunt message: "This is your chance. Don't question our resolve. Don't think that this is going to end any way other than Qaddafi leaving power." Qaddafi's emissaries were distraught. For nearly four hours, they lamented how the United States had turned on them and complained that the rebels were actually terrorists linked to al-Qaeda. It was clear they were psychologically incapable of contemplating the departure of the man they called "the Brother Leader."

Five weeks later, the rebels did it for them. Advancing from their base in the Berber highlands with a speed that stunned everybody, they seized an oil refinery ninety minutes west of Tripoli on Monday, August 15, 2011. NATO warplanes smoothed the way for them, bombing tanks and artillery batteries on the road to the capital. By nightfall on Saturday, the rebels were clashing with regime forces throughout Tripoli; defections from the regime's ranks swelled. By the following Tuesday, they had overrun Qaddafi's compound and driven him into hiding. War planners at NATO and in the Pentagon had expected a bloody siege for Tripoli, lasting perhaps six months. Qaddafi folded in less than thirty-six hours.

It was a heady moment for Clinton, who had been one of the loudest voices for regime change, and her lieutenants wanted to make sure she got full credit for it. On August 21, at the request of Cheryl Mills, Jake Sullivan sent an email to her and the State Department spokeswoman, Toria Nuland, listing Clinton's accomplishments on Libya, going back to February. It showcased her "leadership/ownership/stewardship of this country's Libya policy from start to finish," Sullivan wrote. The next day, Sid Blumenthal chimed in. His email, titled "Your statement post-Q," advised her on how to reap maximum political dividends from the rebel advances. "First, brava!" he wrote. "This is a historic moment and you will be credited for realizing it." When Qaddafi was finally removed from the scene—which didn't happen for another two months, and in bloody fashion—he urged her to make a statement, "wherever you are, even in the driveway of your vacation house. You must go on camera. You must establish yourself in the historic record at this moment." There was a clear White House versus State Department subtext: Blumenthal told Clinton to be wary of attempts by "junior types on the NSC" to claim Qaddafi's fall vindicated the "flamingly stupid 'leading from behind' phrase." Her record on Libya refuted that concept and could remove it as an "albatross" for the president in the coming election. The key was to explain "that the US had a clear strategy from the start, stuck with it and has succeeded."

Clinton was intrigued. But she worried in an email to Sullivan that if she waited for Qaddafi's demise, she might miss her chance. He replied that her staff was already drafting an op-ed article, under her byline, that would summarize her role in the Libya intervention. Sullivan was thinking big: "It makes sense to lay down something definitive—almost like the Clinton Doctrine," he wrote. Bill Clinton did not, like Ronald Reagan or George W. Bush, have a clearly articulated foreign policy doctrine. But in February 1999, near the end of his presidency, he laid out an argument for humanitarian intervention in the Balkans that anticipated Obama's case for limited action in Libya. "We cannot, indeed, we should not, do everything or be everywhere," Clinton declared. But "where our values and our interests are at stake, and where we can make a difference, we must be prepared to do so."

Obama was on vacation in Martha's Vineyard the day Tripoli fell, and he did go on camera to speak about it. "Your courage and character have been unbreakable in the face of a tyrant," he said to the rebels, urging them to pursue a peaceful transition to democracy. "True justice will not come from reprisals and violence. It will come from reconciliation and a Libya that allows its citizens to determine their own destiny.

"In that effort," the president went on, "the United States will be a friend and a partner."

Obama's tone was noticeably more subdued than that of Clinton and her aides, and it spoke to the differences between them. He'd only reluctantly gotten involved in Libya, and he was more skeptical than Clinton of the power of the West to shape events there. In general, he kept a distance from the Libyan conflict. Right after his brief remarks that day, Obama went back to his vacation, playing basketball with his aides; David Cameron canceled his holiday to return to meetings in London. He and Sarkozy would make a joint visit to Tripoli the following month. On September 1, 2011, more than fifty world leaders convened in Paris for a Friends of Libya meeting; Obama sent Clinton in his place. Taking her seat at a long table in the Élysée Palace, she was one of the only non–heads of state. "I remember thinking, 'Thank God we have Hillary Clinton as secretary of state,'" said Chollet, who went with her.

While Clinton's aides mused about making Libya a plank in an emerging Hillary Clinton Doctrine, Obama put it in the context of his counterterrorism successes. When Qaddafi finally was killed in October, the president explicitly linked it to the commando raid that killed Osama bin Laden five months earlier, as well as to the deaths of other al-Qaeda leaders. It showed America's muscle in confronting tyrants and terrorists, but a very different kind than that exercised by George W. Bush. "Without putting a single U.S. service member on the ground," he said in the Rose Garden, "we achieved our objectives, and our NATO mission will soon come to an end. We've demonstrated what collective action can achieve in the twenty-first century."

Even Obama's critics were unstinting in their praise. "The administration deserves great credit," John McCain said on CNN. "Obviously, I had different ideas on the tactical side, but the world is a better place." David Rothkopf, a foreign policy analyst often critical of the administration, told me on the day of Qaddafi's death, "It's time to set aside the snide interpretations of 'leading from behind,' and simply call it leading. This was the kind of multilateral, affordable, effective endeavor that any foreign policy initiative aspires to."

The swiftness of Tripoli's fall, however, carried with it the seeds of future problems. It threw postconflict planning in Washington, such as it was, into disarray; the planners had been expecting a more prolonged battle for the capital. It also emboldened the rebels to reject suggestions of a multinational peacekeeping force, because Tripoli was comparatively peaceful in those early days. That suited Obama fine: He had been dealing with enough Libya-related headaches, not least a nasty tussle with lawmakers in Congress over whether he should have sought their authorization for military action.

Amid all the uncertainty about what a post-Q Libya would look like and what role the United States would play in it, one thing was clear: the president did not want "CPA, Take Two"—the sprawling Coalition Provisional Authority set up by the Bush administration in post-Saddam Iraq. Given the backseat that the United States had taken in the NATO operation, there was little risk of that. With a decade of nation-building behind it, the United States could easily have sent SWAT teams of Treasury officials to help Libya rebuild its financial system, or USAID specialists to advise on public works projects. But with no equivalent of Camp Victory, the colossal military base outside Baghdad, there was nowhere to house them safely. The size of the American footprint in Libya, officials liked to say, correlated to the number of beds the American embassy kept for visitors in its compound in Tripoli. Which is to say: minuscule.

When Clinton visited Tripoli in October 2011, two days before Qaddafi's death, she got a taste of the anarchic Libya to come. She was greeted at the steps to her C-17 military plane by fighters of the Zintan militia. Bearded and armed to the teeth, they controlled the airport. A rival militia, from Misrata, controlled large parts of the city. "My security detail was as nervous as I had ever seen them," she wrote later. "I took a deep breath and started to walk down the stairs." Unlike the fighters who attacked the American compound in Benghazi eleven months later, these men were friendly. They chanted "USA!" and posed for pictures with Clinton, making the "V for victory" salute. At the time, the images seemed a validation of Clinton's risk taking in Libya. Years later, they could have provided the raw material for a political attack ad.

It was in this inchoate atmosphere that Clinton was digesting emails from Sid Blumenthal. To people in the clubby, small-circle world of Barack Obama, the notion of a secretary of state maintaining a running correspondence with an old friend on a topic like Libya was bizarre. Obama read widely, usually at night in his private study, and he had foreign policy experts in for lunch occasionally. But he kept his own counsel, especially on matters of national security. In Hillary's world, however, the peanut gallery has its place. Clinton insisted Blumenthal was one source in a vast stream of information she received every day. And yet the sheer volume of emails, plus the fact that they went directly to her, suggested his voice must have carried weight.

"He's been a friend of mine for a long time," Clinton told reporters in Cedar Falls, Iowa, in May 2015. "He sent me unsolicited emails which I passed on in some instances, and I see that that's just part of the give and take. When you're in the public eye, when you're in an official position, I think you do have to work to make sure you're not caught in a bubble, and you only hear from a certain small group of people."

Nobody could accuse Blumenthal of being blinkered by politics. On March 26, 2011, a week after the NATO bombardment began, the man credited with propagating the notion of a "vast right-wing conspiracy" during the Clinton administration, emailed Hillary with a suggestion to use the "Shock & Awe" strategy that George W. Bush employed in Iraq, in Libya. It was "a possibly counterintuitive notion and option," he granted, but the morale and cohesion of Qaddafi's troops "might be conclusively shattered by another round or two of ferocious bombing targeting concentrations of his military assets. This might just be the ideal moment for it."

At times, Blumenthal's emails, channeling Tyler Drumheller, contained pertinent information. On April 8, 2011, he drew attention to the threat of radical Islamists, which was then of concern mostly to Egypt. "Traditionally, the eastern part of Libya has been a stronghold for radical Islamist groups," the email said. "While Qaddafi's regime has been successful in suppressing the jihadist threat in Libya, the current situation opens the door for jihadist resurgence." Other times, the intelligence was just sketchy. In March 2012, he passed along a report that France and Britain were colluding secretly with tribal contacts in eastern Libya to convince them to split from Libya and create a semiautonomous region in the province of Cyrenaica, home of Benghazi. Citing "extremely knowledgeable sources," he wrote that the French were especially keen on the idea because they felt burned that Libya's new rulers hadn't properly rewarded French firms with contracts after everything France had done for them.

"This strains credulity based on what I know," Clinton replied. "Any other info about it?"

"Will seek more intel," he answered.

That did not stop Clinton from forwarding it to Jake Sullivan.

"What do you think?" she asked.

"I can share around if you like," he replied, "but it seems like a thin conspiracy theory."

Clinton forwarded dozens of Blumenthal emails to Sullivan, for whom, his friends said, they were a groan-inducing addition to the torrent of information that flowed through his BlackBerry every day. (He dismissed one email, purporting to discuss Bashar al-Assad's plans in Syria, as being "reverse-engineered from conventional wisdom.") For Sullivan, as for many younger Clinton aides, Blumenthal was not the feared consigliere he had been in the 1990s; he was more a character in a Clinton-family drama that had long ago gone into reruns. Yet he was still a close friend of the boss, so Sullivan dutifully circulated the most credible ones—discreetly marked from an "HRC friend"—to other senior State officials, such as Jeff Feltman, Gene Cretz, and Chris Stevens, to solicit feedback. Their ginger responses, a mix of raised eyebrows and pulled punches, attested to the quality of their diplomatic training and to the perils of openly questioning Clinton or her kitchen cabinet.

In an email dated April 3, 2012, for example, Blumenthal described jitters in Tripoli that the Muslim Brotherhood was growing popular and could be a major factor in parliamentary elections that July. "Very interesting report," Stevens replied agreeably, and then went on to eviscerate it. He cited an "insightful" Libyan contact who told him he did not believe the Brotherhood would win much support because "they don't have a strong organization and because most Libyans view the LMB as a branch of the Egyptian MB, and Libyans don't want to be ruled by Egypt." To people who knew him, it was vintage Chris Stevens: dignified, with a touch of mischief. Above all, it was informed by his own contacts on the Libyan street.

There is no record during this period of emails or phone calls between Stevens and Clinton. The contrast with Blumenthal was striking, given that Stevens was a Libya expert, her "handpicked" choice, and had been a favorite of hers since she first sent him to Benghazi in April 2011 aboard a Greek cargo ship to establish contact with the rebel leaders. Clinton later told the House Benghazi committee that Stevens had not been disregarded, that he communicated regularly with the State Department officials who were relevant to his assignment. "I was the boss of ambassadors in 270 countries," she said, explaining their lack of contact but understating the importance of Libya at that time. (Clinton had direct contact with ambassadors in other sensitive posts—Chris Hill in Baghdad, for example.)

Had Clinton been in touch with Stevens, she would have found a diplomat who had deep affection for Libya and savored his work there, but was worried about security threats, which began to multiply in the summer of 2012. "Too many militias running around, and some of them are starting to morph into criminal gangs," Stevens emailed a colleague on August 7, after gunmen in Tripoli tried to carjack a vehicle with U.S. diplomatic plates. "We have to be vigilant despite signs of normalization."

On the day after Stevens was killed, Blumenthal was Clinton's constant digital companion. He sent her a stream of emails with analysis and intelligence about the attack, supposedly from inside the Libyan government. Some of what he passed on was accurate: Libyan security officials said the assault was carried out by the Ansar al-Shariah brigade, an Islamist militia group based in East Benghazi; it had been planned for about a month and set in motion after the anger in Egypt over the video denigrating the Prophet Muhammad. But other information was faulty: Libyan officials also said there was a demonstration in front of the compound that numbered about two thousand people; the militants had blended into the crowd before opening fire on the facility. Surveillance video showed no such gathering.

Clinton forwarded the email about Ansar al-Shariah to Sullivan at 11:25 P.M. on Wednesday night.

"We should get this around asap," she wrote.

Blumenthal continued to feed Clinton intelligence about Libya after the Benghazi attack. As the days wore on, however, he began to pay more attention to the political fallout from the attack, which he predicted would be troublesome for the president. On October 1, as Obama entered the final stretch of his reelection campaign, Blumenthal sent Clinton an article from *Salon,* which he took credit for planting. It said Mitt Romney planned to use the Benghazi attack to paint Obama as weak on terrorism in the upcoming presidential debates. "GOP strategists referred to their new operation as the Jimmy Carter Strategy or the October Surprise," the article said. Blumenthal and Clinton could not have missed the irony: The political operative once accused of dishing dirt on Obama was now passing Clinton helpful tidbits to win him a second term. It reflected a recognition on his part that his friend's fortunes were now tied inextricably to Obama's. If the president was defeated, it would complicate Clinton's own path to the White House.

"Thanks. I'm pushing to WH," she replied.

Forwarding it to Sullivan, Clinton wrote, "Be sure Ben knows they need to be ready for this line of attack."

Ben Rhodes, who was responsible for prepping the president on foreign policy issues, didn't need Blumenthal to warn him; the political team was already devising ways for Obama to parry the issue. Sure enough, Benghazi came up as a topic two weeks later, when Romney confronted Obama in the second debate at Hofstra University in New York. "It took the president fourteen days before he called the attack in Benghazi an act of terror," Romney thundered. Actually, Obama did call it an "act of terror," said the moderator, Candy Crowley of CNN, in an awkward interruption; the day after it happened. Romney was flustered. Obama, who was ready for the attack, turned the tables on him: Romney, he said, had crassly politicized Benghazi by issuing a press release that condemned the White House's handling of the attack even before it was clear that Chris Stevens and the others were dead.

By then, however, Benghazi had already been politicized, a failure for which Obama also deserves blame. Clinton's email to her daughter on the night of the attacks, in which she said Stevens had been killed by an "Al Queda–like group," made clear the administration suspected from the start it was terrorism. (Ansar al-Shariah immediately claimed responsibility, then retracted its claim a day later.) But the White House dodged and weaved about what to call the attack, desperate to fend off charges that Benghazi vitiated its claims of dismantling al-Qaeda. Obama's reference to it as an "act of terror," which he made in the Rose Garden with Clinton on September 12, was so fleeting his aides didn't seem to remember he'd said it until weeks later.

Susan Rice's notorious claim—that Benghazi was a protest against the anti-Muhammad video that spiraled out of control—was based on CIA intelligence believed to be accurate at the time.

But her remarks were carefully massaged by other government agencies, including the State Department and the White House, to put as benign a spin as possible on a malignant situation. Among the goals Ben Rhodes set out in an email for Rice's interviews that Sunday: "To underscore that these protests are rooted in an Internet video, and not a broader failure of policy." (Clinton turned down a White House request to do the shows, suggesting she knew a trap when she saw one.)

Unwittingly, Rhodes's email gets at the central question about Benghazi: Did the deadly events of 9/11/2012 reflect a failure in the way Obama and Clinton handled Libya?

Trey Gowdy is much more likable in person than the partisan bully who presided over the Benghazi hearing. In this, he is not unlike Hillary Clinton, the target of his investigation. When we met for breakfast at the Capitol Hill Club, a Republican watering hole hung with portraits of Lincoln and Reagan, Gowdy came across as an unlikely Javert: soft-spoken and charming, with a tangle of gray hair and a day's growth of beard, like that of a man who sleeps in his office—which, in fact, he often does. A former federal prosecutor and district attorney in South Carolina, Gowdy laid out a lawyerly, methodical argument for why a proper investigation of Benghazi needed to take into account American policies toward Libya in the months leading up to the attack.

The House leadership, he said, had empowered him to investigate "all policies, decisions, and activities" that contributed to the attack. The White House, in legal documents filed by the Justice Department, cited anti-Western sentiment as a root cause of it. So what caused that anti-Western sentiment? Did it go back to decisions made at the time of the military intervention? "If I'm being asked," he said, "to figure out what policies led to the attacks, and my own government is telling me it was anti-Western sentiment, then am I not entitled to find out, 'Did that anti-Western sentiment arise twenty-four hours before the attacks? Was it six months before the attacks?'

"A cynic would say, 'How much of that should you have figured out before you did what you did?' " Gowdy continued. "If the goal is to overthrow Qaddafi, OK, then that was your goal. You can check that off. If your goal was to overthrow Qaddafi and leave something more stable in place, more orderly in place, then maybe you didn't accomplish that.

"I don't know what her goal was," he said.

Under the cameras and klieg lights in the Cannon House Office Building, Gowdy didn't put any of those questions to Clinton. Instead, he hectored her over whether she had "solicited" the emails from Sid Blumenthal, and why it took her only four minutes to reply to an email from Huma Abedin about delivering medicine, gasoline, diesel, and milk to the Libyan people, when she didn't respond to months of requests for beefed-up security from her own diplomats. By turning his investigation into a taxpayer-funded fishing expedition to discredit a potential Democratic president, Gowdy squandered perhaps the last chance Congress had to shed light on what the United States could have done differently to prevent Libya from sliding into anarchy.

Among those who advised Obama and Clinton, this is a question that still torments them.

"It drives me crazy when people say, 'It was a good idea to intervene in Libya, but the president should have had a plan,' " said Philip Gordon, who coordinated Middle East policy at the White House. "Well, tell me what the plan to achieve harmony between Libya's disparate factions should have been? We had lots of plans. People worked hard to implement them. The problem was, they didn't work because there was nothing there to build on." The bitter irony was that Obama learned from his two predecessors, Bill Clinton and George W. Bush, and yet still he stumbled. "Libya was an attempt to apply both the lesson of the Balkans—the humanitarian intervention in Srebrenica—and the lesson of Iraq, which is

'Don't go in and try to rebuild a country by coercion,'" Derek Chollet said. "And the end result is Libya today."

There are even questions about Obama's original casus belli: that Qaddafi was about to carry out a genocide in Benghazi. The colonel was mad, to be sure, and had warned that his troops would go house-to-house to "capture the rats." Yet there was nothing in his history to suggest he would kill tens of thousands of people, as Hafez al-Assad of Syria did in crushing the Muslim Brotherhood in the Sunni city of Hama in 1982, or between three thousand and five thousand, as Saddam Hussein did in gassing the Iraqi Kurds in 1988. A more likely scenario, according to some experts on Libya, would have involved rounding up and shooting the rebel leaders—still chilling, but not enough to warrant another American war in the Middle East. Obama, as Alan J. Kuperman, professor of public affairs at the University of Texas, wrote in *Foreign Affairs* magazine, must "accept responsibility for spearheading a disastrous intervention on phony grounds." A high-ranking former administration official involved in the debate told me he shared those doubts; others conceded that in the heat of the moment, the White House was dealing with imperfect information.

Like all counterfactuals, it is impossible to test. With Qaddafi's threats and images of panicked families on the run, it is hard to fault Obama for acting when he did. But having decapitated the country's leadership, he owed it to the Libyan people to do more to clean up the mess. Obama conceded as much, saying Libya weighed on his subsequent thinking about interventions, from Syria to Ukraine. "It's the day after Qaddafi is gone, when everybody is feeling good and everybody is holding up posters saying, 'Thank you, America,'" he told Thomas Friedman of *The New York Times*. "At that moment, there has to be a much more aggressive effort to rebuild societies that didn't have any civic traditions. So that's a lesson that I now apply every time I ask the question, 'Should we intervene, militarily? Do we have an answer for the day after?'"

For Obama, Libya was less a loss of innocence than a confirmation of what he had always believed: that American military interventions, more often than not, end in ashes. He told Gates privately that joining the NATO operation "had been a 51–49 call for him." Another former senior official reached for a different analogy— that of an alcoholic falling off the wagon. "It was like, in a moment of weakness, he had a drink because his friend persuaded him it would be a good idea," the official said. "And then it turned out exactly as he thought it would."

For Clinton, Libya ended up being more traumatic, more personal, and ultimately more perilous for her future. She had, after all, been the chief advocate for the intervention. She had "leadership/ownership/stewardship" of the policy. It was to be a cornerstone of a Hillary Clinton Doctrine, her blueprint for how America could apply itself in the world. "I have NEVER been prouder of having worked for you," wrote Anne-Marie Slaughter, her former director of policy planning, in an email on March 22, 2011, three days after the NATO intervention began. "Turning POTUS around on this is a major win for everything we have worked for." Clinton wrote back, "Keep your fingers crossed and pray for a soft landing for everyone's sake."

On the day she was told about Qaddafi's death, Clinton joked rather gracelessly with a CNN reporter, "We came, we saw, he died." Less than a year later, she stood next to Obama on the polished floor of an open hangar at Joint Base Andrews, as marine pallbearers carried in the flag-draped caskets of four Americans. A military band played the mournful strains of "Nearer, My God, to Thee." Ashen-faced and exhausted, Clinton paid tribute to Chris Stevens and his three colleagues, before introducing the president. "Their sacrifice will never be forgotten," he declared. "The flag they served under now carries them home."

Afterward, Obama put his arm around Clinton, as if to steady her. Rarely had they seemed so close.

# Nine

## Red Lines

Barack Obama wanted to get out of the office. The West Wing, air-less and tense at the best of times, felt like it was going to war footing. So shortly after six P.M. on the last Friday of August 2013, the president asked his chief of staff and closest aide, Denis McDonough, to join him for one of their periodic end-of-the-day strolls around the South Lawn. In his office just down the hall from the Oval Office, Dan Pfeiffer, Obama's senior adviser, was heading out to what he figured would be his last dinner date with his girl-friend for a while. He'd already canceled his Labor Day plans on the Outer Banks. Downstairs in his windowless cubbyhole, Ben Rhodes, having cut short a vacation with his wife in Oregon, was fine-tuning a communications rollout for the hectic days to come. Across West Executive Drive, in the Eisenhower building, Philip Gordon, the NSC's coordinator for the Middle East, was hunkered down, having broken the news to his daughter that he couldn't take her to the Nationals game and fireworks show to celebrate their shared birthday that night.

As Obama and McDonough circled the South Lawn, their path took them past symbols of the Obama presidency, public and pri-vate: the Rose Garden and the Oval Office, but also the swing set the president had installed for his daughters, now rarely used; the White House beehive, yielding honey that darkens in color through-out the summer; the vegetable patch planted by his wife, which supplied the heirloom tomatoes for the First Family's table. The circuit takes only a few minutes to complete, so the two men did multiple laps, with Obama doing most of the talking.

The president was having second thoughts about the missile strike against Syria he had vowed to carry out if it was determined that Bashar al-Assad had used chemical weapons against his own people. Obama told McDonough he wanted to pull back and seek congressional approval first. He ticked off his reasons: a growing sense of isolation after British prime minister David Cameron, who'd pledged to join the United States in the military operation, had suffered a stinging defeat in Parliament when he put the matter to a vote; a fear that acting without approval might undermine him if he needed congressional backing for the next military crisis in the Middle East, perhaps one involving Iran; and, not least, his own record. At an NSC meeting earlier that afternoon, the White House counsel, Kathy Ruemmler, speaking on a video screen, pointedly reminded him that as a senator, he had called for presidents to seek the buy-in of Congress for military operations.

"I'm well aware of what my position is," Obama replied curtly.

McDonough was receptive to his boss's doubts. More so than anyone but Obama himself, he thought that American presidents had reached too reflexively for the military lever over the last decade. From the start of the Arab uprisings, McDonough had resisted the interventionist instincts of his colleagues, whether it was close advisers such as Ben Rhodes and Samantha Power or cabinet members such as Hillary Clinton and David Petraeus. On a trip with lawmakers to the military prison at Guantánamo Bay, Cuba, in June 2013, McDonough told them he thought the conflict in Syria suited America's purposes just fine because it entangled two longtime American foes, Hezbollah and Iran, in a proxy war. Tom Donilon shared McDonough's skepticism. "You could read the president's position through Tom and Denis," one aide said.

With shadows lengthening across the lawn, Obama and McDonough ambled back up the flagstone path to the Oval Office shortly before seven P.M. Word of the walk had spread rapidly in the West Wing, and when the president's secretary, Anita Decker Breckenridge, began calling aides to a meeting, they knew something was up. She summoned Pfeiffer; Rhodes; Susan Rice, who had recently replaced Donilon as national security adviser; Tony Blinken; Rob Nabors, the legislative liaison; Brian McKeon, executive secretary of the NSC; and Brian Egan, the NSC's legal adviser. McDonough, hands jammed in his pockets, stood silently behind one of two beige couches in the office that flanked a marble fireplace with George Washington's portrait above the mantel. Obama, his tie loosened and shirtsleeves rolled up, sat in one of two leather wing chairs, facing the group. Aides offered various accounts of his opening line.

"I have a pretty big idea I want to test with you guys," he said, according to one.

"I've got a crazy idea I want to talk about," he said, according to another.

In truth, it was both big and crazy.


Hillary Clinton had been gone for nearly seven months by the time Obama held that fateful Friday night meeting, but there's little to suggest that her presence would have made any difference. Obama didn't bother to include her successor, John Kerry, or his defense secretary, Chuck Hagel, in the discussion; the two hours of emotionally charged debate did nothing to dissuade him from shelving his promised missile strike to seek congressional approval. He called the two men at nine P.M., after the meeting had ended, and told them of the change in plans. Hagel was dining with his wife at an Italian restaurant in McLean, Virginia, when Obama reached him; Kerry was at home in Georgetown. (He phoned Hagel afterward to commiserate. "What the hell's going on?" Kerry asked.) The heavyweight war council of Obama's first term had given way to an inner circle of advisers who called the shots on critical issues. In this case, where the president essentially presented his decision as a fait accompli, the circle had shrunk to one: Denis McDonough.

There's equally little doubt that Clinton would have opposed Obama's decision to forgo the attack. It was a terrible mistake, she told friends and former colleagues. "The Syrians were shaking in their boots at what the Americans were going to do," a person close to her said. "At a minimum, you would have responded to the chemical weapons, but you also would have created leverage for diplomacy." Obama had drawn a red line against Assad over his use of chemical weapons—it would be a "game changer," he warned—and then he had watched Assad trample across that line with an indiscriminate poison-gas attack on civilians. By failing to make good on his threat to retaliate militarily, Obama had eroded the authority of his presidency, weakened the credibility of the United States with allies and enemies, and unwittingly reinforced the perception in the Muslim world that America had no staying power. Clinton had policy differences with the president over Syria during her final months in office, but this was different.

And yet, when Clinton turned up at the White House ten days after Obama's about-face to take part in a meeting on wildlife trafficking, she was the picture of solidarity. She publicly urged Congress to give the president the authorization he sought for military action. She offered more qualified support for an idea tossed out by John Kerry earlier that day in London and quickly embraced by the Russians: that Syria give up its arsenal of chemical weapons to an outside authority. (Kerry said he had been batting around the idea with the Russian foreign minister, Sergey Lavrov, for a couple of weeks.) "This cannot be another excuse for delay, for obstruction," Clinton said. Whether through diplomacy or military force, she warned, "the world will have to deal with this threat as swiftly and comprehensively as possible."

There was nothing accidental about Clinton's show of support. The day after Obama announced he would go to Congress for approval, McDonough called to brief her about the decision and ask her advice. Clinton, noting the president was headed to a G-8 meeting in St. Petersburg, Russia, later that week, told McDonough it was important for Obama to have credibility when he met Russian president Vladimir Putin, who opposed any action against Assad, a longtime Russian ally. Support for military action in Congress, thin to start with, was withering fast; Obama could not afford to look as if he had no juice. Clinton's suggestion was small ball—persuade the Senate Foreign Relations Committee, which has authority in matters of war and peace, to hold a vote in favor of military action—but McDonough, who had taken charge of the Sisyphean lobbying campaign, seized it gratefully. He put Obama on the phone with her and arranged for the two to talk again in the Oval Office on September 9, the day of the wildlife meeting.

Rarely had the president so needed his former secretary of state. Isolated at home and viewed as irresolute abroad, Obama was desperate for an ally with domestic and international standing. Clinton felt loyalty to the president; with her own presidential bid still twenty months away, she could afford to line up with him, even in an unpopular cause. But throwing her support behind Obama was not without risk: Opponents of military action were already likening Syria to the Iraq War vote in 2002. "She went out on a real limb in saying she supported the president," one aide said, ignoring the fact that Obama had vowed to act if Assad crossed the red line he had drawn.


The Syrian civil war was to become the sharpest line separating Clinton and Obama on national security. Her support for funneling weapons to moderate Syrian rebels in the summer of 2012 put her at odds with the president in the last major debate of their years together. At the time, the split seemed a telling, if not theological, disagreement over how deeply to get involved. (Obama eventually did authorize limited covert aid to the rebels.) In hindsight, it looms larger: The inability of the moderate opposition to coalesce as a fighting force opened the door to the Islamic State, which conquered a large chunk of Iraq and established a caliphate in the desert that straddles Iraq and Syria.

Three years later, Syria was more tangled and hopeless than ever.

Russia had entered the war on Assad's behalf, bombing the remnants of anti-Assad rebels that the United States was trying to help. Iran battled the Islamic State in Iraq while aiding Assad in Syria directly and through its client, Hezbollah. The United States headed a loose coalition, including Turkey and the Gulf states, that was fighting ISIS in Syria and Iraq. What began as a pro-democracy uprising had mutated into a region-wide proxy war involving nearly a dozen countries, whose interests simultaneously overlapped and conflicted. And four years of grinding civil war had produced a grim tide of desperate refugees who were flooding into a panicked Europe.

Against that stygian backdrop, Clinton gave an interview to a Boston television station in October 2015. Asked about the situation, she said, "I personally would be advocating now for a no-fly zone and humanitarian corridors to try to stop the carnage on the ground and from the air." Again, she split with Obama: He remained opposed to such large-scale American military involvement. Russia's entry into the conflict was impossible for him to ignore, however. So he opted, characteristically, for a more limited option: deploying a few dozen special operations troops to northern Syria to help the rebels, mostly ethnic Kurds, combat the Islamic State.

Few people, Clinton included, argue that running guns to the rebels back in 2012 would have prevented the rise of ISIS. But Obama, by balking at his own red line and by refusing to arm the moderates when they still had a chance on the battlefield, diminished America's ability to shape the war or a potential political settlement. Other countries were then able to hijack the conflict by arming more radical insurgent groups, not least the brutal warriors who raised the black flag of the Islamic State. The United States, in Clinton's oft-used phrase, had not put skin in the game.

"The failure to help build up a credible fighting force of the people who were originators of the protests against Assad—there were Islamists, there were secularists, there was everything in the middle—the failure to do that left a big vacuum, which the jihadists have now filled," she told the journalist Jeffrey Goldberg in August 2014.

Strong words from someone who, as a rule, soft-pedaled her differences with Obama—in public, at least. Not surprisingly, the president's aides were angry. Clinton had not, they said, been as passionate an advocate for aiding the rebels in 2012 as she was after the fact, when the Islamic State had become a terrifying media spectacle and a looming political issue in the 2016 campaign. "She never went to the mat on anything that I recall," one Obama aide told me. Nor was the protracted arming debate as black-and-white as she portrayed it. The president thought the initial proposal—devised by David Petraeus, the CIA director, and seconded by Clinton—was half-cooked and unlikely to alter the course of the war. But he didn't reject it so much as kick it down the road. Eight months later—after he had been reelected, Clinton and Petraeus were out of the cabinet, and the agency's new interim director, Michael Morell, had retooled the plan—Obama signed off on a covert program to ship small arms and ammunition, with the help of the Saudis, to Jordan, where it was parceled out to carefully vetted rebel groups.

While Clinton did dramatize her advocacy, the White House narrative diminishes a debate that still ranks as one of the most revealing of the Obama presidency. Clinton and Petraeus were joined by Leon Panetta, the secretary of defense, and General Martin Dempsey, the chairman of the Joint Chiefs of Staff, in supporting the plan. That meant the commander in chief overruled his entire war cabinet, something that had not happened in any other such debate, from Afghanistan to Libya. The fissures flowed downward into the rank and file: The CIA and the State Department did not share their plans for aiding the rebels with the NSC because they knew the White House wouldn't be receptive. When Obama finally came around, the program he secretly approved in April 2013 was so small and slow to get off the ground that the rebel commanders complained later they never got the guns they needed.

For years afterward, Obama was angry at the way the debate

over Syria was framed. He often raised it, unprompted, with reporters. The argument that arming the rebels could have changed the direction of the war, he told Thomas Friedman in August 2014, was ludicrous. "This idea," he said, "that we could provide some light arms or even more sophisticated arms to what was essentially an opposition made up of former doctors, farmers, pharmacists and so forth, and that they were going to be able to battle not only a well-armed state but also a well-armed state backed by Russia, backed by Iran, a battle-hardened Hezbollah, that was never in the cards."

In its anguish and ambiguity, the debate over Syria offers perhaps the clearest window into how Clinton and Obama wrestled with America's role in a fracturing Middle East. Both were appalled to watch Bashar al-Assad, a man they had once hoped would be a reformer, drop barrel bombs and fire poison gas at his people. Both were confounded by the geopolitics of Syria: at once a sectarian civil conflict and a proxy war, involving Russia, Iran, Saudi Arabia, Turkey, and others. Both, but especially Obama, were haunted by Libya, where American intervention had only sowed more chaos and death. Both, but especially Clinton, were mindful of past horrors—Rwanda, the Balkans—where the United States had waited too long or done nothing at all.

"Kosovo, despite the brutality and the horrors of what was happening in the Balkans, was immensely simpler in lots of ways than what we're talking about with Syria," Clinton told me in 2013. "There will always be regret when you're in positions like this when it comes to the horrific slaughter of people trying to express themselves and defend themselves from a government that seems to have lost all sense of responsibility toward their own population."

Clinton called Syria a "wicked problem," a phrase used by strategic planning experts to describe "particularly complex challenges that confound standard solutions and approaches." Obama, in private conversations, referred to it as a "shitty problem," an equally apt description. Their subtle difference in language laid bare an essential divide between how they viewed Syria: She kept casting about for solutions, however far-fetched. He concluded that there were no solutions—at least none that could be imposed by the United States—and, hence, no case for meaningful military intervention.

"She thought the Syrian crisis is like a raging bull that threatens the China shop," said Robert Ford, the last American ambassador to Syria. "Success is not guaranteed, but if we don't try to throw a rope around it, if we don't try to get a grip on it somehow, we have no chance of steering it at all. My sense of Obama is that he thought, 'It's a raging bull, there's not a lot we can do. Stay the hell away from it.'"

For Hillary Clinton, Syria began as an opportunity rather than a threat. On March 2, 2009, during her first visit to Jerusalem as secretary of state, she stood next to the Israeli foreign minister, Tzipi Livni, and announced that the United States would send two emissaries to Damascus. It was the biggest headline of her trip, and with reason. She and Obama were betting that Syria, which had not had a resident American ambassador since George W. Bush recalled the last one in 2005, was the key to unlocking three of the thorniest challenges in the region: a nuclear deal with Iran, a peace accord between Israel and the Palestinians, and a reduction of tensions between Israel and Syria.

Over the next two years, a small circle of American diplomats traveled the road to Damascus, meeting with the stork-like Assad and his corpulent foreign minister, Walid al-Moallem. Also making the pilgrimage was Senator John Kerry. He had cultivated his own relationship with Assad, a fifty-year-old ophthalmologist whose British medical pedigree fooled many into thinking he was a new kind of Arab leader. Some of the issues on the table were unpleasant: reports that Syria was transferring Scud missiles to Hezbollah and Hamas; others less so: a potential peace deal with Israel. Assad was intrigued by the possibility of reclaiming the Golan Heights, the five hundred square miles of rocky highlands seized by

Israel in the 1967 war. The White House viewed peace talks as a way to draw Syria out of the orbit of Iran and its terrorist proxy, Hezbollah. Frederic Hof, a seasoned Middle East expert who handled the Syria file for the administration's special envoy George Mitchell, said that by February 2011, Assad had cleared away most of the obstacles to the Syrian side of a deal with Israel.

"I certainly would not have bet a sizable amount of money that we'd be in the Rose Garden by the end of 2011," Hof said. "But we were definitely making serious progress."

Kerry told me that Assad had agreed to the terms of a U.S.-drafted letter, dated May 22, 2010, that sketched out a peace treaty between Syria and Israel. Syria would restore diplomatic relations with Israel and pledge to stop funneling weapons to Hamas, while Israel would return the Golan Heights. Assad hoped this breakthrough would open the door to aircraft parts and other Western technology, as well as help in building an oil pipeline from Syria to Iraq. Kerry took the letter with him to Jerusalem and showed it to Benjamin Netanyahu, who was intrigued but noncommittal.

The portents were good enough for Obama to name Ford as the first U.S. ambassador to Syria in five years. A soft-spoken Arabist with tours in Algeria, Bahrain, and Iraq, Ford was a diplomat out of central casting: genteel but adventurous, Lawrence of Arabia with the voice of a librarian. When he arrived in Damascus in January 2011, his first meeting with Assad was civil. While Assad didn't give an inch on human rights, he was perfectly charming. "He didn't want to have a stinky meeting," Ford recalled.

Even after protests erupted across Syria in March, and Assad's security forces fired into crowds in the southern city of Daraa, Clinton clung to the idea that Bashar was a reformer, not simply a Western-friendly version of his father, Hafez, author of the Hama massacre, in which tens of thousands of Sunnis had been slaughtered. "There's a different leader in Syria now," she told a leery Bob Schieffer on *Face the Nation* on March 27, 2011. "Many of the members of Congress of both parties who have gone to Syria in recent months have said they believe he's a reformer."

By summer, with crowds chanting in the heart of Damascus and the Syrian army turning its guns on them, nobody had illusions about Assad any longer. On July 8, Ford paid a risky visit to Hama, site of the 1982 massacre, where five hundred thousand people had gathered to protest against the regime. As the ambassador's gray SUV inched through the crowd, it was strewn with roses and olive branches. Assad was livid, accusing Ford of inciting antigovernment rage. But the State Department, which had run out of patience with the Syrian leader, was pleased. So was the White House, for which the incident was proof that sending a diplomat did not mean caving in to the regime.

"Well done," Bill Burns, the State Department's top career diplomat, told Ford in a phone call.

Emboldened by her envoy, Clinton declared three days later that the Syrian leader had lost legitimacy. "We have absolutely nothing invested in him remaining in power," she said to reporters. A month later, Obama went further. "For the sake of the Syrian people," he said in a written statement, "the time has come for President Assad to step aside." Obama saw no need to back up his demand with the threat of military action. A stream of American intelligence reports was predicting that the regime's days were numbered, although analysts differed on the numbers.

Not everybody in the White House was convinced. Steven Simon, an NSC senior director who worked on the Middle East, cowrote a memo with Dennis Ross on the likely trajectory of the Arab uprisings. Nursing doubts that Assad was about to fall, Simon added a section warning that the White House's hands-off strategy in Syria might not work. It was stripped out before the report went to the president. Sure enough, Assad was still in power at the beginning of 2012. Bolstered by Hezbollah and Iran, he carried out a systematic campaign of torture and killing of demonstrators. At that point, John McCain and other lawmakers called for the United States to intervene.

Obama, however, was deeply reluctant, and any thoughts of military action to protect civilians were dispelled by a slide show in the Situation Room early in 2012, given by Marty Dempsey. A low-key, publicity-shy Irishman who had replaced the more extroverted Mike Mullen as chairman of the Joint Chiefs the previous October, Dempsey would become one of Obama's most trusted generals. It was easy to see why: He was an articulate, effective advocate for avoiding rash military action in Syria—the same role Mullen had tried to play on Libya. In a set of slides showing Assad's air defenses, Dempsey warned that it would take as many as seventy thousand American servicemen to dismantle the antiaircraft system and enforce a no-fly zone over the country.

With American military action off the table, Clinton returned to a familiar slog of urgent diplomatic meetings in European capitals about Arab wars. Only Syria wasn't going to unspool like Libya: Russia had a naval base in the country and viewed Bashar al-Assad as a strategic ally; still seething at how NATO's humanitarian intervention in Libya had turned into a campaign of regime change, it had no plans to sanction a pressure campaign against Assad at the United Nations. The Russians vetoed even a watered-down Security Council resolution condemning the regime's violence. As the Syrian uprising metamorphosed into a full-fledged civil war with a shifting cast of rebel groups, Clinton was pressed by the Saudis, Turks, Qataris, and Emiratis to supply arms to the opposition. Robert Ford, now effectively the ambassador to the rebels, was hearing the same plea for weapons from leaders on the ground.

In February 2012, the State Department shut down the American embassy in Damascus, evacuating Ford and his staff. It cited the escalating violence in the capital but did not mention the source of that violence: Jabhat al-Nusra, a well-financed, frighteningly successful militant group linked to al-Qaeda (doing so would have undercut the White House narrative that it had degraded al-Qaeda). To Ford, the inroads made by al-Nusra drove home the need for the United States to get weapons into the hands of more moderate rebels, chiefly the Free Syrian Army. Soon after he got back to Washington, he paid a call on Dave Petraeus at the CIA. The two were old friends from Iraq: Ford had run the political office at the Baghdad embassy while the general was making plans to reach out to Sunni tribal leaders in Anbar Province.

"You guys have got to get into the game in Syria," Ford told Petraeus. "We've got to be helping the opposition because it's going to get really ugly."

"Let me get back to you," Petraeus said.

Until then, the White House had justified its refusal by saying it did not want to further "militarize" the conflict. Obama and Clinton both worried that the United States did not know the rebels well enough to tell the good guys from the bad guys. They feared that weapons would fall into the wrong hands. Their nightmare scenario was a Syrian jihadi armed with an American antiaircraft gun taking out an El Al passenger jet.

The United States had been delivering nonlethal assistance to the Syrian opposition since the summer of 2011. At the University of Aleppo, which had become a hotbed of anti-Assad activity, the State Department was taking small groups of students to Turkey for training in the techniques of nonviolent resistance. In a heartbreaking turn, Syrian security forces stormed the campus in May 2012, killing at least four activists; one was hurled to his death from a fifth-floor window. It was a chilling demonstration of what Tom Friedman once called the "Hama Rules," the scorched-earth tactics that Assad's father used so effectively to crush dissent. That Assad's troops would hunt down and kill young activists this way suggested a regime with no shame. For many in the State Department, it sealed the argument that American aid should no longer simply be nonlethal or humanitarian.

Over the next few months, staffers at State and the CIA quietly worked together to develop an arming proposal. For an administration that prided itself on tight coordination—a "robust inter-agency process," to use Tom Donilon's preferred term—there was remarkably little discussion about these plans between the two agencies and the NSC. The diplomats knew their ideas were not likely to get a warm reception from the president, so they were not very forthcoming with their White House counterparts. Some in the White

House viewed the State Department as clueless, fixated with planning for a post-Assad Syria when it was far from clear that Assad was going anywhere.

While the planning occurred well below Clinton's level, she was undergoing her own change of heart on the arming concept. As with Libya, she kept hearing from leaders in the Persian Gulf that if the United States did not start backing the opposition, it would have no ability to control events. On a Saturday afternoon in July 2012, Clinton invited Petraeus to lunch at her home in Washington. There were several items on the agenda; Ford and his colleagues made sure one of them was arming the rebels. "He had already given careful thought to the idea," Clinton wrote in her memoir, "and had even started sketching out the specifics and was preparing to present a plan."

In fact, Petraeus was way ahead of Clinton. A few months earlier, he had met quietly in Istanbul with the heads of twelve intelligence services from America's allies and countries in the region. The subject was Syria, and the goal was to better coordinate efforts to aid the rebels. Afterward, the CIA began secretly advising on a military airlift operation in which Saudi, Qatari, and Jordanian cargo planes would transport arms and equipment for various opposition groups to airports in Turkey or Jordan. Though the United States was not supplying weapons itself, the agency's advisory role allowed it to keep tabs on where the arms were flowing—and to steer them away from malefactors.

At other meetings in Jordan and Saudi Arabia, Petraeus kept getting pressure from Arab officials to begin funneling weapons directly to the rebels. In July 2012, he met with King Abdullah of Saudi Arabia, who bore a deep hatred of Assad. The next day, the king named Prince Bandar bin Sultan, the flashy, cigar-smoking former ambassador to Washington, as the head of the Saudi intelligence service. Bandar's desire to oust Assad was well known; putting him in that job was an unmistakable sign that the House of Saud would aggressively lobby the United States for help in doing that. The CIA director's enthusiasm for arming the rebels was heavily stoked by Prince Bandar, according to a senior American official. (Saudi Arabia would later end up bankrolling much of the CIA program, under a secret arrangement code-named Timber Sycamore.) Petraeus declined to discuss his role in the debate over arming or training the rebels.

Meanwhile in Syria, the war took an ominous turn. Intelligence agencies began intercepting communications that suggested Syria was moving and mixing chemical weapons agents, a prelude to a possible attack. On August 20, 2012, taking the podium in the White House briefing room, Obama made one of the most fateful statements of his presidency. "We cannot have a situation in which chemical or biological weapons are falling into the hands of the wrong people," he said. "We have been very clear to the Assad regime but also to other players on the ground that a red line for us is, we start seeing a whole bunch of weapons moving around or being utilized.

"That would change my calculus," the president added. "That would change my equation."

For Obama to draw a red line against chemical weapons, even if he did not act against Assad's barrel bombing of Aleppo, was less surprising than it might have appeared. The use of these weapons violated the Geneva Protocol and the Chemical Weapons Convention. That was something that Obama the lawyer and custodian of international norms could not abide. But the president, his aides conceded later, should have been more careful about using the phrase "red line." He had boxed himself in.

It was at this moment that Petraeus, backed by Clinton, made his pitch for arming the rebels. People who were in the Situation Room that September day recalled the CIA director dominating the proceedings. He leaned so far forward across the table, his head cocked toward the president, that he blocked Obama's view of everybody sitting on the far side of him. His presentation was vigorous, detailed, and self-confident, reflecting the experience of a commander who had championed covert paramilitary operations in Iraq. Some found it over-the-top, given that the director of the CIA is supposed to offer the president dispassionate assessments of the intelligence, not be a policy advocate. Petraeus used "hot rhetoric," one person recalled, emphasizing the need to move "now versus later."

Obama listened quietly, leaning to one side in his leather chair in what one aide described as his "senior executive mode." He asked a few questions but did not challenge Petraeus. Afterward, he went around the table and polled the team. Clinton said she favored the plan as a way to force Assad into negotiations. To some in the room, her emotion didn't match the case she was making. "You had the libretto and then you had the notes," one said. Panetta threw in his support, as did Dempsey, even less fervently than Clinton. Panetta summed up the case in his memoir, *Worthy Fights.* "All of us believed that withholding weapons was impeding our ability to develop sway with those groups and subjecting them to withering fire from the regime," he wrote. The president, he added, was "initially hesitant."

So was most of the White House. Biden thought arming the rebels was a "stupid idea," said a person in the room. (He had also advised Obama against laying down a red line.) Donilon and McDonough were both skeptical, though Donilon's position evolved over the coming months while McDonough's did not. Susan Rice spoke out most forcefully against it. Appearing on a video screen from the United Nations, she argued it would draw the United States into a quagmire and muck up Obama's second-term agenda. It was a remarkable turnabout for someone who had led the charge on using force in Libya, and had cultivated a reputation as an advocate of humanitarian interventions generally. This time, she was in lockstep with the boss.

"We asked a lot of questions," a senior White House official recalled. " 'What would be the assessment of the impact this would have? What would be the chain of custody the weapons would have? Who trains the people to use the weapons? Is there a command-and-control structure around these people? Or are we just dumping the weapons in?' There weren't a lot of clear answers to those questions."

For the pro-arming camp, the case came down to a process of elimination. " 'We tried a range of options and nothing has worked. So why not try this?' " said Steven Simon, who watched from a chair along the wall. "You could sense what the president was thinking: 'For something with such a vague, speculative outcome, I'm going to get the United States involved in a civil war in Syria?' " Clinton and Panetta both fell back on the need to get "skin in the game." It didn't help that neither meant it in the Wall Street context in which the phrase is commonly understood—investors putting their own money into a deal to limit the risk they are willing to take. In Clinton's use of the term, having skin in the game would increase, not limit, the risk.

Then there were the inconvenient facts of history. The CIA, at the behest of Michael Morell, had taken a hard look at its record of running guns to insurgent fighters—a murky trail that ran from the Bay of Pigs in Cuba to the contras in Nicaragua. "Needless to say, it was just a concatenation of miserable failures, of backfiring policies, and all kinds of mayhem," Simon said. There was one notable exception: Afghanistan in the 1980s, where the agency funneled weapons to the mujahedeen fighting their Soviet occupiers, but that only worked because the agency had Pakistani intelligence officers on the ground in Afghanistan, helping the mujahedeen. (And even then, many of those fighters ended up, years later, with the Taliban or al-Qaeda.) There was no equivalent in Syria.

Finally, there was an election in two months. If Obama was reluctant on the merits to get drawn into Syria, he was certainly not going to do it just before he faced the voters. He thanked Petraeus for his presentation and ended the meeting without a decision. "In Arab culture," Robert Ford observed, "they have a saying: 'No answer is the answer.' "

• • •

Days after that meeting, Islamic militants attacked the U.S. compound in Benghazi and killed four Americans, confronting Obama and Clinton with an election-year crisis that overshadowed Syria. Petraeus, meanwhile, had become embroiled in a personal crisis over an affair with his biographer, which would precipitate his resignation the day after the election. In early December, an ill, dehydrated Clinton slipped and fell in the bathroom of her house, suffering a concussion and blood clot. She was sidelined for a month. Arming the rebels had lost its moment and its main advocates.

Yet in December, Obama convened another NSC meeting, without Petraeus or Clinton, to debate the issue once again. The CIA's chair was now occupied by Morell, a career intelligence analyst who had briefed George W. Bush on the day of the 9/11 attacks and became the acting director after Petraeus left. Low-key, with none of his predecessor's star power, Morell nonetheless brought strong opinions and a fierce loyalty to his institution. He had retooled the Petraeus plan to address Obama's skepticism, sharpening U.S. control over the weapons. He dialed back claims that it would be a panacea for the rebels and conceded the risks, particularly those of a Sunni slaughter of Syria's Alawite minority. "If a group of armed rebels went back to an Alawite village and killed a bunch of women and children," he warned, according to a person in the room, "the U.S. would have blood on its hands."

The same questions swirled: How would this alter the war? What were the risks? Obama thanked everybody again and said he wanted to think about it, but his body language gave him away. He still wasn't satisfied with the level of vetting for the rebels or with assurances that this would not be a slippery slope for the United States, one that led to direct American military involvement. "They could have tweaked this thing until kingdom come," said a former White House official. "It wouldn't have made any difference. He just didn't think it was a good idea, period."

By early 2013, however, things had changed dramatically on the battlefield in Syria. Assad was no longer on his heels; intelligence reports said he had regained the offensive. His patron, Iran, had come to his rescue, replenishing his munitions depots. The Free Syrian Army was in disarray, running low on guns, while militant groups, chiefly the Qaeda-linked Jabhat al-Nusra, were in the ascendancy, drawing recruits from more moderate groups who sometimes brought foreign-supplied weapons with them.

Until then, Obama had viewed Syria only from the distant vantage point of the Situation Room, in the basement of the West Wing. But in March 2013, he went on a three-day trip to the Middle East that included his first stop as president in Israel. His travels exposed him to the fears of Syria's neighbors. The Israelis were ambivalent about Assad; they disliked him but feared that what followed his regime could be worse. In a meeting in Jerusalem, Benjamin Netanyahu warned Obama that Assad's chemical weapons could fall into the hands of Hezbollah. Speaking afterward to reporters in the courtyard of the prime minister's residence, the president reiterated his warning that the "use of chemical weapons is a game changer."

The next day, in Jordan, Obama got an earful. King Abdullah II, who also despised Assad, hosted the president at a late-night dinner in his palace in Amman, along with Tom Donilon and John Kerry, who had replaced Clinton two months earlier. Jordan, the king told his guests, was buckling under more than one hundred thousand Syrian refugees. He urged Obama to do more to end the war. Jordan was already the site of a secret camp where the CIA was training small cadres of moderate rebels. It had offered the United States bases to carry out drone strikes in Syria, which the White House refused.

All these issues were on the president's mind the next morning as he took a solitary walk through the rose-hued canyons of the ancient city of Petra.

Back in Washington, the CIA kept tinkering with its proposal to arm and train the rebels. In April 2013, the NSC staff sent the president a decision memo, a document that laid out the arguments for a covert program, giving Obama another chance to review his thinking. The basic rationale for aiding the opposition had changed little from the previous year, though the memo punched up the need for the United States to have a seat at the table in deciding Syria's future—something it would get by being more involved in the war. This time, to the surprise of NSC staffers, Obama sent it back with the box checked, "Approved." Normally, there would have been an NSC or deputies meeting to debate such a change in policy. In fact, Obama's check mark was slightly below the "Approved" box, leading some staffers to muse, half in jest, that maybe he had meant to check "Disapproved." The CIA called the White House to make sure the decision had come directly from him.

Obama's shift coincided with new intelligence reports: The Syrian regime had used the chemical agent sarin in small-scale attacks the previous month, in a village near Aleppo and on the outskirts of Damascus. Outside agencies had tested soil samples from the site and blood taken from the victims; there was little doubt that Assad had crossed Obama's red line. Inside the White House, nobody was explicitly linking the WMD attack with the decision to arm the rebels. And regardless of the reports, nothing more happened for three months after Obama approved the CIA's covert program: No weapons flowed, no public announcement was made, no funding was requested from Congress. The program was not only clandestine, it was invisible.

Certainly, Obama's reticence about being drawn into a civil war was at the root of his halfhearted approach to Syria. But in a White House where many of the top officials, including the president, had law degrees, the lawyers played an important, underappreciated role. They curbed efforts to bolster nonlethal aid for the Syrian opposition (covert aid came under less scrutiny). The legal argument was this: Even though Obama had called on Assad to step down, the United States was not at war with Syria. Providing night-vision goggles, communications gear, or even food rations to those trying to oust him therefore could be a violation of international law.

Weren't Assad's barrel-bomb attacks on civilians also a violation of international law? the diplomats replied incredulously. At one State Department meeting about a scheme to transport aid across the Syrian border, a department lawyer warned, "You guys all think you're James Bond, but I'm telling you, if we do this, we're going to go to jail."

By now, the ragtag state of the Free Syrian Army was less of a problem than the threat from Assad's chemical weapons, and the debate in the White House shifted from aiding the rebels to direct military action. Over four decades, the CIA estimated, Syria had accumulated large supplies of sarin, mustard gas, and cyanide, which it could deliver by aerial bombs, ballistic missiles, and artillery rockets. These were stored in depots scattered throughout the country, some close to populated areas. The Pentagon prepared a menu of options for Obama that included commando raids to secure the stockpiles and strikes on Syrian planes from American ships in the Mediterranean. Securing all the known weapons sites, Panetta wrote in his memoir, would have necessitated 75,000 to 90,000 troops, as many as were in Afghanistan. "I considered that impossible," he said, "and my colleagues agreed."

As spring turned to summer, however, the war drums were beating again—and again, Bill Clinton was adding to the din. On June 12, 2013, he sat on a flag-draped stage in Manhattan with John McCain, who had been castigating Obama for months for his lack of action. During the Q&A session at the gathering, sponsored by the McCain Institute for International Leadership, the subject of Syria came up. "Some people say, 'OK, see what a big mess it is? Stay out!' I think that's a big mistake. I agree with you about this," Clinton told McCain. "Sometimes it's just best to get caught trying," he added, using a well-worn Clinton line that was nevertheless widely reported.

The same day, Obama's war council held another meeting in the Situation Room. The intelligence assessments were now definitive: Assad had used sarin gas on his people. Estimates put the number killed at between 100 and 150. John Kerry, who lobbied more aggressively than Hillary Clinton for increased aid to the rebels, brandished a State Department document that warned if the United States did not impose consequences on Syria for these attacks, Assad would view it as a "green light for continued CW use." Obama remained opposed to military action, but the White House knew it had to do *something* to look responsive. On June 13, it scheduled a press call with Ben Rhodes that may qualify as the most oblique declaration of war since Lyndon Johnson asked Congress to pass the Tonkin Gulf Resolution. Confirming the decision that Obama had made two months earlier, Rhodes said the United States would provide "assistance that has direct military purposes" to the Supreme Military Council, the armed wing of Syria's opposition. Reporters peppered him with questions: What kind of assistance? He wouldn't say. Who would provide it? He wouldn't say. How would it be provided? Again, he wouldn't say.

The president said nothing at all.

The truth is, the plan was a baby step—or, as a former State Department official less delicately put it, a case of him "salami-slicing the baby." When the CIA's weapons finally began flowing several months later, it was a trickle. A rebel leader told Robert Ford that at the end of 2014, his men were receiving about 36,000 bullets a month from the United States. In combat, a soldier fires between 100 and 200 bullets a day. That meant the CIA was arming between six and twelve fighters. "It's sort of stupid," the rebel leader told him. The ambassador agreed: A few months earlier, Ford had resigned from the Foreign Service in protest. "I found it ever harder to justify our policy," he wrote in a *New York Times* op-ed. To alter the state of the war and force Assad into a negotiation, the Free Syrian Army needed heavier weapons: mortars, rockets, even surface-to-air missiles.

"Dribbling in little bits of aid wasn't helping them or helping efforts to find a political solution through negotiation," Ford told me.

Obama's halfhearted approach was causing strains at higher levels, too. Chuck Hagel, the Republican former senator from Nebraska whom Obama had asked to replace Leon Panetta as defense secretary in 2013, became frustrated the following year because he could not extract a pledge from the White House to defend the rebels it had trained and armed if they came under attack by Assad's forces. In an angry two-page memo to John Kerry and Susan Rice that October, Hagel complained about this lack of American commitment and the absence of a broader political strategy toward Syria, which he said was hampering efforts to line up support from allies such as France and Turkey for the military campaign against the Islamic State. Hagel copied Denis McDonough, and asked him to hand the memo to the president.

"I could never get anything out of the White House," Hagel said in an interview after he left the administration. "They had these never-ending meetings, which would never get to the real issues. They never looked down the road or anticipated anything."

A war hero in Vietnam who made a fortune in cellphones, won election to the Senate, and then defied his party's president on the Iraq War, Hagel was not used to failure. He thought he had a personal bond with Obama, having befriended him in the Senate and traveled with him to Iraq and Afghanistan during the 2008 campaign. But Syria would drive a wedge between them: White House officials told reporters he was a cipher during policy debates; he concluded the president was captive, as he put it, "to a very incompetent, inexperienced White House staff." A month after Hagel wrote the memo complaining about the Syria policy, he resigned under pressure—the fall guy, he believed, for a national security team in disarray.

Across the administration, there was a disquieting sense that Syria could end up as Obama's Rwanda. Samantha Power, speaking at the Holocaust Memorial Museum in Washington, defended her boss's record in fighting atrocities in Libya and central Africa. "But against all of this," she said, "there is Syria." Tom Malinowski, at his swearing-in ceremony as the assistant secretary for democracy and human rights, noted it was the twentieth anniversary of the Rwandan genocide. "What will our kids and grandkids ask us about our time here twenty years from now?" he asked. The reference to Syria was clear, if unspoken.

Just after two A.M. on August 21, 2013, the Syrian army fired rockets tipped with sarin gas into rebel-controlled suburbs of Damascus. By dawn, the hospitals were overflowing with victims, their mouths foaming and bodies convulsing. The dead piled up by the hundreds, covered in ice to prevent their corpses from rotting in the heat. This was not an isolated attack, with a few dozen victims. It was an atrocity, the worst chemical weapons assault since the Iran-Iraq War, and it was precisely what Obama had in mind when he drew his red line the previous summer. Speaking to half a dozen aides in the Oval Office the next morning, the president ordered them to present him with military options at an NSC meeting that afternoon.

"I set out a red line," he said. "It looks like he crossed it. If that's the case, we need to respond forcefully."

The aides nodded in agreement—except for McDonough, whose furrowed brow gave him away.

"You don't agree, Denis?" Obama asked.

"I don't," he replied.

"I figured you would say that, but why?"

"Our position all along has been not to get involved," McDonough said. "We shouldn't get involved."

"Denis," Obama said, "Assad just carried out a chemical weapons attack. I was pretty clear about what that would mean."

At the NSC meeting that afternoon, and every meeting over the coming week, the discussion was about selecting targets for Tomahawk missile strikes. The Pentagon's plan was to hit four of Assad's main command-and-control centers; the missiles would be fired at three A.M. to keep casualties as low as possible. Which is why Obama's aides were so stunned on the evening of August 30 in the Oval Office, when the president, after his walk with McDonough, told them he was holding off on a strike until he got congressional approval. The pushback from the staff was intense: Dan Pfeiffer told him there was only a fifty-fifty chance he would win a vote in Congress on military action, a prediction that proved wrong by 100 percent. Susan Rice told him it was important, as a matter of executive privilege, that he not back down. A picture taken by White House photographer Pete Souza captured the anguish in the room: Pfeiffer leaning forward on the sofa, chewing on a fingernail; Rhodes slumped back, resting his head on his hand, a legal pad on his lap.

Lawyerly as always, Obama laid out his case. His backing of the NATO air campaign in Libya had left a sour taste among many in Congress. Moving swiftly there had been vital to avert a slaughter in Benghazi, but that wasn't the case here. General Dempsey had told his commander in chief that the two or three days of strikes he was planning would be just as effective "in three weeks as in three days." David Cameron's defeat on the war vote in Parliament had given him pause. Yes, the president granted, Cameron had handled the vote clumsily. But it accurately reflected public sentiment in Britain. "We similarly have a war-weary public," Obama pointed out. Ordering another military action over the heads of Congress, he told his aides, would contradict the spirit of his speech the previous spring, in which he tried to move America off the perpetual war footing of the post-9/11 era.

To many, even former cabinet members, Obama was simply looking for an excuse to avoid pulling the trigger. Throwing himself at the mercy of a risk-averse Congress, Panetta wrote, was "an almost certain way to scotch any action," as the president "well knew."

"You cannot say things like 'a red line' or 'Assad must go' as a throwaway line," Hagel told me. "The president of the United States can't do that." Clinton was more diplomatic, though her neutral, just-the-facts description of the episode in her book suggests someone who had no intention of sharing her true feelings. A more accurate gauge of Clinton's position on Syria came at the one hundredth anniversary gala of *The New Republic* in November 2014, when the magazine's former literary editor, Leon Wieseltier, barged into a cocktail conversation Bill Clinton was having with two of Wieseltier's colleagues about macroeconomic policy.

"Excuse me, Mr. President," he asked. "If you were still in office, you would have intervened in Syria, right?"

"Yes," he replied. "That's the family policy."

Hillary's lobbying on Capitol Hill helped Obama eke out a minor victory in a 10–7 vote in favor of military action on the Senate Foreign Relations Committee. But facing a solid wall of opposition in the broader Congress, the president grabbed a diplomatic lifeline: a proposal the Russians made, seizing on John Kerry's comment, to have Assad surrender his chemical weapons to an outside authority. Months later, Obama and his lieutenants would point to the success of that agreement as vindication of his decision not to strike. "If the president had bombed for ten hours or two days," Kerry told me, "he would not have gotten all the weapons out of Syria."

Yet the red line wouldn't fade. "I've heard it a hundred times if I've heard it a dozen times," Kerry said of his exchanges with foreign ministers. "'Gee, the president announces a red line and then he didn't bomb.' It has entered into the ether of diplomatic mythology."

Fairly or not, the symbolism of Obama drawing a line and failing to enforce it far outweighed the tangible dividends of the chemical weapons deal. It dismayed his friends, disgusted his critics, rattled the nation's allies, and perhaps emboldened its adversaries. "There was a fear," said Wolfgang Ischinger, a prominent German diplomat who served as ambassador to the United States, "that if the U.S. doesn't act, then who else will?" Some point to that weekend, when the guns of August did not sound, as an irreparable blow to America's credibility.

George Mitchell, the Senate elder and frustrated peacemaker of Obama's first term, has watched presidents since Reagan struggle to square agonizing real-world decisions with the enormous symbolic power of their office. "The American people," he said, "are very fortunate that we don't have a president who will push the military button the first chance we have."

Still, Mitchell said, "Making the statement about the red line in Syria, then not following through on it, clearly has had an adverse effect. You cannot view each decision in isolation. Everything a president says or does affects everything else he does. It's important to keep in mind the assembling of power and influence, both internally and externally, and to gauge actions in that context. The president hasn't focused as much on that as on the detail and nuance of each of the issues that he's faced. It may sound harsh, but that's the reality of being a leader."

# Part III

**Diplomacy**

# Ten

## The Back Channel

"All right," Barack Obama said to Hillary Clinton and a handful of advisers as he pulled up a chair at the long conference table in the Roosevelt Room, barely a month into his presidency. "How do we think about Iran? How do we approach it? How do we structure things?" He wasn't looking for a briefing about specific policy options, nor was he interested in reopening the bitter campaign debate between him and Clinton about the wisdom of engaging with Iran's mullahs. That had been settled by the election. His first letter to the supreme leader of Iran, Ayatollah Ali Khamenei, would go out the following month.

Instead, he wanted to try to understand the motives of Iran, a country that had bedeviled his predecessors going back to Jimmy Carter, and remained a bundle of contradictions. Brutal theocracy and prolific sponsor of terrorism, but also a proud, ancient civilization and leader of the Shiite world. Mortal enemy of Israel and purveyor of weekly chants of "Death to America," but home to a large, educated middle class and a generally pro-American younger generation. Why do they approach things the way they do? he wanted to know. Were they capable of changing their behavior?

From above the marble fireplace, a young Teddy Roosevelt looked out over the group, which included Joe Biden; the national security adviser, Jim Jones; his two deputies, Tom Donilon and Denis McDonough; and Clinton's lead Iran diplomat, Bill Burns. The twenty-sixth president, famous for saying "Speak softly and carry a big stick," was a Rough Rider in this equestrian portrait, gripping the reins of his rearing steed, its black tail flying behind it—a warrior calling his cavalry to the glory of battle. One couldn't imagine a less appropriate image for the discussion Obama wanted to have that day.

The forty-forth president, after all, had begun his term declaring, "We will extend a hand if you are willing to unclench your fist." It was the signature foreign policy line in his inaugural address, and an explicit repudiation of Roosevelt's swaggering military adventurism, not to mention George W. Bush's Axis of Evil. Above all, it was a challenge to Iran. More so than Cuba, more so than Burma, more so than Syria or North Korea, Iran was the archenemy that Obama wanted to disarm. The president's offer of a hand was to be the ultimate test of his faith in a form of reasonable, respectful engagement that could—just maybe—wash away decades of enmity and mutual distrust.

In another way, though, the Roosevelt Room was the perfect place to plot a new start with Iran. TR's grandson Kermit Roosevelt, Jr., was the CIA officer who had helped orchestrate the 1953 coup that ousted Iran's democratically elected prime minister, Mohammed Mossadegh, reinstalling the Western-friendly shah Mohammed Reza Pahlavi. Roosevelt's bribery and propaganda campaign is a footnote to the Cold War, but for the mullahs who overthrew the shah in 1979, it planted the narrative of American perfidy that fueled their Islamic Revolution for thirty years—leaving Obama to wonder, on this March day, how to break the cycle of loathing.

To kick off the conversation, Clinton had brought along Dennis Ross, her special adviser on Iran. The choice was telling. Like Clinton, Ross was a confirmed Iran skeptic; his analysis was not encouraging. The Iranian regime, he said, had meaningfully changed its behavior only three times since 1979: after a decade of bloody stalemate in the Iran-Iraq War, when the Islamic Revolutionary Guard Corps told Ayatollah Khomeini he did not have enough troops to fight on forever; during the 1990s, when major European countries threatened Iran with sanctions for assassinating dissidents in Europe; and in 2003, when the United States ousted Saddam Hussein in three and a half weeks, leaving the Iranians to worry that they could be next. In each case, Iran felt forced to take a more pragmatic course.

"The implication," Ross recalled, "was 'You're not going to be able to *induce* them to change their behavior. This is a regime based on deep-seated suspicions, almost a sense of paranoia.'"

Obama listened intently, not pushing back. Even in small groups, he did not want to look like a naïf. But he picked up on the silver lining in Ross's presentation: Iran *had* changed course, even if temporarily, in response to outside forces before. It hadn't happened often, but it had happened. "I think the odds are low," Obama said, "but I really think we ought to engage them."

Then it was Clinton's turn to weigh in. She seconded the president, but with less enthusiasm. "Look," she said, "I think the odds of achieving anything with them are close to nil. But we have to try." The way to do that, she added, was less to cajole than to coerce them.

"The odds are long," Obama agreed.


Barack Obama and Hillary Clinton both thought that engaging the Iranian regime was the best, perhaps the only, way to prevent it from obtaining a nuclear bomb. Both shared the goal of striking a comprehensive, verifiable nuclear agreement. But their instincts about the nature of the regime and its capacity for change differed profoundly. Obama was the first president to refer to Iran as the Islamic Republic, lending the revolution legitimacy and ruling out an American need for regime change. He was the first to publicly admit America's complicity in the 1953 coup. It gave the Iranians, he said, a legitimate historic grievance against the United States. Clinton, on the other hand, was the first top Obama official to publicly accuse Iran of turning into a "military dictatorship." Speaking to students in February 2010 in Qatar, she urged Iran's political and religious leaders to rise up against the Islamic Revolutionary Guard Corps—a statement that, if not a call for regime change, sounded awfully close to it.

Circumstances drew them close for a time. Clinton, serving the man who had defeated her, embraced a policy that initially placed more value on extending an olive branch than wielding a club. Obama, having watched his early efforts at diplomacy collapse amid the repression of the Green Movement, shifted to a sanctions strategy that more closely aligned him with Clinton. Their differing instincts made Clinton and Obama perfect partners for a two-track policy of pressure and engagement. She played bad cop to his good cop, enlisting a coalition of countries to impose punishing sanctions on Iran, while he sent letters to the supreme leader or videotaped greetings to the Iranian people on the Persian New Year. He pitched in on sanctions from time to time, particularly in bringing along the Russians, and she did her part for diplomacy, sending a team of trusted lieutenants to Oman in July 2012 to explore a secret back channel with the Iranians. As Clinton later put it, she "set the table" for the nuclear talks that John Kerry conducted.

Yet the comparison to Kerry is instructive: While Clinton was folding napkins and laying out silverware, he was itching to break bread with the Iranians. In December 2011, when he was still in the Senate, Kerry held his own secret talks in Oman, which created the predicate for the State Department's channel. "Hillary and company were skeptical," Kerry told me. She worried that he had promised the Iranians concessions that the White House was not yet willing to make. Her decision to send her own team to Oman was motivated as much by her desire to corral Kerry as to reach out to the Iranians. Kerry's hunger to cut a deal would manifest itself again in the summer of 2015 when, as secretary of state, he spent weeks in Vienna hammering out the final terms of the historic agreement on Iran's nuclear program.

Would Clinton have played Kerry's role had the diplomacy matured enough before she left office? Quite possibly. But if Clinton had been elected in 2008 instead of Obama, it's not clear the two sides would ever have gotten to Vienna.

After she left the State Department, Clinton diverged from the president on a key tactical question: whether to impose a harsh new round of sanctions on the Iranians after they elected Hassan Rouhani, who had run for president on a platform of seeking better relations with the West as a way of easing Iran's economic isolation. Clinton was swayed by the argument made by many in Congress— as well as by Benjamin Netanyahu—that Iran was on the ropes, so desperate for a deal that tightening the vise would have extracted better terms. "She would have squeezed them again," a person close to her said, "and the only debate is what they would have done." Obama thought ratcheting up the pressure would have undercut Rouhani, emboldened the hard-liners in Tehran, and unraveled the sanctions coalition. He persuaded the Senate to hold off on new sanctions, even after the House had passed legislation designed to drive Iran's oil exports to zero.

"They shared the same tactic, which was engagement, but they envisioned different endgames," said Karim Sadjadpour, a leading analyst on Iran at the Carnegie Endowment for International Peace. "The president's endgame was, 'I'm a guy who can bridge differences. I've bridged races and countries all my life, so I'm going to be able to resolve this.' Clinton had a more cynical view of the endgame. 'We're going to engage them not because we think they're going to reciprocate, but because when they rebuff us, it will expose the fact that the problem lies in Tehran, and not in Washington.'"

In the end, of course, Obama's hope prevailed over Clinton's cynicism, at least to the extent that Iran finally signed a deal in July 2015. It is without a doubt Obama's most significant foreign policy legacy, the once-in-a-generation achievement he had spoken of with reporters on Air Force One three years earlier. To reassure dubious lawmakers at home and rattled friends abroad, the president defined the deal on the narrowest possible grounds, as an arms control agreement. Yet his unspoken hope was that it would have "tacit transformational potential," in the words of Robert Litwak of the Woodrow Wilson International Center for Scholars, empowering Iran's moderates and setting the country on a new course. The 1979 revolution was a hinge event in the Middle East, redrawing alliances, planting the seeds of future wars, and pulling the United States into decades of military entanglements that Obama hoped, finally, to end. Bringing Iran in from the cold could realign the region more profoundly than anything since Britain and France secretly struck the Sykes-Picot Agreement, drawing the borders of the modern Middle East, in 1916.

The focus in the aftermath of the diplomacy, however, was on a less grandiose matter: enforcing the terms of the deal amid deep suspicion on the part of Israel and America's Sunni allies in the Persian Gulf. Iran, pushed by hard-liners at home, continued to support Hezbollah, Hamas, Bashar al-Assad in Syria, and the Houthi rebels in Yemen—only now it was able to finance its terrorist proxies with the billions of dollars that had been freed up by the lifting of sanctions. European countries were eager to get back into business with Iran, raising doubts that those sanctions could ever be reimposed. These challenges, Clinton made clear, suited a cynic better than an optimist. "There is absolutely no reason to trust Iran," she declared at the Brookings Institution in September 2015. "It's not enough just to say yes to this deal. Of course it isn't. We have to say 'yes, *and*.' 'Yes, *and*' we will enforce it with vigor and vigilance. 'Yes, *and*' we will embed it in a broader strategy to confront Iran's bad behavior in the region. 'Yes, *and*' we will begin from day one to set the conditions so Iran knows it will never be able to get a nuclear weapon, not during the term of the agreement, not after, not ever."

Clinton's track record as secretary of state gave her unique credibility to act as Iran's overseer, said Jake Sullivan. "She's built one coalition that was tremendously effective in imposing sanctions," he said. "If it comes to it, she can rally the world to both deter and punish Iran."

At the State Department, Sullivan was a member of the three-person team that conducted the back-channel talks with Iran; he stayed on the team for several months after John Kerry took over the negotiations as secretary of state in 2014. His altar boy demeanor makes him an unlikely heavy, but Sullivan shares Clinton's suspicion of Iran, and he often played the bad cop to Kerry's good cop in the talks, much as Clinton had done on sanctions during the first term. In the early days of the Oman channel, he was Clinton's eyes and ears on the most sensitive diplomatic gambit of her tenure as secretary of state—one in which she had no direct role.

For all the haggling in Vienna, the basic framework of the nuclear deal was laid down in the back-channel talks that began in July 2012 in Oman and continued, on-again, off-again, through much of 2013 in Oman, Geneva, and New York. The twisted path to a deal reveals more about the roles of Clinton and Obama than the deal's final terms. Recounting the secret history of America's diplomacy with Tehran sheds light on how they—and Kerry, the critical third leg of this stool—approached Iran, the most complicated, politically vexed foreign policy issue of their administration.

It was Memorial Day weekend in May 2009 and the State Department was deserted when the phone rang in Ray Takeyh's office. The secretary of his new boss, Dennis Ross, was calling. Would he like to sit in on a meeting Ross was about to have with a special visitor from Oman? Born in Tehran and educated at Oxford, Takeyh had joined the government from the Council on Foreign Relations to advise Ross on Iran policy. He combined his boss's skepticism of Iran with a contrarian perspective. He wrote, for example, that the CIA had little to do with the ouster of Mossadegh; most of the blame lay with Iran's clerics—which implied that their grievances against the United States were both self-serving and bogus. Takeyh agreed to sit in on the meeting, though he worried that it would be a waste of time.

The moment the president said he was ready to extend a hand to Tehran, everyone and his brother began showing up at the State

Department with ideas about how to grease the handshake. The Turks, Western-friendly Iranians, a Canadian diplomat, a former Spanish prime minister—all claimed links to Iranians who were ready to talk. "You had people like that all the time," Takeyh recalled. "I got a message, I got a deal, someone's cousin was with my mother's boyfriend." Takeyh went down to the lobby of the State Department to fetch the visitor. At first glance, the smiling man with the salt-and-pepper beard who was standing beneath the lobby's wall of flags looked no different than any other would-be intermediary.

Salem ben Nasser al-Ismaily was a fifty-one-year-old Omani developer, corporate director, and philanthropist. Well connected in the United States, he was the kind of fellow who could switch from Arabic to English as easily as he did from the robes and headdress of his native land to a Savile Row suit. He was bearing books—he has written several about the history and culture of the Arabian Gulf—which he handed out as gifts. But he was also carrying a sheet of paper that contained an offer by Iran to negotiate with the Obama administration on a range of issues, from the nuclear program to Iran's support for Hezbollah. Ismaily assured Ross he could bring the Iranians to the table.

Oman, he said, would be an ideal venue for secret negotiations: sleepy, off the beaten track, with few journalists to report on the comings and goings of foreign diplomats. A desert sultanate at the mouth of the Persian Gulf, it had long prided itself on its role as mediator between the West and the mullahs. It lies only fifty miles from Iran, across the Strait of Hormuz, the world's most strategic waterway. Oman is ruled with a benign but iron hand by Qaboos bin Said, the well-coiffed sultan who overthrew his father in 1970 in a palace coup. Qaboos is the only game in town: When Clinton paid him a visit in January 2011, his five-hundred-foot yacht, *Al Said*, floated majestically, all by itself, in the sparkling harbor of Muscat, the well-kept capital. The sultan's unchallenged rule allowed him to play the maverick in foreign affairs. He was alone among Arab leaders in not cutting off ties to Egypt after it signed a peace treaty with Israel in 1979; played host to multilateral meetings of the Arab states and Israel; and visited Ayatollah Khamenei in 2009 at a time when Iran was a pariah because of its crackdown on pro-democracy protesters.

Salem Ismaily was the sultan's personal emissary. Born in 1958 to a well-known Arab family, he grew up in Zanzibar, the island off East Africa that had long been a possession of Oman and remained under Omani influence until 1964. He was orphaned when his family home was destroyed in fighting over control of Zanzibar. Ismaily was taken under the wing of the royal family, which underwrote his education in Britain and the United States. With his education and connections to the sultan, he amassed a tidy business empire, starting a bank and building industrial estates outside Muscat.

In 1996, Ismaily became the executive president of the Omani Center for Investment Promotion and Export Development. He traveled widely, proposing joint oil-exploration projects with American firms or pitching aluminum companies to open rolling mills in Oman. His name surfaced in a State Department cable in 2006, when he declined an invitation to attend a U.S.-Arab economic forum because Congress had not yet ratified a trade agreement between Oman and the United States. He also became a roving fixer for the sultan, interceding with foreign governments to help Omanis who got into trouble abroad. It was this moonlighting that would put him in the middle of the most sensitive diplomacy of the Obama presidency.

In October 2015, Salem and I met for dinner in Dallas, where he was on a business trip. He was charming company, with a dry wit, a gentle manner, and a deep knowledge of Oman's history. With his polished loafers and tailored jacket worn over a golf shirt, he fit in well with the manicured clientele at the Mansion on Turtle Creek, where we dined. As is typical of people who do most of their work in the shadows, he was also elusive, declining to speak on the record about his role in the secret talks. (The account below is drawn from half a dozen officials who took part in the negotiations.)

When Ismaily made his first approach to the State Department in May 2009, Ross peppered him with questions. Who had written the Iranian offer of negotiations that he was carrying? Ismaily and his Iranian contacts had written it together, he said (not very comforting). Which Iranians was he talking to? Ismaily mentioned the head of a religious trust that had close links to the supreme leader (a little more comforting). Normally, Ross told me, he viewed these proposals, "not with a grain of salt, but a small ton of salt." But Ross had gotten to know the Omanis through his work on Middle East peace issues in the 1990s, and he knew their ties to the Iranians were genuine. He decided to pass along Ismaily's proposal, with a caveat-laden cover memo, to Hillary Clinton. She told Ross to keep talking to him.

While Ross cultivated his new Omani friend, the president sent two secret letters to Ayatollah Khamenei. The first, which laid out the possibility of a fresh start between the two countries, drew a querulous, multipage response from the supreme leader. (Obama was right about the Iranians having grievances.) Khamenei's reply was enough, however, to embolden the president to send a shorter follow-up letter, in which Obama proposed direct talks over the nuclear program. He even named the two diplomats he would dispatch: Bill Burns and Puneet Talwar, the senior White House official working on Iran. Khamenei never wrote back.

Then, in June 2009, Iran erupted in fury. Mahmoud Ahmadinejad was reelected president in a vote that clearly had been rigged, and angry crowds poured into the streets of Tehran to protest—the greatest act of defiance against the regime since the revolution. The police and a paramilitary group known as the Basij began a vicious crackdown. The unrest reached a bloody climax on June 20, when a twenty-six-year-old philosophy student, Neda Agha-Soltan, was fatally shot in the chest on her way to an anti-government rally. Her death, caught on amateur video and beamed worldwide on YouTube—her eyes rolling back in her head, blood gushing from her mouth and nose—became an iconic moment in the doomed struggle for democracy. Throughout the days and weeks of rage, neither Obama nor Clinton spoke up on behalf of what became known as the Green Movement. The Iranian authorities, they were told by dissidents, would use Uncle Sam's endorsement to discredit the protesters. Obama went a step further in his equivocation: He said there wasn't much difference between Ahmadinejad and his closest rival in the election, Mir Hussein Moussavi. "Either way," Obama said, we're "going to be dealing with a regime that has historically been hostile to the United States."

Clinton, characteristically, didn't challenge the White House's edict of noninterference. The only time she ever showed any public daylight with Obama on Iran was in July 2009 when she said, during a trip to Thailand, that the United States would consider extending a "defense umbrella" over its allies in the Middle East to shield them from a nuclear-armed Tehran. That phrase rattled Obama's aides because it suggested the White House was laying plans to contain the Iranians when its stated policy was to prevent them from getting a bomb. It also harkened back to hawkish remarks she had made during a campaign debate with Obama, when she said that if Iran were to attack Israel, "We would be able to totally obliterate them."

Privately, however, Clinton showed frustration with the hands-off approach. A revealing moment came early in the uprising, after officials at the State Department began noticing that the protesters were using social media sites such as Twitter to share information about rallies. Twitter had scheduled routine maintenance on its network, which required taking down the site for several hours. A young State Department official, Jared Cohen, emailed Twitter's cofounder Jack Dorsey to ask him to defer the work so Iranians would not lose the ability to swap messages. Dorsey agreed. Clinton's aides were angry that Cohen had contravened the White House's orders, fearing it would cause trouble for their boss. But she dismissed the complaints; this, she said, was exactly what the State Department should be doing.

With the benefit of hindsight, Clinton concluded that the administration botched its response to the Green Movement. "I came to regret that we did not speak out more forcefully and rally others to do the same," she wrote. For her, Iran's brutal suppression of the uprising marked the welcome end of Obama's diplomatic overture and the beginning of a phase more suited to her: building support for sanctions. Dennis Ross, meanwhile, had left the State Department for the White House. The Omani channel was not closed, but it was dormant, a tantalizing opportunity still untested.

For the first half of 2010, Clinton was a dark evangelist, preaching a message that Iran could be brought to heel if its economy were squeezed hard enough. Her goal was to rally support for a UN Security Council resolution that would impose harsh new oil and banking sanctions on the Iranian government. In Brasília, she pleaded with President Luiz Inácio Lula da Silva not to pursue his own nuclear diplomacy with Tehran because it would undercut the sanctions. (A deal that Brazil cooked up with Turkey fell apart.) In Doha, she tried to buck up Arab allies by issuing her warning that Iran was "moving toward a military dictatorship." In Beijing, she pressed the Chinese leaders to cut their commercial ties with Iran.

It was a tough job against long odds, said Tom Donilon, because it meant persuading Asians and Europeans, huge trading partners of Iran, to agree to steps "that had a real cost." India, Japan, and South Korea were major importers of Iranian oil; Germany sold the Iranians machinery; Russia had built them a nuclear plant. But it was the right job for Clinton, given her obvious preference for sticks over carrots in dealing with the mullahs. David Miliband, the former foreign secretary of Britain, admired how she was able to turn what had been a political rift between her and Obama ("there had obviously been the spat in the campaign," he said) into a common cause. "Her focus was on coalition building," he told me. "She could throw herself into that." Clinton's aides joked about how she had developed a crush on Miliband: Tall and trim with dark good looks, he was young enough to be her son and articulate in the effortless way of many British public officials. She also valued his opinion, so she listened in the days leading up to the UN vote when he warned her that if China did not vote for the resolution, other undecided members might peel off, leaving the sanctions short of the minimum nine votes in the Security Council.

Much of the lobbying was being done in New York by Susan Rice, the UN ambassador. But Clinton's chance to cement the deal with Beijing came on June 7, 2010, in a most unlikely place: Lima, Peru. Ostensibly, she was there for a meeting of the Organization of American States, which was then squabbling over whether to readmit Honduras after a coup in which its leftist president had been bundled out of the country. As news events go, it was a bust. After unenthusiastically filing our stories, the reporters traveling with her decamped to an outdoor cantina on the bluffs of Lima, overlooking the Pacific. It was four P.M. Low clouds blotted out the view. We ordered a round of *pisco* sours, a potent local cocktail made with *pisco,* a Peruvian liquor; lemon juice; egg whites; and bitters. Then we ordered another round.

Thinking Clinton might be similarly at loose ends, we invited her to join us for drinks. It was something we did from time to time to get past the formality of news conferences and photo ops. Her aides responded positively: Clinton liked a drink after work, and the OAS meeting hadn't exactly been heavy lifting for her, either. At six P.M., we settled our checks and shambled across the road to the J. W. Marriott Hotel, where we rendezvoused in a bar off the lobby with Clinton, Huma Abedin, and Philippe Reines. Clinton was in a buoyant mood and quickly drained her first *pisco* sour. Abedin kept a close eye on her; she was always wary of Clinton letting down her guard with reporters, even impaired ones. Also, Clinton had one more meeting that evening. She had arranged to confer with the Chinese ambassador to Washington, Zhang Yesui, who was at the Lima meeting as an observer. Their plan was to go over some last-minute details in the Iran sanctions resolution before the Security Council voted on it two days later. When Abedin's Black-Berry buzzed to tell her the ambassador was ready, Clinton made a suggestion: Why not invite him to the bar?

Ten minutes later, Zhang turned up. A proper diplomat, he

looked vaguely unsettled by the choice of venue. Clinton gave him an effusive welcome and motioned him to a table in the back. The journalists smelled trouble: Zhang appeared stone-cold sober; Clinton was not. This negotiation was going to be a mismatch, we said, only half in jest; the remedy was to order a round of *pisco* sours for Clinton and Zhang, so he could catch up. I carried the drinks over to the table, crossing a line from covering the news to becoming part of it. Apologizing to Clinton for the interruption, I turned to Zhang and said, "We didn't want you to miss out on the local Peruvian drink, Mr. Ambassador." He murmured his thanks. I set down a frosty glass in front of Zhang, then returned to the bar, leaving the two of them to their negotiation.

In Clinton's account of the episode in her memoir, she described me as ebullient in my role as a waiter (true: I can't help it) and claimed that we reporters "had no idea that negotiations were going on right under their noses" (false: Clinton had told us she was going to discuss Iran-related matters with Zhang, even if she didn't give us any details at the time). As it happened, they were comparing drafts of an annex to Security Council Resolution 1929, which designated which Iranian banks would be sanctioned and which Chinese state-owned enterprises would pull their investments out of Iran. Nailing down these details was vital to securing a yes vote from China.

Two days later, the Security Council, China included, voted 12 to 2 to slap Iran with new sanctions. The UN's action was followed by separate American and European sanctions that crippled Iran's oil exports, depleted its currency, and set the stage for the first serious talks over its nuclear program. Clinton's lobbying campaign, sealed with a drink in a hotel bar in Peru, would be one of her major achievements as secretary of state.

Salem Ismaily never stopped trying to open a channel between the United States and Iran. His next chance came unexpectedly on July 31, 2009, when Iranian guards arrested three young Americans hik-

ing on the border between Iran and Iraqi Kurdistan. The three—
Sarah Shourd, Shane Bauer, and Josh Fattal—were charged with
illegal entry and espionage; they said they did not even realize they
had crossed into Iranian territory. They were held in Tehran's grim
Evin prison, home to political prisoners from the 1979 revolution,
and spent the first four months in solitary confinement.

The hikers' case quickly drew worldwide attention—Obama
and Clinton called for their release, as did Desmond Tutu, Sean
Penn, and Ashton Kutcher—but it just as quickly got tangled up in
the politics of the United States–Iran relationship. The State Department went to work with the Swiss, who have represented
America's diplomatic interests in Tehran since 1979, to no avail.
The months dragged on without any progress. Then Ismaily approached Ross with an offer: Why not have Oman act as a mediator? Ross agreed.

On September 14, 2010, Sarah Shourd was released on bail of
five billion Iranian rial (then roughly $465,000). Iranian officials
said they acted on humanitarian grounds because she had health
problems. The payment was made by Ismaily, who flew to Tehran
in his private jet to pick her up. Bauer and Fattal were less
fortunate—they would be tried and convicted by the Revolutionary
Court—but Ismaily kept working on a similar amnesty for them.
Jake Sullivan briefed Clinton on his efforts, though she never met
the Omani. On July 31, 2011, Sullivan emailed her that a verdict
was expected soon. "Leaves the door open for Salem," he wrote,
suggesting that the Iranians, having made their point, might be
open to a deal. Six weeks later, the two men were released, their
nearly $1 million in bail also picked up by the Omanis.

In a book the hikers wrote about their imprisonment, they por-
tray Ismaily as a kind of mysterious Arab prince who appeared in
the spring of 2010, giving them hope amid grinding despair. "As
soon as he enters the room, the air becomes redolent with sandalwood," Shane Bauer wrote of their first meeting with him in a conference room at the Evin prison. "He walks toward us, smiling
warmly. His lightly bearded face is gentle but self-possessed and

gives off an aura of power—not the same kind of power his Iranian escorts display, but one that is regal." Ismaily introduced himself, bearing the best wishes of Sultan Qaboos. He said nothing about their case, but spoke discursively about other topics, telling them that not all Arabs are terrorists, for example, and talking about the need for Americans to understand the Middle East. Finally, he got around to the point of his visit. "Look, I don't want to get your hopes up," he told them. "Let's just say I'm trying to help you, OK?"

For the White House, the release of the hikers was a major test passed by the Omanis. Ismaily had proved he could deliver with Iran. Now it was his turn to ask for something in return. Iran had its own list of citizens jailed in the United States and Britain, whom it wanted freed. About a year later, three Iranians accused of illegally exporting night-vision goggles and other U.S. military equipment to Iran were quietly released. American officials denied a quid pro quo: the two held in the United States, Shahrzad Mir Gholikhan and Mojtaba Atarodi, had completed their sentences and were awaiting paperwork before being deported. The third, Nosratollah Tajik, was being held in Britain; a British court had decided not to extradite him to the United States, citing delays in his legal case. Still, the timing and symmetry gave the Omanis something to show the Iranians. It helped pave the way for future diplomacy.

Two months after Sarah Shourd was freed, Dennis Ross and Puneet Talwar traveled secretly to Oman to hear from the sultan himself how he thought a channel could work. What Qaboos told them left them impressed: He had visited Ayatollah Khamenei and was confident of Iran's seriousness in seeking a nuclear deal; he was not about to risk his prestige on a failed negotiation. They, in turn, gave the sultan a message to convey to the supreme leader: Obama was determined to prevent Iran from getting a nuclear weapon, but he would prefer to resolve the dispute diplomatically. A month later, Clinton stopped in Muscat for her own briefing with the sultan. She was skeptical the channel would work, but listened. "Even under the best of circumstances, this was a long shot," she wrote.

Obama was more intrigued: He telephoned Qaboos twice over the next few months to probe him on whether he could deliver Iranians who spoke with the authority of Khamenei. The White House, intent on secrecy, did not disclose the calls.

"He was genuinely curious about trying to find an out-of-box approach to change the dynamic," John Kerry told me.

Kerry was by far the most vocal champion of the back channel. He had long nourished the idea of opening lines of communication to Iran, and he saw his chance when he got involved, as chairman of the Senate Foreign Relations Committee, in trying to free the hikers. That put him in contact with Sultan Qaboos and his fixer, Salem Ismaily. It was the kind of assignment that Kerry took on throughout the first term—whether negotiating the release of a jailed CIA contractor in Pakistan or persuading Hamid Karzai to accept a runoff election in Afghanistan—and it made him a valued troubleshooter. But his freelancing was not without its tensions. Among Clinton's aides, the question of whom Kerry was serving—the administration or himself—always hovered. Often, they would insist on sending a State Department official with him to coordinate the message.

In the case of Iran, Kerry was operating on his own. He made several visits to Oman in 2011 and the first half of 2012, during which he spent hours talking to the sultan about the possibility of secret talks with Iran. (The two became so close that in January 2015 Kerry was the only foreign official allowed to visit Qaboos in the German Alpine resort town of Garmisch-Partenkirchen, where he was being treated for cancer.) Kerry also met with Ismaily—sometimes in London and Rome; other times in Washington. Over a long dinner in a private room at Morton's steakhouse, they mapped out what a channel would look like. Kerry became convinced that Oman could deliver Iranians who represented the supreme leader. In any event, he told Obama in a one-on-one meeting in the Oval Office, the only way to test that theory was to meet them.

Clinton and others on the NSC, however, had deep doubts about whether the channel was reliable. They deliberated for months without making a decision. Kerry grew frustrated with what he viewed as foot-dragging by the State Department and the White House. Some on his staff wondered whether Clinton, in her last year as secretary, was content to run out the clock. Briefing her and the president in the Situation Room about his conversations, Kerry warned that if they did not move, the sultan would conclude the United States was not serious about pursuing a diplomatic solution with Iran. The longer they waited, the greater the danger that word of the talks between the Omanis and the Americans would leak out.

"If this is going to go anywhere," Kerry told his Senate chief of staff, David Wade, "we have to get people in a room talking."

He reminded Wade of his own history, as a Vietnam veteran who fought for an end to the war.

"When I was twenty-five years old," Kerry recalled, "reading about the negotiations in Paris over Vietnam, they spent a year and a half negotiating over the shape of the table, and a lot of people died."

In his zeal to jump-start the negotiations, Kerry passed several messages to the Iranians through Ismaily. The senator was coordinating his talking points with Tom Donilon at the NSC, with whom he had a close relationship, but his aggressive approach alarmed Clinton and others at the State Department. Kerry, several officials said, indicated to the Iranians that the United States would acknowledge, at the outset of the talks, that Iran had a right to enrich uranium for a civil nuclear-energy program. Iran had long demanded such a concession, claiming that this right was guaranteed by the Nuclear Non-Proliferation Treaty, of which it is a signatory. But the United States had steadfastly refused, going back to the second Bush administration, and the Obama administration was, at that moment, debating how and when to relax that position.

Kerry denied that he ever signaled to Iranian officials they had a *right* to enrich. "I was very careful from day one," he told me.

"There is no, was no, and never is, within the confines of the NPT, a right to enrich. And we made it crystal clear to them: 'You don't have a right to enrich.'" At the same time, Kerry did hold out the prospect of Iran having a peaceful nuclear program, which the Iranians viewed as being synonymous with possessing an enrichment capacity. He was openly dismissive of hard-liners in Israel and the United States who demanded that Iran dismantle its nuclear infrastructure. "There would have been no negotiation, had the negotiation been to strip them of everything that they had achieved after great difficulty, with assassinations and Stuxnet," Kerry said, referring to two covert and still unacknowledged programs designed to thwart Iran's nuclear ambitions: the alleged killings of Iranian scientists by Israeli agents, and an Israeli-American cyberattack that crippled Iran's centrifuges with a computer worm.

It's quite plausible Kerry never uttered the words "right to enrich" and yet still left the Iranians with that impression. His negotiating style, on public display three years later in the final phase of the talks, was to create a sense of possibility, a win-win atmosphere. He rarely, if ever, played the bad cop. Ismaily may also have embellished Kerry's words. It was generally accepted inside the White House that any comprehensive deal would involve granting Iran some enrichment. In some ways Kerry and his enthusiastic Omani go-between were merely cutting to the chase.

In the fragile atmosphere of early 2012, however, Kerry's forward-leaning style was viewed as a liability. Clinton and Obama worried that the Iranians would believe he was speaking for the White House. He was, after all, a former Democratic presidential nominee, as well as chairman of the Foreign Relations Committee. "The view in the White House was 'Look, John is trying to be helpful here, and he's got good contacts with these people, but it's important that we not mislead them,'" a former official said. Sometime in the spring, Obama decided it was time for the executive branch to take over the secret channel. Kerry didn't protest: As a senator, he knew there was a limit to how far he could take things. He took solace from a casual exchange with Tom Donilon.

Why would he want to keep flying to Oman? Donilon asked Kerry. He might soon be secretary of state, in which case he would have far more on his plate than furtive talks about centrifuges.

"Salem's going to deliver people if you and Puneet can go meet with them," Bill Burns said by phone to Jake Sullivan.

It was the first week of June 2012, and Sullivan was in Scandinavia with Clinton, who was there to talk about the future of the Arctic Ocean. At long last, the Iranians were ready to send emissaries to an exploratory meeting. The White House's goals were modest: to see whether the Omanis could run a secret channel, and to determine if there was enough common ground to justify further meetings. A month later, on July 6, Sullivan quietly left Clinton's side during a visit to Paris and boarded a commercial flight to Muscat. At one level, he was an odd choice for such a sensitive mission. "He didn't have the high profile and years of experience that others had who could have been sent," Clinton told me. "But he had my full confidence, and he was still low-enough profile that he could travel back and forth without inciting undue interest."

Waiting for Sullivan was Ismaily, along with Puneet Talwar and Emmett Beliveau, a White House advance man whose job was to set up secure communications for the meeting. To stay undercover, the three visitors avoided hotels, sleeping on couches in an empty house owned by the American embassy. The next morning, they were ushered into a beautifully appointed room in the royal office. The Iranians asked to come in through a different door than the Americans, and to skip handshakes. With Ismaily, the accommodating host, sitting at the head of a large, polished wooden table, the Americans faced off against four midlevel officials from the Iranian foreign ministry, among them Reza Zabib, who later became ambassador to Cyprus, and Reza Najafi, who became Iran's envoy to the International Atomic Energy Agency. A more senior Iranian, deputy foreign minister Ali Asghar Khaji, was on hand to give instructions to the team. He waited in another room and did not meet the Americans, reflecting Iran's reluctance to invest a preliminary meeting with too much significance.

By all accounts, the meeting was a flop.

The Iranians demanded that the United States recognize their right to enrich uranium, the Americans said no, and the Iranians proposed a variety of formulations to get to the same result, and the Americans said no again. They went around in circles like this for eight hours, punctuated by breaks to sip tea. Finally, Sullivan decided to put an end to it. "We're not going to stay here to keep nickel and diming with these guys," he said to his colleagues. "We need to go."

"If we leave here empty-handed," an Iranian official warned them, "Tehran will never let us come back."

Sullivan had his own misgivings about cutting off the meeting, losing sleep over the decision for a month. He told a crestfallen Ismaily that the United States would be happy to meet again, but only if Iran agreed to negotiate with no preconditions or expectations.

At least the meeting stayed secret. In October 2012, the administration got a scare when Helene Cooper and I got wind of the contacts and reported in *The New York Times* that Iran had agreed to one-on-one nuclear talks with the United States after the presidential election. The White House denied there was any such deal, which we said had come about after "intense, secret exchanges between American and Iranian officials." Our report, landing in the final month of the campaign, became a political hot potato. Mitt Romney accused Obama of appeasement. "Those are reports in the newspaper," Obama said during their final debate. "They are not true."

Four months later, in March 2013, the United States and Iran were back at the bargaining table.

Clinton was gone now, replaced by John Kerry, the tireless booster of the secret channel. Sullivan had grudgingly agreed to stay on in the administration as Joe Biden's national security adviser. Obama had to call him from Air Force One to make a personal appeal that he take the job, which had the added dividend of keeping him on the negotiating team. This time, Bill Burns headed the delegation, which also included Puneet Talwar and Bob Einhorn, an expert in arms-control issues. Einhorn had overseen the State Department's imposition of the sanctions. Renowned for his capacity to drill into the details, he had been nicknamed "the dentist" by the Chinese. Talwar, a former adviser to Biden, was the team's link to the White House; he didn't hesitate to invoke Obama's name. Burns and Sullivan were first among equals, but there was an obvious father-and-son dynamic to their relationship.

A soft-spoken career diplomat whose good manners and wavy gray hair and mustache were equally out of style (the wags in the NSC press shop called him 'Stache), Burns was known for his witty, perspicacious diplomatic cables, which reached a wider audience thanks to WikiLeaks. His account of a booze-soaked three-day wedding reception in Dagestan, Timothy Garton Ash said, was "almost worthy of Evelyn Waugh." His no-drama style appealed to Obama, who liked having him at the table. In Muscat, one of his jobs was to bring down the temperature when tempers flared—often after Sullivan said things like "I'm telling you, this is not going to happen." He sometimes went for walks in the garden with Ali Khaji, who by then was talking to the Americans, not hiding in the next room. Burns was mild-mannered, so when he raised his voice, it got the attention of the Iranians.

This time, Ismaily assured Burns, Iran was ready to negotiate from a "clean baseline." The White House had also decided on a way to address the Iranian demand to keep enriching uranium. "Whether we're prepared to explore the continuation of a domestic enrichment program," Burns told them, "depends upon whether you're prepared to explore the very sharp constraints and verification measures that we and international partners will demand to eventually produce a comprehensive agreement." The key word was "explore," and it had not been chosen lightly.

For two years, the White House had wrestled over how to grant Iran enrichment without giving it a pathway to a bomb. The president, with an interest in nonproliferation that went back to college, threw himself into the nitty-gritty. "We had some extraordinary meetings with Obama," recalled Gary Samore, who coordinated nonproliferation policy at the NSC in the first term, "where we went over with him in great technical detail what the options were for allowing Iran to have some limited enrichment capacity, which we could offer them as a diplomatic overture, but which wouldn't pose a proliferation threat. We went over numbers and types of centrifuges, stockpiles of low-enriched uranium, verification techniques."

The March meeting between the Americans and the Iranians took place in a more relaxed setting: an Omani officers' club, with a complex of villas overlooking the sea. Ismaily made introductions and then withdrew, though he kept vigil outside, checking his cellphone in case they needed anything. Obama had called the sultan beforehand to reinforce his requirements for the negotiations. But again, the session bogged down over enrichment. The Iranians invoked what they said were earlier offers by Kerry, delivered via the Omanis. "We don't know whether you have accurately portrayed what Senator Kerry said, but we can tell you this is our position," one of the negotiators recalled telling them. "We are authorized by the president to say what we're saying. You can take what we say as authoritative statements of the U.S. position."

The Americans also broached a critical issue: They were not going to keep talking unless Iran agreed to place immediate, temporary curbs on its program (the fear being that the Iranians would string out the talks while quietly expanding their enrichment capacity). In effect, the Americans were demanding an interim agreement that would stay in place until the two sides reached a comprehensive agreement. The Iranians said they were open to that, although Iran's political landscape was so murky, with Ahmadinejad in the waning days of his presidency, that it was not clear how solid the Iranian position was. Still, the meeting ended on a better note than the one eight months earlier.

Then, in June, Hassan Rouhani was elected president.

For Obama, this was an opportunity—evidence, perhaps, of the elusive change in Iranian behavior the president and his aides had debated in the Roosevelt Room back in 2009. Over the summer, he sent Rouhani a congratulatory letter and proposed a new diplomatic push on the nuclear issue. Addressing the president rather than the supreme leader was itself extremely significant: It showed that Obama thought Rouhani had been empowered by Ayatollah Khamenei to conduct negotiations with the United States. Speaking to NBC News, Rouhani said Obama's letter "could be subtle and tiny steps for a very important future."

That future began in September 2013 with a new round of talks. The American team was unchanged, but the Iranians now fielded two skilled diplomats, Abbas Araghchi and Majid Takht-Ravanchi, who reported to a new foreign minister, Mohammad Javad Zarif. He was an American-educated former envoy to the United Nations, where he had been involved in an abortive diplomatic effort in 2003 to forge a "grand bargain" with the United States. From the first meeting, it was clear that these Iranians were ready to deal: They accepted the idea of an interim agreement and quickly moved to negotiating a draft text.

After all the uncertainty, the nagging doubts on both sides, the long breaks when the secret channel lay dormant, there were a flurry of meetings between Labor Day and Thanksgiving: three in Oman, one in New York, two in Geneva. As always, there were snags. In one of the first sessions, Takht-Ravanchi overstated Iran's readiness to accept the Additional Protocol, an agreement with the IAEA that granted inspectors broad access to Iran's nuclear facilities. He had to backpedal at the next meeting. The Iranians complained that the United States was being stingy about the Iranian funds it was prepared to free as part of sanctions relief, and they bridled at the list of demands to dismantle or mothball their nuclear equipment. "What else are you going to ask for?" Araghchi asked, staring coldly at the Americans.

Fears grew that the whole exercise would be publicly exposed. I ran into Puneet Talwar in a hotel in Geneva in early November, the day after *The Wall Street Journal* reported that he'd been involved in secret talks with Iran. When I asked him whether the report was true, he laughed it off, but at that very moment, he, Burns, and Sullivan were locked in intense negotiations. When the two sides met during the General Assembly, they steered clear of the UN's Turtle Bay neighborhood, renting rooms at the InterContinental hotel near Times Square. They felt their cover was less likely to be blown in Manhattan than anyplace else. ("Five guys in white shirts buttoned all the way up with no ties can blend in there pretty well," Burns said, referring to the standard business attire for Iranian men.)

While the negotiators were dickering over text, Obama was looking to make history: a meeting with Iran's new president at the United Nations, the first face-to-face meeting of American and Iranian leaders since Jimmy Carter toasted the shah in 1977. He put Sullivan in charge of setting it up. Working with an aide in Rouhani's office whom he had gotten to know through the nuclear talks, Sullivan negotiated what's known in diplomatic parlance as a pull aside—a brief encounter that looks impromptu even if it is anything but. On the evening of Monday, September 23, 2013, Sullivan went to a reception hosted by the president at the residence of Ambassador Samantha Power, a palatial apartment on the forty-second floor of the Waldorf Astoria, to deliver some news: The meeting, he told Obama, looked like it was a go for the next day.

At the last minute on Tuesday, however, the Iranians got cold feet. After a brief debate among Obama's aides, the White House put out word that the president had been receptive to a meeting but that the Iranians had pulled the plug. This leak was designed to put pressure on Rouhani. Critics, even some former administration officials, sniped that Obama's pursuit of the Iranian leader was unseemly. Three days later, the aide to Rouhani called Sullivan, now back in Washington, to propose a phone call. He and Ben Rhodes took the idea to Obama in the Oval Office.

"Yeah, set it up," he told them.

Sullivan had scribbled down two cellphone numbers for Rouhani, whose aides were carrying multiple phones. He sprinted to his office to double-check them. Back in the Oval Office at 2:30 P.M., a panting Sullivan witnessed Obama become the first American president in thirty-four years to speak to an Iranian leader. Their fifteen-minute chat, while Rouhani was in a car being driven to Kennedy Airport, covered a lot of ground. Obama congratulated him on his election and thanked him for encouraging diplomacy at the United Nations. He said he respected Iran's right to civilian nuclear energy, as long as it would accept constraints that would prevent it from manufacturing a bomb. The two lamented the New York traffic, ending the call with good-natured banalities that belied its historic nature.

"Have a nice day," Rouhani said in English.

"Thank you. *Khodahafez,*" Obama replied, using a Farsi phrase for farewell that translates as "God be with you."

A few minutes later, Obama walked to the podium in the White House briefing room to tell the American people. On the way, he passed the Roosevelt Room, where four and a half years earlier he had sat with Hillary Clinton, trying to suss out the opaque motives of Iran. "Just now, I spoke with President Rouhani of the Islamic Republic of Iran," Obama said, characteristically cool, even as he uttered those words. The two leaders had agreed to redouble their efforts to reach a nuclear accord. The president warned of obstacles to come and the possibility of failure, but he remained the cautious optimist he had been, sitting under Teddy Roosevelt's portrait that day in 2009.

"I believe we can reach a comprehensive solution," he said. "I do believe that there is a basis for a resolution."

# Eleven

## Resets and Regrets

Hillary Clinton had come to extend a hand to another old adversary, but he was running late. She perched anxiously on a chair before a Russian Renaissance–style ceramic mantelpiece, waiting for Vladimir Putin. A phalanx of reporters watched from one side of a long table, their cameras and boom mikes craning toward her and the empty seat next to her. Finally, a door swung open on the far side of the room, and in walked Putin (it was more of a saunter, actually). Trailed by his bodyguards—half a dozen guys in ill-fitting suits—Putin loped slowly past the table, shooting a glance at the cameras, which swung toward him like a flock of flamingos abruptly shifting direction. He took his seat next to Clinton and assumed the Putin Slouch—leaning back in the chair, legs splayed, hands planted on his thighs—the posture, Barack Obama once said, that made him look like "the bored kid in the back of the classroom."

Putin, it turned out, had no interest in being a gracious host. The meeting on March 19, 2010, was his first one-on-one encounter with Clinton since she had become secretary of state—added to her schedule at the last minute—and he was squeezing her in at his dacha outside Moscow. The two were sitting for a photo opportunity, a time-honored ritual in which the host welcomes the visitor with a few platitudes while the cameras flash; then the reporters are bundled out the door, and the two leaders can get down to business. But Putin, who was prime minister at the time, had a list of grievances he intended to air with the cameras rolling. The United States, he told Clinton, should lift sanctions against Russian firms that do business in Iran. It should help speed Russia's entry into the World Trade Organization and reduce barriers to Russian companies in America. "A message should be sent that they are welcomed in the economy of the United States," he lectured.

Clinton wore a frozen smile as she listened to the English translation of his remarks. When Putin paused, she began to respond, conceding differences on trade with Russia but saying the Obama administration was eager to solve them. A few moments in, Putin had heard enough. With a jerk of his head, he ordered the cameras ejected from the room. The point of the exercise had been to scold the American secretary of state in front of the Russian media. Once that was accomplished, Putin wasn't about to give her equal time. In a room outside, the bodyguards played a sullen game of pool, while we in the press corps marveled at the sandbagging we had just witnessed—and speculated about how furious Clinton must have been.

If she was mad, she didn't show it.

On the flight out of Moscow that night, the press corps couldn't wait to ask Clinton about the ambush. She had strolled back to the press cabin at the rear of her plane, as she often did, to chew over the events of the day. We crowded around her in the cramped cabin, straining to hear her over the whine of the engines. To our surprise, Clinton laughed the whole thing off. Putin, she said, was just throwing red meat to a domestic audience. Besides, she said, her eyes twinkling, there was a lot more to the story. Putin had kept up his harangue after we left, so she said that she had tried to change the subject. "Prime Minister Putin," Clinton said in a good-natured non sequitur, "tell me about what you're doing to save the tigers in Siberia."

That, she said, snapped him out of his distemper. Putin stood up and motioned for Clinton to follow him downstairs and through a corridor to a private office. Bill Burns, a former ambassador to

Moscow, and John Beyrle, who was then the envoy, tagged along. On his wall, Putin had a map of Russia. Pointing to different regions, he offered a lively, well-informed lecture on the fate of endangered tigers and polar bears. He was planning an expedition to tag bears in Siberia in a few weeks. Maybe Bill Clinton could join him? If not Bill, then Hillary? She promised to check her calendar.

Rather than being thrown off-balance by Putin's fickle treatment, Clinton seemed to revel in it. It was not unlike the response she had to other difficult foreign leaders—Hamid Karzai and Benjamin Netanyahu both come to mind. Clinton seemed to identify with them as fellow political animals, with instincts and patterns of behavior that she not only understood, but on some level, sympathized with.

For the Russia hands traveling with her who had seen Putin play American VIPs going back to George W. Bush, his behavior was a revelation. "I've seen him a lot over the years, and it was interesting to watch," Bill Burns recalled. "It's like he sizes somebody up and sees them as a worthy adversary or counterpart. I've seen him with other people who he didn't see that way, and he'd be much more dismissive and snarky."

Vladimir Putin's tutorial on tigers turned out to be the high-water mark of his relationship with Hillary Clinton. Nineteen months later, at a meeting of European leaders in Lithuania, she excoriated the Russian government—and, by implication, Putin, who by then was planning his campaign to retake the presidency—for holding parliamentary elections that had been marred by allegations of voter fraud and intimidation. "The Russian people, like people everywhere, deserve the right to have their voices heard and their votes counted," she said in a statement. Putin was livid, all but accusing her of fomenting a second Russian revolution. Clinton had sent "a signal" to "some actors in our country," he said bitterly, as crowds poured into the streets in the first major protests of his decade-long rule.

At the White House, Tom Donilon was also annoyed by Clinton's broadside. Relations between Washington and Moscow had grown turbulent in the latter half of 2011, but Donilon was planning a trip to Russia early in 2012 to try to keep things from going completely off the rails. Like others in the president's inner circle, he desperately wanted to salvage the "reset," Obama's cherished effort to defrost relations with Moscow after its invasion of Georgia in August 2008 had threatened to plunge Russia and the West into a new cold war. The policy had produced some tangible benefits—Russia signed an arms-control treaty with the United States, and it supported UN sanctions against Iran—but by the time of the parliamentary elections, the Russians had become embittered over the NATO military intervention in Libya, a longtime Soviet client under Muammar al-Qaddafi. They broke with Washington over Syria, another Soviet ally, funneling arms to Bashar al-Assad and thwarting American efforts to sanction him in the Security Council. Clinton was merely affirming what had been evident for a while: The reset had run out.

Victoria Nuland, the State Department's spokeswoman, was traveling with Clinton in Lithuania at the time of the elections and had drafted her statement. An old-school hawk who learned how to swear in Russian while hitching a ride on a Soviet fishing trawler in her twenties, Nuland was not known for mincing words. ("Fuck the EU," she once told a colleague in a phone call that was intercepted by the Russians—and helpfully leaked by them.) But Toria, as everyone called her, was a skilled diplomat, with the political agility to have worked for both Dick Cheney and Strobe Talbott, a Clinton friend and elder of the Democratic foreign policy establishment. Before she settled on the language, she made sure to run it by Mike McFaul, the NSC's senior director for Russia who was about to be posted to Moscow as the ambassador.

McFaul, the Stanford professor who advised Obama on Russia in 2008, had coined the word "reset," putting it into talking points he wrote for the candidate. (Obama first uttered the phrase, as a verb, on *Meet the Press* on December 7, 2008. "I think it's going to be important for us to reset U.S.-Russian relations," he said.) But McFaul's academic research was in democracy movements—recall his push to dump Hosni Mubarak in Egypt—and he was as appalled as Clinton by the voting irregularities. So he readily signed off on her statement, catching hell later from his boss, the national security adviser. "Donilon was the last holdout in saying, 'Let's just keep this quiet and give them space,'" a State Department official said. "He was going to go negotiate some of these things himself." Clinton had thrown a wrench into his plans.

Russia, like Iran, offers a window into the different worldviews of Obama and Clinton. For Obama, a post–Cold War president, it was a potential partner to realize one of his most cherished goals, dating back to college days: a world in which nuclear weapons are obsolete. For Clinton, a child of the Cold War, it was a lingering reminder of the collapsed Soviet Union and the new world that had confronted her husband as president. Yet though both had thought a lot about how to handle Russia, neither fully appreciated its national narrative—the coercive order that the West had imposed on this proud, humbled giant—which made Putin's aggressive bid to recapture the glory of a lost empire not just plausible but predictable.

After Clinton left the administration, her allies insisted she had always been more skeptical than Obama. While he allowed himself to believe the country was on the cusp of genuine change, she quickly figured out Putin was merely using Dmitri Medvedev, the Western-friendly businessman who was then Russia's president, as a compliant seat warmer before he took back his old job. While Obama's cultivation of Medvedev may have been useful for enlisting Russia's support on Iran or in signing an arms treaty, Clinton viewed this as low-hanging fruit—the most one could hope for in a relationship destined to be chilly, competitive, and adversarial. Exhibit A for this narrative was a three-and-a-half-page memo Clinton sent Obama in January 2013, her last month at the State Department. In it, she wrote that the reset had run its course; that Putin did not share Medvedev's desire for better relations with the

United States; and that Obama should stop playing nice with him. "She always believed Putin would come back, and that when he came back, things would get very difficult," said Jake Sullivan, who wrote the memo.

It's a flattering narrative, which is why Clinton was among the most avid in propagating it. But she *was* ahead of Obama in recognizing how bad things were going to get. Within a few months of her memo, Putin had taken in Edward Snowden, the National Security Agency contractor who fled the United States and leaked details of its domestic surveillance programs. In March 2014, Putin used a dispute with Ukraine over joining the European Union as a pretext to annex Crimea, a Ukrainian province with a large Russian-speaking population. Clinton likened it to Hitler's conquests of Germany's neighbors before World War II, ostensibly to protect the rights of German-speaking minorities in those lands. That was only the beginning of a broader campaign to destabilize Ukraine: By November, Putin had sent artillery and troops across the border to reinforce pro-Russian separatists in the eastern part of the country.

The new cold war that Obama had worked so hard to avoid had arrived, just as Clinton foretold.

The full story, though, is less flattering to Clinton. Apart from Joe Biden, who formally launched the reset with a speech in Munich in February 2009, Clinton was the most visible early exponent of the policy. At her first meeting with Russia's foreign minister, Sergey Lavrov, a month later, she famously presented him with a red plastic button inscribed with the (mistranslated) Russian word for "reset." Biden may claim credit, but it is thanks largely to Clinton that the word entered the lexicon. To some extent, her approach was classic good-lieutenant Hillary: The commander in chief had decided to make this a priority, and by golly, she was going to carry out his orders.

It wasn't just duty, though: Clinton, at least initially, shared Obama's belief that Medvedev had been empowered to cooperate with the United States. While Putin remained Russia's paramount

Barack Obama makes a point to Hillary Clinton as they sit at a picnic table on the South Lawn of the White House in April 2009. They were barely one hundred days into the administration, an adjustment period that proved harder on Clinton than was evident at the time.

Obama and Clinton negotiate with leaders from China, India, Brazil, and South Africa after crashing a meeting at the Copenhagen climate summit in December 2009. The deal on carbon emissions they extracted was paltry, but the bonding experience was important for their relationship.

Senator Hillary Clinton tours a U.S. Army barracks in Iraq in November 2003. "It was the kind of gesture that means a lot to a battlefield commander," said General David Petraeus, who traveled from his field headquarters in Mosul to brief her on the state of the war.

Hillary Clinton was frequently the only person standing between Richard Holbrooke and a White House that wanted to force him out. Here, Holbrooke briefs Obama in the Oval Office in May 2009, while Vice President Joseph R. Biden, Jr., and Clinton look on.

Obama nicknamed his three top national security aides, Tom Donilon, John Brennan, and Denis McDonough, "the grim Irishmen." In March 2011, he spoke to King Abdullah of Saudi Arabia, as Donilon (left) and Brennan listened (the third Irishman, McDonough, is not pictured).

Obama gestures to his first chief of staff, Rahm Emanuel (left), during an Oval Office visit by Prime Minister Benjamin Netanyahu. Emanuel, who acted as Obama's de facto chief adviser on Israel at the start of his administration, brought strong ideas about how to handle Netanyahu.

Clinton confers with her top policy aide, Jake Sullivan, at a meeting in Singapore in 2009. A high school debate champion, Rhodes Scholar, and Yale-trained lawyer, Sullivan conducted the secret nuclear talks with Iran. "He ended up being invaluable," she said.

Ben Rhodes and the president on Air Force One, going over the draft of a speech to the nation that Obama would deliver from Afghanistan hours later. Rhodes's influence went beyond speechwriting: He led the covert talks with Cuba that ended fifty-three years of estrangement.

Obama puts his arm around Clinton after they spoke at a ceremony at Joint Base Andrews to welcome home the caskets of four Americans killed in Benghazi, Libya. It was the end of Clinton's worst week as secretary of state, but only the start of her troubles with Benghazi.

Sidney Blumenthal arrives to testify before the House Select Committee on Benghazi on June 16, 2015. A longtime confidant of Hillary Clinton, Blumenthal sent her hundreds of emails with intelligence about Libya. When her private email server became a scandal, he was at the center of it.

Official White House Photo/Pete Souza

Obama and chief of staff Denis McDonough (left, with arms stretched out and a red folder tucked in the back of his pants), on an end-of-the-day walk on the South Grounds in September 2014. It was on such a walk that Obama told McDonough he was holding off on a military strike against Syria.

Official White House Photo/Pete Souza

Obama gathers his aides in the Oval Office on August 30, 2013, to explain his decision to seek congressional approval before striking Syria. The photo captures the tension: Dan Pfeiffer leans forward on the sofa, while Ben Rhodes slumps back, resting his head on a hand.

Clinton begins to respond after being lectured by Vladimir Putin, then Russia's prime minister, at their first meeting after she became secretary of state, in March 2009. Her host, sitting in his Putin Slouch, listened briefly before ejecting the reporters and cameras from the room.

Obama announces the New START arms treaty with Russia at the White House on March 26, 2010, with Clinton next to him. For Obama, who got into the nitty-gritty of the negotiations, it was the high point of his effort to "reset" relations with Russia.

John Kerry cultivated Sultan Qaboos bin Said of Oman, who became a key middleman for secret nuclear negotiations between the United States and Iran. Here, Kerry meets the sultan at his residence in Muscat in May 2013, while those talks were under way.

Clinton greets Aung San Suu Kyi, the Burmese democracy icon, at her home in Rangoon, as the president looks on. Obama's visit in November 2012 was a farewell road trip for him and Clinton, three months before she left his cabinet and began planning her own political future.

leader, he had clearly given Medvedev the leeway to negotiate deals, large and small, with Washington: from the NATO northern supply route in Afghanistan to the New START arms-control agreement. Given Putin's unchallenged power, the new administration's thinking went, any conciliatory steps taken by Medvedev had to carry his master's imprimatur. "It would be wrong to say that Obama imposed it on her," said Philip Gordon, who served as Clinton's assistant secretary for European and Eurasian affairs before moving to the NSC in 2013. "We saw the logic and bought into it."

The difference was in how they viewed Medvedev's writ: Clinton thought it could be revoked by Putin at any time, as indeed it was after the NATO intervention in Libya, when Putin publicly criticized his protégé's decision not to block a Security Council resolution authorizing military action. The president and his aides, on the other hand, entertained hopes that Medvedev—like Obama, a fit, fortysomething lawyer—embodied a lasting new era of openness and goodwill. In private conversations, White House aides recall, Medvedev was unruffled when Obama brought up the need for democratic reforms. Sometimes the young Russian even sounded like an aspiring Gorbachev. In hindsight, that should have set off alarm bells.

"We, and I think she, did not understand that Medvedev was, in fact, challenging the system and going further than he had been authorized to go," Ben Rhodes told me. "He actually went beyond Putin, and the moment that became clear was the Libya resolution."

To some in the White House, there was more than a whiff of revisionism to Clinton's views of Russia. Her exit memo, for example, merely stated the obvious: Relations with Putin were bad and likely to become worse. As one Obama aide put it, "We didn't need a memo to know Putin is an asshole." Like another exit memo Clinton wrote encouraging Obama to ask Congress to lift the trade embargo against Cuba, it seemed less candid advice from a departing cabinet member than a calculated bid to be on the right side of history in advance of a presidential campaign.

Few dispute, however, that Obama's nonproliferation agenda made him overlook the darker undercurrents in Russian politics. His decision to cultivate Dmitri Medvedev was a bet—rare for him—that nurturing a personal rapport could defrost a chilly geopolitical relationship and, perhaps, remove a lethal vestige of the Cold War. While Clinton supported Obama in his push for arms control, she shared little of his passion for a nuclear-free world, viewing it as a pipe dream. For her, Russia was instead a symbol of how her husband, a southern governor with no foreign policy credentials, managed to unseat George H. W. Bush after he presided over the peaceful end of the Cold War and the collapse of the Soviet empire. When Clinton thinks of Russia, friends say, she harks back to the epochal events of 1989, so masterfully handled by Bush that it opened the door for an upstart Democrat to run on the economy.

"Bill Clinton and Hillary were very, very conscious of the opportunity and the obligation that his administration would have in keeping the Cold War over, helping the reformers, guaranteeing a Europe whole and free, all of that," said Strobe Talbott, a Russia expert who served as deputy secretary of state under Bill Clinton and has known Hillary since she was in law school. "She came into four years as secretary of state with a number of fixed points in her past experience that related to what she would be dealing with, and one of those fixed points was Russia. She was both knowledgeable about what had been the direction of Russia and alert to what was changing."

Hillary Clinton's day-to-day contact as secretary of state, of course, was not Putin, but Sergey Lavrov, the hard-drinking, chain-smoking career diplomat who has been Russia's foreign minister since 2004. In many ways, he was a throwback—"a sophisticated Soviet retread in an Italian suit, an updated Mr. *Nyet*," wrote Susan Glasser, referring to the nickname given to his Brezhnev-era predecessor, Andrei Gromyko. Wily, combative, and relentless, Lavrov, like Putin, sees his role as asserting Russia's power around the globe, more often than not against the United States. His relationship with Clinton's predecessor, Condoleezza Rice, had been testy, with Lavrov bullying her in ways that some around Rice found sexist. When he first met Clinton in a Geneva hotel in the winter of 2009, it looked as if she was in for more of the same.

The reset button, a former State Department official recalled, was a "Philippe special"—as in Philippe Reines, the caustic, canny Senate staffer to Clinton who became her image maker at State, Michael Deaver to Clinton's Ronald Reagan. A forty-six-year-old New Yorker with a wicked sense of humor, clannish loyalty, and impulse-control issues, Reines had nevertheless smoothed the edges of Clinton's serrated image, engineering a series of laudatory magazine profiles and TV appearances that recast the humbled loser of 2008 as a regal stateswoman.

Clinton's reliance on Reines is evident from the hundreds of emails that flowed between them during his four years as her senior adviser for strategic communications. (He was also appointed a deputy assistant secretary of state, to the disdain of some of the career diplomats.) She consulted him on routine issues such as Sunday show interviews and sensitive ones like the politics of appearing on a panel with Henry Kissinger. He could get away with a good-natured impudence that other aides never tried. When an obviously tickled Clinton forwarded Reines an email in April 2012 with the news that she had been inducted into the American Academy of Arts and Sciences, he replied, "This prestigious addition to your otherwise thin résumé could really make THE difference when you're interviewing for jobs next year." More than anything, Reines was loyal, turning his acid pen on anyone he felt had wronged her. His bullying email exchanges with offending reporters were legendary. "Have a good day, and by good day, I mean Fuck Off," he once wrote to Michael Hastings of *Rolling Stone,* at the end of a hostile back-and-forth over Clinton's response to the Benghazi attacks. (Reines apologized for that one.)

For all his quirks and excesses, Reines had one hard and fast rule: He didn't get involved in the substance of diplomacy. He knew what he didn't know. On long flights, when Jake Sullivan and other aides buried themselves in briefing books, Reines would leaf through the latest *Us Weekly*. Ask him what he thought of the latest Quartet statement on the Middle East, and he would fall silent. On Clinton's first trip to Europe as secretary of state in February 2009, however, Reines decided to try his hand at diplomatic stagecraft. It was an ill-fated decision, one that produced the first gaffe of his boss's tenure, antagonized the White House, and revealed Clinton's inner circle to be foreign policy rubes, still using a playbook more suited to a political campaign.

Looking for a way to dramatize Obama's reset policy, Reines had the bright idea of having his boss present Lavrov with a gag gift, a symbol of the new era: a red button with the words "reset" and its Russian equivalent printed on it. Standing with the tall, well-tanned Lavrov before a forest of cameras, Clinton opened a green gift-wrapped box and showed him the button. It had been nicked from Geneva's InterContinental hotel. Above the button was stamped "PEREGRUZKA," in Latin, not Cyrillic letters; below it, "RESET."

"We worked hard to get the right Russian word," Clinton said, turning to Lavrov. As if sensing that the whole idea was half-baked, she added, "Do you think we got it?"

"You got it wrong," he replied. "It should be *perezagruzka*. This means overcharged."

Clinton laughed, a bit too loud. "Well, we won't let you do that to us," she told him. "I promise."

The two got through the moment, though Lavrov, never one to squander a tactical advantage, needled Clinton about it during a press conference after their meeting. He said he hoped the linguistic miscue would "contribute to the advancement of Russian in the United States and English in Russia." Clinton, still trying to make lemonade out of lemons, said the faulty translation was more apt than the correct one would have been. Resetting ties would mean an "overload" of work for both sides. Lavrov, having scored his point, generously agreed. "The load is enormous in terms of our agenda," he said, "but neither Hillary nor I have any desire to get rid of any of that load."

Once the electrical metaphors were exhausted, the finger-pointing began. Reines, State Department officials told reporters, had shown the translation to Mike McFaul, a Russian speaker who was on the trip as the NSC's representative, and he had signed off on it. So had Bill Burns, another Russian speaker who arrived at the hotel separately, twenty minutes before the meeting. Neither disputed that, though their exchanges with Reines were so rushed, and they were so harried, that they didn't think through what he was planning. McFaul, for whom this was an introduction to the Clinton crew, felt aggrieved. Burns, the diplomatic pro, faulted himself for not speaking up to kill the whole escapade. Anyone who knew anything about Sergey Lavrov knew he wouldn't take kindly to a gag gift. He would view it suspiciously, as if the Americans were trying to put one over on him. Such teasing might have worked between Bill Clinton and Boris Yeltsin. Not with Mr. *Nyet*.

At the White House, Denis McDonough and Ben Rhodes were furious that Clinton's people were pinning the blame on McFaul. This was early in her tenure, before they had formed any bonds with Reines or Jake Sullivan; to them, Clinton's circle was still an enemy camp. Not only had Clinton muffed her first meeting with the Russian foreign minister, her people were blaming the debacle on the White House. It all felt like a nasty hangover from the campaign. "They were like, 'Why are you doing antics like this anyway?'" recalled a former administration official. "This is your first meeting with Sergey Lavrov. You're not going to some fundraiser in Detroit."

Weeks later, McFaul got an email from a Russian friend. "You know how you really translate 'reset' in Russian? Reset." It's a computer term, for which there's no Russian equivalent. There was a lesson, perhaps unintended, in that.

However clumsy their start, Lavrov was to treat Clinton more carefully than he had Condi Rice. Like Putin, he respected that she was a global celebrity and a political figure in her own right. But that didn't mean they ended up having a positive relationship. Lavrov's style is to spend forty-five seconds discussing each of the thirty items on his agenda—a formula for grinding, not very productive meetings. Clinton's style is to dig into one or two issues more deeply, in the hopes of achieving a tangible result. She often emerged from discussions with him visibly frustrated. She also had to accept that in those early days, the real business with Russia was being conducted above her pay grade.

Barack Obama began his courtship of Dmitri Medvedev with a multipage letter, hand delivered in February 2009 by Burns and McFaul. The trip was a Burns idea. He said the document was too important to send by email. Indeed, Obama made a newsworthy offer in it: The United States might hold off on deploying a new missile-defense system in eastern Europe if Moscow would help stop Iran from developing long-range weapons. But the letter, written by McFaul, went beyond that, laying out other issues in which the United States and Russia might find common ground, including a new treaty to radically reduce their nuclear weapons stockpiles. Essentially, it was the template for the reset. Medvedev welcomed the overture, and made plans to meet with Obama at a G-20 meeting in London two months later.

Obama's bet on Medvedev was in part generational. Born in September 1965, four years after Obama, he completed his legal studies in 1989, shortly after the fall of the Berlin Wall; Medvedev was a post–Cold War product, unsullied by the "old ways" of thinking that Obama said still plagued Putin. "Those two presidents are a different generation," Pavel Palazhchenko, an interpreter for Mikhail Gorbachev, told Peter Baker of *The New York Times* in July 2009. "Many of the dogs in the old fights are really not their dogs. And they will be willing to take a fresh look at some issues."

The London summit was also the first time that Obama and Clinton were together overseas, and it laid bare the unequal nature of their partnership. As Clinton flew into London from a meeting in The Hague, her plane was put into a holding pattern above Stansted Airport because air traffic had been halted to accommodate Air Force One. Once on the ground, her Boeing 757 taxied past Obama's much larger 747, parking at a respectful distance. On the short flight, a large bouquet of Dutch tulips occupied a seat in the press section, which was empty because most of the reporters had opted to fly home from Holland. (Covering the secretary of state on an Obama presidential trip is about as exciting as covering school board races on election night.) The flowers, a gift from the Dutch foreign minister, were Hillary Clinton tulips, named for her in 1994 when she was First Lady.

The moment Clinton joined Obama in London, however, she went from being a principal—a historic figure worthy of a namesake flower—to a mere staff member. "I was the only woman on either side of the table," Clinton observed about the first meeting between Obama and Medvedev, held at Winfield House, the baronial residence of the American ambassador to the Court of St. James's. That was true, as was the fact that when the two presidents announced they would begin negotiations on an agreement to cut in half the thousands of strategic nuclear missile launchers held by both countries—a bold idea that would require painstaking negotiations by the diplomats in Clinton's department—she said barely a word.

Clinton would scarcely figure in the yearlong drama to come. For Obama, the negotiations with Medvedev that produced New START would be the most hands-on, sustained diplomacy of his presidency. (He spent a comparable amount of time on the Iran nuclear talks, but left the actual bargaining to John Kerry.) Clinton's low profile is even more striking, given that one of her assistant secretaries—Rose Gottemoeller, a nuclear expert who had served in the Clinton administration and headed the Carnegie Moscow Center—ran the day-to-day negotiations.

When these talks required higher-level intervention, it was supplied by Obama. The arms-control wonk who had once written a senior-seminar paper at Columbia about how to negotiate with the

Soviets to reduce their nuclear arsenals was suddenly doing it for real. He threw himself into the technical details of warheads, launchers, heavy bombers, and missiles—to the point that some of his advisers questioned whether this was the best use of a president's time. Obama became particularly engrossed by telemetry: the data that a missile transmits during test flights, which can be used to determine its throw-weight, how quickly it burns fuel, and how many times its flight path shifts before it releases its warhead. The United States and Russia agreed to share this data, but Obama dickered repeatedly with Medvedev over the frequency of the information swap.

"My favorite word in English now is 'telemetry,'" Medvedev said to Obama, after yet another haggling session about it.

All told, the two leaders had fourteen meetings or phone calls about New START, before finally signing the treaty in Prague in April 2010. There were tense moments: In February, as the two sides were getting close, Russia unexpectedly demanded that the United States make concessions in its missile-defense program. "Dmitri, we agreed," Obama said testily. "We can't do this." But there were breakthroughs, as well, which spoke to the deepening sense of trust between them. A major turning point came at the UN climate change summit in Copenhagen in December 2009. This was the gathering at which Obama and Clinton crashed a meeting of China and other emerging economies, forcing them into a face-saving agreement on emissions reduction targets. Before that, Obama and Medvedev had their own meeting of the minds, in another part of the shopping mall where the conference was being held. They had already agreed on the basic terms of the deal: cuts in deployed warheads, missiles, and heavy bombers; and increases in inspections. Now they were finally able to put to bed the pesky issue of telemetry.

"Let's just do it on an annual basis," Obama proposed.

"I don't see any problem with that," Medvedev replied.

• • •

Few speeches mattered more to Barack Obama than the one he gave on April 5, 2009, in a medieval square in Prague. Framed by the spires and domes of a city that had once been a Cold War battleground, the president laid out his vision of a world free of nuclear weapons. It was a vision that Ronald Reagan had once had—one that Obama had nurtured his entire adult life. "Today," he declared, "the Cold War has disappeared but thousands of those weapons have not. In a strange turn of history, the threat of global nuclear war has gone down, but the risk of a nuclear attack has gone up."

Hillary Clinton was in the audience that day, and she agreed with most of what Obama said. He said he would negotiate a deal with Russia to reduce the nuclear arsenals of both nations; she had promised to do the same thing in 2007 as a Democratic candidate. He called on Congress to approve the 1996 Comprehensive Nuclear-Test-Ban Treaty; she, too, supported the treaty, which Russia, but not the U.S. Congress, had ratified. He spoke about the urgent need to secure nuclear weapons in a world where the technology to build a bomb had spread; she was a firm believer in nonproliferation. The safe removal of nuclear warheads from the former Soviet republics had been a signal achievement of her husband's White House.

Yet, on a visceral level, Clinton lacked the no-nukes fervor of Obama. He was itching to rewrite sixty years of Cold War nuclear doctrine from the moment he got into the Oval Office; she thought that was unrealistic. He made absolutist statements—"I state clearly and with conviction America's commitment to seek the peace and security of a world without nuclear weapons"; she stayed away from them. On nuclear issues, as in so many other areas of national security, Clinton's instincts tended to be less radical and more conservative than Obama's. "Giving up nuclear weapons was la-la land," said Ivo Daalder, the president of the Chicago Council on Global Affairs, summarizing her position. "That's what you say, but nobody actually *believes* it. I actually think the president did believe it—does believe it."

A Dutch-born academic who advised Obama on foreign policy

during the 2008 campaign, Daalder was also a true believer. While serving as American ambassador to NATO during the first term, he pushed Obama's nuclear agenda on the side. An early test came in 2009 when Pentagon planners submitted a draft of *The Nuclear Posture Review,* a national security document issued at the start of each administration that lays out criteria for how and when nuclear weapons should be used. Obama's aides disparaged the draft as milquetoast. Far from reflecting the president's bold ideas about disarmament, it protected the prerogatives of a Pentagon that did not want to give up its most fearsome deterrent weapons. From Truman Hall, the elegant Flemish country estate outside Brussels that is the residence of the NATO ambassador, Daalder sent tougher wording to Derek Chollet and Bob Einhorn, who had been drafted to make the paper more ambitious.

Clinton didn't oppose that effort—she was the one who gave the rewrite duty to Chollet and Einhorn—but she also knew that the Pentagon would zealously oppose any attempts to push the United States toward what the nuclear-free crowd referred to as "the logic of zero." And she certainly wasn't going to pick a fight with Bob Gates over it. "I don't think she particularly *believed* in Obama's view," Daalder said. "But that's OK. This was not an issue to go fight over, and, by the way, the Pentagon was going to fight it for her." In the end, *The Nuclear Posture Review* fell short of zero use, even if it did break new ground in narrowing the conditions under which the United States would use nuclear weapons.

Clinton's next major involvement in nuclear policy came in April 2010, when the NSC Deputies Committee recommended unilaterally cutting in half the nation's arsenal of tactical nuclear weapons. These are designed to be used in combat on the battlefield, as opposed to strategic weapons, which are aimed at targets such as factories or cities. Tactical nukes were deployed to defend Europe from a Soviet invasion, and are locked in underground vaults on air bases in five NATO countries. If anything, they are even more outmoded than the strategic weapons Obama and Medvedev had agreed to reduce through the New START treaty. "We should get rid of them," Hoss Cartwright, the iconoclastic general then serving as vice chairman of the Joint Chiefs of Staff, declared at one White House meeting.

Clinton didn't disagree with that assessment, but she had been asked by Obama to lobby her former colleagues in the Senate to ratify New START, which he and Medvedev had just signed. It was going to be a tough sell: Some of the lawmakers were eager to protect strategic nuclear weapons facilities in their states; others worried that Obama had given away too much. For the White House to announce at that moment it was cutting another pillar of its nuclear arsenal would be terrible politics. "I can't unilaterally cut tactical weapons and then convince the Senate to ratify New START," she said at an NSC meeting. "This is a worthwhile proposition, but let's come back to it after we get New START ratified."

The White House never did come back to it. Other priorities soon crowded out Obama's nuclear agenda, as did a hostile Congress. The Republicans captured the House in midterm elections that fall. Clinton threw herself into the New START lobbying campaign, and after weeks of haggling, a lame-duck Senate passed it by a vote of 71 to 26 in December 2010. But Obama's other nonproliferation goals, like ratifying the Comprehensive Nuclear-Test-Ban Treaty, were dead. When he gave a speech about America's Cold War bond with Germany at the Brandenburg Gate in June 2013, Obama repeated his hope for a "world without nuclear weapons." He didn't say a word about tactical nukes, even though his own staff had recommended unilaterally cutting them.

"There was a danger we could end up with the worst of all worlds," said Jim Steinberg, who advised Obama on nonproliferation issues in the 2008 campaign. "A rhetorical commitment to zero, which was unachievable in the foreseeable future, coupled with a reluctance to follow through on concrete reductions, including through unilateral actions, which would have a more powerful impact on achieving nonproliferation goals."

• • •

Obama's relationship with Medvedev reached its chummy apogee in June 2010, in the aftermath of their arms talks. Welcoming him to the White House on a steamy early summer morning, Obama suggested they grab lunch at one of his favorite joints, Ray's Hell Burger, across the Potomac in Arlington, Virginia. Tossing their suit jackets into the limo, Barack and Dmitri strolled into Ray's like a couple of office workers on a casual Friday. Obama did the ordering: cheddar cheeseburger with onions, lettuce, tomato, and pickles for himself; cheddar burger with jalapeños, onions, and mushrooms for Medvedev (both medium well-done, Obama asked, quietly overruling his guest's request for well-done). The rapport between the two men was genuine, even poignant: Dmitri's shy, futile attempts to pay his share of the tab; Barack's graciousness as he introduced his guest to a group of soldiers in uniform. In hindsight, though, one could see ominous clouds in the sunny tableau: the orange Ray's souvenir T-shirts that Obama and Medvedev cheerfully posed with before leaving: "Go to Hell," they said in flame-streaked letters.

Historically, personal diplomacy has mattered more with Russia than in America's relations with most other countries. Richard Nixon wrote of the lengths he went to in wooing Leonid Brezhnev. During a 1973 visit to Camp David, he presented the Soviet leader with a dark-blue Lincoln Continental as a gift. Brezhnev took off in the car, a white-knuckled Nixon in the passenger seat, careering around the hilly presidential retreat. When he finally squealed to a stop, Nixon choked out a compliment on his guest's driving. "Diplomacy is not always an easy art," he wrote. Nixon attributed the emergence of détente with the Soviet Union in part to his rapport with Brezhnev. In 1994, Boris Yeltsin hosted Bill and Hillary Clinton at a banquet for the opening of the new Russian embassy in Washington. A whole stuffed piglet was placed on the table in front of them, she recounted; Yeltsin used his knife to lop off its ears, handing one to Bill and taking a bite out of the other. (Clinton gamely followed suit.) "To us!" Yeltsin toasted, raising the remains of his ear. Meeting eighteen times over the seven years they were both in office, they were able to navigate thorny issues such as securing and dismantling the Soviet nuclear arsenal.

Still, it's easy to overstate the role personal dynamics play. Though Bill Clinton got along famously with Yeltsin, it didn't prevent a rupture between the United States and Russia over the ethnic slaughter in Kosovo. George W. Bush claimed he had peered into Putin's soul, an act of self-delusion that didn't prevent relations from going to hell over Georgia.

Obama, as a rule, invested less in this kind of leader-to-leader diplomacy than other presidents, and when he did, it yielded mixed results. In Angela Merkel, he saw a disciplined, brainy physicist, an outsider from East Germany who made history by becoming her country's first woman chancellor—a female facsimile, in other words, of himself. He showered her with attention: a Presidential Medal of Honor, an invitation to linger for a sunset chat after a meeting at Camp David in 2012, a state dinner in the Rose Garden, at which she was served apple strudel and serenaded by James Taylor with "You've Got a Friend." Still, later that year, Merkel flatly rebuffed Obama's pleas to do more to bail out Greece. And when she discovered in 2013, courtesy of Edward Snowden, that the NSA had been tapping her cellphone, the gemütlichkeit between them deflated faster than whipped cream.

"In Europe, especially, Obama was welcomed with open arms, and some people had unrealistic expectations about him," said Nicholas Burns, a veteran American diplomat who was ambassador to NATO and a top deputy to Condoleezza Rice. "People don't appreciate that American interests continue from administration to administration."

Medvedev, however, was different; Obama thought he was getting a return on his investment. "They had a genuinely good relationship," David Axelrod said. "You could see it. You know when people get along, and you could see that those two guys got along." The personal bond led Obama to spend more time on Russia in those early years than he did on other issues, such as the Middle East peace process. "If you go back and look historically at the deliverables, the actual outcomes of policy, not the chitchat, we probably got more done with the Russians in those three years than at almost any other time in history," McFaul said. "Because we were getting it done, he would invest in it."

That investment also helps explain why Obama was less apt than Clinton to take a hard line against Russia immediately after Putin moved his protégé out and reassumed the presidency in May 2012. So often criticized for being too distant or for not reaching out enough, Obama had done something utterly uncharacteristic with Russia: He had over-personalized the relationship, ignoring the longer history and the larger context.

Putin and Obama never clicked. Before their first meeting in July 2009, the young president said, "Putin has one foot in the old ways of doing business and one foot in the new." After the session—an alfresco breakfast in Moscow, during which Putin delivered an hour-long monologue on Russia's view of the world—Obama hadn't changed his assessment. "I found him to be tough, smart, shrewd, very unsentimental, very pragmatic," he said. "On areas where we disagree, like Georgia, I don't anticipate a meeting of the minds anytime soon." Afterward, he repeated to Axelrod a telling remark that Putin had made during breakfast. "You know," he said, "I'm just an old security guy; you're an educated man."

"There was a message there about what was to come," Axelrod said.

From there, their encounters became a catalog of shrugs and sighs, grim handshakes and sullen photo ops—the exaggerated pantomime of a stilted relationship. Even Obama's rare attempts to warm up Putin went nowhere. At a meeting in Lough Erne, Northern Ireland, in June 2013, he joked that age was depleting their athletic skills. Putin, who is a decade older than Obama and was facing questions about his health at the time, didn't laugh. "The president just wants me to relax," he said, making clear it hadn't worked. Obama insisted the two could do business—they huddled in St. Petersburg in September 2013 over how to deal with Syria's chemical weapons—but he couldn't resist poking him about his posture.

Clinton had taken Putin's concerns to heart after their meeting in March 2010. She pushed the White House to accelerate Russia's entry into the World Trade Organization. On the flight home from Moscow, she mused with aides about his passion for Siberian tigers: Maybe there was a way to take advantage of his interest in wildlife preservation? But having promised to check her calendar for dates to go on a polar bear–tagging expedition with him, she canceled plans to attend a conference he hosted in St. Petersburg in November 2010 to save the tigers. (Her excuse—she had to stay home to lobby senators on the New START treaty—took some of the sting out of it for him.)

Their relationship, though, was destined to end as badly as Putin and Obama's. Even in the heyday of the reset, she didn't hesitate to speak out about civil liberties in Russia (a stark contrast to the gingerly tone she took with China). In October 2009, she addressed nearly one thousand students at Moscow State University, where Ronald Reagan had delivered a bracing lecture twenty-one years earlier on the relationship between freedom and economic prosperity. Clinton echoed Reagan, saying Russia could best fulfill its potential by protecting basic freedoms. "That's why attacks on journalists and human rights activists are such a great concern," she declared, "because it is a threat to progress. The more open Russia will become, the more Russia will contribute."

After Clinton all but accused Putin of rigging the parliamentary elections, their relationship was beyond repair. And once she turned on him, she used far more barbed words than Obama. He likened Putin to a bored schoolkid; she likened him to Hitler.

"It's better not to argue with women," Putin said in an interview with a French television station in June 2014, when he was asked to respond to her comments about the annexation of Crimea. "Ms. Clinton has never been too graceful in her statements."

Clinton's exit memo on Putin—her requiem for the reset—was circulating in the White House at a time when some officials were beginning to question the value of the policy. But that didn't mean her warnings were welcomed by the president's inner circle. When one of Donilon's colleagues asked him early in 2013 if he'd read the memo, he snapped, "Yeah, I've seen it," in a tone that didn't invite further discussion. In the weeks after Obama was reelected, the focus was still on getting things back on track with Russia. There were weekly NSC staff meetings about what new initiatives to propose to Moscow and whom to send as an emissary. (Joe Biden was considered at one point.) Resetting the reset became a running joke. "Hillary's memo wasn't getting that much traction," said Julianne Smith, a former adviser to Biden. "But people were beginning to say, 'Maybe we shouldn't be so needy.'"

Donilon didn't see it that way. He had thought deeply about the role of a national security adviser, and in keeping with his status as the president's senior counselor on foreign affairs, he concluded that his job was to manage the "great power" relationships. That meant regular trips to Moscow and Beijing, where he sat stiffly in vast reception rooms, across from leaders who were seeing him only because he had Obama's ear. Donilon was not a natural diplomat with the intellectual swagger of a Kissinger or Brzezinski, but he was exceedingly well prepared, with an encyclopedic knowledge of the issues between the United States and Russia, from Afghanistan to counterterrorism. He thought the reset was salvageable, that the great-power relationship he had worked so hard to cultivate was not doomed to rupture over the differences in the way the two saw their interests.

In May 2012, Obama sent Donilon to Moscow to meet with Putin. This was the meeting he had been arranging when Clinton blasted the parliamentary elections. With Putin about to reassume the presidency, it was clear the era of goodwill was ending. Mike McFaul, who had taken up his post as ambassador in January, had been pilloried by the Russian press and subjected to Soviet-style harassment after he and Bill Burns met with opposition leaders and human rights advocates. (He got death threats; Russian agents tailed his car and turned up at his children's soccer games.) Before McFaul left, Clinton had given him a spine-stiffening send-off. "Stand firm, Mike," she told him. "Don't let those White House guys take the edge off."

Putin received Donilon in the same dacha where he had scolded Clinton four years earlier. Obama's emissary brought a list of ideas for how the White House could work with Russia's once-and-future czar (a deal on missile defense; a summit meeting for him and Obama in Moscow). Putin was not in a receptive mood: Still smarting over the NATO intervention in Libya, he was convinced the United States planned to continue its imperialist ways in Syria, where Russia has a naval base and a client in Assad. He had already said publicly that the days were over when the United States could use international organizations to take down governments from Kosovo to Libya. With Donilon, as with Clinton, Putin skipped the pleasantries.

"When are you going to start bombing Syria?" he asked.

Still, Donilon didn't leave the session entirely empty-handed. Putin was open to a summit with Obama, and a date was set for the following September. Then, on August 1, 2012, Russia granted temporary asylum to Edward Snowden, who had fled to Moscow from Hong Kong and spent a month sitting in Sheremetyevo International Airport after the State Department revoked his passport. An angry Obama canceled the meeting.

With Russia's slow-motion invasion of Ukraine in August 2014, Clinton's direst prophecies were fulfilled. Not only did the tanks and troops snuff out the last embers of the Obama reset, they put to the test his determination to avoid being drawn into another military conflict. Other former Soviet satellites and republics, such as Estonia and Lithuania, worried they were next in Putin's path; they were members of NATO, raising the prospect that the alliance would have to go to war to defend them. The debate over what to do about a Russia on the march revealed, yet again, how Obama's worldview differed from the Cold War–forged view of Clinton. She took a consistently tougher line than he did.

From the start of the conflict, Obama's response was to hang an economic noose around the necks of Putin and his cronies. Leaning hard on Angela Merkel, the United States and Europe blacklisted Russian banks and energy companies. The Treasury Department imposed travel bans and froze foreign assets belonging to cronies such as Igor Sechin, who ran the oil giant Rosneft. Russia's economy fell into a recession. None of it cowed Putin. With Ukraine's troops being pounded by heavy guns supplied by Russia, Obama came under intense pressure to begin funneling weapons, particulary Javelin antitank missiles, to Ukrainian troops—and not just from reflexive hawks such as John McCain and Lindsey Graham. Madeleine Albright, Mike McFaul, and Strobe Talbott all argued that the United States needed to come to the aid of the Ukrainians. "I very much incline in that direction," Obama's defense secretary, Ashton Carter, said.

Obama did not. Arming the Ukrainians, he told aides, would kick off a cycle of escalation that the West could not win, given that Ukraine lies on Russia's border and means so much more to Moscow than it does to the United States. The depth of Obama's resistance became clear to people outside the government when he invited about a dozen foreign policy experts to dinner at the White House on September 8, 2014. The agenda had been planned down to the minute: one hour of discussion on the Islamic State, one hour on Russia. As the second hour began, Obama said, "OK, now we're going to switch to Ukraine." He threw down a startling gauntlet.

"Will somebody tell me: What's the American stake in Ukraine?" he asked his guests.

Strobe Talbott, who spent much of his professional life studying the Soviet threat during the Cold War, was slack-jawed. Preserving the territorial integrity of states liberated from the Soviet Union was an article of faith in Washington, at least for those of Clinton's generation, who had watched the Soviets invade Hungary in 1956. Talbott argued that the West couldn't simply stand by while Russia had its way with one of its neighbors. Stephen Hadley, who had been George W. Bush's national security adviser, echoed him. "Well, I see it somewhat differently than you do," Obama replied. "My concern is it will be a provocation, and it'll trigger a Russian escalation that we're not prepared to match." That was a legitimate concern, Talbott granted, but not a reason to give Russia a free pass. "Having known Hillary for a long time," he told me, "I'm pretty sure she would have seen the invasion of Ukraine in a different way, namely as a threat to the peace of Europe."

A year and a day after that dinner, Talbott's assumption was borne out. Standing on a stage at the Brookings Institution, of which he is the president, Talbott introduced Clinton for the first major foreign policy speech of her 2016 presidential campaign. During a question-and-answer period afterward, she was asked how the West could put more pressure on Vladimir Putin. The United States, Clinton said, needed to dial up the sanctions and bring other pressure to bear. Though she didn't specify it that day, her aides said that would include providing defensive weapons to the Ukrainians.

"We have not done enough," she said. "I am in the category of people who wanted us to do more in response to the annexation of Crimea and the continuing destabilizing of Ukraine."

Clinton wasn't just talking about guns and blacklists. Washington, she said, urgently needed a new mindset to deal with an adversary that was going to plague the United States for years to come. It wasn't so much new as back to the future: The White House would have to recruit old Soviet specialists—"and I'm looking right at you, Strobe Talbott," she said—to dust off their playbooks and devise new policies for fighting Russian aggression. Like the Soviets, the Russians planned "to stymie and to confront and to undermine American power whenever and wherever they can.

"I don't think we can dance around it very much longer," she continued. "I mean, we all wish it wasn't the case. We all wish it would go away. We all wish that Putin would choose to modernize his country and move toward the West instead of sinking himself deeper into historical roots of czar-like behavior and intimidation along borders and projecting Russian power in places like Syria and elsewhere.

"But I think the jury is in," she concluded.

# Twelve

## The Pivot

As she sat down to a Chinese banquet in the Ming dynasty splendor of the Wanshou Temple in Beijing, Hillary Clinton allowed herself a moment to breathe again. After six days of high anxiety, she thought her diplomats had just pulled off perhaps the most sensitive deal of her tenure at the State Department: an agreement with the Chinese government to allow a blind dissident named Chen Guangcheng to leave the American embassy, where he had sought refuge from police persecution.

A few hours earlier, Chen had hobbled out of a marine barracks in the embassy compound, his right hand gripping a crutch, his left hand held by Kurt Campbell, the American diplomat who had negotiated the arrangement with Chinese officials. Chen was to be treated at a hospital, reunited with his family, and allowed to study law at a Chinese university, before possibly moving to the United States. He was helped into a waiting van, and Jake Sullivan handed him a cellphone: The secretary of state was on the line. Neither he nor Clinton could quite make out what the other was saying, given the background noise and the lack of a translator.

"You might have missed it," Campbell emailed Clinton a few minutes later, as Chen, now in a wheelchair, was entering the hospital, "but when he heard your voice he said, 'I want to kiss you.'"

Later, Chen claimed he had told Clinton, "I want to see you," not "I want to kiss you," having been promised by the Americans that she would meet him in person. It was the first in a chain of misunderstandings, tense moments, and hurt feelings in this ill-starred episode, not just between Chen and Clinton but between Clinton and the White House.

Things went awry as soon as the State Department team left Chen at the hospital on the afternoon of May 2, 2012. He spoke by phone with a friend in dissident circles, Teng Biao, who told him he'd made a terrible mistake in agreeing to leave the embassy; neither he nor his family would ever be safe in China, particularly after media attention shifted away from his case. He should ask to go back to the embassy, and from there directly to the United States. Chen's wife deepened his sense of unease, recounting her own chilling encounters with the Chinese police while the couple had been apart. He immediately began dialing journalists to tell them he didn't feel safe. Clinton's aides had pressured him to leave, he told them, warning that he would be charged with treason if he didn't. He all but accused them of throwing him to the wolves. By the time dinner was over, Clinton knew that the agreement struck by her lieutenants for Chen to stay in China had fallen apart.

Back in Washington, Barack Obama was just returning from a grueling thirty-six-hour trip to Afghanistan. The moment Air Force One touched down at Joint Base Andrews on the morning of May 2, his advisers were engulfed by the Chen drama. "It's going sideways," Denis McDonough said, when I asked him about events in Beijing as he hurried off the plane, a cellphone pressed to his ear. The White House was apoplectic about the unfolding crisis and let Clinton's team know it. In a few days, the United States and China were meeting in Beijing for the Strategic and Economic Dialogue, an annual high-level meeting of dozens of officials from the two governments. A public standoff with the Chinese could blow up not only that meeting, but also America's most important bilateral relationship—one that was already a geopolitical balancing act—in the middle of an election year. The prospect of a Chinese dissident being cut loose by the United States was fast becoming a theme on the campaign trail. Mitt Romney called it a "day of shame" for the administration.

The secretary of state had gotten them into this fix a week earlier when she authorized State Department officials to bring in Chen after he escaped house arrest in his village in eastern China, traveled 350 miles to Beijing on a broken foot, and appealed to the embassy for help. He was a compelling figure, to be sure, his legal advocacy for China's poor earning him the nickname "the barefoot lawyer." But Clinton made the risky decision to pick him up on the streets of Beijing after a tense, profanity-laden phone call between Jake Sullivan and Tom Donilon, in which Donilon, far from endorsing the move, raged about the mess it was going to create (both men declined to discuss their conversation, which was described by other officials). "The secretary has to do what she thinks is right," Donilon told Sullivan before ringing off.

China experts at the White House questioned whether harboring Chen was worth the risk; lawyers at the NSC suggested it would be illegal; political advisers suspected Clinton of grandstanding. When the president's aides told him at his daily briefing the next morning about the new refugee in the Beijing embassy, he was not happy.

"Get him out," Obama ordered.

Clinton's diplomats, in turn, felt hung out to dry by White House officials who anonymously criticized their efforts to carry out Obama's directive to remove Chen. They had not slept for days, negotiating with angry Chinese officials and an emotionally fragile man on the run. Now, with their reputations—even their careers—on the line, they were reading in the newspapers that they had botched his transfer to the hospital. They had failed to leave an American official with him, adding to his sense of isolation. They hadn't adequately briefed his wife, Yuan Weijing, which might have eased the anxiety she expressed to her husband after they were reunited. They hadn't kept an open line to Chen, which meant they couldn't get through to him, even though he was busy talking to reporters on cellphones supplied by the embassy.

Some on her staff thought the target of these whispers was Clinton herself. "They were more than happy to watch her slide on a banana peel," one State Department official said. "The decision that mattered was 'Do you bring the guy into the embassy or not?' When it turned ugly, the White House said, 'Well, you never should have done that, Hillary.'"

The morning after Clinton's dinner at the temple, she went for a walk with Kurt Campbell in the garden of the Diaoyutai State Guesthouse. The Chinese were furious that Chen wanted to renege on the agreement; they were in no mood to negotiate a new one. The White House was furious to be facing both a diplomatic crisis and a domestic political embarrassment. Campbell, a bench-pressing former naval reserve officer from Fresno who plays the violin and rowed crew at Oxford, normally exudes a swaggering air—Richard Holbrooke, by way of California's Central Valley. On this day, though, he was drained and despondent. Having pushed Clinton to take in Chen, Campbell told his boss that he feared he had not served her well. Maybe he should resign his post as assistant secretary of state for East Asian affairs. Clinton told him she had no regrets. "This is a small price to pay to be the United States of America," she declared.

Rather than accepting Campbell's resignation, she told him to go back to the bargaining table—this time with a goal of getting Chen out of China. Over the next three days, as the White House watched nervously, Campbell and Clinton herself would engage in several more grinding rounds of diplomacy with Chinese officials, finally salvaging an agreement for Chen to move to the United States and study law at New York University. China, though bruised by the experience, was not ready to rupture the strategic summit, and perhaps the entire relationship, over a single nuisance case.

For Clinton, the deal was sweet vindication, a dramatic flourish to four years in which she had made Asia a signature priority at the State Department. To her, the Chen affair was evidence of the durable, resilient bonds she had fashioned over many visits to China, during which she spent hours in public and private encounters, pressing common interests from climate change to restraining North Korea's regime. "I believed we were going to figure out a way through this," she told me. "We might never agree on the what or why, but we couldn't allow our relationship to founder over this."

Still, the sniping from the White House stayed with Clinton's aides for years. The anonymous potshots over how the diplomats handled Chen's case belied the esprit de corps that Team Clinton and Team Obama had labored to create. It was a reminder that some senior Obama aides were still ready to blame Clinton for missteps, even four years into a tenure in which she had largely played the loyal lieutenant. The criticism struck Clinton's team as especially unfair, given that her hard-edged diplomacy and heavy focus on Asia had been perhaps her greatest contribution to Obama's foreign policy, the one place in a White House–dominated administration where she indisputably made a mark.

The tension reflected the extraordinary stakes involved for both Clinton and Obama. The Chen Guangcheng affair threatened to undo three and a half years of painstaking work to create a new climate for the relationship between the United States and China. The administration had reasserted America's role as a Pacific power by stiffening its spine with Beijing and shoring up its Asian alliances. Clinton spearheaded the project, dubbing it the "pivot." The White House then co-opted the approach, preferring to call it the "rebalance." (Even the nomenclature would later prove a source of conflict.) Whatever the name, the policy was a rare example of over-the-horizon thinking by an administration that, in other parts of the world, seemed to lurch from crisis to crisis. The standoff over the blind dissident, by putting that achievement at risk, brought much deeper strains to the surface—long-simmering, never-resolved tensions over who should get credit for turning east.

Barack Obama and Hillary Clinton both fancied themselves Asia hands, but they came about their status differently. For Clinton, who had little cultural or emotional affinity for the region, her expertise was the result of conscious choice, methodical deliberation, and hard work. For Obama, who spent his childhood in Indonesia and Hawaii, it was more instinctive, almost a reflex. For both, Asia was a Shangri-la, shimmering in the distance, an opportunity to shift America's focus from the hopeless quagmires of the Middle East.

Unlike in the Middle East, where they had clear differences over policy and strategy, Clinton and Obama agreed on the growing centrality of Asia—and, more specifically, China—and the need to reclaim America's place there after nearly a decade of neglect. In October 2011, Clinton wrote a long article in *Foreign Policy* magazine that, apart from lacking the grace notes found in Obama's prose, could have been written by the president. "As the war in Iraq winds down and America begins to withdraw its forces from Afghanistan," she declared, "the United States stands at a pivot point." Just as the post–World War II Atlantic alliance "has paid off many times over," Clinton wrote, "the time has come for the United States to make similar investments as a Pacific power."

As with Clinton, Obama's bias toward the region was not driven by any special affection for China. He came into office as a former Illinois senator, viewing the Chinese primarily as a threat to Midwestern manufacturing. Clinton, the former New York senator, shared those suspicions, but on behalf of her home-state constituents such as Corning, a maker of fiber optics. Both were intent on making the Chinese obey the international rules of the road on trade. This cold-eyed, domestically driven view was important because it helped wean the United States away from the China-centric approach to the region that had prevailed since Nixon went to Peking in 1972. That approach reached its peak under George W. Bush, whose Treasury secretary, Henry Paulson, dominated Asia policy. Paulson liked to boast that, as a Goldman Sachs investment banker, he had made seventy trips to China.

For all the common ground, there were subtle differences between the two, which spoke to their distinct experiences. Clinton, with her exposure to her husband's rocky dealings with China and her own history dating back to the 1995 UN women's conference, tended to view China through the prism of "great power" politics— a complex relationship to be managed rather than a partnership filled with promise. Obama, with little hands-on experience of China and childhood roots in Jakarta, tended to view it from the perspective of Southeast Asia, where the Chinese were feared for imperial ambitions and resented for their commercial success. Both views had merit.

The president's Southeast Asian perspective surfaced in unexpected ways. In October 2009, Lee Kuan Yew, the founder of Singapore, paid a visit to the White House. Revered at home for building an immaculate, well-functioning, multiethnic city-state, he was much more controversial in the West, where Singapore was notorious as a nanny state that outlawed chewing gum and caned criminals. Briefing Obama before the meeting in the Oval Office, two of his aides reminded him of Lee's less-than-pristine human rights record. "I spent some of my formative years in Indonesia," he replied, "and this man was a hero. He was a heroic figure."

Though Obama had no such reverence for China, he heeded the advice of his campaign advisers on Asia, Jeff Bader and Jim Steinberg, who were determined to get him off on the right foot with Beijing. They shunned the China-bashing approach that George W. Bush and Bill Clinton had taken during their presidential campaigns and which had haunted them once in office. Steinberg coined the phrase "strategic reassurance" to describe how the United States and China could manage the inevitable tensions between an established power and a rising one. (The White House later disavowed the term when critics branded it overly conciliatory.)

For the first year of his presidency, Obama was too preoccupied by the financial crisis and the wars in Iraq and Afghanistan to pick a fight with China, even if he'd wanted to. Nor did he have the flexibility to play the roving statesman elsewhere in Asia. Three times, he was forced to cancel a visit to his boyhood home of Indonesia: a healthcare vote, the Gulf Coast oil spill, and the government shutdown all got in the way. This gave Clinton a rare chance to claim some foreign policy turf of her own in an administration that ran most of the major portfolios, from Iran to Russia, out of the West Wing. With the president sidelined by one thing after another, she plunged into the geopolitics of this far-flung region.

"While their goals might have been the same, stylistically, they were quite different," said Jon Huntsman, Obama's ambassador to China. "One was detached, reserved, more strategically focused; the other was on the front lines, trying to execute and get some things done."

Clinton's effort got off to a shaky start.

To underline the new focus, Clinton chose Asia rather than Europe for her first overseas trip. No secretary of state had done that since Dean Rusk in 1961. The idea had been suggested by Steinberg, whom the White House had installed as her deputy after his work for Obama during the campaign. He viewed the Asia trip as a part of a three-pronged diplomatic campaign in which Obama would invite Japan's prime minister, Taro Aso, to be the first foreign leader to visit the Oval Office, and host a private lunch for President Lee Myung-bak of South Korea. Clinton's four-country, eight-day itinerary in February 2009 sent a clear message: The United States was going to pay attention to the whole region, not just the Middle Kingdom.

Her first two stops, in Japan and Indonesia, were a model of campaign-style public diplomacy. At the University of Tokyo, she spoke to a standing-room-only audience about how the United States hoped to rebuild its ties to the Muslim world. In Jakarta, Clinton appeared on a popular variety show, *Awesome*, confessing to the young host that her favorite musicians were the Beatles and the Rolling Stones, and then inspected a water-treatment project along a canal in a working-class neighborhood, a small crowd trailing her like the Pied Piper. "People are very excited to see Hillary Clinton," said Daniel Sitorus, a twenty-four-year-old lawyer. "It doesn't matter that she isn't Barack Obama; she is one of the most famous women in the world."

Meeting with reporters halfway through the trip in a hotel conference room in Seoul, Clinton was energized. The cautious figure we saw in Washington had given way to an intrepid diplomat, full of plans. She was going to redefine the job of secretary of state, pulling it from the sterile confines of bilateral meetings into the rough-and-tumble arena of people-to-people encounters. She was going to dispense with the opaque language of diplomacy. "I don't think that it's a forbidden subject to talk about succession in the hermit kingdom," she said, referring to North Korea's ailing dictator, Kim Jong-il. (She learned quickly that it was, in fact, verboten; she never broached the topic again.) On her last stop, in Beijing, Clinton said she planned to have a meaty exchange with Chinese leaders on climate change and North Korea, issues where the two sides could work together. That meant not haranguing them with a perfunctory, predictable American lecture about their poor human rights record, which would draw a perfunctory, equally predictable reply.

"We pretty much know what they're going to say," she explained. "We know that we're going to press them to reconsider their position about Tibetan religious and cultural freedom, and autonomy for the Tibetans and some kind of recognition or acknowledgment of the Dalai Lama. And we know what they're going to say, because I've had those conversations for more than a decade with Chinese leaders." (She might as well have added, "Yadda yadda yadda.") The woman who had once declared that "human rights are women's rights and women's rights are human rights" was saying, in effect, that pushing China on this was a waste of time.

As soon as Clinton's comments were reported, Amnesty International and lawmakers cried foul. Representative Chris Smith, a New Jersey Republican and frequent critic of China's human rights violations, called it a "shocking display of pandering." Her aides quickly huddled in a staff room at the Westin Hotel in Beijing, debating whether the comments constituted enough of a gaffe that they needed to be walked back. The next morning, Jeff Bader approached her gingerly. He was not an obvious choice for an intervention: A seasoned China hand, Bader was an Obama loyalist who had been critical of Clinton during the campaign. Now he was the NSC's senior director for Asia, traveling with her. In those early days especially, White House officials on the secretary's plane were sometimes viewed as spies. Though Bader raised her remarks with the White House, Obama's aides were not particularly concerned, suggesting they had little problem with Clinton's nonconfrontational approach.

Bader decided on his own that she needed to clarify the American position. He met with Clinton at her hotel the next morning and told her that her comments, "while the absolute truth, were unduly provocative," presumably to human rights groups and lawmakers who liked lecturing China. He handed her a yellow sheet with a few points scrawled on it. The Obama administration, the statement said, viewed the protection of human rights as a "critical global priority," and American officials planned to raise the issue in every meeting, public and private, with Chinese officials. Clinton took the paper and put it in her pocket. When she was asked about her comments later that day at a news conference with the Chinese foreign minister, Yang Jiechi, she rather ostentatiously pulled out the sheet, put on her reading glasses, and read the talking points verbatim.

For Clinton, it was a rookie error, and one she would not repeat. She did not dwell on the episode in her memoir, but some believe it had lasting consequences. "I always felt that she tried to overcome that weakness or deficiency later on with a harder line toward China," Huntsman said. "Because she really did amp up her volume and her assertiveness."

Clinton wasn't the only one struggling to get the tone right with China in those early days. At the White House, the emphasis on a smooth relationship tripped up Obama as well. Eight months after Clinton's trip, he postponed a meeting with the Dalai Lama when he visited the United States, a courtesy that American presidents customarily extended to Tibet's exiled spiritual leader, even though it always drew protests from the Chinese government. The problem wasn't the meeting, per se, but the timing: The following month, Obama was making his first trip as president to China, and the White House didn't want to poison the atmosphere. Critics, however, pounced on Obama for kowtowing to Beijing. "We hadn't reckoned with the way people in Washington set up litmus tests," a frustrated Bader said. "Maybe we should have."

The White House had good reason to worry about the optics of Obama's visit. He was traveling to China at a time when the financial crisis had tarnished the reputation of the United States throughout Asia. Suddenly, America seemed a declining power, its housing and financial markets in shambles, its political system paralyzed, a debtor nation in hock to Beijing for a trillion dollars in Chinese-owned Treasury bills. China's economic ascendancy, on the other hand, awakened a latent nationalism, making heightened tension with the United States almost inevitable. That complicated the strategy of Bader and Steinberg, which was to break a long-established pattern of newly elected presidents going through a bad first year with the Chinese, largely because of the anti-China rhetoric they had used to get elected.

In the 1992 campaign, three years after the massacre in Tiananmen Square, Bill Clinton referred to the Chinese as the "butchers of Beijing"; in 2000, George W. Bush criticized President Clinton for calling China a "strategic partner," saying it was more of a "strategic competitor"; in 2008, Hillary Clinton demanded that Bush boycott the opening ceremony of the Beijing Olympics to protest China's treatment of Tibet and its failure to press Sudan to stop the killing in Darfur. Obama, however, declined to join her call. "I'm hesitant to make the Olympics a site of political protest," he said at the time, "because I think it's partly about bringing the world together." His fence-sitting, combined with his thin foreign policy résumé, made him a mysterious figure in China. "We tried to introduce him as the first Asia-Pacific president," Huntsman recalled.

"But the Chinese were perplexed. Where does he come from? What does he think? He remained a bit of a cipher."

Obama's trip, in November 2009, was a public relations fiasco. He and President Hu Jintao held substantive talks about the world economy and the nuclear ambitions of Iran and North Korea, but the Chinese relentlessly stage-managed Obama's public appearances. They allowed no questions after his joint news conference with Hu. They refused to broadcast his town-hall meeting in Shanghai on state television, depriving him of a nationwide audience for his remarks; then they packed the hall with members of the Communist Youth League, which guaranteed he wouldn't get the kind of questions that opened the door to provocative answers. And they crudely censored an interview Obama gave to a Chinese alternative newspaper, *Southern Weekend,* in which he talked about trade, the bilateral relationship, and the rise of China. At a time when the United States was on its back foot, the treatment he endured seemed a metaphor. American press coverage was withering.

Obama was angry at the Chinese but equally frustrated by the bad press, which he felt substituted score keeping for analysis. His angry response to my coverage during his trip to Asia five years later—when he told me he had not gone to Japan expecting to sign a trade deal—reflected a concern, his aides told me, that *The New York Times* was yet again going to establish a narrative that Obama was floundering in the region, when the facts on the ground showed otherwise. That sensitivity is understandable: Daily news can sometimes slight genuine progress. But as Obama came to appreciate over time, the symbolic power of the presidency is crucial for setting the tone. And in the fall of 2009, the new president was cast in the role of supplicant in China; that, more than his private exchanges with Hu, drove the coverage.

Clinton recognized the challenge for the United States. Over a long lunch with Prime Minister Kevin Rudd of Australia in Washington in March 2009, she asked him for advice on dealing with China. "How do you deal toughly with your banker?" Clinton said, according to a State Department cable released in December 2010 by WikiLeaks. Rudd, describing himself as a "brutal realist on China," told Clinton that the United States should adopt a policy of "multilateral engagement with bilateral vigor"—a polite way of saying "Make friends with China's neighbors and get tough on China." Whether Rudd knew it or not, he was describing the outlines of a policy already taking shape in the State Department.

"China badly misread the United States, believing we were in a downward spiraling decline," said Kurt Campbell, one of the principal architects of that new approach. "On that first trip, they did not treat Obama as well as they should have."

China's position was never as strong, nor America's as weak, as it looked in 2009. The $800 billion fiscal stimulus that Obama negotiated with Congress pulled the United States back from the brink—quieting talk of America's decline—and China's vast holdings of Treasury bonds and other U.S. debt meant it could not afford a collapse of the American economy any more than America could. As the situation in the United States stabilized, the White House decided to stiffen its posture toward the Chinese. Three months after his trip, Obama approved a sale of weapons to Taiwan and met the Dalai Lama, both of which drew spluttering outrage from Beijing.

Obama also began acting on his well-founded suspicions that China didn't play by the rules in global trade. He imposed a 35 percent tariff on the country for dumping tires into the American market. (One Obama aide called this "showing his Chicago pol side.") When Bader tried to brief him on Asian security issues before a visit by Hu Jintao in 2010, Obama waved him away impatiently. "Nobody cares about security," he said. "They only care about the economy." During the Clinton administration, Bader had actually worked with Obama's economic wise man, Larry Summers, to negotiate China's entry into the World Trade Organization. Rather than being impressed by that achievement, Obama liked to needle them about it. "Did you guys give away too much?" he asked more than once. So hawkish was Obama on trade that

Summers and Tim Geithner, his Mandarin-speaking Treasury secretary, would team up to parry his instincts to strike back at Beijing.

An emboldened China, meanwhile, was playing a dangerous game in the security sphere. The People's Liberation Army had grown much more assertive and independent under Hu, a cautious, colorless leader. Chinese warships began harassing Japanese ships in its coastal waters, raising tensions with an old enemy. During one dispute in 2010, China halted the export of rare-earth minerals, critical for the manufacture of technology equipment, to Japan. Farther south, China began bullying its neighbors over ancient territorial disputes in the South China Sea. That left allies such as the Philippines, and erstwhile enemies such as Vietnam, eager for American support.

They were about to get some—not from Obama, but from Clinton.

One by one, the foreign ministers leaned into their microphones: Vietnam, Malaysia, the Philippines—twelve of the twenty-seven countries present at the Asian summit meeting, held on July 23, 2010, beneath the vast, wavelike roof of Hanoi's convention center. The ministers complained about China's claims to a string of islands and reefs in the South China Sea, which conflicted with their own claims and were causing tensions. They urged China to accept a multilateral approach to settling these disputes rather than its preferred method of dealing with (read: strong-arming) the smaller countries one-on-one. Clinton, by prearrangement, spoke last. America wasn't taking sides in these conflicts, but after years of watching from the sidelines, it would help facilitate efforts to settle them. "The United States," she said, "has a national interest in freedom of navigation, open access to Asia's maritime commons, and respect for international law in the South China Sea."

For Beijing, which claims vast swaths of the South China Sea as a "core interest" of the Chinese state, those were fighting words.

Yang Jiechi, a stiff, suspicious diplomat at the best of times, felt sandbagged. Clinton had not warned him in advance, a breach of diplomatic etiquette that troubled some in her delegation. He stormed out of the room to get instructions from Beijing about how to respond. When he returned an hour later, he fixed Clinton with a glare and condemned those who tried to meddle in Asia's affairs. Turning to the Vietnamese foreign minister, he asked how a socialist country could be in league with a country that considered socialism an epithet. He was even less subtle with the rest of the group. "China is a big country," Yang warned them. "Bigger than any other countries here."

For the United States to thrust itself into this Asian Great Game was a risky proposition. Not everyone was happy about it. Richard Holbrooke, who began his career in Vietnam and was assistant secretary of state for East Asian affairs in the 1970s, worried about antagonizing the Chinese. "Why would you do this?" he asked Clinton after she got back from Hanoi. "For years, we never took a position on the Spratly Islands."

To casual observers of foreign affairs, the South China Sea is one of those distant, arcane issues that are difficult to fathom. It lies on the other side of the world; the legal issues are fiendishly complicated; few, if any shots, have been fired; even the names of the disputed territories—the Spratly Islands, Mischief Reef, Scarborough Shoal—are charmingly obscure, like something out of a *Pirates of the Caribbean* movie. Yet Clinton's intervention in this dispute may have been one of the most consequential actions in her time as secretary of state. If there is a military clash between the United States and China in the next decade, it is likely to break out in the South China Sea or the equally troubled waters to the north, in the East China Sea.

To assert hegemony over those waters, China is pursuing a twenty-first-century version of gunboat diplomacy. At Mischief Reef, which is part of the Spratly archipelago (claimed by China and the Philippines), Chinese ships are dredging white sand and piling it on top of the partly submerged reef. The vast reclamation project—two thousand acres and growing—has created artificial islands large enough to support harbors and military installations; one even has a three-thousand-yard airstrip on it. The goal of this frenetic activity is access to natural resources: Those reefs and islands sit atop vast untapped reserves of oil and natural gas—at least sixty-one billion barrels of petroleum—which China, Vietnam, and other fuel-hungry countries are racing to lock up.

Clinton thought this contest could be the next major source of conflict, just as gunboat diplomacy had been in the nineteenth century, when the United States, Britain, and other naval powers extracted concessions from weaker countries by sending warships to menace them. (China, ironically, was originally a victim of gunboat diplomacy: In 1840, during the First Opium War, a British gunboat sailed up the Yangtze River to put down a rebellion against the opium trade.) "This hunt for resources is going to consume large bodies of water around the world for at least the next couple of decades," Clinton said in 2011. While the race has drawn in many countries, China was the prime antagonist. Clinton recalled how, during a meeting in 2009, Dai Bingguo, the top Chinese foreign policy official, brandished a map to show her his country's historic claim to the South China Sea. The U-shaped boundary, known as the nine-dash line, extends hundreds of miles south of China's southern coast, gobbling up most of the waterway shared by seven countries.

Clinton's statement in Hanoi might have caught the Chinese off guard, but it had been weeks in the making. Campbell, working with Bader, had quietly laid the groundwork at lunches with ambassadors from Southeast Asia. The roots of the effort went back to a dinner Clinton hosted in the State Department early in her tenure. One of the guests, J. Stapleton Roy, a respected former ambassador to China, Indonesia, and Singapore, urged her to sign a long-shelved treaty with a group of Southeast Asian nations that would knit the United States more fully into their security. That dovetailed with Campbell's plan to shift the center of gravity of

American diplomacy from China and its East Asian neighbors—Japan and South Korea—to Southeast Asia.

"This was Kurt's great insight," Jim Steinberg said.

Steinberg had written a book with Campbell about the foreign crises that trip up new presidents—the Bay of Pigs for Kennedy, Black Hawk Down for Bill Clinton—and he recommended Campbell to run the East Asia bureau. A defense expert who knew more about Japan than China, Campbell did not have much entrée in the White House. But he quickly won favor with Clinton, who liked his enterprising approach to policy. He made the case to her that, with his help, she could put a Clinton stamp on Southeast Asia. "We can claim more territory in Asia," Campbell told her. "If you give me the time, if you give me the space, I can deliver success there." So Clinton threw herself into a region that had been neglected by the United States since Vietnam, burrowing into the commercial byways of the Mekong Delta and visiting obscure destinations such as Port Moresby in Papua New Guinea.

"The thing about Hillary is that she adopted the style," said Kim Beazley, Australia's ambassador to Washington. "The style is, number one, you turn up; number two, you respect the local culture. She understood that Southeast Asia doesn't move to the Confucian rhythms of North Asia."

Clinton got approbation wherever she went. "Time and time again," she told me, "I had leaders—I mean, I'm talking about the highest leaders—essentially say: 'Thank goodness. Thank you. I'm so pleased you're here. We were worried about America.'"

Two tangible achievements flowed out of the new policy. First, Campbell began talks with the military dictators in Burma about a rapprochement with the country the generals had renamed Myanmar and ruled brutally for half a century. Burma was the only diplomatic opening of the Obama years to be almost entirely a Clinton project. Second, restoring America's bonds with the region it once called Indochina gave Obama the framework for his most consequential trade initiative, the Trans-Pacific Partnership. The project began modestly in 2006 as a pact among four Pacific Rim countries—Australia, Brunei, Singapore, and Chile—but grew to encompass twelve countries that account for nearly 40 percent of the world's gross domestic product. It became the centerpiece of Obama's pivot to Asia.

The TPP was almost strangled in its crib by Obama's economic brain trust, led by Larry Summers. They thought it was too small—a boutique agreement that was a distraction from a bigger Asian free trade deal (with South Korea), and a luxury at a time when the United States had other economic problems to fix. Leading the campaign for it were Steinberg, Campbell, and other State Department officials. They were backed by Bader and Tom Donilon, who viewed the Trans-Pacific Partnership as the third leg of the pivot, along with Clinton's diplomatic outreach and new military commitments in the region. After six months of rancorous internal debate—"It took more shouting and screaming than I would have hoped for," Steinberg said—Obama sided with his foreign policy team over his economic team in making the agreement a priority. He asked Michael Froman, a law school classmate who had worked with him on the *Harvard Law Review*, to conduct the painstaking multiparty negotiations to produce an agreement.

Obama's decision to stick with the Trans-Pacific Partnership turned out to be even more important than it appeared at the time. With budget cuts and the demands of Afghanistan and Iraq constraining how many ships or soldiers the United States could move to Asia, and with diplomacy, by its nature, making only incremental progress, trade became the driving force of the pivot. Clinton predicted that the TPP would be "important for American workers" and lauded it as a "strategic initiative that would strengthen the position of the United States in Asia." She spoke out in favor of the agreement no fewer than forty-five times while secretary of state, according to CNN.

Then, as her presidential campaign gathered steam in the fall of 2015, Clinton abruptly reversed course. She said she could no longer support TPP for a variety of reasons, including its failure to protect American exporters from countries such as China that manipulate their exchange rates. "The bar here is very high," she said, "and, based on what I have seen, I don't believe this agreement has met it." Her political calculations during a Democratic primary were clear. But the about-face antagonized the White House, weakened Obama's case for the deal in Congress, and bitterly disappointed Bader, Campbell, and others who had fought for it.

While Clinton and Campbell led the tougher approach toward China, they were helped by a president whose instincts were leaning in that direction anyway. Throughout 2010, Obama's patience with Hu Jintao had been fraying. China was unwilling to discipline its client state North Korea even after it torpedoed a South Korean navy ship, killing forty-six sailors. If China did not help curb Pyongyang's belligerence, Obama warned Hu at a G-20 meeting in Seoul, he would not hesitate to take steps to protect America from a nuclear missile attack. Dropping his talking points and looking at Obama, Hu asked him to clarify what he meant. His answer carried an ominous hint: The United States would move navy warships into the waters off China.

"Obama pulled back the veil," said Jeff Bader, who was in the room with the two presidents that day.

Beyond his frustration with Beijing, the president was naturally inclined to a policy that shifted America's focus southward. Obama's Asia lay not on the thirty-eighth parallel or the windswept ramparts of the Great Wall but in the tropical swelter of Indonesia. He identified more with the dozy pace of Jakarta than with the crackling energy of Shanghai. At breakfast one morning in 2010, during a summit in Toronto, Obama sat down with Susilo Bambang Yudhoyono, a Javanese former army general, known by his initials SBY, who was then serving as Indonesia's president. The two leaders chatted softly, their conversation punctuated with long silences that left neither uncomfortable. To Rahm Emanuel, the president's hyperactive chief of staff, it was a revelation.

"I think I understand you better now," he said to Obama afterward. "You've got this whole Asian thing going."

Obama smiled. "The wave comes in, the wave goes out, and another wave comes in," he said. "Just be calm and relaxed."

By the time Obama returned to Asia again in the fall of 2011, the White House had all but co-opted Clinton's strategy. At an economic summit in Honolulu, on his way to the region, Obama made an impassioned case for the Trans-Pacific Partnership. In Darwin, Australia, he announced he would deploy a rotating force of 2,500 marines to underline America's security commitment to the region. (The idea originated with Kurt Campbell, who sold it to Defense Secretary Leon Panetta.) During his last stop, on the island of Bali, Obama made the biggest news of the trip, announcing he would send Clinton to Burma to test her theory that this beguiling land of Buddhist temples, so long under the military's boot, was ready to open up.

Each of these moves posed a direct challenge to Beijing. The Chinese were not eligible to join the TPP because they did not meet its labor and environmental requirements. The marine force in Darwin, while small, was the advance guard of a potential American military presence throughout the region that could defend friends and allies from a predatory China. Bringing Burma's generals in from the cold would allow them to reduce a reliance on China that had turned their country into a vassal. While Obama and Clinton shunned the term "containment"—insisting they welcomed a rising China—their demurrals fooled no one. "Have a good trip building the de facto China containment alliance," Sidney Blumenthal emailed Clinton before one of her Asian tours.

At the same time, both kept doggedly engaging China's leaders. Clinton, on repeated trips to Beijing between 2009 and 2012, deepened her relationship with Dai Bingguo, the Communist Party elder who told her the first time they met that she was "much prettier and much younger" than her pictures. Dai was instrumental in clearing the way for Chen Guangcheng to leave China for the United States, averting a broader rift. Obama, frustrated by the stilted relationship he had with Hu Jintao, set out to develop a more personal rapport with Hu's successor, Xi Jinping. In June 2013, he hosted Xi at the "shirtsleeves summit" in Rancho Mirage, California, a self-conscious effort to cut through the formal rituals of great-power diplomacy.

In eight hours of ostensibly informal but meticulously staged conversation, Obama went toe-to-toe with China's formidable new leader on vexing issues, from China's rampant cyber espionage and theft to its slow-motion conquest of the South China Sea. The choice of venue felt like a throwback: Walter Annenberg's two-hundred-acre Sunnylands estate—Camp David West, with its yellow cactuses, midcentury modern architecture, and manicured golf course, all bathed in the sun-faded glow of Republican money. Bobby Flay grilled porterhouse steaks in the evening, after the two men had gone for strolls in the desert heat. Squint, and you could almost see Nixon and Reagan in their V-neck sweaters and high-waist slacks, whizzing by in their golf carts.

At one level, the results were disappointing: Xi was scarcely less stiff than Hu. He was never going to become the soul mate that Obama had hoped. But he was a pragmatist who recognized the benefits of cooperation. When Obama went back to Beijing in November 2014, the two signed a landmark agreement to cap and later reduce greenhouse gas emissions—a victory that made up for the lack of progress on issues such as Chinese hacking. Avoiding a replay of 2009, the White House persuaded Xi to take questions at his news conference with Obama in the Great Hall of the People. Josh Earnest, the press secretary, called first on *The New York Times* for symbolic reasons: The Chinese government had declined to renew the visas of *Times* correspondents in China as a reprisal for its coverage of the financial dealings of Chinese leaders and their families. I stood up and, with a wall of camera bulbs flashing, asked Xi two questions: Did he view Obama's pivot as a threat to China? And would China ease its refusal to give visas to correspondents in light of a broader visa agreement it had just signed with the United States?

At first, the Chinese president looked like he was going to simply ignore the impudent foreigner. (The agreement, Chinese officials complained, was that each reporter was to address only his or her president; the White House said there had been no such deal.) Xi ordered the moderator to move on, taking a scripted question from a state-owned paper. Obama, who was clearly eager to hear Xi's answer, smiled at me and shrugged, the presidential equivalent of "nice try, buddy." It turned out that Xi was merely biding his time. After he answered the Chinese journalist, he circled back to me and delivered a curt lecture. No, the pivot was not about containment. And the visa problems of *The Times* were of our own making. "In Chinese," Xi said, "we have a saying: The party which has created the problem should be the one to help solve it."

Two days later, Obama stood next to the Burmese democracy icon Aung San Suu Kyi in the garden of her lakeside house in Rangoon. He was there to build on Clinton's historic opening to Burma four years earlier, but he patted himself on the back for the exchange in the Great Hall of the People earlier in the week. If there was a common thread to his efforts in Asia, Obama said, it was his campaign to advance American values, as well as interests. That Xi answered my question was a small victory for his cause.


Success, the saying goes, has a thousand fathers.

While Asia was a healthy collaboration for Obama and Clinton, it became a bitter tug-of-war between those who tried to claim authorship of the pivot. The tensions that flared during the Chen episode had been building for months. The men who made Asia policy—and they were, with the exception of Clinton, men—were a close-knit, competitive fraternity. Donilon, Campbell, Steinberg, and Bader had worked together in previous administrations, written books together, even gone on fly-fishing holidays together in Sun Valley. In many ways, they resembled the cadre of American envoys who worked on Middle East peace. The difference was, these guys hadn't failed.

"It's attractive because it's nonpartisan, and it's the most well-regarded strategic move by the Obama administration," Steinberg said. "Who wouldn't want to be associated with it?"

A few months before the 2011 trip in which Obama laid out the elements of the pivot, Donilon told his staff he wanted to write an article in *Foreign Affairs* magazine articulating the policy. He had a credible claim to being one of its architects: After all, he fought for TPP, he flew to Beijing multiple times to develop his own ties with China's leaders; and he popularized the phrase "rebalance," saying the United States needed to rebalance from Iraq and Afghanistan to more promising places such as Asia. But Donilon, while smart, hardworking, and well organized, was an administrator, not a grand strategist. He was also a chronic worrier—a "bed-wetter" in the unkind description of a former State Department official—who drove his staff batty with demands for reams of briefing papers every time he appeared on *Meet the Press*. Aides were soon churning out endless drafts. "It became a joke because every month there'd be meetings about the *Foreign Affairs* article," one told me. "But he'd never pull the trigger because he was so nervous."

Clinton, meanwhile, was writing her own article for *Foreign Policy*, a rival publication. It was a Kurt Campbell initiative, clearly designed to put a State Department imprimatur on the Asia policy. When Jake Sullivan told Ben Rhodes in September 2011 that it was scheduled to be published in two weeks, Donilon hit the roof. He told one of his deputies, Derek Chollet, to order Clinton's drafters to narrow its scope. What followed was a bureaucratic tussle, at once petty and revealing, over how the nation's most important policies are communicated. The NSC suggested that Clinton write about multilateralism, a theme too wonky even for her. What they really wanted, Campbell joked to his colleagues, was for her to confine herself to "Indonesian agriculture between 1860 and 1890."

With the president's trip looming and Donilon's essay stuck in rewrites, the White House green-lighted Clinton's article. It appeared on October 11, 2011, under the headline "America's Pacific Century." It might as well have said, "Clinton's Pacific Century." In it, she boasted of making her first trip as secretary of state to Asia, and seven more in the two years after that. She wrote of the need for "forward-deployed" diplomacy and made clear she was on the vanguard of that effort, working to build trust with the Chinese. She even said, "We have made very clear, publicly and privately, our serious concerns about human rights"—showing how far she had come since that first trip when she said such protests were a waste of time.

While Clinton was in Asia with the president, the White House asked her to sit for five TV interviews, officially making her the face of the policy. Days later, Obama sent Clinton on her historic mission to Rangoon, eclipsing other news, including the wrap-up press conference by Donilon the next day, which he had viewed as a chance to finally put his stamp on Asia. He hadn't counted on speaking poolside at the W Retreat and Spa in Bali, steps from the turquoise waters of the Indian Ocean. Five minutes into his twenty-minute opening statement, restless reporters began messaging White House aides: "Why can't you end this thing so we can go back to the beach?"

Donilon had a particular animus against the word "pivot," which appeared in the first sentence of Clinton's *Foreign Policy* article. The phrase, he said, needlessly antagonized America's European allies, who assumed it meant the United States was pivoting *away* from them. It was also easy to mock, given the gap between rhetoric ("America's Pacific Century") and reality (a few hundred marines sitting in Australia). But the word stuck, and that was fine with Clinton. In May 2012, she emailed Jake Sullivan to ask, "Didn't we, not the WH, first use the 'pivot'?" Two months later, after I had left my beat at the State Department for the White House, I called up Clinton to interview her about—"for lack of a better word," I added apologetically—"the pivot."

"Good word," she said. "We like that word."

# Thirteen

## The Lady and Havana

Except for their suits and ties, the two Americans hurrying through St. Peter's Square on the afternoon of October 28, 2014, scarcely stood out from the hundreds of tourists and pilgrims milling about in the shadow of Bernini's colonnades. When the pair reached an alleyway marked for official visitors, they were met by a priest and escorted behind the walls of the Vatican into the private realm of the Roman Curia—a place tourists rarely see. They were led through a series of stately courtyards in the Apostolic Palace, their escort pointing up to the papal apartments, which Pope Francis had shunned in favor of humbler quarters elsewhere in Vatican City, before arriving in a gilded reception chamber in the offices of the secretary of state.

The men from Havana had arrived a few minutes beforehand. By then, the Americans knew them well, having held half a dozen secret meetings with them over the course of eighteen months, several at a Canadian government building in Ottawa. The Americans smiled and shook hands with the Cubans warmly, surprising their Vatican hosts—a team consisting of four senior advisers to Pope Francis, including the secretary of state, Cardinal Pietro Parolin. Each delegation was to brief the Vatican alone, so when the cardinal and the two Cubans disappeared into another smaller room, the Americans—Ben Rhodes and his White House colleague Ricardo Zuniga—waited outside. When the Cubans walked back out of the room thirty minutes later, Rhodes and Zuniga were ushered in to find their hosts in a state of mild shock.

"I can't believe this," one said.

"Is this really happening?" another asked, as the Americans took their seats at the table.

It is, the Americans told the pope's men. Cuba and the United States were about to reestablish diplomatic relations, ending fifty-three years of bitter estrangement. They had come to ask for a papal blessing, a symbolic step that would give crucial political cover to both sides.

Once they had gone over the basic terms—a prisoner exchange in which an American development worker jailed in Havana, Alan Gross, would be swapped for three Cuban agents held in the United States, as part of a broader restoration of diplomatic relations— Rhodes and Zuniga joined their Cuban counterparts back in the reception room. All four sat down at a long table, across from the Vatican officials. The Americans recited their obligations again, out loud. The Cubans, who were from the Interior Ministry and the office of President Raúl Castro, did the same. Afterward, Cardinal Parolin offered a few words about what he had just witnessed. "In a world that has very little good news," he declared, "this will be welcomed around the world. It shows that people can make peace with one another."

A few minutes later, Rhodes and Zuniga were back in St. Peter's Square. They walked across the sea of cobblestones in a daze as the reality sank in: They had just sealed the biggest diplomatic coup of the Obama presidency so far. Rhodes was still terrified it would all fall apart, that they would slip up in some way. He asked the Cubans to leave the Vatican first so they wouldn't be spotted together by some journalist or Brookings analyst on holiday, wandering through the square—blowing the lid on an eighteen-month covert operation. Suddenly famished, the two men found a neighborhood place a block from the Tiber and ordered a little comfort food: tomato and mozzarella, pasta Bolognese, fried artichoke, a bottle of Chianti.

As they toasted their history-making day, Rhodes's thoughts ran to one of his White House colleagues back home, the chief of staff Denis McDonough—a man whose caution was perhaps surpassed only by his Catholicism. "Denis will never be able to undo this decision," he joked, "now that we have a commitment from the pope."

The diplomacy of the Obama years may have been a team sport—the Asia pivot, the Iran nuclear deal, the Middle East peace process—but Barack Obama and Hillary Clinton can each lay claim to one diplomatic opening that was uniquely theirs. Obama's was Cuba; Clinton's Burma. Each bore the unmistakable imprint of its author: how they approach problems, how they manage colleagues and subordinates, how they tolerate risk—in short, the habits and instincts that have defined their public careers.

Obama's overture to Cuba was conducted by a tiny circle of trusted White House aides. The State Department was entirely cut out, except for John Kerry, who was annoyed that Foggy Bottom had nothing to do with it. The president announced the news to an unsuspecting world on the morning of December 17, 2014. It's not a stretch to call it his diplomatic equivalent of the bin Laden raid, a spectacular deal blessed at the top levels of the Holy See but cut in the shadowy netherworld of espionage.

Clinton's cultivation of Burma, on the other hand, was the opposite: a painstaking, public three-year-long process, in which she enlisted the support of influential constituencies in Washington, carefully tested the waters with the heroine of Burma's democracy movement, Aung San Suu Kyi, and then finally approached the generals, who had seized power in 1962, turning the country into a hermetic dictatorship. By the time Clinton met Suu Kyi in person for the first time, at a lakeside villa in Rangoon in December 2011, she had read several books about her and they had spoken multiple times by phone. "I felt," Clinton recalled, "as if we had known each other for a lifetime."

Beyond the differences in style, Cuba and Burma also offer an insight into their different views of the world.

For Obama, Cuba was another in the rogues' gallery of old adversaries he was ready to engage. As with Iran, he felt that America's long-standing policy of isolation was obsolete, self-defeating, and played into the hands of its repressive rulers. Cuba was less strategically important than Iran, to be sure, but it had political resonance in the United States, particularly in the electoral battleground of Florida. As a candidate, he had started with a cautious proposal, promising to ease restrictions on the travel of Cuban-Americans. But in July 2007, at a debate in Charleston, South Carolina, he famously pledged to meet the leader of Cuba—and for that matter, the leaders of Venezuela, Syria, Iran, and North Korea—without preconditions, during his first year in office.

Clinton's views on Cuba were those of a standard-issue 1990s Democrat, one still running for her party's nomination. They had been shaped by the Cold War and hardened during her husband's presidency, when a Cuban fighter jet shot down two planes belonging to a Miami-based organization that helped people trying to escape Cuba on rafts. In the ensuing furor, Bill Clinton signed the Helms-Burton Act, which extended the reach and duration of the trade embargo, perpetuating Cuba's poverty and becoming a reviled symbol of American obduracy. As a candidate in 2008, Hillary had stuck to a familiar script, one poll-tested not to offend Cuban American voters. An opening to Cuba, she said, could come only if Cuba changed first. "Unless there is some recognition on the part of whoever is in charge of the Cuban government that they have to move toward democracy and freedom for the Cuban people," she said, "it will be very difficult for us to change our policy."

Clinton had a change of heart after becoming secretary of state. Part of it was simply the difference between being a diplomat and a politician, but part of it was also that whenever she traveled to Latin America, she got a lecture about how retrograde the half-century-old embargo looked to people there. Cuba policy, she concluded, was becoming an impediment for the United States across the region. She came back from those trips convinced that the State Department should, at the very least, loosen rules for people to travel to and from Cuba. At times, she ran into resistance from a White House that was balancing Obama's pro-engagement instincts with a fear that he would alienate Cuban American voters in the process. Before leaving her job, Clinton wrote an exit memo to Obama, in which she recommended that he push Congress to lift the embargo.

If Cuba appealed to Obama because of the tug of history, Burma appealed to Clinton for classic geopolitical reasons. It sits between India and China, giving China access to the Bay of Bengal and a strategically important trade route that Chinese officials hope to turn into a maritime Silk Road. Burma's profound isolation bred a deep economic dependence on the Chinese; they built dams across the Irrawaddy River and hemmed in the crenelated redbrick walls of Mandalay's fort with garish concrete-and-glass hotels. During Clinton's first year at the State Department, there were also alarming reports that Burma was trying to buy nuclear parts and expertise from North Korea—an unholy alliance between two of the world's pariah states.

Reaching out to the Burmese regime could check China's influence in the region *and* make the world a safer place. Clinton, moreover, admired Aung San Suu Kyi, both for the dignity that had earned her the sobriquet "the Lady" and for the steeliness that lay beneath her elegant demeanor. At their historic first meeting in 2011, they each wore white. Once the gauzy photo op was completed, the two women got down to the kind of pragmatic, no-nonsense relationship that Clinton had with the likes of Bibi Netanyahu.

Clinton also intuited that Burma offered her a chance to make history in a way that Cuba did not. Despite the president's emotional connection to Southeast Asia, Burma was not a priority for Obama when he came into office. He cared about the region, but mostly in the context of trade and China. On Cuba, however, he signaled his readiness to change the status quo early on. Speaking to Latin American leaders at his first regional summit meeting in

Trinidad and Tobago on April 17, 2009, Obama declared, "I'm prepared to have my administration engage with the Cuban government on a wide range of issues—from drugs, migration, and economic issues to human rights, free speech, and democratic reform." Clinton immediately picked up on his word choice. "It was 'my administration,' which may mean they'll pursue out of WH," she wrote in a prescient email to Jake Sullivan that evening.

"With Burma, she was in the lead, and State did a lot of the work," Ben Rhodes told me. "In Cuba, we did the work. With Burma, it was a more methodical effort to bring along Congress, to make sure you look before you leap. With Cuba, it was a big bang."

Rhodes had a unique vantage point on both projects. Before his work on Cuba, he had acted as Clinton's biggest White House advocate on Burma. Though formally just a speechwriter, his influence in the West Wing went far beyond channeling the president on foreign policy. With personal ties and a philosophical kinship that dated back to the 2008 campaign, Rhodes saw himself as a keeper of the flame for his boss. Reaching out to closed societies, he thought, was exactly what a history-making president like Obama should be doing. At the request of Sullivan and Kurt Campbell, Rhodes helped overcome the resistance to the Burma opening from NSC staffers, like Samantha Power, who worried about dealing with the generals, given their decades of human rights abuses. When Clinton was proposing her first visit to the country, Rhodes suggested that Obama speak by phone with Aung San Suu Kyi to give him the confidence to sign off on the idea. He was on hand a year later, in November 2012, when the president traveled to Rangoon with Clinton just before she left his cabinet—a celebration of her diplomatic breakthrough that doubled as a farewell tour for two people who surely never expected to have warm feelings for each other.

Clinton cherished her achievement in Burma. But after she left the State Department and began plotting her White House run, she had few opportunities to talk about it. Cuba, on the other hand, remained a live political issue. In July 2015, Clinton went to Miami, the heart of Cuban-exile country, to repeat what she had told the president three years earlier in her exit memo: The embargo needs to go. "The Cuban people want to buy our goods, read our books, surf our web, and learn from our people," she said. "They want to bring their country into the twenty-first century. That is the road toward democracy and dignity and we should walk it together." But as with her reaction to the Iran nuclear deal, Clinton qualified her support with a warning. "We should be under no illusions that the regime will end its repressive ways any time soon, as its continued use of short-term detentions demonstrates," she said. Her call to give Cubans access to more cellphones, computers, and satellite television carried a subversive overtone. These are the tools that a restless, disenfranchised population uses to throw out its government. "Engagement is not a gift to the Castros," Clinton told her audience. "It is a threat to the Castros."

It was a far cry from the upbeat, embracing tone the president struck when he first announced the opening. "To the Cuban people," he said in a brief address from the Cabinet Room of the White House that December morning, "America extends a hand of friendship. Some of you have looked to us as a source of hope, and we will continue to shine a light of freedom." As with Iran, Obama conceded the grievances that Cubans still had—in this case over America's colonial legacy. "We can never erase the history between us, but we believe that you should be empowered to live with dignity and self-determination," he said. "Cubans have a saying about daily life: 'No es fácil'—it's not easy. Today, the United States wants to be a partner in making the lives of ordinary Cubans a little bit easier, more free, more prosperous."

His words were not all that different than Clinton's. But the tone was day and night.

Mitch McConnell, the Republican senior senator from Kentucky, kept a handwritten thank-you note from Aung San Suu Kyi framed and hanging in his office. Hillary Clinton knew this because when she went to see him in early 2009, he showed it to her. Clinton had asked for the meeting because she wanted to review the long-standing American policy of refusing to engage the Burmese government. McConnell, then the Senate minority leader, was a leading voice in Congress for that policy—in 2007, he had helped pass sanctions to punish the military junta, and had become a faithful advocate of the pro-democracy movement, winning the gratitude of Suu Kyi. This was the kind of courtesy call that Barack Obama almost never made on Capitol Hill, especially on someone like McConnell, a skilled GOP warrior who once said his number-one goal was to make Obama a one-term president. Clinton wasn't particularly chummy with McConnell, either, but she knew that unless she obtained his acquiescence, if not his support, her effort to reach out to the Burmese would run into a buzz saw of opposition in Congress.

"I said, 'This is off the record; this is just me talking to you, Mitch,'" Clinton told me. "I want to tell you that I'm trying to put together an effort to test what's happening in Burma."

"Well, I don't think that'll work," he replied.

"It may or may not work," she said, "but what I want to know is whether you would support us trying."

They went back and forth for a while. Clinton pointed to a few promising signs in Burma. The government, for example, had announced plans to hold elections in 2010 under a new constitution. McConnell was skeptical, but he couldn't argue that George W. Bush's strategy of isolating the generals had succeeded. "We talked," Clinton recalled, "and he finally said, 'Well, nothing else has worked. Might as well.'"

She was not finished working her former colleagues. Next, Clinton sought out Jim Webb, the Virginia Democrat who was deeply interested in Asia. (He would later mount a brief challenge to her for the party's presidential nomination.) A Naval Academy graduate and marine who fought in Vietnam, Webb was cocky, temperamental, and iconoclastic, one of the Senate's most idiosyncratic members. When it came to Burma, he was on the other end of the spectrum from McConnell. Sanctions had been an abject failure, he told Clinton. They had done nothing to dislodge the regime, and because China refused to take part in them, they had enabled the Chinese to all but colonize the country. He urged her to move, and fast.

Then, in May 2009, there came an opportunity in the guise of a setback: an American man named John Yettaw was arrested in Rangoon. Yettaw, a mentally disturbed army veteran from Missouri, had become obsessed with Aung San Suu Kyi. Twice, he swam across Inya Lake and entered the heavily guarded compound where she had been living under house arrest since 2003, to try to talk with her. The second time, he was arrested after paddling back across the lake. The authorities, after sentencing Yettaw to seven years in jail, slapped Suu Kyi with an additional eighteen months of confinement. She had violated the terms of her house arrest by letting the intruder stay overnight. The new sentence would remove her from the field for the 2010 election. A frustrated Clinton called McConnell and Webb separately for advice. Webb proposed going to Burma to try to negotiate the release of the American, and Clinton agreed. When he arrived there, he was unexpectedly offered a meeting with Than Shwe, the seventy-eight-year-old "senior general" who headed the military junta and who—in seventeen years in power—had almost never met with Americans. Webb's trip wound up being an invaluable reconnaissance mission for Clinton and the State Department.

Than Shwe was a mystery, even by the mysterious standards of Burmese strongmen. His claim to fame was Naypyidaw, the grandiose, Potemkin village–like capital city that he had carved out of sugarcane fields, in extreme secrecy, a decade earlier. Paid for in part with the proceeds of Burma's thriving heroin trade, it is without a doubt the world's weirdest capital: twenty-lane highways with no traffic, lined by sprawling, cheerfully lighted hotels with no guests; bombastic, deserted government buildings; gardens tended by peasants in conical hats; and, on the edge of town, a majestic, windswept pagoda that is a replica of the much-visited Shwedagon Pagoda in Rangoon.

That August, Jim Webb became the first senior American official ever to set foot in the capital. He was richly rewarded by Than Shwe. Not only did the general agree to release John Yettaw, he allowed Webb to meet with Aung San Suu Kyi. It was a strained encounter: Suu Kyi, not surprisingly, was cross about Yettaw; his unwelcome visit had extended her imprisonment. She was also suspicious of Webb, who had been vocal about easing sanctions and not becoming overly reliant on any single figure in Burma (translation: her). She kept her arms crossed throughout, but she also made clear she would not stand in the way of an American overture to the generals. "Throughout her meeting with Senator Webb, Aung San Suu Kyi emphasized her practicality," read a State Department cable sent to Clinton. "We have a dream list. We have a wish list. But we're practical. We want a solution."

The cable—signed by the deputy chief of mission at the American embassy in Rangoon, Thomas Vajda—thrummed with excitement. The generals, Vajda reported, were plainly receptive to Obama's new era of diplomatic outreach. "It is certain Than Shwe believes he has unclenched its fist," he said of the regime, borrowing a phrase from the president's inauguration speech. The embassy made two recommendations to Clinton: Allow Burma's foreign minister to travel to New York for the UN General Assembly, and have someone make contact with a well-connected Burmese official, U Thaung, who had been appointed as the regime's special envoy to the United States.

Clinton was excited by what she read. Less than thirty minutes after getting a readout of the meeting, she emailed Sullivan and Huma Abedin to ask, "Should I try to call Webb?"

"I think yes," Sullivan replied.


With the United States open to more official contacts, the job of reaching out to Burma's brass moved from Webb to Kurt Campbell. He arranged to sit down with U Thaung in New York on September 19, 2009. Campbell had exhaustively researched his counterpart—or as exhaustively as possible, given the lack of useful intelligence about anyone in the Burmese regime. There were rumors he'd been involved with Burma's nuclear program, and had amassed influence by befriending Than Shwe. But U Thaung seemed less ready to unclench his fist than his boss. He presented Campbell with a laundry list of grievances; it was less a meeting than a lecture.

Still, Campbell got what he wanted: an invitation to visit

Two months later, on a misty November morning, he woke up at dawn in Bangkok and was driven to the airport, where he boarded a U.S. government plane. A vintage 1950s prop, it was less Air Force One than Sopwith Camel. (The State Department's fleet of aircraft was not as up-to-date as the Pentagon's.) Black smoke poured out of the engines when they coughed to life; during the short flight, the pilot warned him not to put his foot on an exposed wire or they might crash. Campbell had no idea what awaited him in Burma, but for a diplomat like him, with a sense of drama, it was an Indiana Jones moment.

After a cordial, if inconclusive, meeting with the generals in Naypyidaw, Campbell was permitted to fly on to Rangoon to meet Aung San Suu Kyi. They were allotted two and a half hours at the Inya Lake Hotel, a low-slung concrete pile built by the Soviets in the 1960s, where he was staying. He planned every detail: an airy room with billowing white curtains; a table set for two in the middle of a parquet floor; homemade brownies, a favorite of Suu Kyi's. At the appointed hour, she pulled up in a little silver car, tailed by the police.

"It was among the more exciting and memorable things in my life," Campbell told me, "and I've done a lot of things in my life."

Suu Kyi told him about her life within four walls. She kept to a strict daily regimen that included reading and listening to the BBC. ("My job," she called it.) They discussed why the Burmese regime suddenly seemed open to a relationship with the United States: It was worried about its dependence on China; it was falling behind its neighbors; it had watched other military regimes, like Indonesia's, make a successful transition to civilian rule. Suu Kyi was open to engagement but only if her party, the National League for Democracy, received certain guarantees. Afterward, Suu Kyi appeared pleased with the meeting; Campbell, she told associates, was "a scholar who displayed goodwill and knowledge of Burma," according to a cable from the American embassy.

Campbell wrote his own thirty-page memo on the meeting for Clinton. She was anxious to keep the momentum going. But his next visit, in March 2010, was a misfire. The generals were consumed by internal strife and seemed to have lost interest in reform. Aung San Suu Kyi, feeling marginalized, had turned against members of her own party who had been released from jail and wanted to run in the elections. She clashed angrily with American officials, who told her they would not condemn anyone who took part in the vote. A picture told the tale: Campbell and his deputy, Scot Marciel, shielded a querulous-looking Suu Kyi from the sun with black umbrellas.

Back home, the Burma opening was encountering growing resistance in the State Department and the White House. Harold Koh and Melanne Verveer, senior State Department officials with human rights backgrounds, were increasingly worried about making a deal with the junta, and had a direct line to Clinton. At the NSC, Tom Donilon shared Samantha Power's reservations. Campbell had a receptive ear in Jeff Bader, but Bader's successor at the NSC, Daniel Russel, was a cautious career diplomat who also harbored doubts. Clinton decided not to scrap the dialogue with the Burmese entirely, but downgraded it to one of Campbell's deputies. She was biding her time.

By the end of 2010, however, the ground began shifting on both sides of the Pacific. In Rangoon, the regime unexpectedly released Aung San Suu Kyi from house arrest. Than Shwe retired and was replaced by Thein Sein, a younger, more cosmopolitan figure who handed in his general's uniform when he became president (and also invited Suu Kyi to his house for dinner). In Washington, Clinton had fully embraced the pivot, settling on Asia as the place where she could make her mark, which turned Burma into even more of a priority. Obama was planning his own trip to Asia in the fall of 2011; Campbell saw this as an opportunity. A breakthrough on Burma would not only make headlines, it also would dramatize America's new presence in the region.

"We're going to throw the long ball," Campbell told colleagues. "We're going to try to do this thing in Burma."

By "this thing," he meant a diplomatic overture capped by a Clinton visit. No secretary of state had traveled to the country in more than fifty years. For Hillary Clinton, a meeting with the Nobel laureate Aung San Suu Kyi would be a personal triumph, a moment even someone as worldly as Clinton would save for her scrapbook. But selling the White House on "this thing" was going to be tricky. Obama's aides still worried about rewarding the generals prematurely. (Besides, they liked to keep the history-making moments for the president.) At NSC meetings, Clinton pressed her case. "We need to test this," she told the group. "Let's take some chances." The White House response was to schedule more meetings. As a frustrated Campbell and Sullivan turned to Rhodes, Clinton took her case directly to Obama.

"I think this is real," she recalled telling him. "We need to test it. The only way for me to feel comfortable advising you is to go." Somewhat to her surprise, Obama quickly agreed. "He basically said, 'Look, I'm behind you,'" she told me. "It was really between the president and me. He trusted me."

Clinton's visit was every bit the triumph that Campbell hoped, arguably the high point of her four years at the State Department. It began quietly, on the last day of November in 2011 when she landed in Naypyidaw to a simple handshake from a deputy foreign minister. There were no crowds waving flags or signs lining the route of her motorcade. (The prime minister of Belarus, who was coming the next day, rated a giant red billboard.) Clinton met first with Thein Sein; as they sat on gold thrones in a vast chamber, she handed him a personal letter from Obama, which encouraged him to persevere with reforms and promised the United States would reciprocate by easing sanctions. "He looked more like an accountant than a general," Clinton wrote.

The next day, she met Aung San Suu Kyi for dinner in Rangoon. Campbell, as usual, had left nothing to chance. He had brought a stack of first-edition copies of books, including a biography of George C. Marshall, for Clinton to give her. In Seoul, where Clinton's delegation had been just prior to Burma, he sent out an aide to buy a chew toy for Suu Kyi's dog. The staff placed candles throughout the colonial villa to create some ambiance, but when Campbell began advising Clinton on what she should wear—colors and numerology are important in Burmese culture, he explained to her—she cut him off in midsentence.

"Kurt," she said, "I can dress myself."

After drinks with Campbell and the special envoy to Burma, Derek Mitchell, the two women sat down alone to dinner. Clinton shared her impressions of Thein Sein; Suu Kyi peppered her with questions about her political ups and downs. Clinton later wrote that she reminded her of other political prisoners like Nelson Mandela and Václav Havel—"the coiled intensity of a vibrant mind inside a long-imprisoned body." At the end of dinner, Suu Kyi gave Clinton a silver necklace that she had designed herself; Clinton gave her the chew toy.

Among those beguiled by the images coming out of Rangoon was Ben Rhodes. He had been developing his own affinity for Southeast Asia, musing about what it would be like to follow his White House days with a posting there. With the diplomatic opening seemingly real, he began laying the groundwork for a visit to Burma by the president and Clinton after the 2012 election. She could introduce Obama to Aung San Suu Kyi, it would serve as a last road trip for Obama and Clinton before she left his cabinet, and it would reaffirm the Asia pivot, their most fruitful collaboration.

Sure enough, almost a year later, just eleven days after he vanquished Mitt Romney, Obama was in Thailand, preparing to fly to Burma. Given all they'd done to get the president to this moment, Rhodes saw to it that Campbell and Sullivan were assigned seats on Air Force One for the short hop from Bangkok to Rangoon. Obama dropped by en route to thank them for their work. For Campbell, who had never enjoyed much access at the White House, this was a rare opportunity, not likely to be repeated. To commemorate it, he set about pocketing every bit of Air Force One memorabilia he could get his hands on: cocktail napkins, glasses, even a flashlight stamped with the seal of the president. After landing in Rangoon, Campbell jogged toward his van at the end of a long motorcade, the bag of loot clanking against his legs.

Suddenly, he heard his name being called. Looking behind him, he saw two Secret Service agents trotting after him on the tarmac. "Dr. Campbell," they shouted. "Dr. Campbell." His stomach clenched; were they after him because of all the stuff he had taken from the plane? "It must be the flashlight," he thought to himself. "I'm going to say I took it accidentally." He jogged faster, but the agents closed the gap. "Dr. Campbell," one said, as he pulled up alongside him, "the president would like you to ride in the limo with him."

Campbell had to hustle back in the direction he had come, under the wing of Air Force One, all the way to the front of the motorcade. Obama and Clinton were waiting for him in the air-conditioned comfort of "the Beast," the president's armored Cadillac. Campbell settled on a jump seat facing the president and the secretary of state. The car began to roll silently.

"So tell me about the country," Obama said.

For visiting American VIPs, Latin America holds far less mystery than Southeast Asia. As far back as the Monroe Doctrine and the imperialism of Teddy Roosevelt, the United States has been a constant, proprietary presence in a region it considers its backyard. The two sides share colonial legacy freighted with all the vestigial ties and familial resentments that Britain has with Burma or France with Vietnam. When American officials call on their neighbors south of the border, the reception they get is often rocky, but rarely is it revelatory. And yet when Hillary Clinton attended her first meeting of the Organization of American States in Honduras on June 2, 2009, she was stunned to learn just how much the region had changed, particularly in how it viewed the long grudge between Cuba and the United States.

The venue was a country club in San Pedro Sula, a mangy industrial city known for clothing factories, rampant drug violence, and a string of strip malls pocked with McDonald's, KFC, and Taco Bell franchises. Her host was Manuel "Mel" Zelaya, the mustachioed businessman who had run Honduras for the past three years. (He would be forced out of the country a few weeks later, wearing only his pajamas.) Arriving dog-tired at eleven P.M., Clinton was immediately ushered into a room for a one-on-one meeting with Zelaya. He had gathered his entire extended family—wife, children, in-laws, and grandchildren. After two granddaughters presented Clinton with handmade headbands, she sat down awkwardly facing the president, and they began exchanging pleasantries. Five minutes later, the foreign minister of Honduras entered the room, saw that there was no chair for him, and left. Thirty seconds later, he returned carrying his own chair. The same exercise was repeated over the next fifteen minutes with three other senior Honduran officials. Finally, after what one aide described as a "completely surreal" conversation with Zelaya, the meeting was over, and Clinton was able to retire for the night.

The next morning, as Clinton was being driven to the opening session of the OAS general assembly, Jake Sullivan briefed her on the day ahead. "If everything goes according to plan—"

Clinton interrupted him with a laugh.

"Jake, were you paying attention yesterday?" she said. "Nothing's going to go according to plan."

Sure enough, Clinton soon had a mess on her hands. What was supposed to be her debut as a diplomat in Latin America turned into a free-for-all over Cuba that threatened to become a public relations nightmare for the Obama administration. Venezuela, Nicaragua, Bolivia, and Ecuador were agitating to readmit the country to the OAS. (It had been expelled in 1962.) Brazil and Chile were sympathetic, as well. All felt that the suspension, like the American embargo, was a Cold War relic. But the United States opposed readmitting Cuba unless it agreed to abide by the organization's democratic principles (not that Venezuela did, either).

Clinton spent the day pleading with the Brazilians and Chileans to accept what she billed as a compromise: The United States, she reminded them, had always opposed letting Cuba back in, regardless of the commitments it made. She also said the Obama administration was planning to increase its engagement with Havana. "The OAS continues to be an instrument of domination of the United States," railed Daniel Ortega of Nicaragua, the former Sandinista guerrilla leader. Zelaya undermined her as well; he called the decision to suspend Cuba "that other day that will live in infamy."

By nightfall, the United States remained isolated. The meeting was shaping up as an early diplomatic setback for Clinton. (In my news story that day, I wrote that she had "failed to hash out a compromise," which prompted anxious emails between Clinton and her aides.) Complicating matters, she had to leave Honduras early to join Obama in Cairo for his speech to the Islamic world. But overnight, as Clinton was flying to Egypt, the diplomats she left behind in San Pedro Sula managed to turn the tide in America's favor. Over endless pots of coffee, they persuaded a majority of the thirty-four OAS members to make Cuba's readmission contingent on its accepting democratic principles. (The Cuban government later angrily refused the offer.) Clinton was relieved, but still rankled by the press coverage, which she thought painted her as having stumbled in what was an impossible situation.

"I'm usually the pessimist, but I'm not sure this is as dire as it seems in the moment," Philippe Reines wrote her in a soothing email that night.

Reines was right, of course, but his email was a revealing snapshot into Clinton's fragile state of mind. With Obama dominating the great issues of the day—from Afghanistan to Iran—she was desperate for any victory she could find, even one on a rather poky debate over letting Cuba into a club it didn't want to join. Still, San Pedro Sula ended up being a valuable learning experience for her. It showed Clinton just how superannuated America's Cuba policy had become, and how much resentment it was stirring up in the region. Even if her diplomats had fended off Hugo Chávez and other leftist leaders this time, she knew that Cuba would continue to haunt the Obama administration. When she got back to Washington, she told the president that she was appalled by how much grief the United States had taken over it.

"She came out of that recognizing that Cuba was a problem," said Dan Restrepo, the NSC's senior director for Western Hemisphere affairs, who was on the trip. "The antiquated nature of the relationship allowed leaders like Chávez to paint the Obama administration as something other than it was."

In fact, the White House was interested in opening more channels to Cuba. It just wanted to do so in a way that didn't antagonize powerful Cuban American politicians in Florida, New Jersey, and elsewhere, who could try to sink the effort in Congress. In April 2009, Obama took a first step by fulfilling his campaign pledge to reverse Bush's restrictions on the travel of Cuban Americans. Restrepo made the announcement, in Spanish, from the podium at the White House. Politically, it was low-hanging fruit: Who could object to allowing Cubans living in Florida to visit their aging aunts and uncles in Havana? The next step would be more groundbreaking: expanding the ability of other Americans to visit Cuba. At Clinton's direction, the State Department began drafting plans to loosen restrictions for all sorts of people-to-people exchanges, as well as more flights and direct mail service.

The White House, however, was getting cold feet. On August 18, 2010, Obama flew to Miami Beach to raise money for Democrats running in the midterm elections. He got a friendly reception from the flip-flop-wearing crowds outside Jerry's Famous Deli, where he ordered two corned-beef sandwiches on rye. But the local politicians were frostier: They had gotten wind of the proposed changes and warned the president that any further outreach to Cuba would hurt them with Cuban American voters. Among those traveling with Obama that day was Jim Messina, a White House political operative who would manage his 2012 reelection campaign. (He said he did not recall talking to Florida politicians about Cuba policy.) Still, the announcement of people-to-people exchanges was put off until the following January.

"We were not being pushed back because of any ideological dispute," said Arturo Valenzuela, the assistant secretary of state for Western Hemisphere affairs. "We were being pushed back because they were thinking, 'Oh my God, this is not the right time to do it.'"

The other major impediment to any Cuba opening, of course, lay in Havana. Hard-liners in the Castro government had a long history of sabotaging efforts to thaw the relationship, as Bill Clinton learned in the 1990s with the shootdown of the rescue planes. Barack Obama's ambitious talk of engagement didn't guarantee he would get a receptive response from Cuba any more than he had from Iran. Indeed, at the end of 2009, eight months before the president's trip to Miami Beach, the Obama administration faced a crisis that officials suspected might be evidence of such a backlash: a sixty-year-old government contractor from Potomac, Maryland, had blundered into the biggest trouble of his life in Castro's Cuba.

"Anywhere that I've worked, anywhere that I've traveled, I never felt safer than in Cuba," Alan Gross recalled. "I felt that I could walk anywhere, any time of the day, and I didn't have to worry about being mugged or accosted or whatever. Of course," he added with a laugh, "now I know—I had to worry about being arrested."

Gross was sitting in a glassed-in conference room at the Washington office of his publicist, Jill Zuckman. He was far from the desperate, suicidal figure portrayed in news reports at the time of his release. He had regained much of the weight he had lost in prison. His smile was bright—a temporary bridge replaced the five teeth that had fallen out as a result of subsisting on a grim diet with no fresh vegetables for five years—and he was wearing glasses to correct for the partial loss of vision in one eye. Gross was full of wry recollections about the ordeal he had suffered, and he expressed genuine affection for the Cuban people and culture. (At the end of our meeting, he handed me a *Romeo y Julieta* cigar, cheerfully flouting the embargo.) But he also still bore deep bitterness about the way he was treated, toward the Cuban officials who jailed him and the American officials who took so long to spring him loose.

"I was a prisoner of both governments," he said. "There was a dearth of leadership on both sides. From what I could tell, they were doing nothing to try to correct this terrible situation."

Alan Gross was no dilettante in the risky business of democracy promotion. In a thirty-year career, he had worked in fifty-four countries, including Afghanistan and Iraq. His expertise was in handing out IT equipment that would give people access to the Internet. In Cuba, that was illegal. On December 3, 2009, he was wrapping up his fifth trip to the country, during which he had distributed satellite Internet routers, cellphones, and laptops to members of its tiny Jewish population. At ten P.M., after packing his suitcase, he heard pounding on his door. Four policemen stood outside. "You're coming with us," one said. He was taken away and thrown into a dank cell in Villa Marista, a notorious jail on the edge of Havana that houses political prisoners.

For Hillary Clinton, Gross joined a troublesome list that included three hikers captured in Iran, two Asian American TV journalists arrested in North Korea, and one deluded swimmer in Burma. When American citizens are held abroad for political reasons, it falls to the secretary of state to advocate for their release. In this case, her response was complicated by the fact that Gross clearly had broken Cuban law. He pleaded ignorance, claiming his company had never told him it was illegal to bring this gear into

Cuba. "Had I had that knowledge," he insisted to me, "I would never have done the project. It certainly wasn't worth that risk; nothing would have been worth that risk." (Gross sued, eventually winning a $3.2 million settlement from USAID, which funded the work through a contractor, Development Alternatives.) When an American consular official, Martha Melzow, first visited Gross in jail on December 28, 2009, nearly a month after his arrest, he told her only that he had been arrested for carrying "contraband."

Clinton fell back on standard policy: Demand Gross's return without any conditions. "We are deeply concerned about his welfare and poor health, and we have used every available channel to push for his release," she said after a meeting with his wife, Judy, on June 17, 2010. It was pro forma—and bound to fail. At that moment, Cuba was seeking the release of five intelligence agents who had been arrested in Miami in 1998 and jailed in the United States for infiltrating Cuban American dissident groups. One of them, Gerardo Hernández—who was serving two life terms for his role in shooting down two planes over Cuba in 1996 that had been dropping anti-Castro leaflets—had become a folk hero back home. The idea that the Cubans would release an American who had violated Cuban law, without getting any of the so-called Cuban Five in return, was fanciful.

"There was, politically, no possibility the Cuban government was going to let Gerardo sit in a U.S. prison while my client returned home," said Scott Gilbert, the lawyer who represented Gross. "The Cuban government couldn't tolerate such an outcome, and it didn't take a genius to figure that out. But apparently this was not understood. The State Department really seemed to believe for years that if they pounded the table hard enough, the Cubans would relent."

A onetime partner at the white-shoe firm of Covington & Burling, Gilbert took over Gross's case in December 2011 after Gross and his wife had become disillusioned with Clinton, as well as with his previous lawyers. With a lucrative practice in extracting money from insurance companies, Gilbert was not the most obvious choice to represent an idealistic development worker. But he is no ordinary D.C. litigator: Gilbert is an unapologetic lefty with a deep love for Cuba; above his desk hangs a rare numbered copy of the iconic photo of Che Guevara taken by Fidel's photographer, Alberto Korda. For him, the key was to show Cuba a modicum of respect. He came to view his role as a kind of marriage counselor, trying to get two long-estranged partners to talk to each other. "There was just an appalling lack of understanding of the Cuban people, of their history, of their government, of what makes them tick," he said. "It's a unique country with a very long memory. There's nothing like it in the world in terms of being in the time warp that they're in."

As soon as Gilbert began talking to Cuban officials, it became clear the only way Gross was coming home was as part of a prisoner exchange for the Cuban Five, especially Hernández. That meant persuading the Justice Department to commute the sentences of the Cuban agents. There were legal grounds for doing so: The convictions of *Los Cinco* had been overturned by a federal appeals court, which ruled that they had not received a fair trial in a Miami court. (A higher court later reinstated them.) Senator Patrick Leahy of Vermont, who had made a crusade of restoring relations with Cuba, urged Obama and Attorney General Eric Holder to swap the Cubans for Gross. But the White House told Leahy and Gilbert this was impossible. *Los Cinco* were acknowledged spies, after all; Obama wasn't ready to make a gesture like that.

"I didn't want to give them false hope," said Ricardo Zuniga, the traveling partner of Ben Rhodes, who had moved from being a Cuba expert at the State Department to taking Dan Restrepo's place as the NSC's director for Latin America. "I wanted to make it clear that getting Gross out was a top priority, but we didn't know at that point where we were going to land in our talks. Believe me, if we could have gotten Alan out earlier, we would have."

Leahy would not let the matter drop. He and his wife, Marcelle, had visited Fidel and Raúl Castro several times in Havana over the years. They had shared photos of their grandchildren and talked about what might finally break the ice between their countries. If Obama was reelected, Leahy confided to Raúl in the summer of 2012, there might be an opening. Back home, he pestered the president every time he saw him. "When Obama saw me," Leahy said, "he would ask, 'Are we going to talk about Cuba again?'"

Cartagena is a charming Colombian port with a walled old city, balconies draped in bougainvillea, and the misfortune of being the place where eleven Secret Service agents famously cavorted with prostitutes in their hotel rooms on the eve of a visit by President Obama in April 2012. It is less well known as the place where Obama promised to hasten the end of a half century of Cuba policy. The moment came at the Summit of the Americas, a gathering at which he had gotten a messiah's welcome on his first visit in 2009; this time, however, the Latin American leaders lined up to pillory him for his refusal to allow Cuba to join the group. No one spoke more forcefully about the need for change than Colombia's president, Juan Manuel Santos, who was about to undertake his own risky overture to antigovernment guerrillas in his country. He pressed the president to do likewise with the Cubans.

"If I'm reelected," Obama told Santos, "I'll do something on Cuba."

"We all heard that and kind of filed it away," Ben Rhodes said.

Indeed, a few weeks after he was reelected, the president told his advisers he wanted to do "something big on Cuba." In April 2013, Rhodes and Zuniga went to the Oval Office to present a detailed plan to negotiate a prisoner swap as part of a diplomatic opening. Obama was wary: There had been secret overtures to Cuba in the past; they usually ended in failure, with crossed wires or missed signals. The president wanted to keep this effort small so that if it failed, it could be easily shelved. Still, he authorized the pair to open a secret channel to Havana.

For Rhodes, who was bone-tired and ready to leave after six years in the White House, this felt like a new lease on life. "Cuba changed something about this presidency," he said. "The idea that we're going to normalize relations with Cuba seemed nuts to a lot of people around here in 2014. Now we break taboos all the time. It was a breaking of the seal." For Zuniga, it was the start of an intense period in which he closeted himself in his office with the door closed, poring over the maze of regulations, some dating from the Kennedy administration, that would have to be dismantled to end a half century of estrangement. He likened it to sifting through an archaeological dig.

Zuniga had a fascinating provenance. He is the grandson of Ricardo Zuñiga Augustinus, a right-wing politician in Honduras who ran a failed campaign for president in 1981, having supported its military rulers for the fifteen years before that. Young Ricardo was born in Tegucigalpa, the Honduran capital, but grew up in the United States. After graduating from the University of Virginia, he joined the Foreign Service. Among the older Latin America hands at the State Department, Zuniga's family lineage was a source of fascination: His grandfather had tense relations with American diplomats in Honduras over labor rights. "What are you doing working at the State Department?" a few teased him. But Zuniga was tireless, discreet, and a quick study. Assigned to the U.S. Interests Section in Havana, a sort of shadow embassy in countries with which the United States doesn't have formal relations, he developed the expertise in the licenses and regulations that was to come in so handy later.

A few weeks after their meeting with Obama, Rhodes and Zuniga sent a message to officials in Raúl Castro's office, bypassing diplomatic channels to keep it secret. The Cubans responded positively. Two months later, the pair began making furtive trips to Ottawa, where they would meet in offices provided by the Canadian government, which has long had relations with Cuba. They flew on commercial flights from Washington and made up cover stories to explain their absences to colleagues. The Cubans showed up with boxes of cigars and bottles of Havana Club rum for the Americans, which they had to leave behind in Canada because of the embargo. "Someone in Canada is very well stocked," Rhodes said. Much later, when the White House began planning the announcement, Rhodes brought a handful of colleagues into his confidence. To email about it without having to resort to cumbersome classified computers, the NSC's spokeswoman, Bernadette Meehan, took to calling it Project Ardilla, the Spanish word for squirrel, the swashbuckling, buck-toothed rodent in the Hanna-Barbera cartoon *Secret Squirrel*.

While John Kerry had been told of the back channel early on, no one else at the State Department knew about it—not even Roberta Jacobson, the assistant secretary who was leading the negotiations to release Gross. Scott Gilbert was also in the dark. The downside of not cluing him in was that, from Gilbert's vantage point, the effort to free his client was going nowhere. Gross, who had been moved early on from the Villa Marista prison to a locked room at the Carlos J. Finlay Military Hospital in Havana, was losing hope that he would ever see home again. He had lost seventy pounds during his first year of imprisonment. ("The food sucked," he said. "If anything moved in it, I wouldn't eat it.") Every month or so, he was transferred back to the prison for a meeting with U.S. consular officials. (Each trip necessitated a SWAT team and a five-vehicle convoy.) Aside from a couple of courtesy calls with Clinton, the State Department gave little comfort to Judy Gross.

"My wife received nothing—no support whatsoever, no information from the government," he said. "And she got more than I got. I was never angry at Obama; I was angry at the government."

What about Hillary Clinton?

"I'll reserve comment," he said.

Clinton's team worked harder on his behalf behind-the-scenes than Gross may have realized. Her chief of staff, Cheryl Mills, had gotten to know the Cubans through her work in earthquake-stricken Haiti. Several times, she met with the foreign minister, Bruno Rodríguez, in Port-au-Prince or New York to lobby for Gross's release. In early 2012, Jake Sullivan made the case for trading *Los Cinco* for Gross in a memo that he wrote for Clinton and copied to Rhodes. The exchange, he wrote, could be the basis for a "big bang"—a rapprochement between Cuba and the United States. When Rhodes sounded out Sullivan about coming to the White House as an adviser to Joe Biden after Clinton departed, they talked about making Cuba one of their pet projects.

Ultimately, though, the decision to approve a swap was Obama's, and he still wasn't ready to take the leap.

Unaware that the president had authorized a secret channel, the pro-Cuba contingent in Congress cast about for ever-more-inventive ways to pressure him. Patrick Leahy enlisted other lawmakers, including Chris Van Hollen, the House Democrat who represented Gross's district in Maryland; Jeff Flake, a Republican senator from New Mexico; and Dick Durbin, the Illinois Democrat who is close to the president. At a White House meeting on Cuba policy with Susan Rice and Denis McDonough, Durbin offered a fateful suggestion. "Maybe we should ask the pope to help," he said.

Tim Rieser, a foreign policy aide to Leahy, sensed an opportunity. His boss was one of the most prominent Catholics on Capitol Hill; Obama was scheduled to have his first meeting with Pope Francis that spring. Rieser drafted letters from Leahy to two politically connected cardinals, Jaime Ortega of Havana and Sean Patrick O'Malley of Boston. Leahy asked them to try to turn the pontiff into a lobbyist. On March 27, 2014, the president arrived to pay his respects at the Vatican. He and the pope shook hands in the same chamber where Rhodes, Zuniga, and the Cubans would meet to present their deal to the Vatican seven months later. Sitting across a simple desk from Obama, Francis made his plea for the prisoner exchange and a new start between the United States and Cuba. The next time Obama ran into Leahy, he teased him that the pope had faithfully delivered the senator's talking points.

Francis reiterated those points in follow-up letters to Obama and Raúl Castro, which he handed to Cardinal Ortega when the cardinal made his own visit to the Vatican later. The question was, how could Ortega hand deliver the letter to Obama? That would involve the efforts of a third cardinal, Theodore McCarrick of Washington. He arranged for Ortega to speak at a symposium at Georgetown University, giving him an excuse to fly up from Havana. Afterward, McCarrick spirited him to the White House, where he met Denis McDonough. While he was there, Obama dropped by to pick up the letter.

The clerical skulduggery was straight out of a Dan Brown novel, but none of it was helping Alan Gross.

In April 2014, having heard nothing about his case, Gross went on a nine-day hunger strike. The White House had long fretted about his physical and mental condition; McDonough sent him a brief handwritten note, imploring him not to lose hope. But that spring, things took a sharp turn for the worse. Gross's mother, Evelyn, became seriously ill with cancer. (She died in June.) The Cubans rejected his requests to visit her while she was sick or to attend her funeral. Gross's sixty-fifth birthday loomed; he vowed he would not spend another year behind bars. Gilbert warned Rhodes and Zuniga that his client might kill himself. Gross spoke ominously about attacking one of his guards, a move that would almost certainly have gotten him shot. Despite his weight loss, he was robust, clocking a daily exercise routine of fifty pull-ups and five miles of walking in a circle in his cell. "I knew exactly who I would have taken out," Gross told me, "and I knew exactly how I would have done it."

The threats of suicide, he said, were mainly designed to scare the White House. "I did say I wasn't going to have another birthday in jail, but that didn't mean I was going to kill myself," Gross explained. "It meant I was going home, one way or the other. I was being purposefully ambiguous. The White House interpreted it exactly as I wanted them to."

There is more than a little bravado to Alan Gross, and perhaps a hint of revisionism. Gilbert and Zuckman both took his threats to kill himself seriously, as did the White House, especially after his mother died. "If I bring him out on the plank," Gilbert warned Zuniga, "you'll have to live with this." John Kerry sent Gross a multipage handwritten letter to buck up his spirits. The president even sent him a typewritten letter of condolence—the gist of which, Gross said, was, "Please hold on. Don't do anything drastic."

"Scott, we have a problem," Ricardo Zuniga told Gilbert one day in the late summer of 2014.

"What's the problem?" Gilbert asked.

"Adriana's pregnant," he replied.

Adriana Pérez was the wife of Gerardo Hernández, the most famous of the Cuban Five. Desperate to have a child with her husband, she had asked Pat Leahy for help when he visited Havana the previous summer. This was no simple request: Hernández was locked away in the Victorville federal penitentiary in Southern California, 2,300 miles from Havana, serving a life term for espionage and conspiracy to commit murder. Leahy turned again to his aide, Tim Rieser. He researched the precedents with the Bureau of Prisons and wangled approval for an unorthodox mission, the strangest twist yet in this saga: Cuban officials went to Hernández's cell, picked up a vial of his sperm, and flew it to a clinic in Panama. There, Adriana was impregnated.

"The first time, it didn't take," Leahy said with a sheepish smile. "They had to do it a second time."

The problem was that Adriana was now showing, and the Cubans wanted to announce her pregnancy. If the artificial insemination ever became public, Zuniga told Gilbert, it would provoke a storm of questions on Capitol Hill. Hard-liners like Democrat Robert Menendez of New Jersey and Marco Rubio, Republican of Florida, would hold hearings and the White House's secret negotiations with Havana would inevitably be exposed. (By that time, Rhodes and Zuniga had briefed Gilbert about the back channel.) It all seemed rather surreal to Gilbert, but he offered a solution to Zuniga and his White House colleagues: Hide Adriana in his vacation house in Miami Beach until she had her baby. "Nobody will even know who she is," he said. "There's so many Cuban Americans down there."

The next time Gilbert sat down with Zuniga, he asked, "Did you convey my message?"

"Yes, I did," he replied. "They're very appreciative, and they think you're insane."

The Cubans, however, agreed to keep Adriana's pregnancy under wraps. The secret talks were safe, for now. Cuba reciprocated for the American gesture toward Hernández by improving the treatment of Gross and allowing two American doctors to visit him. An even bigger breakthrough had come a few months earlier, shortly after Obama's trip to the Vatican. Upon his return, the president quietly commuted Hernández's sentence, as well as those of the other two remaining *Cinco*. (Though they were always referred to as the Cuban Five, two of the Cubans had completed their sentences before Obama took his action.) This meant that Rhodes and Zuniga could finally put Hernández and his comrades on the table as a quid pro quo for Gross. A deal suddenly seemed within reach.

But there was one more twist: The president walked out to the Rose Garden on May 31, 2014, to announce a different prisoner swap on the other side of the world. Army sergeant Bowe Bergdahl had been freed by the Taliban in Afghanistan in exchange for five Taliban fighters held in the military brig at Guantánamo Bay. From his cell in Havana, a bitter Allan Gross watched the images of Obama standing with the soldier's father on Cuban television. "I was pissed when they made a big deal of it," he recalled. With reason, it turned out: The Bergdahl trade threw a wrench into the negotiations over his fate. At their next meeting, in early June, the Cubans told the Americans that Bergdahl should pave the way for a straight prisoner swap. In fact, it did the opposite. Obama was facing a barrage of criticism on Capitol Hill for trading a soldier who had walked off his post in Afghanistan for five battle-hardened Taliban fighters. The last thing he could afford at this moment was trading three Cuban spies for a hapless development worker.

"We made the point: 'This shows you how controversial swaps are. This is something we are only willing to consider in the context of an appropriate exchange,'" Rhodes told me. "The important thing was not to see the swap as the end, but the gateway to the policy changes."

Even the policy changes, by themselves, weren't going to be enough. The White House needed to find another way to justify releasing the three Cubans. The solution came from Eric Holder, people involved in the case said. The Justice Department identified a Cuban man, Rolando Sarraff Trujillo, who had worked as a high-level spy for the CIA and been jailed in Cuba for nearly two decades. By persuading the Cubans to release Trujillo as part of the package, the United States was able to present the prisoner exchange as a spy swap—and the liberation of Alan Gross as a humanitarian gesture by the Castro government. It was window dressing, of course, but that hardly mattered to Gross, when his Air Force 757 landed at Joint Base Andrews, shortly after eleven A.M. on a brisk December day. After five years, he was finally home.

A couple of days after his return, Gross and his wife sat in Scott Gilbert's office, under the prized photo of Che. The phone rang, and the lawyer pushed a button to put it on speaker.

"Hi, Alan," said Hillary Clinton.

"Hello," he replied.

"I'm glad you're home," she said.

Clinton might not have succeeded in winning Gross's freedom, but she had a stake in his case, too, and she wanted him to know she cared. The perfunctory nature of their exchange summed up her less-than-satisfying role on Cuba. As with Burma, Clinton's instincts about Cuba were right: The country's relationship with the United States was ripe for a change. As with Iran, she helped lay the groundwork for Obama's diplomatic overture. But the big risks were taken by the president—it was not clear, in fact, that she would have taken them if she had been in his place—and so the recognition rightly went to him.

The Cuba breakthrough marked the end of a trying year for

Obama, one in which many had questioned his leadership in confronting the war in Syria, the threat of the Islamic State, and Vladimir Putin's aggression in Ukraine. It was the first of a pair of landmark achievements: The Iran nuclear deal would come seven months later. At the State of the Union address on January 20, 2015, the sixth of his presidency, Obama claimed the mantle of a statesman. Diplomacy, he asserted, had halted Iran's nuclear program; Iran and the West stood on the cusp of a lasting agreement to curb its nuclear ambitions. The release of Alan Gross was part of a long-overdue reconciliation with Cuba. "We are ending a policy that was long past its expiration date," he said. "When what you're doing doesn't work for fifty years, it's time to try something new." Three years after Clinton proposed it in her exit memo, Obama challenged Congress to lift the trade embargo. "As His Holiness Pope Francis has said," the president observed, "diplomacy is the work of 'small steps.'"

With that, the president looked up at a special guest, seated behind the First Lady in the balcony of the House chamber. "Welcome home, Alan," he said. "We're glad you're here."

Flashing a gap-toothed smile, Gross thrust his fists upward in triumph. The audience rose in a standing ovation.

# Epilogue

## Two Campaigns

"There's no doubt that Hillary Clinton's more muscular brand of American foreign policy is better matched to 2016 than it was to 2008," said Jake Sullivan, her top policy adviser at the State Department who played the same role in her presidential campaign.

It was the second Thursday in December 2015, fifty-three days before the Iowa caucuses, and Sullivan was sitting down in Clinton's headquarters to explain how she was shaping her message for a campaign suddenly dominated by concerns about national security. Clinton's strategy, he said, was twofold: Explain to voters that she had a clear plan for confronting the threat posed by Islamic terrorism, and expose her Republican opponents as utterly lacking in experience or credibility on national security.

Nobody was better placed than Sullivan to help Clinton defend her record. He had run her Policy Planning shop at the State Department, traveled with her to all 112 countries she visited as secretary of state, been on hand for the triumph in Burma and the tragedy in Benghazi. Sullivan had left the government in 2014 for a teaching job at Yale Law School, but there was never any doubt he would return to Clinton's orbit. (The betting was he would be the national security adviser in a Hillary Clinton White House.) For now, Sullivan had traded the suit and tie he wore at the State Department for jeans and a button-down shirt, which made him look barely older than the young campaign workers sitting outside the conference room where we met.

Clinton's millennial army was arrayed across a converted trading floor that had the dingy aesthetic of a Wall Street back office. Bathed in the glow of iMac screens, some rocked silently to music streaming through brightly colored earbuds; a few had traded desk chairs for ergonomically correct exercise balls. The campaign offices, occupying two floors of a hulking redbrick tower in Brooklyn Heights, New York, bore an uncanny resemblance to Barack Obama's 2012 headquarters in Chicago. That was no accident: Obama had set the standard for political campaigns in the digital age; Clinton's team was eager to borrow his techniques, as well as the start-up vibe.

Color-coded signs marked the various departments, with the digital team occupying a large section near the entrance. State flags hung from the ceiling, identifying clusters of desks where volunteers were organizing field operations for the individual Democratic primaries: Iowa, New Hampshire, South Carolina. Heroic posters of the candidate papered the walls. An air-hockey table stood in a break room, next to a sink filled with dirty coffee mugs. An in-house store sold merchandise—plastic cups, glasses, and a T-shirt that looked like a pantsuit jacket—all emblazoned with Hillary's corporatist logo, soon to be as ubiquitous as Obama's rising sun.

Clinton's challenge, her advisers acknowledged, was how to stake out her own positions without disavowing the president's. She could not afford to alienate the racially and ethnically diverse coalition that had vaulted Obama to victory in 2008; she needed those voters to thwart the progressive insurgency of Senator Bernie Sanders of Vermont during the Democratic primaries, and she would need them again in the general election. "There's going to be a huge amount of interest in the press to score-keep," Sullivan said. "It just so easily can become a sport that distracts from her ability to make an affirmative case."

Yet as he talked about how Clinton planned to persuade voters that she was the right commander in chief for a dangerous age, the paradox was hard to miss: While she was copying Obama's tech-

niques and staying close to him on domestic issues, she was beginning to distance herself from a foreign policy she once helped
shape, and energetically promoted around the world.

In a series of policy speeches throughout the fall, Clinton had
reasserted her hawkish credentials. She said the United States
should consider sending more special operations troops to Iraq
than Obama had committed, to help the Iraqis and Kurds fight the
jihadi warriors of the Islamic State. She came out in favor of imposing a partial no-fly zone over Syria, which he opposed. And she
described the threat posed by ISIS to Americans in starker terms
than he did. As was often the case with Clinton and Obama, the
differences were less about direction than degree. She wasn't calling
for ground troops in the Middle East, any more than he was. She
insisted her plan was not a break with his, merely an "intensifica-
tion and acceleration" of it.

There were good reasons for Clinton to let her inner hawk fly. Jitters about terrorism had transformed a campaign the analysts once
predicted would be driven by the economy. After Paris and California, Americans were more worried about a major attack on the
homeland than at any time since 9/11. Polls taken after the attacks
showed that a majority favored sending ground troops to Iraq and
Syria, a remarkable, though perhaps temporary, shift from the war-
weary sentiment that had prevailed during most of Obama's presidency. The GOP candidates reached for apocalyptic metaphors to
demonstrate their resolve. Senator Ted Cruz of Texas threatened to
carpet bomb ISIS until the desert sand glowed; Donald Trump called
for the United States to ban all Muslims from the country "until we
are able to determine and understand this problem and the dangerous threat it poses." Both assailed Obama for policies they claimed
had left Americans at the mercy of a borderless jihadi army. His reluctance to acknowledge the public's fears about terrorism, they
said, was yet more evidence of his failure to lead.

Clinton, too, thought the president had not summoned enough
feeling to match the moment. Campaigning in diners and high
school gymnasiums across Iowa and New Hampshire, she spoke

bluntly about how the Islamic State was exporting its war to the United States by using social media services to recruit fighters in San Bernardino as well as Syria. Clinton did not pander to the public's anxieties as shamelessly as the Republicans. But neither did she, like Obama, attempt to minimize them.

Their contrasting approaches were on vivid display when both spoke in the capital on December 6, 2015, six hours apart and two blocks from each other. Clinton, addressing an audience of think tankers at the Willard InterContinental hotel, said jihadi extremism posed a threat "not just in far-off lands, but right here at home." Americans, she said, "are anxious and fearful, and we have reason to be." A subdued Obama, speaking from the Oval Office for only the third time in his presidency, implored the public not to give in to fear, because sowing fear was what the extremists wanted. "Instead," he declared, "we will prevail by being strong and smart, resilient and relentless, and by drawing upon every aspect of American power."

"Here's how," he added, sounding less like Winston Churchill than the host of a home-improvement show.

The strategy Obama proceeded to outline was more or less the one he had been using against the Islamic State since it declared a caliphate and began publicly executing Americans in 2014: air strikes in Iraq and Syria, along with a small contingent of special operations troops to train Iraqi and Kurdish fighters. Again, he ruled out ground troops, saying the United States would defeat the enemy without having to send "a new generation of Americans overseas to fight and die for another decade on foreign soil." ISIS, he said, accounted for a tiny fraction of the world's Muslims, and was not worthy of being the spark for a civilizational conflict between the West and Islam.

Nor was Obama going to exaggerate the danger of terrorism in a country where 406,000 people were killed by guns between 2001 and 2013, compared to 3,000 by acts of terrorism. "If you define the challenge as being an existential threat to the United States," Ben Rhodes told me, "you put yourself into the position of doing stupid things, like suspending civil liberties or barring Muslims from the country. The interesting thing in looking back on 9/11 is that Bush was very effective rhetorically in rallying the nation. But it might have set in motion the snowball that led to Iraq."

Clinton and Obama were in different places, of course: She, in the heat of a campaign that had been upended by concerns about national security; he, in the fourth quarter of a presidency, campaigning for his legacy. It was yet another turn in the cycle of their singular relationship: from rivals to colleagues, and now to partners in a delicate succession dance. Obama, whatever his frustrations with Clinton's opportunism and hawkish proclivities, viewed her as the best hope to secure his foreign policy achievements; Clinton, by drawing close to Obama on some issues and pulling away from him on others, hoped to find the balance that would lead her into the White House.

When an annoyed Barack Obama walked to the back of Air Force One in the spring of 2014 to defend his foreign policy to the press corps, his career as a statesman was arguably at its low ebb. He had squandered the credibility he had gained among hawks in his first term after having ordered the troop surge in Afghanistan, the raid on Osama bin Laden, and the NATO air strikes in Libya (even if that intervention looked ill-considered in hindsight). His refusal to enforce his own red line in Syria—combined with the lightning rise of the Islamic State and the unchallenged aggression of Vladimir Putin in Ukraine—had put him on the defensive with Republicans and even Democrats, not least Hillary Clinton. To some, his speech on the limits of American power at West Point that May carried echoes of Jimmy Carter's doleful declaration in July 1979 that the United States faced a "crisis of confidence."

"Since World War II," he said, "some of our most costly mistakes came not from our restraint, but from our willingness to rush into military adventures without thinking through the consequences—without building international support and legitimacy for our action; without leveling with the American people about the sacrifices required."

"Just because we have the best hammer," he observed, "does not mean that every problem is a nail."

By the spring of 2016, though, Obama had reason to feel much better about his standing. He had engineered the breakthroughs with Cuba and Iran, the climate change agreement in Paris, and the Asia-Pacific trade pact, though the latter remained hostage to the ill winds of politics (Clinton's politically motivated about-face on the deal being the most rank example). The Islamic State, while casting a shadow over the West, was mired in a war of attrition with Iraqi and Kurdish forces, and had lost nearly half the territory it had seized in Iraq. Putin remained a menace, though the White House held out hope that he might eventually come around on Syria. (In March 2016, he announced a partial withdrawal of Russian forces from the country.) Obama had even defied his own observation that seminal achievements in foreign policy were once-in-a-generation events. With Iran and Cuba, he could claim two in as many years.

At heart, though, Obama's legacy depends on whether the simple principle he articulated in 2014 will outlast his presidency. Certainly, his views have not changed. In his final year in office, Obama still thought that foreign policy was fundamentally about the prudent calculation of risk, about avoiding reckless adventures in places where the nation's core interests were not at stake—about, in short, not doing "stupid shit." If anything, his diplomatic successes had made him *more* secure in a policy that sought to preserve the liberal world order, even at the cost of sacrificing the nation's peripheral interests. The singles and doubles that Obama swung for may have appeared modest but they rested on what Gideon Rose, the editor of *Foreign Affairs,* described as "an immodest sense that time and tide are generally on the side of the order rather than the side of its remaining enemies."

His critics hadn't changed their views, either. Many in the foreign policy establishment predicted Obama would leave few footprints in Washington, that future presidents wouldn't need to measure their policies against an Obama Doctrine. His presidency would be remembered as a reaction, perhaps an overreaction, to that of his overreaching predecessor. His advisers, a clannish, untested circle, never shook off the post-Iraq-traumatic-stress disorder they brought into office, and they would probably scatter to the winds when their leader returned to private life. Even some Democrats who had thrived in the Obama administration relished the prospective return of Bill Clinton's foreign policy circle, a seasoned, self-confident crowd that had more in common with Richard Holbrooke than with Denis McDonough.

Obama, his aides said, was at peace with the fact that he would never be embraced by those who held a more traditional view of American power. "Our foreign policy establishment becomes deeply uncomfortable when they are aware that we're recognizing American limits," Ben Rhodes said. "That's not in the career manual for a foreign policy commentator or thinker."

By his last year in office, the president was wearing the establishment's disdain as a badge of honor. "There's a playbook in Washington that presidents are supposed to follow," he said in a much-discussed interview in *The Atlantic*. "The playbook prescribes responses to different events, and these responses tend to be militarized responses. Where America is directly threatened, the playbook works. But the playbook can also be a trap that can lead to bad decisions."

There was a deeper reason for Obama's serenity: He believed that he, not the foreign policy elite, was in sync with the American people. He had, after all, knocked off Clinton in 2008 by lashing her to Iraq. He had won the White House by promising to end George W. Bush's wars, and then won reelection after trying to deliver on that promise. Obama had tapped into something more profound than mere war weariness: He was reflecting a country, a decade into the twenty-first century, that had lost its rationale for playing the global policeman, for carrying the world, Atlas-like, on its shoulders.

"We'd been living on strategic fumes since the end of the Cold

War," said the historian Robert Kagan of the country that elected Obama. "Even though we had three presidents in a row who were raised, in their bones, in the America-as-indispensable-nation tradition, there is no reason to think the American people necessarily bought into that.

"The only thing that has changed since then," Kagan continued, "and it's significant, is ISIS."

For those trying to divine the differences between Obama and Clinton, Bob Kagan serves as something of a weather vane. A leading light of neoconservative thinking, he is perhaps the most influential advocate of the need for a continued Pax Americana. In books and articles, Kagan has made the case that, as he wrote for *The New Republic* in May 2014, "Superpowers don't get to retire." Obama's inward turn, he wrote, went against not only seventy years of history but also America's basic instincts. Obama invited him to lunch after the article appeared for a conversation that Kagan likened to defending a doctoral thesis. The two did not see eye to eye.

Kagan, however, is largely at home with the views of Hillary Clinton. His wife, Toria Nuland, served as her press secretary at the State Department. He was a member of her foreign policy advisory board, which included both Democrats and Republicans. For him, Clinton fits snugly in a tradition of hawkish Democratic foreign policy that goes back to Dean Acheson and Harry Truman. "Clinton will represent a turn back toward the idea of the U.S. as the indispensable nation whose responsibility it is to uphold the liberal world order," Kagan said. "That is where the heart of the bipartisan foreign policy consensus is. One of the interesting things about Obama has been his indifference to this consensus and his willingness to proceed almost entirely according to his own different perspective."

The day after their dueling speeches on the Islamic State, Obama invited Clinton to lunch in his private dining room. The press secretary described it as "mostly a social occasion," a statement that seemed even less credible than the usual banalities the White House issued about private meetings between Obama and Clinton. This would be the last time they got together before 2016, and the race to succeed Obama, officially began. They had much to discuss; their fortunes were more closely intertwined than ever.

Despite his string of late-term successes, Obama recognized that much of his legacy could quickly be undone by a Republican president. The Iran deal and the climate change pact were particularly vulnerable. Clinton had a stake in both: She had done the spadework on sanctions that helped bring Iran to the negotiating table; climate change was the issue that first brought her and Obama together in Copenhagen, and one that may have greater long-term consequences for the planet than anything else Obama has done. "What we were able to do in Copenhagen made Paris possible," the president told Ben Rhodes, after the agreement was signed there. Preserving those gains would likely require her involvement again.

That is why her campaign is Obama's as well.

On the eve of the election, the two were unquestionably in a better place than in the summer of 2014, when Clinton's stinging criticism of Obama for his Syria policy led to a frosty encounter at a party on Martha's Vineyard. They met there again in August 2015, this time for Vernon Jordan's eightieth birthday, and the temperature was noticeably warmer. Obama arrived first. When Clinton walked into the tent at the Farm Neck Golf Club, he gave her a hug. "It seemed very heartfelt," said a person who was at both evenings. "The body language seemed much more casual, more friendly."

After running against her, recruiting her, mourning the lost diplomats of Benghazi with her, and wrestling with her on issues from Syria to Richard Holbrooke, Obama seemed to have accepted Clinton for the political animal she was. When his aides told him that she had come out against the Trans-Pacific Partnership, the president merely rolled his eyes. They remained very different people with very different instincts about how to wield American power—

like Truman and Acheson, the plainspoken Missouri haberdasher and the aristocratic Connecticut Yankee, who together embodied the idealism and realism of America in the twentieth century.

Acheson was an unwaveringly loyal lieutenant to Truman, much as Clinton had been to Obama. "The most important aspect of the relationship between the president and the secretary of state," he once observed, "is that they both understand who is president." But Acheson had a darker view of the post–World War II world than his boss. Like Clinton, he believed that an expansionist Russia needed to be resisted, "with force of arms," if necessary. Like Clinton, he was skeptical that the United Nations would ever be enough to keep the peace among nations. Like Clinton, he viewed statecraft less as an idealistic enterprise than a cold-blooded exercise in balancing power.

Perhaps it was no accident that Clinton invoked Dean Acheson more than her other predecessors. She extolled his brand of "good, old-fashioned diplomacy" as a way to preserve America's primacy in world affairs. "Beneath his formal exterior," she wrote, "he was a highly imaginative diplomat, breaking protocol when he thought it was best for his country and his president." As a young woman, she met him fleetingly the night before she delivered the graduation speech at Wellesley College that would make her famous.

On her way to dinner, Clinton ran into a classmate, Eldie Acheson, who was with her grandfather.

"This is the girl who's going to speak tomorrow," she told him.

Peering down at Hillary, Dean Acheson said, "I'm looking forward to hearing what you have to say."

# Acknowledgments

Authors like to think of themselves as lonely heroes. Most, of course, have a supporting cast—in my case, a great many people who helped me at every step of this journey, from the first glimmerings of the idea to the frantic final days of editing.

My agent, Will Lippincott, was there at the start, drawing out and refining my ideas, prodding me to think big, refusing to let me lose my nerve. He is a gentleman and a consummate pro. Will introduced me to Andy Ward, who proved to be that rarest of species among editors: relentlessly demanding, yet unfailingly upbeat and constructive. He and his crack team at Random House made every page of the book better.

I have been privileged to call *The New York Times* my professional home for nearly twenty-five years; many people there deserve my gratitude. Dean Baquet gave me a soft landing in the Washington bureau after a decade overseas, then handed me two of the bureau's prized beats, which became the foundation for the book. Later, as executive editor, he granted my request for a leave at an inconvenient moment for the paper.

Dean's three successors in Washington, Carolyn Ryan, David Leonhardt, and Elisabeth Bumiller, were unstintingly supportive. Carolyn championed the project, which grew out of a story she assigned on Hillary Clinton's record as secretary of state; David suggested I write a weekly online column, *Listening Post,* which sharpened my thinking on foreign policy; Elisabeth offered sound advice from her book-writing experience and tolerated my preoccupations after I returned to work. Thanks also to Bill Hamilton, a first-rate editor and confidant for reporters-turned-authors.

Helene Cooper and Mark Mazzetti, friends and bestselling authors in their own right, encouraged me to take the plunge, saw me through the emotional spin cycle of pitching a book, and never tired (at least visibly) of hearing about my small triumphs and lingering anxieties.

As a White House correspondent covering foreign policy, I've gotten to be part of two of the best teams in journalism. Peter Baker, Michael Shear, Jackie Calmes, Julie Hirschfeld Davis, and Gardiner Harris have been my partners in the exhilarating, infuriating job of trying to decipher 1600 Pennsylvania Avenue. David Sanger, Eric Schmitt, Scott Shane, Thom Shanker, Charlie Savage, Michael Schmidt, and Matt Rosenberg have been my teammates in the even murkier business of writing about national security. Particular thanks to Michael Gordon and Steve Myers, who collaborated with me on some of the stories that appear in these pages, and to Jennifer Steinhauer, who kept reminding me there's more to life than work.

Two other institutions were critical: the Woodrow Wilson International Center for Scholars and the German Marshall Fund of the United States, both of which granted me writing fellowships that provided more than just office space. At the Wilson Center, thanks to Jane Harman, Caroline Scullin, and especially Robert Litwak, who was a patient, perceptive sounding board for my ideas. At the German Marshall Fund, my gratitude goes to Karen Donfried and Derek Chollet, a gifted foreign policy thinker who challenged my assumptions and deepened my understanding of events.

My work was helped enormously by two research assistants, Arnab Datta and Joseph Federici, graduate students at my alma mater, Georgetown's School of Foreign Service. From running down obscure facts and combing through emails to organizing my research and critiquing the manuscript, Joe and Arnab embraced this project, bringing to it their own insights and fresh perspectives. They both have big futures.

John Walcott, an editor who holds the uncommon distinction of having gotten the Iraq War right from the beginning, brought his discerning eye to the manuscript. Thanks also to Bill Antholis and the faculty of the Miller Center at the University of Virginia for reminding me of the broader historical context.

Kim Ghattas, who wrote her own insightful book on Hillary Clinton, was an unflagging source of encouragement. Thanks, as well, to Nicole Gaouette, Matt Lee, Glenn Kessler, David Ignatius, Jennifer Tung, Kate McNamara, and Larry Downing, who shot the image on the back cover. Eric Weiner and Sharon Moshavi were vital suppliers of spirit and spirits during the long months of writer's isolation, while Dan Wilhelm, Courtney O'Malley, Martin Regg Cohn, Karen Mazurkewich, and Randall Rothenberg cheered from afar. So, too, did my in-laws, Kenneth and Mimi Tung.

I owe an everlasting debt to my parents: my brave, indestructible mother, Brigid, from whom I got a love of writing and a curiosity about foreign affairs; and my steadfast, thoughtful father, Paul, with whom I've been having a conversation about America's role in the world since high school. Thank you, too, to my brother, Philip, and sister, Juliet, for a lifetime of support.

My children, Caroline and Nicholas, cheerfully endured the distractions and periodic bouts of solipsism that overtook me during a year of writing. Caroline worked as a researcher and photographer for the book, even as she was riding the roller coaster of college applications. Nicholas matched my daily output for his own study of World War II aircraft.

Finally, my wife, Angela, without whom this project, like so many other things in my life, would simply not have happened. Her brilliant mind and impeccable taste saved me from an assortment of blunders; her love and confidence sustained me through the darkest nights; her superhero energy propelled me across the finish line.

Our partnership, thankfully, endures beyond presidencies.

# Bibliography

Allen, Jonathan, and Amie Parnes. *HRC: State Secrets and the Rebirth of Hillary Clinton*. New York: Crown, 2014.

Axelrod, David. *Believer: My Forty Years in Politics*. New York: Penguin Press, 2015.

Bader, Jeffrey A. *Obama and China's Rise: An Insider's Account of America's Asia Strategy*. Washington, D.C.: Brookings Institution Press, 2012.

Baker, Peter. *Days of Thunder: Bush and Cheney in the White House*. New York: Doubleday, 2013.

Bauer, Shane, Joshua Fattal, and Sarah Shourd. *A Sliver of Light: Three Americans Imprisoned in Iran*. New York: Eamon Dolan, 2014.

Bernstein, Carl. *A Woman in Charge: The Life of Hillary Rodham Clinton*. New York: Alfred A. Knopf, 2007.

Burton, Fred, and Samuel M. Katz. *Under Fire: The Untold Story of the Attack in Benghazi*. New York: St. Martin's, 2013.

Chandrasekaran, Rajiv. *Little America: The War Within the War for Afghanistan*. New York: Alfred A. Knopf, 2012.

Chayes, Sarah. *Thieves of State: Why Corruption Threatens Global Security*. New York: W. W. Norton, 2015.

Chen, Guangcheng. *The Barefoot Lawyer: A Blind Man's Fight for Justice and Freedom in China*. New York, Henry Holt, 2015.

Chivvis, Christopher S. *Toppling Qaddafi: Libya and the Limits of Liberal Intervention*. New York: Cambridge University Press, 2014.

Chollet, Derek. *The Road to the Dayton Accords: A Study of American Statecraft*. New York: Palgrave Macmillan, 2005.

Chollet, Derek, and James Goldgeier, *America Between the Wars*. New York: Public Affairs, 2008.

Chollet, Derek, and Samantha Power, eds. *The Unquiet American: Richard Holbrooke in the World*. New York: Public Affairs, 2011.

Clinton, Hillary Rodham. *Hard Choices*. New York: Simon & Schuster, 2014.

———. *Living History*. New York: Scribner, 2003.

Cooper, John Milton, Jr. *The Warrior and the Priest: Woodrow Wilson and Theodore Roosevelt*. Cambridge, Mass.: Harvard University Press, 1983.

Dallek, Robert. *Nixon and Kissinger: Partners in Power*. New York: HarperCollins, 2007.

Gates, Robert M. *Duty: Memoirs of a Secretary at War*. New York: Alfred A. Knopf, 2014.

Gerth, Jeff, and Don Van Atta, Jr. *Her Way: The Hopes and Ambitions of Hillary Rodham Clinton*. New York: Little, Brown, 2007.

Ghattas, Kim. *The Secretary: A Journey with Hillary Clinton from Beirut to the Heart of American Power*. New York: Times Books, 2013.

Gordon, Michael R., and Bernard E. Trainor. *Endgame: The Inside Story of the Struggle for Iraq, from George W. Bush to Barack Obama*. New York: Pantheon Books, 2012.

Haqqani, Husain. *Magnificent Delusions: Pakistan, the United States, and an Epic History of Misunderstanding*. New York: Public Affairs, 2013.

Hill, Christopher R. *Outpost: Life on the Frontlines of American Diplomacy*. New York: Simon & Schuster, 2014.

Holbrooke, Richard. *To End a War*. New York: Random House, 1998.

Ikenberry, G. John. *Liberal Leviathan: The Origins, Crisis, and Transformation of the American World Order*. Princeton, N.J.: Princeton University Press, 2011.

Indyk, Martin. *Innocent Abroad: An Intimate Account of American Peace Diplomacy in the Middle East*. New York: Simon & Schuster, 2009.

Isaacson, Walter, and Evan Thomas. *The Wise Men: Six Friends and the World They Made*. New York: Simon & Schuster, 1986.

Ismaily, Salem Ben Nasser Al, with Richard A. Tzudiker. *The Sultanate of Zanzibar*. Indianapolis: Dog Ear Publishing, 2014.

Kagan, Robert. *The World America Made*. New York: Alfred A. Knopf, 2012.

Khalidi, Rashid. *Brokers of Deceit: How the U.S. Has Undermined Peace in the Middle East*. Boston: Beacon Press, 2013.

Kissinger, Henry. *World Order*. New York: Penguin Press, 2014.

Mann, James. *The Obamians: The Struggle Inside the White House to Redefine American Power*. New York: Viking Penguin, 2012.

Maraniss, David. *Barack Obama: The Story*. New York: Simon & Schuster, 2012.

Marton, Kati. *Paris: A Love Story*. New York: Simon & Schuster, 2012.

Mazzetti, Mark. *The Way of the Knife: The CIA, a Secret Army, and a War at the Ends of the Earth*. New York: Penguin Press, 2013.

Miller, Aaron David. *The Much Too Promised Land: America's Elusive Search for Middle East Peace*. New York: Bantam Dell, 2008.

Morell, Michael, with Bill Harlow. *The Great War of Our Time: The CIA's Fight Against Terrorism from Al Qa'ida to ISIS*. New York: Twelve, 2015.

Nasr, Vali. *The Dispensable Nation: American Foreign Policy in Retreat*. New York: Doubleday, 2013.

Nixon, Richard M. *RN: The Memoirs of Richard Nixon*. New York: Grosset & Dunlap, 1978.

Obama, Barack. *The Audacity of Hope: Thoughts on Reclaiming the American Dream.* New York: Crown, 2006.

———. *Dreams from My Father: A Story of Race and Inheritance.* New York: Times Books, 1995.

Oren, Michael B. *Ally: My Journey Across the American-Israeli Divide.* New York: Random House, 2015.

Panetta, Leon, with Jim Newton. *Worthy Fights: A Memoir of Leadership in War and Peace.* New York: Penguin Press, 2014.

Pederson, Rena. *The Burma Spring: Aung Sang Suu Kyi and the New Struggle for the Soul of a Nation.* New York: Pegasus Books, 2015.

Ross, Dennis. *Doomed to Succeed: The U.S.-Israel Relationship from Truman to Obama.* New York: Farrar, Straus and Giroux, 2015.

Rothkopf, David. *National Insecurity: American Leadership in an Age of Fear.* New York: Public Affairs, 2014.

Sanger, David. *The Inheritance: The World Obama Confronts and the Challenges to American Power.* New York: Harmony Books, 2009.

Savage, Charlie. *Power Wars: Inside Obama's Post-9/11 Presidency.* New York: Little Brown, 2015.

Schweizer, Peter. *Clinton Cash: The Untold Story of How and Why Foreign Governments Helped Make Bill and Hillary Rich.* New York: HarperCollins, 2015.

Shane, Scott. *Objective Troy: A Terrorist, a President, and the Rise of the Drone.* New York: Crown, 2015.

Todd, Chuck. *The Stranger: Barack Obama in the White House.* New York: Little Brown, 2014.

Woodward, Bob. *Obama's Wars.* New York: Simon & Schuster, 2010.

# Notes

This book is based on six years of coverage of Hillary Clinton and Barack Obama for *The New York Times,* as well as on extensive original reporting. That includes 142 interviews with 127 people, including John Kerry, Robert Gates, Chuck Hagel, David Petraeus, Rahm Emanuel, Tom Donilon, Madeleine Albright, David Miliband, and many others. Several consented to multiple interviews, lasting several hours, for which I am deeply grateful. In cases where I reconstructed scenes or dialogue, I sought to confirm the account with multiple sources. I have tried to put as much information as possible on the record. In some cases, involving discussions of covert programs or sensitive internal debates, the sources insisted that their comments remain on background or, in a few cases, that they remain unidentified.

The book draws on nine interviews I conducted with Hillary Clinton between 2009 and 2014, three with colleagues from *The New York Times.* Clinton did not agree to an interview for the book, nor did President Obama. The White House and the Clinton campaign both cited a lack of comfort with drawing contrasts between Obama and Clinton in an election year. But their senior advisers cooperated and did not block my access to friends or former staffers. In addition to my own reporting, I have drawn on the work of colleagues and competitors, as noted below.

The book was helped immeasurably, and fortuitously, by the scandal over Clinton's use of a private email account and server while secretary of state. Her request that the State Department release her work-related email from 2009 to 2013 made available a trove of primary-source material the likes of which is not usually accessible to historians or journalists until years later. The fifty-five thousand pages of email, released by the State Department in monthly installments between May 2015 and February 2016, provide a rare window into Clinton's thinking, the deliberations among her senior staff, and her relations with the White House. I also made use of emails from other officials, which were released in response to requests by the House Select Committee on Benghazi or to requests by journalists and watchdog groups under the Freedom of Information Act.

My understanding of the foreign policy of President Bill Clinton was deepened by my reading of the oral histories of his cabinet members and senior advisers, which were compiled by the Miller Center at the University of Virginia. The first batch of these transcripts, released in November 2014, offers a remarkably candid portrait of the president and the First Lady as they wrestled with issues that remain relevant today.

### Prologue **The Warrior and the Priest**

xii **The impromptu visit** Obama's visit was off-the-record, and I have not reported on it until now. The president's remarks were reported by David Rothkopf in *Foreign Policy* magazine on June 4, 2014, and, in more detail, by Reid Cherlin in *Rolling Stone* on August 4, 2014.

xiv **"not an organizing principle"** Jeffrey Goldberg, "Hillary Clinton: 'Failure' to Help Syrian Rebels Led to Rise of ISIS," *The Atlantic,* August 10, 2014, http://www.theatlantic.com/international/archive/2014/08/hillary-clinton-failure-to-help-syrian-rebels-led-to-the-rise-of-isis/375832/.

xvii **"I have made clear"** Hillary Clinton, speech to the Council on Foreign Relations, November 19, 2015.

xix **"it's been a mixed record"** Author interview, Leon Panetta, for *NYT.* Published in Mark Landler and Amy Chozick, "Hillary Clinton Struggles to Define a Legacy in Progress," *The New York Times,* April 14, 2014.

xix "her basic instincts" Author interview, Dennis Ross.

xx "She takes the position" Author interview, Leslie Gelb.

xxi "It leads you in a different direction" Author interview, Ross.

xxi "transformational and maximalist" Author interview, Joseph Nye.

xxii "the warrior and the priest" John Milton Cooper, Jr., *The Warrior and the Priest* (Cambridge, Mass.: Harvard University Press, 1983).

xxii "working in tandem" G. John Ikenberry, *Liberal Leviathan* (Princeton, N.J.: Princeton University Press, 2011), xiv.

## Part I **Worlds Apart**

### One **From Cairo to Copenhagen**

3 "very good rapport" Author interview, Hillary Clinton, for *NYT.* Published in Mark Landler and Helene Cooper, "After a Bitter Campaign, Forging an Alliance," *The New York Times,* March 19, 2010.

5 "She couldn't, wouldn't, and didn't" Author interview, former administration official.

6 "foundational document" Author interview, Michael Oren.

6 "fair share of lumps on it" Author interview, Rahm Emanuel.

7 "C'mon, let's just do this" Author interview, Clinton, for *NYT.*

8 "Yes, there's *history*" Author interview, Emanuel.

8 "each had an *aha* moment" Author interview, Jake Sullivan.

9 "He didn't view her negatively" Author interview, David Axelrod.

10 "Whoa, just present it to him" Author interview, Joseph Biden, for *NYT.*

10 "Secretary of Awesome" Email, Cheryl Mills to Hillary Clinton, August 6, 2009.

11 "I heard on the radio" Email, Clinton to Lona Valmoro and Huma Abedin, June 8, 2009.

11 "No independent dialing allowed" Email, Clinton to Abedin, February 10, 2010.

11 "People are deeply unhappy" Email, Sullivan to Clinton and Philippe Reines, December 11, 2009.

11 "There's no way" Email, Reines to Clinton and Sullivan, December 11, 2009.

12 "You magnify differences" Author interview, Tommy Vietor.

12 "It was weird" Author interview, Dan Pfeiffer.

14 "This is a woman" Author interview, Anne-Marie Slaughter.

14 "You tell Hillary" Author interview, former administration official.

15 "He is louche, alcoholic, lazy" Email, Sidney Blumenthal to Clinton, November 2, 2010.

15 "Make Steinberg tell Donilon" Email, Blumenthal to Clinton, March 17, 2010.

16 "blithe liberal cultural imperialism" Email, Blumenthal to Clinton and Mills, July 9, 2009.

16 "Just knock on the door" Email, Clinton to Abedin, November 2, 2009.

17 "Not President Obama" Author interview, former administration official.

17 **"He ended up being invaluable"** Author interview, Clinton, for *NYT.* Published in Mark Landler, "Biden Adviser Leaving Washington, but It May Not Be for Long," *The New York Times,* June 20, 2014.

18 **"taking a break from peeling potatoes"** Email, Sullivan to Clinton, November 25, 2010.

18 **"Jake just never stopped"** Author interview, Melanne Verveer.

20 **"vacuous cipher"** Tweet from @NatSecWonk.

20 **"Look, Issa is an ass"** Tweet from @NatSecWonk, September 15, 2013.

21 **"heroic vision of diplomacy"** Author interview, James Steinberg.

22 **"Shared personality traits"** Robert Dallek, *Nixon and Kissinger* (New York: HarperCollins, 2007), 92–93.

22 **"Baker used to say"** Author interview, Aaron David Miller.

22 **"I see the president"** Author interview, Clinton, for *NYT.*

23 **"K saw Nixon every day"** Email, Clinton to Reines, December 13, 2009.

23 **more than ten times its size** David Rothkopf, *National Insecurity* (New York: Public Affairs, 2014), 207–8.

24 **"This micro-management"** Author interview, Douglas Frantz.

24 **"I am very proud"** Email, Clinton to Neera Tanden, January 8, 2012.

25 **"If it does break that way"** Email, Tanden to Clinton, May 25, 2009.

25 **she woke up early** Email, Clinton to Miguel Rodriguez, December 24, 2009.

25 **"What does that say?"** Author interview, Clinton, for *NYT.* Published in Mark Landler and David Barboza, "For Shanghai Fair, Famous Fund-Raiser Delivers," *The New York Times,* January 2, 2010.

25 **"Great news from Chevron!"** Email, Elizabeth Bagley to Mills, July 14, 2009.

26 **"I didn't want McNerney"** Author interview, Jon Huntsman.

26 **"It's fine"** Author interview, Clinton, for *NYT.* Published in Mark Landler, "Clinton Sees U.S. Pavilion at China Expo," *The New York Times,* May 22, 2010.

27 **"wait until 19 million people"** Email, Reines to Clinton, March 16, 2011.

28 **"a strong friend"** Barack Obama and Hillary Clinton, interview by Steve Kroft, *60 Minutes,* CBS, January 27, 2013.

## Two **Origins**

31 **"wrath of our country"** Jeff Gerth and Don Van Natta, Jr., *Her Way* (New York: Little, Brown, 2007), 228–29.

31 **"wrong, plain and simple"** Hillary Rodham Clinton, *Hard Choices* (New York: Simon & Schuster, 2014), 137.

32 **"endless possibilities of America"** Hillary Rodham Clinton, *Living History* (New York: Scribner, 2003), 2.

32 **"psychodrama of the baby boomers"** Barack Obama, *The Audacity of Hope* (New York: Crown, 2006), 36.

33 "he could not be of one place" David Maraniss, *Barack Obama* (New York: Simon & Schuster, 2012), 431.

34 "The scope of that power" Obama, *Audacity of Hope,* 274–75.

34 as much harm as good Maraniss, *Barack Obama,* 429.

34 "lonely witness for secular humanism" Barack Obama, *Dreams from My Father* (New York: Crown, 1995), 50.

34 "extras on a Hollywood set" Ibid., 312.

35 wander the streets of Nairobi Peter Baker, "Obama Delivers Tough-Love Message to End Kenya Trip," *The New York Times,* July 27, 2015.

35 "It's all there" Obama, *Audacity of Hope,* 273.

36 "on the outside looking in" Author interview, Mike Ramos.

36 "the ugly conquest" Obama, *Dreams from My Father,* 23.

37 "a naïve faith in American ability" Maraniss, *Barack Obama,* 354–55.

37 "better dead than red" Clinton, *Living History,* 21.

38 "rooted in the conservatism" Clinton, interview by Scott Simon, *Weekend Edition,* NPR, January 13, 1996.

38 "America was lagging behind Russia" Ibid., 20.

38 "'character building'" Carl Bernstein, *A Woman in Charge* (New York: Knopf, 2007), 15.

38 "She was Methodist" Author interview, Lissa Muscatine.

38 "your talents lie elsewhere" Clinton, *Living History,* 27.

39 "I don't remember Hillary" Author interview, Greg Craig.

39 "give voice to children" Clinton, *Living History,* 50.

40 "I didn't want to be a hindrance" Ibid., 261.

41 "You and Chelsea rode an elephant" Ibid., 278, 283.

41 "They were rather bureaucratic" Author interview, Sandy Berger.

42 "'This is why I do this'" Author interview, Muscatine.

42 "human rights are women's rights" Speech by Hillary Clinton to the United Nations Fourth Conference on Women, Beijing, September 5, 1995.

43 "mind conservative and a heart liberal" Bernstein, *Woman in Charge,* 50.

43 "We have to act" Author interview, Verveer.

43 "stop the genocide" Clinton, *Living History,* 169–70.

43 "I urged him to bomb" Lucinda Franks, "The Intimate Hillary," *Talk* magazine, September 1999, 169.

44 "'Why wouldn't you name Madeleine?'" Author interview, Madeleine Albright.

44 "each of us connected" Albright, interviewed for the William J. Clinton Oral History Project, Miller Center, University of Virginia, August 30, 2006.

45 "some echoes of Hillary" Berger, interviewed for the Clinton Oral History Project, March 25, 2005.

45 "very emotionally involved" Author interview, George Mitchell.

46 "a reluctant warrior" Author interview, Bruce Riedel.

48 "he got an A" Maraniss, *Barack Obama,* 460.

49 "Was I going to give in" Ibid., 449.

49 "lacked any overarching theme" Obama, *Audacity of Hope,* 290.

49 "borscht, vodka, potato stew" Ibid., 312.

50 "I said to myself" Author interview, Zbigniew Brzezinski.

51 "linger on such thoughts" Obama, *Audacity of Hope,* 322.

## Three **Hillary and the Brass**

52 "she's the secretary of state" Author interview, David Petraeus.

54 "Hillary had Stan's back" Michael Hastings, "The Runaway General," *Rolling Stone,* July 8, 2010, http://www.rollingstone.com/politics/news/the-runaway -general-20100622.

54 "This is a tough lady" Author interview, Robert Gates.

55 "never would have tolerated" Author interview, Geoff Morrell.

55 "CIA gave Obama an angle" Author interview, Vali Nasr.

56 "one of the surprises for Gates" Author interview, Bruce Riedel.

57 "Maybe the dogs will take you" Maureen Dowd, "Hillary Clinton Says She Once Tried to Be a Marine," *The New York Times,* June 15, 1994.

57 "I don't think it's made up" Author interview, Ann Henry.

58 bouquets of spring flowers Author interview, Chris Hill.

58 "left lasting impressions" Clinton, *Living History,* 345.

59 "gal can get a cold beer" Author interview, Franklin Hagenbeck.

60 lined up ten experts Author interview, Andrew Shapiro.

61 "I read people" Author interview, Jack Keane.

61 "that Irish gruff thing" Author interview, Kris Balderston.

63 "I want to see Jack Keane" Email, Clinton to Lauren Jiloty, June 27, 2010.

64 "She was full of questions" Author interview, Petraeus.

66 opposed it for political reasons Robert M. Gates, *Duty* (New York: Alfred A. Knopf, 2014), 376.

66 "This is not politics" Hillary Clinton, interview by Diane Sawyer, ABC News, June 9, 2014.

67 "Hillary was adamant" Author interview, Gates.

68 "Four Horsemen of national security" Author interview, Morrell.

68 "dirty little secret" Author interview, Tom Nides.

68 "give them every troop" Author interview, David Axelrod.

69 "the dilemma *you* face" Bob Woodward, *Obama's Wars* (New York: Simon & Schuster, 2010), 222.

69 "not an adequate strategic partner" Classified cable, Ambassador Karl Eikenberry to Clinton, November 6, 2009.

69 the cable was leaked Eric Schmitt, "U.S. Envoy's Cables Show Worries on Afghan Plans," *The New York Times,* Jan. 25, 2010.

70 "umbrella of protection" Gates, *Duty,* 483.

71 "even if we achieve this much" Author interview, Karl Eikenberry.

72 "doesn't have the derring-do" Author interview, Sarah Chayes.

74 **"run it up the gut!"** Author interviews, former administration officials.

74 **"audibles with aircraft carriers"** Author interview, former administration official.

## Four **Holbrooke Agonistes**

79 **"game he wanted to play"** Author interview, Vikram Singh.

79 **"asset to be used"** Author interview, Derek Chollet.

79 **"greatest collective security failure"** Richard Holbrooke, "America: A European Power," *Foreign Affairs,* March–April 1990, 40.

79 **"cannot on the presidency,"** Derek Chollet, *The Road to the Dayton Accords* (New York: Palgrave Macmillan, 2005), 42.

79 **"ferociously intelligent"** Clinton, *Living History,* 453–54.

80 **"freight train of negatives"** Author interview, Frank Wisner.

81 **"I feel trapped"** Richard Holbrooke, *To End a War* (New York: Random House, 1998), 50.

82 **"I don't work for you"** Author interview, Tom Nides.

83 **"If you want farmers"** Author interview, Robert Gates.

83 **"a waste of money"** Rajiv Chandrasekaran, *Little America* (New York: Alfred A. Knopf, 2012), 112.

84 **" '*Stop,* Richard' "** Author interview, Rosemarie Pauli.

85 **"Excuses were made"** Richard Holbrooke, "The Longest War," *The Washington Post,* March 31, 2008.

85 **"There can't be a runoff"** Author interview, Richard Holbrooke, for *NYT.*

86 **"John performed brilliantly"** Author interview, Clinton, for *NYT.*

87 **" 'Don't listen to me' "** Author interview, Vali Nasr.

87 **"general's wingman"** Author interview, Kati Marton.

88 **"like the Balkans"** Author interview, David Petraeus.

89 **"The UN had convening power"** Author interview, Douglas Lute.

89 **"This is screwed up"** Author interview, administration official.

90 **"It sounded quite ominous"** Email, Strobe Talbott to Clinton, March 20, 2010.

90 **"Jim Jones can't fire"** Author interviews, former administration officials.

90 **"Richard strayed"** Email, P. J. Crowley to Cheryl Mills et al., September 17, 2009.

92 **"We had to get napkins"** Author interview, Wisner.

93 **subdued and tired** Author interview, Michael Abramowitz.

93 **"a beautiful woman"** Dr. Jehan El-Bayoumi, interview by David Holbrooke for *The Diplomat,* HBO Documentary Pictures, 2015.

95 **"a big-picture guy"** Author interview, Husain Haqqani.

96 **" 'I wish you had made that offer' "** Author interview, Marton.

96 **"on the front lines"** Roger Cohen, "Diplomat and Warrior," *The New York Times,* August 31, 2014.

96 **"Any time you want to ball up"** Author interview, David Holbrooke.

97 "**institutional memory and history**" Author interview, Dan Feldman.

98 "**Obama having a one-hour lunch**" Author interview, Ben Rhodes.

98 "**I'm sick of people**" Author interview, former administration official.


## Part II **War and Peace**

### Five **Below the Waterline**

101 "**Is anyone reading the newspaper?**" Author interviews, former administration officials.

102 "**She was supportive**" Author interview, Leon Panetta, for *NYT.*

104 "**She doesn't believe they are a strategy**" Author interview, Harold Koh.

104 "**a left-right coalition**" Speech by Harold Hongju Koh to the Oxford Union, May 7, 2013.

105 **257 strikes** Statistics are drawn from the Bureau of Investigative Journalism, a London-based nonprofit organization that has tracked drone strikes in Pakistan since 2004.

105 "**a bunch of strikes, willy-nilly**" President Obama, speaking during a Google Hangout, January 30, 2012.

106 **erased his early ambivalence** Charlie Savage, *Power Wars* (New York: Little Brown, 2015), 35.

107 "**option of last recourse**" Jo Becker and Scott Shane, "Secret 'Kill List' Proves a Test of Obama's Principles and Will," *The New York Times,* May 29, 2012.

107 **Neither decision was straightforward** Mark Mazzetti, *The Way of the Knife* (New York: Penguin, 2013), 228.

107 "**The politics in Pakistan**" Author interview, Leon Panetta, for *NYT.*

107 "**shrewd, blunt, and colorful**" Clinton, *Hard Choices,* 187.

108 "**I've been asking for this**" Ibid., 190.

108 "**in the awkward position**" Author interview, Daniel Benjamin.

108 "**It was the mantra**" Author interview, Dennis Blair.

111 "**Do we have good answers**" Emails between Jake Sullivan and Clinton, October 25, 2009.

113 "**so much collateral damage**" Town hall at Government College University, Lahore, October 29, 2009.

113 "**What's important here**" Town-hall interview hosted by Pakistani women journalists, Islamabad, October 30, 2009.

114 "**Maybe they're not getable**" Roundtable with senior Pakistani editors, Lahore, October 30, 2009.

114 "**Right on the target**" Email, Anwar Iqbal to Huma Abedin, October 29, 2009.

115 "**Mrs. Clinton challenged**" "Mrs. Clinton in Pakistan," editorial board, *The New York Times,* October 29, 2009.

115 "**Because the program remained classified**" Clinton, *Hard Choices,* 184.

115 **"Because we were keeping things covert"** Author interview, Michael Leiter.

116 **"I hit the effing roof"** Author interview, John Kerry.

116 **"Who are the drone strikes killing?"** Author interview, Husain Haqqani.

117 **"No terrorist attacks"** Author interview, Cameron Munter.

118 **"one man's combatant"** Tara McKelvey, "A Former Ambassador to Pakistan Speaks Out," *The Daily Beast,* November 20, 2012, http://www.thedailybeast .com/articles/2012/11/20/a-former-ambassador-to-pakistan-speaks-out.html.

119 **"it's you who are flat wrong"** Mazzetti, *Way of the Knife,* 292.

120 **"I'm not a pacifist"** Author interview, Munter.

120 **"My good friend"** Clinton, *Hard Choices,* 187.

120 **"a luminous representative"** Leon E. Panetta with Jim Newton, *Worthy Fights* (New York: Penguin Press, 2014), 199.

121 **"That would end it"** Author interview, Bill Daley.

121 **"He basically threatened to bomb Pakistan"** Hillary Clinton during a Democratic primary debate, Cleveland, Ohio, February 26, 2008.

122 **"it's probably fifty-fifty"** Author interview, Leiter.

122 **"the chance to get bin Laden was worth it"** Clinton, *Hard Choices,* 193.

123 **" 'my suggestion is, don't go' "** Mark Landler, "From Biden, a Vivid Account of Bin Laden Decision," *The New York Times,* January 30, 2012.

124 **"It's enough"** Author interview, former administration official.

124 **"To say a military tactic is legal"** Speech by President Obama at National Defense University, May 13, 2013.

125 **"He really does see it"** Author interview, Ben Rhodes.

126 **"the drone president"** Author interview, Vali Nasr.

## Six Peacemakers

128 **"keep a distance"** Author interview, Michael Oren.

128 **Obama chided her** Author interviews, former administration officials.

128 **"continue the same pattern"** Remarks by the president at the beginning of the trilateral meeting with Prime Minister Netanyahu and President Abbas, September 22, 2009.

129 **"There was a tension"** Author interview, Martin Indyk.

130 **"very little action"** Elizabeth Dias, "Jimmy Carter Talks About Iran, Campus Rape, Jesus Christ and the Paintings of W.," *Time,* April 10, 2014, http://time .com/56770/jimmy-carter-jesus-christ-iran-putin-clinton-kerry/.

130 **"never stop working"** Hillary Clinton, "How I Would Reaffirm Unbreakable Bond with Israel—and with Benjamin Netanyahu," *Forward,* November 4, 2015.

132 **"The lesson of history"** Author interview, Malcolm Hoenlein.

132 **"continue that conversation"** Peter Wallsten, "Allies of Palestinians See a Friend in Obama," *Los Angeles Times,* April 10, 2008.

133 **"examination of the record"** Rashid Khalidi, *Brokers of Deceit* (Boston: Beacon Press, 2013), 68.

133 **"Chicago Jewish community"** Author interview, David Axelrod.

134 **"the only way to deal with Bibi"** Author interview, Dennis Ross.

134 **"hostility was so high"** Author interview, George Mitchell.

136 **The full import** Author interview, Robert Malley.

137 **"core-course curriculum"** Author interview, Denis McDonough, for *NYT*.

137 **"that doesn't mean"** Remarks with Israeli foreign minister Tzipi Livni, March 3, 2009, State Department.

138 **Clinton gave Peres** Martin Indyk, *Innocent Abroad* (New York: Simon & Schuster, 2009), 178–80.

138 **"Who's the fucking superpower"** Aaron David Miller, *The Much Too Promised Land* (New York: Bantam Dell, 2008), 273.

138 **"a stop to settlements"** Mark Landler and Isabel Kershner, "Israeli Settlement Growth Must Stop, Clinton Says," *The New York Times,* May 27, 2009.

141 **"we know the reason"** Helene Cooper and Mark Landler, "Obama's Peace Tack Contrasts with Key Aide, Friend of Israel," *The New York Times,* May 21, 2011.

141 **"That turned out to be wrong"** Dennis Ross, *Doomed to Succeed* (New York: Farrar, Straus and Giroux, 2015), 343.

142 **"pretty worked up"** Author interview, former administration official.

143 **"choose the interlocutor"** Author interview, Steven Simon.

144 **"This was a big surprise"** Author interview, Mitchell.

144 **"always sound cocky"** Emails between Clinton and Jake Sullivan, March 22, 2010.

146 **"nasty business"** Clinton, *Hard Choices,* 329.

148 **"these lines are indefensible"** Remarks by President Obama and Prime Minister Netanyahu of Israel after Bilateral Meeting, May 20, 2011, White House Press Office.

149 **"He can beat Hillary"** Peter Baker and Jodi Rudoren, "Obama and Netanyahu: A Story of Slights and Crossed Signals," *The New York Times,* November 8, 2015.

150 **"he's a chickenshit"** Jeffrey Goldberg, "The Crisis in U.S.-Israel Relations Is Officially Here," *The Atlantic,* October 28, 2014, http://www.theatlantic.com /international/archive/2014/10/the-crisis-in-us-israel-relations-is-officially-here /382031/.

151 **"not just another few houses"** Jodi Rudoren and Mark Landler, "Housing Move in Israel Seen as Setback for Two-State Plan," *The New York Times,* November 30, 2012.

151 **"we could just watch that video"** David Remnick, "Hillary Is Running: A Dispatch from the Saban Forum," *The New Yorker,* December 2, 2012, http://www .newyorker.com/news/news-desk/hillary-is-running-a-dispatch-from-the-saban -forum.

152 **"constructive footing"** Author interview, Hoenlein.

## Seven **Sinking Sands**

153 "give us a hand" Author interview, Frank Wisner.

154 "It will do no good" Email, Bill Burns to Hillary Clinton et al., January 29, 2011.

156 "what I said yesterday" Email, Clinton to Jake Sullivan, February 4, 2011.

156 "took me to the woodshed" Clinton, *Hard Choices*, 345.

158 "a State-WH rift story" Email, Clinton to Jake Sullivan, February 5, 2011.

158 "threw a huge dust cloud" Author interview, Brian Katulis.

158 risks for violent upheavals The classified report, PSD-11, was first reported in Mark Landler, "Secret Report Ordered by Obama Identified Potential Uprisings," *The New York Times*, February 16, 2011.

159 "the anchor of the region" Author interview, Samantha Power, for *NYT*.

159 "sinking into the sand" Mark Landler, "Clinton Assails Arab Leaders, Urging Reform," *The New York Times*, January 14, 2011.

160 he agreed to add a short coda Author interview, Michael McFaul.

161 "searching for a way" Mark Landler, "Obama Seeks Reset in Arab World," *The New York Times*, May 11, 2011.

162 "This is like my dad" Author interview, Bill Daley.

164 demonstrators chanted "Monica" Arshad Mohammed, "Egyptians Pelt Clinton Motorcade with Tomatoes," Reuters, July 15, 2012.

164 "How do I correct?" Author interview, Dennis Ross.

165 she was frustrated Kim Ghattas, *The Secretary* (New York: Times Books, 2013), 226.

167 "cling to the status quo" Forum for the Future, Partnership Dialogue Panel Session, Doha, January 13, 2011.

167 "I see the glass as half full" Mark Landler, "U.S. Offered Rosy View Before Bahrain Crackdown," *The New York Times*, February 18, 2011.

169 "They made exactly the same mistake" Author interview, Robert Gates.

169 "how our military feels" Clinton, *Hard Choices*, 366–67.

169 "it's not a fair fight" Peter S. Green and Nicole Gaouette, "Bill Clinton Says U.S. Should Support a No-fly Zone in Libya," Bloomberg, March 10, 2011.

169 "What do you think of this idea?" Email, Clinton to Jake Sullivan, February 21, 2011.

170 "airplanes are allowed to bomb and strafe" "Careful with Qaddafi," editorial board, *The Philadelphia Inquirer*, March 4, 2011.

171 "dramatic and stylish figure" Clinton, *Hard Choices*, 360.

171 "I think Harvey" Email, Clinton to Philippe Reines and Huma Abedin, September 11, 2012.

171 "She was impressed" Author interview, Bernard-Henri Lévy.

172 "I looked them in the eye" Author interview, Clinton, for *NYT*.

172 "They grumble that we dominated Dayton" Derek Chollet and James Goldgeier, *America Between the Wars* (New York: Public Affairs, 2008), 131.

172 "I swore to myself" Samantha Power, "Bystanders to Genocide," *The Atlantic*, September 2001.

173 **"a new chapter"** Author interview, former administration official.

173 **"Some nations may be able"** Remarks by the President in Address to the Nation on Libya, March 28, 2011, National Defense University.

174 **"I have regretted it"** Samantha Power, interview by Savannah Guthrie, *Today*, NBC, October 3, 2013.

174 **"she was prepared to act"** Author interview, James Steinberg.

175 **"You're not going to drag us"** Colum Lynch, "The Libya Debate: How Fair Is Obama's New Claim That the U.S. Led from the Front?," *Foreign Policy*, October 23, 2012, http://foreignpolicy.com/2012/10/23/the-libya-debate-how-fair-is-obamas-new-claim-that-the-u-s-led-from-the-front/.

175 **"OK, we're a go"** Author interview, Gérard Araud.

176 **"leading from behind"** Ryan Lizza, "The Consequentialist," *The New Yorker*, May 2, 2011, http://www.newyorker.com/magazine/2011/05/02/the-consequentialist.

177 **"still a constant struggle"** Author interview, Jeremy Shapiro.

177 **full-blown psyops campaign** Eric Schmitt, "U.S. Gives Its Air Power Expansive Role in Libya," *The New York Times*, March 28, 2011.

## Eight **Post-Q**

178 **"Did we survive the day?"** Email exchange between Hillary Clinton and Jake Sullivan, October 10, 2012.

179 **dead of smoke inhalation** Account of the assault is drawn from Fred Burton and Samuel M. Katz, *Under Fire* (New York: St. Martin's, 2013), 91–130, and from Sean Flynn, "The Murder of an Idealist," *GQ Magazine*, December 2012, 282–86.

179 **fled to the airport** Account of the assault at the CIA annex is drawn from the report of the State Department's Accountability Review Board, December 18, 2012.

180 **"Very hard day"** Email, Hillary Clinton to "Diane Reynolds" [Chelsea Clinton], September 11, 2012.

181 **"Pat helped level set things"** Email, Sullivan to Clinton, October 10, 2012.

182 **a rich new vein** Michael Hirsh, "The Benghazi-Industrial Complex," *Politico Magazine*, May 4, 2014, http://www.politico.com/magazine/story/2014/05/hillarys-nightmare-the-benghazi-industrial-complex-106332.

182 **These details emerged** Michael S. Schmidt, "Hillary Clinton Used Personal Email Account at State Department, Possibly Breaking Rules," *The New York Times*, March 2, 2015.

184 **"didn't seem like an issue"** Amy Chozick and Michael S. Schmidt, "Hillary Clinton Tries to Quell Controversy Over Private Email," *The New York Times*, March 10, 2015.

184 **"Look, she hates you"** Glenn Thrush and Maggie Haberman, "What Is Hillary Clinton Afraid Of?," *Politico Magazine*, May 1, 2014, http://www.politico.com/magazine/story/2014/05/hillary-clinton-media-105901.

185 "you're such good journalists" Transcript of Clinton's farewell interview with State Department press corps, January 31, 2013.

185 "fueled in large part by anger" David Kirkpatrick, "A Deadly Mix in Benghazi," *The New York Times,* December 28, 2013.

186 "Do we want to badger you" Transcript of the House Select Committee on Benghazi hearing, October 22, 2015.

187 "We need partners" Remarks by the President at the United States Military Academy Commencement Ceremony, May 28, 2014.

188 "Obama was reluctant" Author interview, Dennis Ross.

189 "a strategic tautology" Author interview, Derek Chollet.

189 "private security experts" Email, Clinton to Sullivan, April 8, 2011.

189 "wouldn't shut the door to it" Bill Clinton, interviewed by Bianna Golodryga, *Good Morning America,* ABC, April 5, 2011

190 "balance of power" Author interview, Ross.

190 a secret order Jo Becker and Scott Shane, "Hillary Clinton, 'Smart Power' and a Dictator's Fall," *The New York Times,* February 28, 2016.

191 folded in less than thirty-six hours Christopher S. Chivvis, *Toppling Qaddafi* (New York: Cambridge University Press, 2014), 162.

191 "leadership/ownership/stewardship" Email, Jake Sullivan to Cheryl Mills and Victoria Nuland, August 21, 2011.

191 "This is a historic moment" Email, Sidney Blumenthal to Clinton, August 22, 2011.

192 "like the Clinton Doctrine" Emails between Clinton and Sullivan, August 22, 2011.

192 "We cannot, indeed, we should not" Remarks by the President on Foreign Policy, San Francisco, February 26, 1999.

192 "in the face of a tyrant" Mark Landler, "For Obama, a Moment to Savor, If Briefly," *The New York Times,* August 22, 2011.

193 "we have Hillary Clinton" Author interview, Chollet.

193 "we achieved our objectives" Remarks by the President on the Death of Muammar Qaddafi, Rose Garden, October 20, 2011.

194 "simply call it leading" Mark Landler, "For Obama, Some Vindication for His Much-Criticized Approach to War," *The New York Times,* October 21, 2011.

194 seeds of future problems Chivvis, *Toppling Qaddafi,* 162.

194 "I took a deep breath" Clinton, *Hard Choices,* 378–79.

195 "He's been a friend of mine" Adam B. Lerner, "Hillary Clinton Downplays Sidney Blumenthal's Influence," *Politico,* May 19, 2015.

195 "Shock & Awe" Email, Blumenthal to Clinton, March 26, 2011.

196 "jihadist resurgence" Email, Blumenthal to Clinton, April 8, 2011.

196 "a thin conspiracy theory" Emails, Blumenthal to Clinton, Clinton to Sullivan, March 8–9, 2012.

196 "reverse-engineered from conventional wisdom" Email, Sullivan to Clinton, September 18, 2012.

197 "Very interesting report" Emails between Sullivan and Chris Stevens, April 3, 2012.

197 **"I was the boss"** Transcript of the House Select Committee on Benghazi hearing, October 22, 2015.

197 **"militias running around"** Email, Stevens to a State Department colleague, August 7, 2012.

198 **"We should get this around asap"** Email, Clinton to Sullivan, September 12, 2012.

198 **"the Jimmy Carter Strategy"** Craig Unger, "GOP's October Surprise?" *Salon,* October 1, 2012.

199 **"I'm pushing to WH"** Emails between Blumenthal, Sullivan, and Clinton, October 1, 2012.

199 **"It took the president fourteen days"** Mark Landler, "Attack on U.S. Mission in Benghazi Becomes Subject of Strongest Words," *The New York Times,* October 17, 2012.

200 **"rooted in an Internet video"** Email, Ben Rhodes to David Plouffe et al., September 14, 2012.

201 **"A cynic would say"** Author interview, Trey Gowdy.

201 **"It drives me crazy"** Author interview, Philip Gordon.

202 **"end result is Libya"** Author interview, Chollet.

202 **"a disastrous intervention"** Alan J. Kuperman, "Obama's Libya Debacle," *Foreign Affairs,* March–April 2015, https://www.foreignaffairs.com/articles/libya/obamas-libya-debacle.

202 **"a lesson that I now apply"** Thomas Friedman, "Obama on the World," *The New York Times,* August 8, 2014.

203 **"a 51–49 call"** Robert M. Gates, *Duty,* 519.

203 **"a moment of weakness"** Author interview, former administration official.

203 **"NEVER been prouder"** Email, Anne-Marie Slaughter to Clinton, March 22, 2011.

203 **"We came, we saw, he died"** Clinton, interview by CBS News, October 20, 2011.

## Nine **Red Lines**

206 **"a crazy idea"** The reconstruction of the red-line decision is based on interviews with multiple current and former administration officials.

206 **"What the hell's going on?"** Author interview, Chuck Hagel.

207 **"cannot be another excuse"** Steve Holland, "2016 Repercussions? Hillary Clinton Backs Obama on Syria Action," Reuters, September 9, 2013.

209 **"I personally would be advocating"** Clinton, interview by WHDH-TV, Boston, October 2, 2015.

209 **"failure to do that"** Jeffrey Goldberg, "Hillary Clinton: 'Failure' to Help Rebels Led to the Rise of ISIS," *The Atlantic,* August 10, 2014.

211 **"never in the cards"** Friedman, "Obama on the World."

211 **"There will always be regret"** Author interview, Clinton, for *NYT.*

211 **"wicked problem"** Clinton, *Hard Choices,* 461.

212  "a raging bull" Author interview, Robert Ford.

213  "making serious progress" Author interview, Fred Hof.

213  sketched out a peace treaty Author interview, John Kerry.

213  "he's a reformer" Clinton, interview by Bob Schieffer, *Face the Nation,* CBS, March 27, 2011.

214  "nothing invested in him" Arshad Mohammed, "Syria's Assad 'Is Not Indispensable,' Clinton Says," Reuters, July 11, 2011.

214  "the time has come" Statement by President Obama on the Situation in Syria, August 18, 2011.

216  "get into the game" Author interview, Ford.

217  "preparing to present a plan" Clinton, *Hard Choices,* 462.

217  away from malefactors C. J. Chivers and Eric Schmitt, "Arms Airlift to Syria Rebels Expands, with Help from CIA," *The New York Times,* March 25, 2013.

218  Timber Sycamore Mark Mazzetti and Matt Apuzzo, "U.S. Relies Heavily on Saudi Money to Support Syrian Rebels," *The New York Times,* January 23, 2016.

218  "change my calculus" Remarks by the President to the White House Press Corps, James S. Brady Briefing Room, August 20, 2012.

219  "All of us believed" Leon Panetta, *Worthy Fights,* 449–50.

219  "a lot of questions" Author interview, senior administration official.

220  "why not try this?" Author interview, Steven Simon.

221  "blood on its hands" Author interviews, former administration officials.

221  "He just didn't think" Mark Mazzetti, Robert F. Worth, and Michael R. Gordon, "Obama's Uncertain Path Amid Syria Bloodshed," *The New York Times,* October 22, 2013.

222  "a game changer" Mark Landler and Rick Gladstone, "Chemicals Would Be 'Game Changer' in Syria, Obama Says," *The New York Times,* March 20, 2013.

224  "we're going to go to jail" Author interview, former administration official.

224  large supplies of sarin Neil MacFarquhar and Eric Schmitt, "Syria Threatens Chemical Attack on Foreign Force," *The New York Times,* July 23, 2012.

224  "considered that impossible" Panetta, *Worthy Fights,* 448.

224  "get caught trying" Maggie Haberman, "Clinton Splits with Obama on Syria," *Politico,* June 12, 2013.

225  he wouldn't say Mark Mazzetti, Michael Gordon, and Mark Landler, "U.S. Is Said to Plan to Send Weapons to Syrian Rebels," *The New York Times,* June 13, 2013.

225  "I found it ever harder" Robert S. Ford, "Arm Syria's Opposition," *The New York Times,* June 10, 2014.

226  "these never-ending meetings" Author interview, Hagel.

226  "against all of this" Samantha Power, Remarks at the U.S. Holocaust Memorial Museum's National Tribute Dinner, April 30, 2014.

226  "What will our kids and grandkids ask us" Mark Landler, "U.S. Envoys See a Rwanda Moment in Syria's Escalating Crisis," *The New York Times,* May 13, 2014.

227  "You don't agree" Author interview, former administration official.

228 **Throwing himself at the mercy** Panetta, *Worthy Fights,* 450.

228 **"a throwaway line"** Author interview, Hagel.

229 **"the family policy"** Author interview, Leon Wieseltier.

229 **"the president had bombed"** Author interview, John Kerry.

229 **"There was a fear"** Author interview, Wolfgang Ischinger.

230 **"It may sound harsh"** Author interview, George Mitchell.

## Part III **Diplomacy**

### Ten **The Back Channel**

235 **"The odds are long"** Author interview, Dennis Ross.

235 **America's complicity** Remarks by the President at Cairo University, June 4, 2009.

235 **"military dictatorship"** Mark Landler, "Clinton Raises U.S. Concerns of Military Power in Iran," *The New York Times,* February 15, 2010.

236 **"Hillary and company"** Author interview, John Kerry.

237 **"squeezed them again"** Author interview, person close to Clinton.

237 **"different endgames"** Author interview, Karim Sadjadpour.

238 **"tacit transformational potential"** Author interview, Robert Litwak.

238 **"not enough just to say yes"** Hillary Clinton Addresses the Iran Nuclear Deal, Brookings Institution, September 9, 2015.

238 **"She's built one coalition"** Author interview, Jake Sullivan.

239 **For all the haggling in Vienna** The meetings in Oman were first reported by Bradley Klapper, Julie Pace, and Matthew Lee of the Associated Press in "Secret US-Iran Talks Set Stage for Nuclear Deal," November 24, 2013. Laura Rozen also reported elements of the talks in *Al-Monitor.*

239 **self-serving and bogus** Ray Takeyh, "What Really Happened in Iran," *Foreign Affairs,* July–August 2014, https://www.foreignaffairs.com/articles/middle-east/2014-06-16/what-really-happened-iran.

240 **"You had people like that"** Author interview, Ray Takeyh.

241 **declined an invitation** Cable from U.S. Embassy in Muscat to State Department, June 4, 2006, released by WikiLeaks.

241 **he was also elusive** Author interview, Salem Ismaily.

242 **"a small ton of salt"** Author interview, Ross.

243 **"historically been hostile"** President Obama, interview, CNBC, June 16, 2009.

243 **"defense umbrella"** Mark Landler and David Sanger, "Clinton Speaks of Shielding Mideast from Iran," *The New York Times,* July 22, 2009.

243 **"totally obliterate them"** Clinton, interview, *Good Morning America,* ABC, April 22, 2008.

243 **routine maintenance** Mark Landler and Brian Stelter, "Washington Taps into a Potent New Force in Diplomacy," *The New York Times,* June 16, 2009.

243 **"I came to regret"** Clinton, *Hard Choices,* 424.

244 "that had a real cost" Author interview, Tom Donilon, for *NYT*.

244 "spat in the campaign" Author interview, David Miliband

246 "under their noses" Clinton, *Hard Choices*, 433.

247 "Leaves the door open" Email, Sullivan to Clinton, July 31, 2011.

247 "redolent with sandalwood" Shane Bauer, Joshua Fattal, Sarah Shourd, *A Sliver of Light* (New York: Houghton Mifflin Harcourt, 2014), 134–36.

248 "this was a long shot" Clinton, *Hard Choices*, 436.

249 "out-of-the-box approach" Author interview, Kerry.

250 "get people in a room" Author interview, David Wade.

251 "'not mislead them'" Author interview, former administration official.

252 "Salem's going to deliver people" Author interviews, Jake Sullivan, Bill Burns, Puneet Talwar.

252 "my full confidence" Author interview, Clinton, for *NYT*. Published in Mark Landler, "Biden Adviser Leaving Washington, but It May Not Be for Long," *The New York Times*, June 20, 2014.

253 the meeting stayed secret Helene Cooper and Mark Landler, "U.S. Officials Say Iran Has Agreed to Nuclear Talks," *The New York Times*, October 20, 2012.

254 "worthy of Evelyn Waugh" Timothy Garton Ash, "US Embassy Cables: A Banquet of Secrets," *The Guardian*, November 28, 2010.

254 "prepared to explore" Author interview, Burns.

255 "extraordinary meetings" Author interview, Gary Samore.

256 "subtle and tiny steps" Hassan Rouhani, interview by Ann Curry, NBC News, September 18, 2013.

257 involved in secret talks Jay Solomon and Carol Lee, "U.S.-Iran Thaw Grew from Years of Behind-the-Scenes Talks," *The Wall Street Journal*, November 7, 2013.

258 "Yeah, set it up" Author interviews, Jake Sullivan and Ben Rhodes.

258 "God be with you" Peter Baker, "U.S. and Iran Agree to Speed Talks to Defuse Nuclear Issue," *The New York Times*, September 27, 2013.

## Eleven **Resets and Regrets**

259 the Putin Slouch Mark Landler, "Clinton Calls Israel's Steps to Cool Housing Dispute 'Useful,'" *The New York Times*, March 20, 2010.

260 "save the tigers" Clinton, *Hard Choices*, 242.

261 "he sizes somebody up" Author interview, Bill Burns.

261 "their voices heard" Paul Richter and Sergei L. Loiko, "Vladimir Putin Accuses Clinton of Inciting Protests in Russia," *Los Angeles Times*, December 9, 2011.

262 Soviet fishing trawler Mark Landler, "From 'Least Diplomatic Diplomat,' Salty Peek at Trans-Atlantic Strains," *The New York Times*, February 10, 2014.

262 "important for us to reset" President-elect Obama, interviewed by Tom Brokaw on *Meet the Press*, December 7, 2008.

263 "the last holdout" Author interview, senior administration official.

264 **"Putin would come back"** Author interview, Jake Sullivan.

265 **"We saw the logic"** Author interview, Philip Gordon.

265 **"went beyond Putin"** Author interview, Ben Rhodes.

266 **"keeping the Cold War over"** Author interview, Strobe Talbott.

266 **"sophisticated Soviet retread"** Susan B. Glasser, "Minister No: Sergei Lavrov and the Blunt Logic of Russian Power," *Foreign Policy,* April 29, 2013, http://foreignpolicy.com/2013/04/29/minister-no/.

267 **"This prestigious addition"** Email, Philippe Reines to Clinton, April 18, 2012.

267 **"Have a good day"** Email, Reines to Michael Hastings, September 23, 2012.

268 **"Do you think we got it?"** Mark Landler, "Lost in Translation: A U.S. Gift to Russia," *The New York Times,* March 6, 2009.

269 **"how you really translate 'reset'"** Author interview, Michael McFaul.

270 **"different generation"** Peter Baker, "Obama Resets Ties to Russia, but Work Remains," *The New York Times,* July 7, 2009.

271 **"the only woman"** Clinton, *Hard Choices,* 232.

272 **"I don't see any problem"** Peter Baker, "Twists and Turns on Way to Arms Pact with Russia," *The New York Times,* March 26, 2010.

273 **"strange turn of history"** Remarks by President Barack Obama in Prague, April 5, 2009, White House Press Office.

273 **"la-la land"** Author interview, Ivo Daalder.

275 **"the worst of all worlds"** Author interview, James Steinberg.

276 **"not always an easy art"** Richard M. Nixon, *RN* (New York, Grosset & Dunlap, 1978), 880.

276 **A whole stuffed piglet** Clinton, *Living History,* 412.

277 **serenaded by James Taylor** Mark Landler, "One Casualty of Eavesdropping on Merkel: A Warm Rapport," *The New York Times,* November 1, 2013.

277 **"People don't appreciate"** Author interview, Nicholas Burns.

277 **"those two guys got along"** Author interview, David Axelrod.

278 **"he would invest in it"** Author interview, McFaul.

278 **"tough, smart, shrewd"** Peter Baker, "Obama Resets Ties to Russia, but Work Remains," *The New York Times,* July 7, 2009.

278 **"president just wants me to relax"** Remarks by President Obama and President Putin of Russia After Bilateral Meeting, Lough Erne, Northern Ireland, June 17, 2013.

279 **"The more open Russia will become"** Mark Landler, "In Moscow, Clinton Urges Russia to Open Its Political System," *The New York Times,* October 14, 2009.

279 **"better not to argue with women"** Vladimir Putin, interview by Jean-Pierre El-kabbach and Gilles Bouleau, Radio Europe 1 and TF1 TV, June 4, 2014.

280 **"'we shouldn't be so needy'"** Author interview, Julianne Smith.

281 **"When are you going to start bombing"** Peter Baker, "U.S.-Russian Ties Still Fall Short of 'Reset' Goal," *The New York Times,* September 2, 2013.

282 **"I very much incline"** Confirmation testimony of Ashton Carter, Senate Armed Services Committee, February 4, 2015.

282 **"Will somebody tell me"** Author interview, Talbott.

284 **"the jury is in"** Clinton at Brookings Institution, September 9, 2015.

## Twelve **The Pivot**

285 " 'I want to kiss you' " Email, Kurt Campbell to Clinton, May 2, 2012.

285 "I want to see you" Chen Guangcheng, *The Barefoot Lawyer* (New York: Henry Holt, 2015), 303.

286 "It's going sideways" Author interview, Denis McDonough, for *NYT.*

287 "Get him out" Author interview, former administration official.

287 botched his transfer Mark Landler, Jane Perlez, and Steven Lee Myers, "Dissident's Plea for Protection from China Deepens Crisis," *The New York Times,* May 3, 2012.

288 "slide on a banana peel" Author interview, senior administration official.

289 "might never agree" Author interview, Clinton. Published in Michael R. Gordon and Mark Landler, "Backstage Glimpses of Clinton as Dogged Diplomat, Win or Lose," *The New York Times,* February 2, 2013.

290 "a pivot point" Hillary Clinton, "America's Pacific Century," *Foreign Policy,* October 11, 2011, http://foreignpolicy.com/2011/10/11/americas-pacific-century/.

292 "they were quite different" Author interview, Jon Huntsman.

293 "a forbidden subject" Mark Landler, "Clinton Reshapes Diplomacy by Tossing the Script," *The New York Times,* February 20, 2009.

294 "unduly provocative" Jeffrey A. Bader, *Obama and China's Rise* (Washington, D.C.: Brookings Institution Press, 2012), 16.

295 "litmus tests" Mark Landler, "Obama's Evolution to a Tougher Line on China," *The New York Times,* September 20, 2012.

295 "bringing the world together" Obama, interview by Harry Smith, *The Early Show,* CBS, April 2, 2008.

296 "deal toughly with your banker" State Department cable from Clinton, March 28, 2009.

297 "China badly misread" Author interview, Kurt Campbell.

297 "Did you guys give away too much?" Author interview, Jeff Bader.

298 "freedom of navigation" Mark Landler, "Offering to Aid Talks, U.S. Challenges China on Disputed Islands," *The New York Times,* July 23, 2010.

299 "China is a big country" Bader, *Obama and China's Rise,* 105.

300 "hunt for resources" Mark Landler, "A New Era of Gunboat Diplomacy," *The New York Times,* November 12, 2011.

300 a long-shelved treaty Author interview, Stapleton Roy.

301 "Kurt's great insight" Author interview, James Steinberg.

301 "The thing about Hillary" Author interview, Kim Beazley.

301 " 'Thank goodness' " Author interview, Clinton, for *NYT.*

302 "important for American workers" Clinton, *Hard Choices,* 77.

303 "bar here is very high" Hillary Clinton statement on the Trans-Pacific Partnership, October 7, 2015.

303 "pulled back the veil" Mark Landler, "Obama's Evolution to a Tougher Line on China," *The New York Times,* September 20, 2012.

304 "this whole Asian thing" Author interviews, Rahm Emanuel and Jeff Bader.

304 **"China containment alliance"** Email, Sidney Blumenthal to Hillary Clinton, October 28, 2010.

305 **asked Xi two questions** Mark Landler, "Fruitful Visit by Obama Ends with a Lecture from Xi," *The New York Times,* November 12, 2014.

308 **"We have made very clear"** Clinton, "America's Pacific Century."

308 **"Didn't we, not the WH"** Email, Clinton to Jake Sullivan, May 14, 2012.

308 **"We like that word"** Author interview, Clinton, for *NYT.*

## Thirteen **The Lady and Havana**

311 **"Denis will never be able"** Author interview, Ben Rhodes.

311 **"known each other for a lifetime"** Clinton, *Hard Choices,* 101.

312 **"it will be very difficult"** Clinton, speaking during a Democratic primary debate in Des Moines, Iowa, December 4, 2007.

314 **"engage with the Cuban government"** Remarks by the President at the Summit of the Americas Opening Ceremony, Trinidad and Tobago, April 17, 2009.

314 **"pursue out of WH"** Email, Clinton to Jake Sullivan, April 17, 2009.

314 **"she was in the lead"** Author interview, Rhodes.

315 **"threat to the Castros"** Speech by Clinton at Florida International University, Miami, July 31, 2015.

315 **" 'No es fácil' "** Statement by the President on Cuba Policy Changes, Cabinet Room, December 17, 2015.

316 **"me talking to you"** Author interview, Clinton, for *NYT.*

318 **her arms crossed** Rena Pederson, *The Burma Spring* (New York: Pegasus Books, 2015), 316.

318 **"unclenched its fist"** State Department cable from U.S. Embassy in Rangoon to Clinton, August 18, 2009.

318 **"I think yes"** Email, Sullivan to Clinton, August 15, 2009.

319 **"exciting and memorable"** Author interview, Kurt Campbell.

320 **"a scholar who displayed goodwill"** State Department cable from U.S. Embassy in Rangoon to Clinton, November 10, 2009.

321 **"We need to test this"** Author interview, Clinton, for *NYT.*

321 **no crowds waving flags** Steven Lee Myers, "Greeted Quietly, Clinton Arrives in Myanmar," *The New York Times,* December 1, 2011.

322 **"more like an accountant"** Clinton, *Hard Choices,* 116.

322 **"coiled intensity of a vibrant mind"** Ibid., 101.

323 **"tell me about the country"** Author interview, Campbell.

324 **"were you paying attention"** Author interview, Dan Restrepo.

325 **"that other day"** Mark Landler, "American Nations Debate Readmitting Cuba," *The New York Times,* June 2, 2009.

325 **"usually the pessimist"** Email, Philippe Reines to Clinton, June 3, 2009.

327 **"not the right time"** Author interview, Arturo Valenzuela.

327 **"never felt safer"** Author interview, Alan Gross.

329 **"We are deeply concerned"** Statement by Clinton after meeting Judy Gross, June 17, 2010.

329 **"didn't take a genius"** Author interview, Scott Gilbert.

330 **"if we could have gotten Alan out"** Author interview, Ricardo Zuniga.

331 **"When Obama saw me"** Author interview, Patrick Leahy.

331 **"I'll do something on Cuba"** Author interview, Rhodes.

333 **"very well stocked"** Julie Hirschfeld Davis and Peter Baker, "A Secretive Path to Raising U.S. Flag in Cuba," *The New York Times,* August 13, 2015.

334 **"we should ask the pope"** Author interview, Tim Rieser.

337 **"We made the point"** Author interview, Rhodes. First reported in Mark Landler, "U.S. Swap for Bergdahl Shook Up Secret Talks with Cuba," *The New York Times,* December 30, 2014.

338 **"glad you're home"** Author interview, Gross.

339 **"glad you're here"** Remarks by the President in State of the Union Address, U.S. Capitol, January 20, 2015.

## Epilogue **Two Campaigns**

341 **"There's no doubt"** Author interview, Jake Sullivan.

344 **"right here at home"** Speech by Clinton to the Saban Forum, Brookings Institution, Washington, D.C., December 6, 2015.

344 **"Here's how"** Address to the Nation by the President, Oval Office, December 6, 2015.

344 **"existential threat"** Author interview, Ben Rhodes.

346 **"the best hammer"** Remarks by the President at West Point, May 28, 2014.

346 **"time and tide"** Gideon Rose, "What Obama Gets Right," *Foreign Affairs,* September–October 2015, https://www.foreignaffairs.com/articles/what-obama -gets-right.

347 **"There's a playbook"** Jeffrey Goldberg, "The Obama Doctrine," *The Atlantic,* April 2016, 76, http://www.theatlantic.com/magazine/archive/2016/04/the-obama -doctrine/471525/.

347 **"strategic fumes"** Author interview, Robert Kagan.

348 **America's basic instincts** Robert Kagan, "Superpowers Don't Get to Retire," *New Republic,* May 26, 2014, https://newrepublic.com/article/117859/allure-normalcy -what-america-still-owes-world.

350 **"force of arms"** Walter Isaacson and Evan Thomas, *The Wise Men* (New York: Simon & Schuster, 1986), 371.

350 **"good, old-fashioned diplomacy"** Speech by Clinton to the Council on Foreign Relations, September 8, 2010.

350 **"Beneath his formal exterior"** Clinton, *Hard Choices,* 21.

350 **"This is the girl"** Clinton, *Living History,* 39.

# Index

## About the Author

MARK LANDLER has covered American foreign policy for *The New York Times* since the inauguration of Barack Obama, first as diplomatic correspondent and since 2011 as White House correspondent. In twenty-four years at the *Times,* he has been the newspaper's bureau chief in Hong Kong and Frankfurt, European economic correspondent, and a business reporter in New York. He lives with his family in Chevy Chase, Maryland.

@MarkLandler